Date: 8/12/21

BY SHIRLEY JACKSON

# The
# Letters of
# Shirley Jackson

# The
# Letters of
# Shirley Jackson

. . .

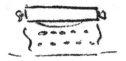

Edited by Laurence Jackson Hyman

In consultation with Bernice M. Murphy

RANDOM HOUSE

NEW YORK

Published in the United States by Random House, an imprint and
division of Penguin Random House LLC, New York.

RANDOM HOUSE and the HOUSE colophon are registered
trademarks of Penguin Random House LLC.

Line drawings throughout are by Shirley Jackson.
Photograph credits appear on page 603.

LIBRARY OF CONGRESS CATALOGING-IN-PUBLICATION DATA
Names: Jackson, Shirley, 1916–1965, author. | Hyman, Laurence Jackson, editor. |
Murphy, Bernice M., editor.
Title: The letters of Shirley Jackson / Shirley Jackson; edited by Laurence Jackson
Hyman in consultation with Bernice M. Murphy.
Description: First edition. | New York : Random House, [2021] | Includes index.
Identifiers: LCCN 2020045797 (print) | LCCN 2020045798 (ebook) |
ISBN 9780593134641 (hardcover) | ISBN 9780593134665 (ebook)
Subjects: LCSH: Jackson, Shirley, 1916–1965—Correspondence. |
Authors, American—20th century—Correspondence.
Classification: LCC PS3519.A392 Z48 2021 (print) | LCC PS3519.A392 (ebook) |
DDC 813/.54—dc23
LC record available at https://lccn.loc.gov/2020045797
LC ebook record available at https://lccn.loc.gov/2020045798

Printed in the United States of America on acid-free paper

randomhousebooks.com

2 4 6 8 9 7 5 3 1

First Edition

Book design by Caroline Cunningham

To Shirley, for her enduring wit and wisdom

# CONTENTS

. . .

# PREFACE

. . .

## Portrait of the Artist at Work

*Laurence Jackson Hyman*

My mother was a writer. That's what she did. She loved nothing more than writing, though she certainly also loved her children, cooking, friends, cats, music, and playing bridge. I can picture her sitting on her beloved red kitchen stool, spiced meatballs simmering on the stove, making a shopping list—with scribbled asides of insight into or warnings for her characters in whatever novel she was working on. She might even stop one of us kids, whichever one was walking by, to try out a story idea.

From her early childhood, Shirley knew she wanted to write, and she managed to find some hours in most days to do just that—first handwritten poems and short vignettes, then long letters to friends and journals, then, when she met her first typewriter in her teens, a flood of poems, stories, and letters. Later, of course, came short stories, novels, family chronicles, plays, children's books, and letters. Many more letters.

Shirley loved writing letters as much as she liked to write fiction, and later in her life, when she had become an established professional author, the two would often vie for her time and attention. She would sit down at her typewriter and contemplate the surface of her desk and worktable, covered with a dozen letters to be answered, a note to be written to her agent, an overdue letter to her parents—already eight pages—waiting to be finished and mailed off, and many single paragraphs on otherwise blank sheets: starts of stories, ideas for stories, character ideas, or fragments of dialogue. Looking over this array of papers, she would often choose to spend a couple of hours banging out a long letter on her typewriter, at times feeling a little guilty because Stanley, listening downstairs, would assume that she was "really working" on a story, to sell to a magazine, to help support our household.

Whenever my siblings and I were away—at camp or school or college—we would eagerly anticipate the familiar typewritten yellow pages from our mother. She would be funny, warm, chatty, and would walk us through family triumphs and mishaps with the same amused tone and wit she often brought to her published work. Both my parents were dutiful and skillful letter writers, and they passed on the habit. I became fond of writing to friends and relatives from a young age. Writing back to my parents in particular was, for me, a chance to try to juggle language and humor as brilliantly as they did. In our family, we were always expected to hold up our ends of the conversation.

Shortly after I moved to San Francisco in the early 1970s my grandmother, Shirley's mother, Geraldine Bugbee Jackson, presented me with a shallow box, solid but worn, and told me it held all my mother's letters to her and my grandfather (whom Shirley always called Pop), after they began saving them in 1948. She said she hoped I would publish them someday. I was honored, but it took me a while before I worked up the courage to read them; it was startling to see those familiar yellow folded pages and Shirley's instantly recognizable typewriter font. But once I started reading them I was completely transported, re-experiencing events in our lives as she recounted them, and remembering our household, with all its nuttiness and intellectual sparring, its pets and books, its music and parties. Now, nearly fifty years later, most of my mother's letters to her parents, together with many other letters she wrote, are being published for the first time in this collection.

Spending so much time with these letters during the past few years, as I assembled and edited this collection, has been an important per-

sonal journey for me. Among the photographs on the walls of my office are two of Shirley: in one, she is twenty, laughing while leaning
against a mid-1930s roadster, a girl I never knew. The other is taken in
the early 1960s; she sits with Stanley, both of them smiling, Shirley
holding her beloved cat Applegate, just as I remember them. Both
pictures appear in this book. Every now and then I catch a glimpse of
one photograph or the other, and I become more determined in the
effort at hand, reminded that my task now is to let my mother tell her
own story.

My hope is that this book serves as both a wonderful literary document and the self-reported account of a short but extremely creative
life. Shirley regarded letter writing as an art form as well as a mode of
communication, and she excelled at it. Her letters are fun to read; they
are constructed like marvelous miniature magazines, full of news and
gossip, recipes, sports updates, jokes, childrearing concerns, tips and
recommendations, with tantalizing glimpses of herself, the artist at
work. And she took obvious joy in writing them. Many of these letters,
especially those to her parents, run deliciously long, sometimes a dozen
or more pages, typewritten, usually single-spaced, most done with total
avoidance of the shift key.

Shirley's own speaking voice really comes through to me when I
read her letters, her natural ways of phrasing, and pausing, her choice
of words and inflection, her use of language. And her letters, even to
her agents, were always well-seasoned with gags. Shirley was at heart
a vaudeville comedian, and she could find a funny side to almost anything. Consider her description in a letter to me in the early 1960s of
Stanley's desk chair breaking: "dad's chair fell apart again. you remember how it happens; first the chair cracks and joggles and then slowly
comes apart and dad leaps up and the chair goes out from under him
and he leans over and his lighter falls out of his pocket and he leans
over to pick up the lighter and his cigarettes fall out of his pocket and
he leans over to pick up his cigarettes and cracks the side of his head
against the desk . . ."

Shirley's habit of writing most everything in lowercase has been
preserved here because it reflects her personality nearly as much as the
letters' content. When, during my youth, drawings and notes would

suddenly appear on the refrigerator, or on a kitchen cabinet, or in the hallway near the telephone table, or on the study doors, they would almost always be typed lowercase, often with her playful abbreviations, run-ins, and deliberate misspellings, sometimes even cryptograms, puzzles, and silly poems. For Shirley, language was play. That same playfulness is abundant in the many *New Yorker*-style drawings and cartoons she loved to draw, some of which are included here.

Shirley wrote for most of her life on manual typewriters—distrusting anything electric—and often claimed nobody could read her handwriting. Shirley named her first typewriter "ernest" and gave him a jokester personality of his own, complete with mood swings. Subsequent typewriters shared the same name, and she often refers to "ernest" in her letters, and blames him for any revealing typos or pun-play misspellings. She was a rapid typist, usually firing a flurry of punches lasting half a minute or less, followed by brief silence, then another loud barrage. I remember coming home from school with friends who were startled at the percussive sound of my parents' type-writers both going at once, pounding away in different rooms.

Shirley herself always expected her letters to be published one day, and wrote as much to her parents several times, at one point observing wryly that she wouldn't relish the job of editing them since she customarily did not date her letters (and indeed I am grateful that many of her recipients did so). At the start of this project, I had managed to gather about five hundred Shirley Jackson letters—some thirteen hundred typewritten pages—from a variety of sources, including many from biographer Ruth Franklin, whose research uncovered the letters to Jeanne Beatty, Louis Harap, and Virginia Olsen. Many others came from the voluminous Brandt & Brandt Literary Agency files, and personal family files. In this volume, I have included nearly three hundred of Shirley's letters, written to nearly twenty different recipients.

In order to include as many letters as possible, some have been shortened, eliminating, for instance, paragraphs describing, in detail, the four children's clothing sizes at holiday time or misbehavior of the cats (and even those paragraphs were often hard to let go of). Many others were left virtually intact, especially her wonderfully crisp notes to her agents. Unfortunately, some letters could not find a place in this collection but will undoubtedly be studied by future literature schol-ars, who may indeed uncover still others.

Despite the long hours arm-wrestling myself over the selection and editing, it has been a warm pleasure getting to know my mother so much better, in all the various stages of her life, some of which I re-member, some not. Beginning work each day has been like entering a time machine and setting the date on the dial, instantly to be trans-ported to a day in, say, 1939 or 1950, or 1963. It is refreshing to hear my mother sounding so happy, so excited about her work and her children and her well-earned successes as a writer, even in the face of the many challenges she faced and the family troubles we all brought her. Together with her drawings, these letters take us on a bumpy, poignant, hilarious ride through Shirley's version of life as an artist, a woman, and a mother in small-town mid-twentieth-century America.

It would be disingenuous not to acknowledge that I am a player in all of this. Since childhood I have been asked how I felt being a char-acter in my mother's short stories and books. My answer: I never minded appearing in Shirley's stories, though for many years as a kid I didn't pay much attention to them. As an adult, I learned to have fun with my fictional early life. Sometimes I wonder whether my own childhood memories are real, or as Shirley told them. I think my mother always treated me fairly as a character, in both stories and drawings—and she gave me some great lines. Among many other things, this collection of letters is my own childhood, documented by one of the iconic writers of the past century. I remain her character.

# INTRODUCTION

. . .

## "It Is a Wonderful Pleasure to Write to You..."

In early 1960, Shirley Jackson wrote the following to a fan named Jeanne Beatty, with whom she had recently established a friendship that was conducted entirely through the mail:

> it is a wonderful pleasure to write to you. i go from month to month and year to year never writing letters because i cannot write little letters which are polite and unnecessary mostly because i can't stop, as you see. You provoked me, you did; if you write to a professional writer a lovely long letter you are apt to get a rambling long letter back. it's like sitting down to talk for an hour, and far more agreeable than most conversations.

The Beatty letters—which were brought to light by Jackson's most recent biographer, Ruth Franklin—are spontaneous, playful, confessional, witty, and forthright. They provide us with an invaluable insight into Jackson's state of mind at a time when she was at the peak of her literary prowess and illustrate the vitally important role that letter writing played in her personal and professional existence. Through their letters, the Baltimore housewife and the bestselling author established an apparently genuine rapport, which came to serve as a significant emotional and intellectual outlet for Jackson.

As the Beatty correspondence underlines, the selected letters assembled in this volume give one of the most versatile and influential American authors of the twentieth century the chance to speak once again for herself. They provide revealing insights into Jackson's remarkable body of work and vividly dramatize her efforts to reconcile domestic responsibilities with the creative impulse and a busy professional life. Her fierce intelligence, endlessly percolating imagination, genuine delight in the company of family and friends, and unique worldview are evident on every page.

Jackson's husband, the literary critic Stanley Edgar Hyman, was the first to recognize that his wife's correspondence represented an important strand of her literary output. In a March 1960 letter to her parents, Leslie and Geraldine, Jackson mentions that the couple have been discussing what will happen to her private papers after her death:

> anyway the important thing is my letters to you over these years, which i pray you have kept, and will arrange for them to get back to me. stanley is most urgent about this, since he puts a higher value on them than i do [...] since I hope i have a couple of years still to go the problem is not very pressing, but the vital thing is that you not throw them out. since I only write long letters to you they must be a long detailed record of many years. i am almost embarrassed when I think of the mountains of pages they must make.

Jackson's hope that she has "a couple of years still to go" is poignant. Although she was only forty-three, she had a little over five years to live. As she anticipated, her surviving letters do indeed make "mountains of pages." Jackson downplays their significance, noting that Stanley values them more than she does, but it is easy to understand why he felt they were worth preserving. The relationship between authors' family lives and their creative endeavors is frequently a close one, but for Jackson, the two were often one and the same.

In order to understand why Shirley Jackson and her work still matter, it is necessary to mention the tale which made her one of the most talked about writers in the United States. Along with *The Haunting of Hill House* (1959), "The Lottery," which was printed in *The New Yorker* in June 1948, secured Jackson's reputation as a writer of elegantly written but viscerally unsettling fiction.

In this exquisitely controlled short story, ordinary people do terrible things because tradition demands it, and communal murder is an apparently unremarkable fixture in the local events calendar. "The Lottery" has for decades been a staple of short-story anthologies and high school English classes, and its classic status perhaps obscures just how shocking the story was considered when it first appeared. It has also been enduringly influential. Echoes of "The Lottery" can be found in Stephen King's "Children of the Corn" (1977), Thomas Tryon's 1973 bestseller *Harvest Home*, and more recently, in some of the most prominent exemplars of the current "Folk Horror Revival": see, for instance, Ari Aster's 2019 film *Midsommar*.

However, despite the considerable critical and commercial success Jackson attained during her lifetime, and the high esteem she has long been held in by aficionados of horror and gothic fiction, the true scope of her literary significance was, in the decades immediately following her death, often overlooked. This likely had much to do with the fact that her writing both evaded and traversed conventional generic and audience categories.

Jackson's work appeared in a wide range of publication outlets, amongst them *The New Yorker, Harper's Magazine, Charm, Ladies' Home Journal, Mademoiselle, Good Housekeeping, The Magazine of Fantasy and Science Fiction, McCall's, Reader's Digest,* and *The Saturday Evening Post*. Although her six published novels share obvious thematic consistencies—in particular, a profound interest in the relationship between living spaces and the women who inhabit them—they also utilized a wide range of premises. The novels encompass a panoramic critique of a Californian suburb (*The Road Through the Wall,* 1948); an intense and original campus novel (*Hangsaman,* 1951); a furiously inventive psychiatric case study (*The Bird's Nest,* 1954); an apocalyptic satire (*The Sundial,* 1958); a classic of supernatural horror fiction (*The Haunting of Hill House,* 1959); and a first-person narrative related by a teenager whose skewed perspective is simultaneously chilling and captivating (*We Have Always Lived in the Castle*, 1962).

Jackson remains best known as the author of nuanced and elegantly written works of fiction which often contain gothic elements. However, she also wrote numerous stories inspired by experiences as a wife and mother. These comic tales quickly became a staple fixture in the most prominent women's magazines of the era. Readers may even recognize early versions of some of this material in this volume. As Jackson says in a 1955 letter to her parents: "i guess the reason i always think i have written you is because i write the same material in stories; if i sent you the first drafts of all my stories you would have twice as many letters but i guess not as much true news." Many of these stories were revised for publication in *Life Among the Savages* (1953) and *Raising Demons* (1957). Jackson's family stories became so well known during her lifetime that she was singled out for criticism by Betty Friedan in *The Feminine Mystique* (1963) as one of the female authors of what Friedan scathingly characterized as "Happy Housewife" magazine stories.

Jackson's family stories likely contributed to the surprising lack of critical attention her work received in the decades following her death. As scholar Lynette Carpenter has persuasively argued: "traditional male critics could not, in the end, reconcile genre with gender in Jackson's case; unable to understand how a serious writer of gothic fiction could also be, to all outward appearances, a typical housewife, much less how she could publish housewife humor in *Good Housekeeping*, they dismissed her." Jackson's popular fiction associations were also seen as problematic. Lenemaja Friedman, the author of the first academic study of her work (*Shirley Jackson*, 1975), considered Jackson to be an undeniably interesting but ultimately minor writer because she "saw herself primarily as an entertainer, as an expert storyteller and craftsman."

Nor did Jackson appear to fit neatly in with the dominant postwar trends in the literary gothic. By dint of her California birth and strong New England associations, she certainly could not be classified as a product of the American South. This distinguished her from Carson McCullers, Truman Capote, and Flannery O'Connor, all of whom were considered to be key exemplars of the "New American Gothic." Furthermore, although, as critic John Parks has noted, she certainly had numerous thematic and symbolic elements in common with these writers, Jackson's blurring of the boundaries between reality and fantasy invariably leaned more towards the subtly uncanny than to the overtly grotesque.

Within a popular fiction context, Jackson was again often left out of the critical conversation, until recently seldom discussed alongside the male writers more usually associated with the postwar boom in fantasy, horror, and science fiction (although Stephen King extensively praises *The Haunting of Hill House* in *Danse Macabre*, and Mark Jancovich has effectively situated Jackson alongside other genre 1950s writers such as Charles Beaumont, Richard Matheson, and Robert Bloch). Jackson was also often only briefly referenced in discussions of the so-called *New Yorker* School during the 1940s and 1950s, despite the fact that she wrote one of the most (in)famous stories ever printed in the magazine. In summary, her gender, versatility, professionalism, and commercial popularity meant that Jackson was frequently deemed less worthy of serious scholarly and critical inquiry than many of her contemporaries.

Times have changed, and a new wave of academic interest in Jackson's oeuvre has emerged, supplementing excellent work carried out in the 1980s and 1990s. Since 2000, there have been four edited essay collections, two monographs, dozens of book chapters and journal articles, and numerous dissertations and PhD theses. Although "The Lottery," *We Have Always Lived in the Castle*, and *The Haunting of Hill House* remain the most frequently discussed texts, a much wider selection of Jackson's work is now being studied than was previously the case.

Jackson's back catalogue has been attractively repackaged and relaunched for a new generation of readers. It is now much easier to find her lesser-known works than before, particularly outside of the United States. In 2010, Jackson's selected works were published in a Library of America anthology compiled by Joyce Carol Oates, one of her most accomplished literary successors, with a second volume, edited by Ruth Franklin, following in 2020. Franklin's award-winning 2016 biography, *Shirley Jackson: A Rather Haunted Life*, marked another significant milestone in the author's return to critical and popular prominence. It inspired numerous reviews and articles enthusiastically reappraising Jackson's literary legacy. Jackson's estate has played an important role in keeping interest in her work alive, encouraging publishers to reprint her work and releasing two volumes of previously uncollected and unpublished writings: *Just an Ordinary Day* (1995) and *Let Me Tell You: New Stories, Essays, and Other Writings* (2015), which were both edited by Laurence Jackson Hyman and Sarah Hyman DeWitt. The Jackson-Hyman family's promotion of the author's work and legacy has carried over to the next generation. Jackson's grandson, visual artist Miles Hyman, illustrated an edition of her children's story *9 Magic Wishes* in 2001 and adapted "The Lottery" as a graphic novel in 2016.

Renewed interest in Jackson's life and work has now extended to a new wave of visual adaptations. A film version of *We Have Always Lived in the Castle,* directed by Stacie Passon, came out in 2018. In that same year, Mike Flanagan's horror series *The Haunting of Hill House,* inspired by Jackson's most famous novel, was released on Netflix. In a turn of events which would probably have both amused and horrified Jackson (she was notably camera-shy), in 2020, *Handmaid's Tale* actor Elisabeth Moss played a fictionalized version of the author in the film *Shirley,* which is based on Susan Scarf Merrell's 2014 novel.

It is fair to say, then, that Jackson is most definitely back in the spotlight. That being said, this is the ideal time to publish this carefully selected and abridged collection of her correspondence. The letters provide a wealth of illuminating insights into Shirley Jackson's professional and personal life as it unfolded over the course of twenty-seven years.

The volume opens in June 1938, with one of the many love letters Jackson wrote to Stanley when they were undergraduates at Syracuse University. It concludes with a note to her literary agent Carol Brandt which Jackson sent little over a week before her death on August 8, 1965. Unfortunately, no letters written by Jackson before 1938 have yet been found. The 1950s is the most well documented decade here.

Although it appears that Jackson did not ask her parents to start saving her correspondence until 1960, it is interesting that the earliest letter we have from her to them was sent in 1948—the year she came to national prominence with "The Lottery."

The letters are addressed to a relatively small circle of regular correspondents. Those most frequently featured here are Stanley (almost all of these letters were written between June 1938 and May 1940), her parents (from 1948 onward), and from the early 1950s, her agents—first, Bernice Baumgarten and later, Carol Brandt. There are also letters to her children, Laurence, Joanne, Sally, and Barry, and to friends such as Louis Harap, Walter Bernstein, Ralph Ellison, Virginia Olsen, Libbie Burke, and Jeanne Beatty, as well as assorted other business contacts and acquaintances.

The letters featured in the first part of this volume, "From Debutante to Bohemian: 1938–1944," depict a side of Jackson that has often been overlooked. The title is entirely apt. We first encounter the author as a madly-in-love college student who is only too aware that she is living a decidedly bourgeois existence. As well as depicting her intense early relationship with Stanley, these letters amusingly reference the day-to-day realities of college life—whimsical conversations with friends, frequent parties, romantic misunderstandings and passionate reconciliations. There are also references to Jackson's literary interests, college classes, and contemporary political debates. Jackson's clashes with her fiercely anti-Communist and politically conservative father, Leslie, come up on several occasions.

There are also letters documenting Jackson's return to her native state of California during the summer of 1939, during which she writes movingly about the joy of once again seeing San Francisco. Jackson pines for Stanley throughout the trip, repeatedly declaring her love for him in extravagant terms. It is clear that the stay in California consolidated her already strong feelings for him. Jackson felt that she had found in him a true intellectual equal, and someone who supported her creative ambitions. These early letters also explain the idiosyncratic formatting style Jackson deployed in her letters to family and friends (and in first drafts of her writing) throughout the rest of her life: "notice if you haven't already that i have borrowed your distinctive writing style with ideas of my own such as no punctuation which is a good idea since semi-colons annoy me anyway."

There are many passages of interest pertaining to Jackson's development as a writer. These include references to *Anthony*, the unfinished novel that she worked on during this time, as well as brief mentions of poems and stories written while she was a teenager. Jackson also displays a keen awareness of her aptitude for conflating the everyday with the uncanny. In a letter to Stanley written in December 1938, she declares:

christmas is incredibly horrible when seen from the jacksonian leaping-at-sudden-fears angle. for example, wandering happily along, in a daze of beatific peace-on-earthness, i found myself face to face with a windowful of monstrous bells tolling horribly right before my nose. to my mind there is something dreadful about large objects moving silently and somehow ominously, particularly when, like these, they were swinging slowly back and forth . . .

Readers familiar with the later fiction will recognize this as a superb early instance of Jackson's unrivaled ability to imbue inanimate objects with malevolent qualities. It is hard not to flash forward to 1959, and to Eleanor Vance's first, repulsed impression of Hill House: "The house was vile. She shivered and thought, the words coming freely into her mind, Hill House is vile, it is diseased; get away from here at once."

We have no letters written between the end of May 1940 and January 1942. During this time, Jackson and Hyman graduated from Syracuse, moved to New York City, married (in August 1940), and had their first child, Laurence. The correspondence starts back up again with a series of letters and notes to their friend Louis Harap. Jackson was already beginning to sell stories to magazines such as *Mademoiselle* and *The New Yorker*, and confident enough in her talent to chastise Harap when he provided literary feedback that she clearly disagreed with "i don't think you're any kind of judge of what i'm trying to do."

We also find here the first of many references to the practicalities of balancing motherhood with a literary career. Jackson explains to

Harap in a July 1944 letter that the nocturnal wanderings of their young son mean that "my usual time for writing—the evening—has been curtailed, and i do even less." This same letter references an event of great historic import—the Allied invasion of Normandy—and an intriguing career opportunity for Stanley. It seems that Bennington, a small liberal arts college in the wilds of rural Vermont, is looking for young instructors. Jackson's closing remarks are typically droll: "if they should offer stanley a job it means i would be married to a college professor, doesn't it, unless i got wise in time? and can't you just see stanley teaching a seminar in a girl's college? whee."

There was indeed a job in Bennington, and the young family's move from the city to the countryside would have lasting personal and professional consequences for Jackson. Despite the fact that she seldom referenced a specific geographical setting in her fiction, thanks in part to the flurry of attention generated by "The Lottery," her writing soon became irretrievably associated with New England. Apart from a two-year stint in Saugatuck, Connecticut, she spent the rest of her days living in North Bennington. As Jackson's subsequent letters illustrate, her life, Stanley's life, and the lives of their young children became intrinsically connected with Bennington College and the surrounding community.

From the late 1940s onward, publishing deadlines vie with the due dates and demands of Jackson's human offspring. In the earliest surviving letter to her parents, written in October 1948, Jackson mentions juggling proof corrections for *The Lottery and Other Stories* (1949) with preparations to give birth to her third child, Sally. A rather flustered letter written to her mother, Geraldine, in April 1949 details the origins of a delicious (but untrue) story that dogged her thereafter: the rumor that Jackson had cast a hex on publisher Alfred A. Knopf, causing him to break his leg while on a skiing trip in Vermont. Jackson's evident dismay here is compounded by the flippant response she gave to a reporter who asked her to expound upon her supposed expertise in witchcraft: "fortunately he had just bought me two drinks, so i was able to tell him, very fluently indeed, about black magic and incantations and the practical application of witchcraft in everyday life, most of which i remembered out of various mystery stories."

Jackson's family stories became an increasingly important facet of her creative output during this period. We find in the letters from this time considerable delight in the fact that they are an obvious popular and financial success and came to constitute a vital source of income for their growing household. It is therefore striking to see her critique the quality of this material in letters to her parents, as in this October 1949 missive:

> I quite agree with you about the recent stories. they are written simply for money, and the reason they sound so bad is that those magazines won't buy good ones, but deliberately seek out bad stuff because they say their audiences want it. i simply figure that at a thousand bucks a story, i can't afford to try to change the state of popular fiction today, and since they will buy as much of it as i write, i do one story a month, and spend the rest of the time work-ing on my new novel or on other stories. [. . .] this sort of thing is a compromise between their notions and mine, and is unusual enough so that i am the only person i know of who is doing it. that's why i can sell them.

Contrastingly, in a letter written a few years later to her editor at *Good Housekeeping,* Jackson persuasively defends the originality and social importance of these stories:

> i suppose that essentially what i am saying is that there is just so much fun and satisfaction in day-to-day life in a family that maybe it's time someone wrote about that, and shouted down the children-are-monsters people. some articles, perhaps, on the infu-riating things, like bullies and outsiders and meanness, but always stressing the notion that things are fundamentally nice. i get many letters from women who feel that they are buried hopelessly under the endless problems of a family, and have found that just one humorous article has given them enough of a brief new glimpse so that they can dig in again and get the laundry done in half the time, or get through dinner one more night without screaming. i

admit it's a subject important to me. i'd like to know what you think.

This obvious contrast between the ways in which Jackson characterizes her magazine writing in these quotes is one of several intriguing instances in this volume in which we see her express different shades of opinion about her own works (or their filmic adaptations) depending upon whether she is addressing her parents or discussing them with a professional contact. Jackson's letters to Geraldine and Leslie frequently itemize the financial and reputational rewards of her literary endeavors. Yet at the same time, she could downplay the significance of work which her parents (and perhaps even she herself) seemed to perceive as being motivated less by artistic inspiration and more by practical commercial imperative. This critique of the family stories may suggest that Jackson had on some level internalized the wider societal feeling that explicitly "domestic" and female-focused material was of course meant to be taken less seriously than challenging, intense works of fiction such as "The Lottery" and *The Road Through the Wall* (both of which were published during the late 1940s, at much the same time that Jackson's family tales started to become an increasingly important facet of her output).

The same reasoning may also explain the negativity Jackson later expresses towards the film adaptations of *The Bird's Nest* (*Lizzie,* Dir: Hugo Haas, 1957) and *The Haunting of Hill House* (*The Haunting,* Dir: Robert Wise, 1963) in letters home. It's almost as if she's reluctant to be seen to endorse these "Hollywood" versions of her work despite the apparently sincere excitement she expresses elsewhere (particularly in letters to her agents). Throughout their correspondence, it is obvious that Jackson wanted her work to be a source of pride and satisfaction to her parents, and this may explain why she sometimes self-deprecatingly preempts (or agrees with) their potentially critical response to the more "commercial" side of her career.

Jackson's works in progress (particularly the novels) are often referenced in the 1950s letters, particularly those written to Baumgarten and Brandt. Highlights include a witty aside about the unexpected side effects of writing a novel about a protagonist with multiple personalities—"The trouble, I find, with writing and being absorbed in a book about dissociated personality is that after a while you begin to dissociate yourself"—and Jackson's hilarious account of a business meeting she and Baumgarten had with the wildly enthusiastic actor-producer Franchot Tone, who wanted her to write a film about Isadora Duncan.

There are letters here which highlight Jackson's attention to detail and absolute certainty regarding the effect she wanted her work to exert upon readers. For instance, in a 1957 letter to her publishers correcting misleading jacket copy for *The Sundial,* Jackson demonstrates a keen awareness of the delicate sense of equilibrium associated with her work: "I realize that this must sound like a childish temper tantrum, but it seems to me that <u>Sundial</u> is so precariously balanced on the edge of the ridiculous that any slip might send it in the wrong direction; I tried to keep it on that uneasy edge because I thought it made the book more exciting, but I wouldn't like to see anyone breathe on it too hard." We are also privy to some tantalizing insights into the research Jackson conducted when in the early stages of planning her most famous novel. In January 1958 she writes to her parents to ask if they have any information about the Winchester Mystery House:

> the reason for this is my new book; it is to be about a haunted house, and i can't seem to find anything around here; all the old new england houses are the kind of square, classical type which wouldn't be haunted in a million years. i have half a dozen sketches of california houses which look right, but remember the winchester house as a good type house for haunting.

The new book was, of course, *The Haunting of Hill House.* We later see Jackson's evident satisfaction with the rapid progress of her exciting new project, and her empathy for the characters as the plot trajectory arcs inexorably towards tragedy: "The novel is getting sadder. I suppose it's because of a general melancholy, leaves turning red and a frost last night, but a general air of disaster is slowly settling over Hill

House. It's always such a strange feeling—I know something's going to happen, and those poor people in the book don't; they just go blithely on their ways."

There are fascinating glimpses here too of works that might have been, including several unfinished novels. These include her early 1950s effort *Abigail,* the college novel *Anthony,* the fantasy novel *The Fair Land of Far,* and of course, *Come Along with Me.*

Work on Jackson's final published novel, *We Have Always Lived in the Castle,* had begun by early 1960, but it was to prove a more protracted process than the composition of *Hill House.* As Jackson explained to Jeanne Beatty, "the heroine is named merricat; do you like it? mary catherine really, but we who know her best say Merricat." As detailed by Ruth Franklin, Beatty had sent a "simple fan note" to Jackson in December 1959. This led to an intense and intimate correspondence, which lasted for much of the writing process of *We Have Always Lived in the Castle.*

In the Beatty letters, Jackson enthusiastically discusses her opinions on literature and, in particular, her thoughts on fantasy, science fiction, and children's fiction. She is often humorously frank here about her personal preferences: "and i think i am probably the only person around these days who reads samuel richardson for pleasure; SIR CHARLES GRANDISON is perhaps my dearest book. i don't recommend it however unless you are in jail or somewhere else where you have plenty of time. mystery stories i read all the time and stanley gets furious because he is always reading something like ULYSSES which i frankly regard as a great bore." A particular high point is her droll analysis of the reasons why J. R. R. Tolkien has such evident difficulty in writing about women.

Jackson also discussed the evident difficulties she was having with her promising but difficult new novel, of which "four people" had now read the first two chapters:

> and all independently announce that it is the best work i have ever done so if i could only stop with the first two chapters and publish those it would be fine but no they want another two hundred pages. it is hard. very hard. i finally got it into a kind of sustained

taut style full of images and all kinds of double meanings and i can manage about three pages a day before my eyes cross and my teeth start to chatter, and i shall be late i shall be late.

The number of letters written by Jackson from the late 1950s onward appears to have decreased significantly. Conversations with Laurence Jackson Hyman about this issue have raised the possibility that a reduction in the price of long-distance phone calls to California meant that lengthy digests of the latest family news for her parents were no longer a practical necessity. There is also a strong likelihood that the issues that impeded Jackson's progress on *We Have Always Lived in the Castle* also affected her correspondence. She wrote to her friend Libbie Burke in October 1963, "Part of my current writing bloc is a complete inability to write letters; I can barely manage." As has been documented by her biographers, this was a difficult time for Jackson, who had to contend with marital problems, physical ailments, and episodes of severe anxiety. Jackson's female protagonists often found home to be both a sanctuary and a prison: one of the most moving sentences in this volume is therefore surely the author's weary admission, in a 1962 letter to her daughter Sally, that "i no longer go out of the house." Another is found in a heartbreaking letter written to Stanley (probably) in 1960, which concludes with the lines: "you once wrote <u>me</u> a letter (i know you hate my remembering these things) telling me that i would never be lonely again. i think that was the first, the most dreadful, lie you ever told me."

It is for these reasons then that Jackson's final years are amongst the most sparsely covered here. As with the makeup of her selected letters throughout this volume, this state of affairs accurately reflects the composition of her entire body of (known) correspondence. Jackson's last known letter was written to Carol Brandt only a few days before her death and ends with the unintentionally moving line "everything this summer seems to have been conspiring to keep me from working, but I do make progress."

It is clear that Jackson relished every opportunity to tell a good story. Many of the anecdotes contained in these letters are comic gems in their own right. A personal favorite is her account of the night when, tired of "hovering between three and four children," Jackson resorted to drastic, doctor-prescribed measures. She vividly describes forcing down a vile concoction of castor oil and cream soda (followed by a whisky chaser), as Stanley and their close friend Ralph Ellison—who was supposed to drive her to the hospital—looked on with horror and "real respect." The frustration caused by the baby's stubborn refusal to appear despite these heroic efforts is accentuated by a twist in the tale. Little Barry wasn't overdue at all: they'd miscalculated his due date.

As a Jackson scholar (and a Jackson fan), it has been a pleasure to consult with Laurence Jackson Hyman throughout the editing and selection process for this volume. The letters featured here deserve to stand alongside her previously published writings as works of considerable literary merit and interest in their own right, and I have no doubt that they will inspire further critical and academic interest in Jackson's entire oeuvre. Even more importantly, I know that they will fascinate, delight, and move her readers.

It seems appropriate, then, to leave the final words here to Shirley Jackson, for whom writing (of every kind) constituted such an essential component of her personal and professional identity. As she wrote toward the end of an April 1962 letter to her parents: "keep well. write soon. keep soon. write well."

> Bernice M. Murphy
> School of English,
> Trinity College Dublin

Note: I would like to thank Janice Deitner and Dara Downey for their invaluable feedback on this introduction.

## WORKS REFERENCED

Carpenter, Lynette. "Domestic Comedy, Black Comedy, and Real Life: Shirley Jackson, a Woman Writer." In *Faith of a Woman Writer*, eds. Alice Kessler-Harris and William McBrien. New York: Greenwood Press, 1988.

Franklin, Ruth. *Shirley Jackson: A Rather Haunted Life.* New York: Liveright Publishing, 2016.

Friedan, Betty. *The Feminine Mystique.* New York: W. W. Norton, 1963.

Friedman, Lenemaja. *Shirley Jackson.* Boston: Twayne, 1975.

Jackson, Shirley. *The Haunting of Hill House.* London: Penguin Modern Classics, 1959; 2009.

Jancovich, Mark. *Rational Fears: American Horror in the 1950s.* Manchester, UK: Manchester University Press, 1996.

King, Stephen. *Danse Macabre.* New York: Simon & Schuster, 1981; 2011.

Parks, John. "Chambers of Yearning: Shirley Jackson's Use of the Gothic." In *Shirley Jackson: Essays on the Literary Legacy,* ed. Bernice M. Murphy. Jefferson, N.C.: McFarland, 1984; 2005.

# ONE

· · ·

## From Debutante to Bohemian: 1938–1944

I must stop writing letters and get to writing a novel. If you think of any good scenes for a novel covering about forty pages send them right along. I can use anything I get.

—To Louis Harap, May 11, 1944

*Shirley Jackson is born in San Francisco, California, on December 14, 1916. Her father, Leslie, emigrated from England at age twelve with his mother and two sisters and became a self-made successful business executive with the largest lithography company in the city. Her mother, Geraldine, is a proud descendant of a long line of famous San Francisco architects and can trace her ancestry back to before the Revolutionary War.*

*Shirley grows up primarily in Burlingame, an upper-middle-class suburb south of the city. But when she is sixteen, Leslie is promoted and transferred, and the family moves—luxuriously, by ship, through the Panama Canal—to Rochester, in upstate New York. The Jacksons quickly join the Rochester Country Club and become well-established in the city's active society world. The move is very hard on Shirley, who misses California and her friends there, especially her best friend, Dorothy Ayling. She finishes high school in Rochester (where one of her classes is once interrupted for a few minutes so that Shirley can marvel at snow falling outside the window), then attends the University of Rochester for one difficult year, before deciding to spend the next year writing alone in her room at home, with the lofty goal of producing a thousand words a day. Little of what Shirley writes during that period is believed to have survived.*

*She then enrolls at Syracuse University, where she enjoys literature classes, and where the university's journal,* The Threshold, *publishes her story "Janice," a one-page conversation with a young woman who brags that she has that day attempted suicide. Another literature student, Stanley Edgar Hyman, from Brooklyn, New York, the brash, intellectual son of a Jewish second-generation wholesale paper merchant, reads her story and vows on the spot to find and marry its author.*

*Shirley and Stanley meet on March 3, 1938, in the library listening room, and an intellectual connection quickly develops into a romantic one. These letters begin just three months after they've met, when both Shirley and Stanley are on summer break, she at home in Rochester, and he at first at home in Brooklyn and then rooming with his friend Walter Bernstein at Dartmouth, then working at a paper mill in Erving, Massachussetts.*

*This is the earliest known surviving letter of Shirley's. She is twenty-one, and Stanley is about to turn nineteen.*

### [To Stanley Edgar Hyman]

tuesday [June 7, 1938]

portrait of the artist at work. seems i brought a collection of miscellaneous belongings home from school, among them a c and c hat* which bewilders goddamnthatword my little brother. he says if it's a hat why doesn't it have signatures all over it. mother seems to think i'm insane, and closes her eyes in a pained fashion when i call her chum. she also tells me that love or no love i have to eat and when i say eatschmeat she says what did you say and for a minute icy winds are blowing. there has been hell breaking loose ever since mother woke me this morning by telling me that that was a letter from dartmouth that the dog was eating.† when she came in an hour later and found me reading the letter for the fifth time she began to be curious and asked me all sorts of questions about you. yes, she got it all. consequently there was a rather nice scene, me coming off decidedly the worse, since mother quite unfairly enlisted alta's‡ assistance and alta went and made a cake and i like cake. mother says, in effect: go on and be a damn fool but don't tell your father. i had to cry rather loudly though. which means that you are going to meet a good deal more opposition than i had counted on. i think mother was mad because she took your long distance call the other day and the big shot was expecting an important business call and he was quite excited when the operator said that the party at the other end of the line wasn't going to pay. yes, and mother says to tell you that any more

---

* A plush beanie hat, still popular today, named "c and c" after the French cheveux corp, or "body of hair."
† Stanley is staying with Walter Bernstein at Dartmouth for the summer.
‡ Alta is the Jacksons' live-in maid and cook.

letters arriving with postage due and she will either steam the letters open since they belong to her since she practically bought them or she will start taking the postage out of my allowance.

however all in all she is being rather sweet, and more intelligent than i gave her credit for, since she absolutely refuses to forbid me to see you which means that now i have no reason to be romantically clandestine. disappointing when i'd already picked out a hollow oak tree. which brings me to the point: if you love me so damn much why don't you come out and say so? looked all through your letter to find out if you loved me and you refuse to say. damn you anyway. i love you you dope.

notice if you haven't already that i have borrowed your distinctive writing style with ideas of my own such as no punctuation which is a good idea since semi-colons annoy me anyway. and incidentally i read mother the poem at the top of the pages in your letter and she translated it for me, she knows french and i don't but even then it wasn't such a good idea. i also told father all about communism which was wrong, wasn't it. he said re-ally in a whatthehelldoyou-knowaboutlifeyoushelteredvictorianflower sort of voice.

also. y* snarls deep down in her throat whenever i mention you which idoratheroftenchum. she thinks you're a nice sweet child, only it's too bad you had to fall into my clutches. i managed to get to talking before she did so now she knows all my troubles and i don't know any of hers. 'tanley . . . i think i'll come to new york and get laid. ooooooooooh yes. my mother mayhertribeincrease had been reading liberty† that oracle of the masses and has discovered that eight out of ten college students are all for immorality. she has been asking me leading questions until i came out and said that if she meant had i preserved the fresh bloom of dewy innocence yes i had but it hurt me a damn sight more than it ever hurt liberty. mother is reassured but not too happy about the whole thing, having doubts.

i didn't know y was an ardent communist but she is, but then she

---

* Elizabeth Young, nicknamed y ("ee") by Shirley, was her best friend in Rochester.
† *Liberty* magazine was a general-interest weekly that was started in 1924 and lasted until 1950.

was a vegetarian once too. we're going to drink beer, and i mean that we're going to drink lots of beer. but quantities. we have sorrows to drown.

about our mutual friend Michael.* he brought the scamp . . . boat . . . in fifth in saturday's race and mother saw him that night and he was plenty drunk and getting drunker and the damnfool insulted mother in some way and now she's mad and michael can't come see me till mother is appeased and he'll never remember that he said anything wrong till someone meaning me reminds him. are you happier than formerly?

s.edgar. it's so silly to write this junk when all i want to say is i can't stand it i won't wait four months i love you. what am i going to do? it's not going to be long, is it? it'll be september soon, won't it? like hell it will.

shan't go on like that. i'm going to Be Brave. bloody, but unbowed. going to be a debutante. yeah. i'm going to count the days and minutes till september. think of me sometimes, won't you, chum. hell. wish i could think of a good quotation to top that paragraph off with.

i shall go on writing revolutionary poetry as long as i damn well please. i just thought of a good line: capitalists unite you have a world to win and nothing to lose but your chains . . .

dearest, <u>be</u> a good boy, and <u>do</u> wear your rubbers, for mother's sake, now won't you?

darling!

p.s. s. edgar; goddamn your lying soul why did you have to go away and leave me? I love you so much.

s.

•  •  •

* Michael Palmer, Shirley's casual boyfriend in Rochester, was from an affluent family, raced boats, and was a member of the Rochester Yacht Club, where his family socialized with the Jacksons.

## [To Stanley Edgar Hyman]

[June 8, 1938]

hawney!

every time i get a letter from you, which seems to be an event happening with astonishing frequency, i think of more things i want to say to you, most of them being i love you but that's beside the point. so it has come to the position where i write you every day because you write me every day and i hope you like the idea. anyway i like to write letters in your style because i don't have to hunt for the shiftkey and because it's easier on ernest, who is typewriter, and makes him very happy because he is lazy too.

this is gibbering

and it looks like e e cummings, who y said my revolutionary poetry reminded her of and when i asked her what that meant she said she didn't like e e cummings either.

i know that should be whom

stop correcting me

you better go easy on my mother. she is getting amused by this faithful in my fashion* idea and says she thinks you must be an awful dope to expect me to learn to cook. moreover she wants to know why she can't read your letters. i told her it was secret propaganda but that didn't help much either. she is having her reading club here this afternoon which means that she expects me to pour tea but that ain't all she expects. she says: now, darling, <u>please</u> for my sake put on a decent dress and do something with your hair, and you might even do your fingernails something quiet if you can, and <u>will</u> you be polite to my guests, after all they may be society but some of them are really quite nice and if you'll only be nice like i said i might buy you that silly book.

---

* "Faithful in my fashion, Cynara" was code between Shirley and Stanley for Stanley's infidelities. The term comes from a poem by Ernest Dowson, with the line "I have been faithful to thee, Cynara! in my fashion."

that silly book being fearing* if i can get it

so i put up my hair

but that ain't gonna stop me from flapping my eyelashes at miss macarty who is the dame what reviews the book and saying sweetly: do you like cathedral close, dear? don't you think it's too, too wonderful, and what about eliot? i adore eliot, but robert frost? so much horse-shit, as i know you will be the first to say. you do have such a wonderful grasp of literature, dear.

if that doesn't finish mother with the reading club i have lived in vain.

my father has taken to reading aloud to me from the nation's business and also donates small booklets which i am to read to rid my mind of the foul decay of communism. he has become convinced that i am a confirmed communist and despairs of my soul. here is one paragraph that you might like. from youthinbusiness, a speech by a man whom the big shot says is really quite intelligent: "The system under which we live is not perfect. of course not. no system yet devised by man is. but it has grown better and better over a long period of time, it is the only one that has done this in so consistent and enduring a fashion . . . the fact that we have come as far as we have doesn't mean, though, that america has now reached a standstill. i said before that the system was far from perfect, but it is constantly getting better as we learn more about its operations. if you retain this system you will find, as you grow older, a constantly expanding opportunity, an enlarging horizon, better times than we have today . . ."

am i the only one then who longs to perpetuate the status quo

by the way, y is a socialist and not a communist, but i suppose it's all the same. all radical. all vegetarians.

dearest. i love you, i love you, and i need you so much. you've got walter and dartmouth to console you but all i have is y, who takes a malicious delight in explaining to people thus: "Well, he's sorta dumb, but he's got a lot of money. they've been secretly married for

---

* Kenneth Fearing, poet.

over a month now. lee* isn't telling people because . . . well, it's a secret. i think he's wonderful. he's taken over the rochester yacht club
and is going to try to run it at a profit . . ." you should see janice
who by the way is not speaking to me anymore. y says that she took
great pains to get a copy of the threshold[†] to janice. y <u>also</u> says that
she's very fond of you and she thinks you're giving me the needles.
y's cute.

s.edgar. i am afraid that you will have forgotten very soon. please,
if you do, don't go on writing and trying to make me think that you
haven't. but, then, too, please don't forget or stop loving me, or learn
to love someone else more. because i love you so much. If I once start
telling you what I really feel you'll see how scared I am, and how
much more I need you than you'll ever need me.

O.K. i'm sorry. i'll shut up, and be a good girl and go pour tea. i
love you. for gods sake write me and convince me you're not lying to
me when you say it's all right. i think i'll tear this damned document
up. it's not very clever is it. not up to the usual jackson standard.
blame it on my misery. or on the reading club.

lee

p.s. i gather that you have managed to find a minute to whisper in
walter's[‡] pearly ear that you love me.

later . . . blessed be the name of my dog. mother took hours to persuade me into a pink dress with dots all over and even got my hair
up, dragged me down to listen to mrs. johnston tell about her trip to
europe . . . so wonderful, all those places, we really enjoyed it sooooo
much, and the boat, so big, and england, so dirty, but charming, and i
picked up the cutest bag in belgium, just like the ones in new york,
only so much cheaper . . . only mother made the mistake of shutting
the dog in my room, and so it became necessary for me to go upstairs

* Lee was a nickname Shirley gave to herself, to rhyme with that of her friend y ("ee").
† Shirley's story "Janice" appeared in *The Threshold* in February 1938.
‡ Walter Bernstein—Stanley is still staying with Walter at Dartmouth.

and speak to him about his howling, and once upstairs, she can't leave to come up and get me, so i grabbed the typewriter quick. debutante, indeed.

have gone back to reading p.g. wodehouse. quiet the nerves. please dear write me soon, i'm afraid that whether i have anything to say about it or not y is going to write you. she says she has a few little things she'd like to tell you. god help <u>you</u>. she had a few little things she wanted to tell me and i'm still raw.

for god's sake can you think of any telepathic way by which i can get myself into your arms and stay there?

· · ·

me.

"Me."

[To Stanley Edgar Hyman]

[June 13, 1938]

sugar,

i forget why i didn't write yesterday; i think i was washing my hair. you ought to have received at least one of my letters by now. i mailed one tuesday night; at least i gave it to a funny little man in a mail-truck who said he was the postman; y was with me and will witness the same. maybe i forgot to stamp them or something equally sta-cian.* i had a letter from shiah† this morning. shiah wants y and me to wander syracuse-wards this summer for a call. mother properly outraged: whatvisita<u>man</u>! perhaps that's because shiah promised beer in his letter.

   also: mother, weakening visibly, asks me to correct an erroneous impression: she likes you, thinks you a dear boy, and, after hearing how you made me eat three hot fudge sundaes, positively dotes on you. she heard properly censored versions of your literary criticisms and thinks you an intelligent young man, but i told her you copied them out of a book.

   y has also asked me very nicely to ask you very nicely to ask walter very nicely if he would mind living in sin with her in new york. she has also taken a fancy to walter who is the only person she has ever heard of who lives in new york where she wants to study the ballet. she is afraid that walter will not look with favor upon her gifts, but says she will always hope and remember him fondly. (i am, s. edgar, worried about her. since her breakdown she has not opened a book and swears she will not read for the next two years, or, if she is not better, never study again. she rejoices at not having her degree, be-cause she hates the university, and hates everyone there. she is begin-ning to hate stepan. she looks like hell, and all her previous

* Another of Shirley's nicknames for herself was Stacia, representing the troublesome side of her personality; she sometimes called her "my demon."
† Shiah is a Syracuse friend of theirs.

knowledge is becoming confused, so that she contradicts herself and forgets what she is talking about. she has this constant deep fear of insanity. i have never known her to be less at ease. she just can't think . . . she wants me to help her, and by helping her she means be with her all the time, and keep her from thinking. i'm scared . . . what can I do with her?)

dear, i can't write letters. the old art has deserted me. you take consolation in reading; i sit for hours at the typewriter and only succeed in composing strange sonnets. think i'll send you a couple. they may not sound eclectic to you, but bear in mind the fact that i have been rereading finnegan. and anyone asking what they mean will be forthwith consigned to dante's lowest level. (of hell, not writing) i personally think they are fascinatingly obscure, and maybe revolutionary. no, certainly revolutionary; maybe leftist. i can't read you know. no concentration. i even abandoned mr. wodehouse. in rochester they don't have mr hemingway in the libraries because they don't think he is fit reading. is that chauvinistic, when they have thomas thackeryswinburne, richester's [sic] own.

y, after hearing your comments on spender and eliot, is seriously considering a long long letter to you. she wants to know how you work in the goldenbough.

darling i haven't remembered for two letters to tell you about this deep passion that i have been cherishing toward you. i tried to tell y and she wouldn't listen. i miss your funny hair. and your dimples. i believe i even miss you a little. dionysius. maudlin hell. i'm in love with the guy. i love you . . . being without you, even for this past week, has been purest hell, and there haven't been many moments when i wasn't thinking about you. i wait for your letters every morning, and when i try to write to you i'm almost afraid to start because there are so many things i want to tell you and i'm scared i'll say them. if only i could see you for even a little while! i could say them then. i'm not used to this business, s. edgar. i don't know how to tell you these things. enough. me, i'll go mad.

darling, this is just what i wanted to tell you over the phone last night and didn't have time to say. i'm not afraid any more, and not worried, and not going to marry any goddamned fool of a michael and i'm only going to love you for ever and ever amen. and don't ever, ever believe anything different. all this nonsense about how i should be gaily having myself a time is to stop at once, because like the silly idiot i am, i am happier sitting around thinking about you all day. i want you more than anything in the world and you needn't imagine that anything you can say or do is going to stop me from getting what i want, and you can't even stop me from wanting it, so stop arguing.

this is the first real love letter i ever tried to write and it's not very good, i need more practice. see that you give me some. practically the only thing i know is that i love you and love you and love you.

s.

. . .

[To Stanley Edgar Hyman]

tues. [June 14, 1938]

hero of m'life,

afternoon of a debutante . . . life is assuming alarming aspects. mad, mad gaiety. things like: fri. nite, bridge, sat. aft. ride to yacht club . . . not with michael . . . to see races, sun. country club, dinner (only i didn't go because i was half-expecting a vereee important phone call), mon. nite, y, tues. ride horseback, wed. calling with mama, thurs. tea, fri. dash off a novel, sat., luncheon, sat. nite, country club dance . . . with michael, sun. baseball game . . . etc. i never plan more than a week in advance. notice, too, that every day leaves at least three hours off to write seh. and another hour each morning to decipher seh's typing.

had no letter from you yesterday, and came down to breakfast and a frown which my small brother aggravated until he was told to gotohellyougoddamlittlebastard, much to mother's unmitigated horror. upon which she came soothingly into the sunroom where i was miserably feeding the dog toast and said poor little girl did she feel terrible because she didn't get a letter? upon which i told her the same thing i had told my brother, with changes made necessary by the dog's presence, and she said that's all right, just be calm, maybe the letter will come this afternoon. so she took me shopping and bought me two new fuzzy sweaters, giggling the while because there was no seh for them to get fuzz all over. this morning mother, with a gleam in her eye that i suspect indicated gratitude to you, threw two letters in my face and said itoldyouso. next time, chum, if you want to keep peace in the jacksonhousehold, you write on monday.

about that telephone call, now. hearing you be speechless for the first time in nineteen years did my heart good. i had been waiting all day for you to call . . . remember i didn't know whether you would or not, and knowing your financial status, suspected not. but mother had me locked in the bedroom with the upstairs phone, so that if you <u>did</u> call . . . (don't blame her. she tells her friends: "I just don't know what to <u>do</u> with the child! seems she's in love!") by the time i got through waiting twenty minutes for you to find the phone after the operator got hold of me i was a nervous wreck, and was dropping ashes from my cigarette all over the phone book. and when i heard your voice . . . goddam you, don't ever do that again. sound so suppressed and unhappy, i mean. and sort of incoherent, too. if you do decide to call again on sunday night, call after nine, anyway. my father was quite upset about being made to stay home from the club because i was waiting for a call. darling, it made a nervous wreck out of me, hearing your voice like that. and you did sound like a little boy . . .

if you must be literary, tell me what to do with my novel, which is coming along fine, thank you. i have been working on anthony,* who has suddenly turned into an emotional weakling, with a very real fear of insecurity. he is afraid of paul and jealous of mary. is that fair. also, from nowhere there has come a wife to anthony, named edith, who just wandered in on page six of anthony and started to talk. i rather like her, though, she's nice.

---

* *Anthony* is the title of a novel Shirley is struggling to write.

last night y took me calling on a sick friend, a mrs. sherwood, a
very charming young woman who had a wrenched back and to
whom we took peonies stolen out of my mother's garden. mrs. s.,
pleased, entertained us with rum toffee, which i adore. also, she is
very interested in astrology, and always tells me how lucky i am to be
a sagittarius, and the typical sagg at that. seems all of those people
are happy, worthless, and lucky. that's me. sun is now opposite my
sign, which means i should be unhappy, only i ain't, which mrs. s. lays
to the fact that i don't know anything about astrology.

my demon returned unexpectedly last night and for two hours
mrs. s. and y had to listen to stacia. i have discovered that you can't be
stacia and plan a luncheon. and mother everlastingly disgraced, taking me shopping. we went to buy shoes and the shoe salesman who
is an old friend of the family and calls me, familiarly, sister, and calls
mother madam, looked upon my darned stockings with distinct dis-
approval. i said defensively that i had mended them myself and after
we had picked the shoeman up and revived him he said all by myself
and i said yes and he said well . . . and turned my foot over and there
was no sole to the stocking. mother swooned and bought me three
new pair of stockings, and then she took me to buy dresses and it
seems that my slip, a subject about which you, as a little gentleman,
should know nothing, had been several inches too long and i had
employed the old dormitory method of tying a string around the
waist and hiking the slip up into a blouse effect so it was short. when
mother saw that, and saw the red and black string i had used, she
tightened her lips and went and bought me two short slips. and
when we met some dar* friends of hers and they looked sort of funny
at my old coat with the lining hanging in shreds and the belt in two
pieces, she made me go and hide behind a rack of dresses until they
were gone and then went and bought me a new coat and two new
dresses. i dunno . . . maybe it's a racket, but it always works.

write me twice a day. i like the idea. you ought to start getting this
week's crop of letters round about wednesday. i'll mail all the old
ones i have lying around. i love you.

* Daughters of the American Revolution. Geraldine's Bugbee-Field family considered
themselves members.

s. edgar: for your info, there is a young female in rochester and i don't mean y who thinks about you a lot and wishes she could see you and loves you very much.

by the way make walter let you steal castaway.* dear walter let stanley steal castaway and i will give you all my oz books. that is a promise. shirley h jackson.

'tanley, i'm getting awfully fond of you.

s.

•    •    •

[To Stanley Edgar Hyman]

wednesday [June 15, 1938]

dear,

monopoly established by mother in the stamp market, raising the price to five cents per, and me in slacks and slippers, so could not get out to buy more. i of course refuse to bow to injustice and so did not mail your letter. i am going on strike or else going to carry the matter to the paternal supreme which will undoubtedly render an oracular decision running roughly: well, if you've got to write to a communist, which is all silliness anyway. why on earth are people communists anyway? thus high finance in the jackson household. my brother has paid me the dollar, under stress. very easy system. i talk to one of his fraternity brothers for a while. then: Oh, so you got stinking at the sigma chi dance, huh? out cold, huh? well, how'd you like to have headquarters hear about <u>that</u>? . . . he gave me the dollar quite easily.

s. edgar, i am bewildered and unhappy, and i don't quite under-stand so many things. you remember my telling you about elizabeth, my college friend who was a philosophy major, phi bete, and then

---

* *Castaway*, a novel by James Gould Cozzens, was very important to both Shirley and Stanley. By odd coincidence, Shirley's agent and friend years later will be Bernice Baumgarten, wife of Cozzens.

couldn't get anything but a factory job and subsequently turned radical? she is out of work again, and is deathly afraid that her younger brother will get a job before she does, because then he will have to support the whole family. she was here last night, and i asked her about this whole radical setup. seems she is a socialistunionworker or something like that, which she says is trotskyist. she bent that whole mighty brain of hers and all her personality to trying to convince me that any radical viewpoint, so long as it was cognizant of the necessity for social change, was right, and i, having listened to my father for lo these many long months, cannot be convinced. i respect elizabeth like i respect you, and believe that you are as right as my father, but why should i have to think one way or the other? do i have to shout and wave my arms in favor of the revolution, or else oppress the poor proletariat? must i be one or the other?

why in hell should i be concerned over humanity, one way or the other? you know my rather passive misanthropic tendencies, and how i hate this whole human race as a collection of monsters. if so, why should i want to save the bastards? why should i worry if half of them are standing on the necks of the other half? i once made a character, my famous Man Who Went Mad From Eating Carrots, who, besides being a nice comedian, also managed to express much of this hatred of mine. he is a portrait of me, anyway, as usual. here's my Man. being a sketch of the author at work, he enters reciting over and over again: A B C D . . . what comes after D? then, after some conversation with lee . . . who is also me . . . he says (still being me):

 . . . i want to reform the things that people hold so dear to their stinking little heads. i want to take something away from all these tiny unimportant creatures that call themselves God's chosen. i wish i could hurt them terribly, terribly . . . i hate them—god, how i hate all people! their insignificance—oh, it's all so funny, deathly funny, because they none of them know. but they'll know how much i hate them. i'll show them, when i take away those things they base their lives on! i'm starting with the alphabet, you see. they'll never know what happened, only that their precious, comfortable alphabet is gone . . . destroyed. i'll laugh—can you hear me laughing? and then . . . their cash-and-carry stores. and street cars. and imitation

flowers and genuine soapstone bookends and cheap fancy letter
paper and china dogs on ashtrays. i'll take all these things, and rip
them to pieces, and people will go mad, and then—then everyone
will be mad, and they'll know how i hate them!

. . . and pictures on sofa pillows . . . sofa pillows with paintings on
them that say: Souvenir of Sioux City . . . and their cheap novels, and
glue, and five-and-ten-cent jewelry and movie stars. god! how i'll
tear their hero-worship to pieces! and their silly clothes, and . . . but
most of all their stupid, stupid smugness! i'll kill them all—but, you
see, i can't start yet, i can never remember what comes after D. if i
could only remember what comes after D, I could . . .

which, seh, is the gentleman's exit line. no doubt very bad writing,
but so heartfelt that, even now, reading over it, it fills me with the
same impotent fury that made me write it before.

can you see any good, valid reason why i should be concerned with
people? thinking of them makes me want to bash my brains out
against the stone wall of their stupidity, trying to murder them all . . .
remember Millay's line: I love humanity, but i hate people? mine is
altered to: i like many people, but god! what i think of humanity! can
you understand my reaction when certain people, whom in individuality i like and admire and respect, like you and lizbeth and y, can,
taken into the abstract, become part of that Masses which you want
to save and i loathe? i like lizbeth and i like y and i love you but
when all of you are withdrawn and become People, indistinguishable
fragments in that great, headless brainless unity which is the race of
man, you leave me screaming and beating helplessly at you with my
lily white paws. oh, hell. it's useless. i can't explain a disgust and hatred like that. just accept it and then wonder why i should embrace
either communism or capitalism. i don't give one little pink damn for
the things my father stands for. he's just as surely People, when you
stand off and look at him. you're all fighting over something i
wouldn't go near. i don't want your filthy old bone.

and this . . . from shirley whore jackson. the great authoress, creator of the incomparable anthony, the magnificent paul, the delightful mary. this, the incoherent babbling of a madwoman crying for
sleep. yeah, and that last line would have read better if it had been

madman, always the artist. but all i can do is justify my position, which is after all the most that any of us can do, and some of us not so well. this, s. edgar, i strongly suspect to be me answering you back, and, also, one of the few times when i can talk without having you interrupt me. consider me as having said all i shall. you may talk now.

i am reading the 42ndparallel.* y (whom you persist in spelling e) is making me. someday i shall tell you why i am so very angry at y right now, and why i think that very soon a beautiful friendship may be terminated abruptly.

i never remember to tell you until the last page that i love you more than anything or anyone in the world. it's because i know it so well and i think you know it so well that it just doesn't seem necessary to tell you, until i realize that i can't stop telling you. i love you, my darling, and always shall. even when you cry over telephones i love you. even when you write stupid things like spender being a better poet than eliot. even when you're a million miles away i love you. if i may coin a phrase, i think you're cute.

s.

•  •  •

[To Stanley Edgar Hyman]

thurs [June 16, 1938]

snookums,

wouldn't you know . . . y has been using ernest again; he jitters. mother has established a system of snatching my letters out of the typewriter page by page, and, when she figures she has enough, slamming them into an envelope and mailing them, saying the while that the poor boy probably expects a letter . . . so if my letters seem somewhat disconnected, realize only that it is mother's fault. she also

* *The 42nd Parallel* is a 1930 novel by John Dos Passos.

closes her eyes politely while she puts them in envelopes. she also
says that one of these days she is going to read all your letters, when
she has lots of time, it having taken her a good month to read just
gonewiththewind.

mail this morning very interesting. letter from brooklyn, letter
from hanover, and invitations to a wedding for barry, mother and me.
barry and i are sending ours back. we have a new toaster which leaps
at one, and barry and i spend hours baiting it from behind the
kitchen door* . . . i have hay fever as usual . . . y and i, stricken with
the artistic fever, spent last evening painting pictures. our respective
personalities betrayed in our art, as usual. i had seven, all horribly
colored, mostly of faces with green eyelids, and one with rose and orange flowers, and y did a very poor impression of nijinsky being harlequin. she learns about these things the hard way. i meet a guy who
has a sailboat, and learn how to sail; y reads a book. she also read a
book about etchings. more hard way. i learned that the easy way
too . . . y is also quite enthusiastic about anthony, wanting me to
throw the rest of the novel away and keep anthony as a short
story . . . we have started our old race for rejection slips. i used to be
about six ahead of her but she has been cheating and getting them
from the new yorker all winter.

you should see my room, seh. the sun is coming in all over, but
simply all over, and the whole damn place is gay and yellow. the
books are glowing, and pan† has sunlight on his nose and ivy in his
hair. he is laughing about something. the bed is not made, there are
letters from seh all over the floor where they fell out of my desk
when i opened it, and the red-brown chair has a raspberry sweater
draped over the back, and a magenta cushion and a blue bathrobe
over the arm. oh, seh, i love my room when it's like it is now. nothing
in it is passive. even the bookends have personalities, and everything
is golden. all the windows are open and the curtains are flapping-
happily. it's wonderful, and all day . . . until three . . . i am going to be
curled up in the redbrown chair, feet on a footstool, with cigarettes
on the table and the bed unmade, and read and at three i go to a tea

---

* A very early example of Shirley's giving inanimate objects malevolent personalities.
† Shirley's pewter mask of Pan.

with y, in starched linen suits and with nice pink finger nails and appropriate white hats over one eye and neat little handkerchiefs, and we will be very polite. like hell we will. we're going as stacia and tanya in dirty old clothes and we'll sit with our legs over the arms of our hostess's best chairs and gibber. you'd think people would stop inviting us to teas.

but we are going to the artgallery tomorrow, to see an old friend of ours, a picture named mood. mood is a lady with a necklace of lima beans, and cruel slanting eyes and a half-smile which depends on whether there are shadows or not, and if we come in very softly she will raise an eyebrow at us and ask us to stay for tea, and if she is annoyed she will smile and curl her long yellow hand and tell us about murder and horror and grief. there is also an exhibit of local painting past which we shall walk with averted eyes. and after, coffee and waiters to frighten. and then, too, there is a secondhandbookshop which y discovered and has not visited because she has been waiting for me. and a concert soon. and people are after us to organize a picnic but we say no very firmly because people bore us. and we're not doing any dancing or any partying or even any dating because we have a new makebelieve which is that we don't know anyone in town and are all alone here with the whole city to play with and no obligations.

seh, seh, life is such fun. even away from you life can be fun.

michael? who's michael? i can't seem to remember . . .

we're going to have a summer that will make recapitulation wednesday seem hysterical. (recapitulation wednesday is always the last wednesday of the summer, because wednesday is our day, and we go to a very special little joint where we can sit all afternoon and drink coffee and we remember the summer, and compare it with all other less pleasant summers and we wonder how we would like to have had it different and we have never found a summer that is pleasanter than the one just over and after recapitulation wednesday the summer is officially over.) and sometime before recapitulation wednesday we are going to get very drunk, and we are going to find a new place to drink coffee and we are going to eat spaghetti all by ourselves and we are going to have collected some money so we can go to ny all by ourselves. we cannot go to salem because we have no money. we cannot even go to a movie.

i'm babbling again. it's because the sun is out and y is coming and i've got to find the reddest nail polish in the house. it's such a long time to recapitulation wednesday. and you send me a letter all about vegetation.

i'm going back to bed. yeah, and I'm taking dospassos with me. that book must be trash, because i can't stop reading it and you know my tastes.

i love you.

s.

•   •   •

*Stanley comes to Rochester for a visit, and while he and Shirley are sitting on the Jacksons' front porch—she thinking her parents are out of town— Leslie and Geraldine unexpectedly drive up. Stanley, terrified of meeting them, jumps over the railing and flees. Shirley, startled and confused, runs after him. They then spend hours walking and arguing.*

[To Stanley Edgar Hyman]

[July 5, 1938]

dear stan,

this may be a cruel and unnecessary thing to do, but i hope you can see that it's my natural reaction under the circumstances. in case you think that my family is responsible, none of them has mentioned you since i came in sunday night, nor will they. evvie has no doubt told you of the scene that took place when i came in at two-thirty after spending five hours with a young man who not only refused to meet them, but took a most idiotic and silly way of indicating that he would have nothing to do with them . . . five hours for which i could account in no way except to say that we had been walking, which my father refused to believe.

understand, i think that the way you acted that night was inexcusable. not that i so much wanted you to meet my father . . . god knows that in your state of mind there was nothing i wanted less . . . but that i resented your making a damn fool out of yourself and creating the worst impression possible. more than that, you made a damn fool out of me, which, since you know me, you will see is another reason why i find your conduct inexcusable. even the fact that i loved you wasn't sufficient. i hated you for that.

it would not be advisable for you to come to rochester again this summer. write to me, of course, but don't try to communicate with me in any other fashion. that is not my family's decree, it is mine. you would certainly not be thrown out of the house if you came here, but i refuse to endure a repetition of such an affair as last sunday's. i won't come to new york, or, needless to say, to massachusetts.

can you see how such adolescent idiocy as that has succeeded in making me doubt that i love you? i am surely in no position to find fault with you, but i may certainly detest your childishness when it puts me in the position where i not only have to make excuses for you to other people, but also have to justify your actions to myself and find that i cannot. let me have until september to realize for sure that i do love you. i know i do, but i must do a little growing myself before i can be sure.

that was the feeling you saw in me that night when you called it insanity. i was trying to reconcile my love for you to the great irritation you produced in me. you were more childish and more incomprehensible every minute, and every time you blamed me for it i wanted to leave you and go off somewhere and think, and try to see things clearly. i knew there was going to be a scene with my family when i got in, and i didn't care, but to have you striking out at me and hurting me all the time i was with you was too much. i didn't even try to tell you, this time. i knew you wouldn't understand at all. so i said nothing about it and let you rave. therefore you were sorry you came. i was sorry too, only i didn't want to hurt <u>you</u>. i wanted to be happy in the few minutes i had left with you, but you didn't want that. you wanted to quarrel. so we quarreled. you did everything in the world to destroy whatever love i had left for you in that time we stood on the corner (where i had to take you because i knew my father was up and would throw you out if he heard us), and i made no attempt to stop you, because i am tired of trying to justify myself in your eyes. whatever attempt i could have made would have been condemned immediately because it did not meet with your ideas. i know that from experience.

however, one thing i know now. you did not, and could not, destroy any of my love for you. i still love you as much as before, only now i am afraid to love you so much because you are so young, and because i am so young. you don't mind my childishness because there are so many other things about me you want to change first, but that strange childishness in you is all that i want to see different. i've never made any attempt to change you . . . you know that. and by september i intend to be reconciled to that in you which i hate, and i shall leave you a clear field in which to change me. all our quarrels and all my "backsliding" have been because i banged my head against this and couldn't accept it. now, i hope, it will be different. i love you and i'm afraid i always shall.

s.

•   •   •

[To Walter Bernstein]

wednesday [July 20, 1938]

dear walter,

first of all, thanks. only you didn't make it harsh enough. what i needed—and still need—is a good talking-to. somebody ought to tell me a few things. i have resented stan's trying to make me over for so long that when there came a chance to point out to him that nobody could boss me i took it and didn't stop to think . . . and look what i started. i've behaved like a sap and i know it. but he still can't be the boss of me, dammit. i got a very wretched letter from him yesterday, and am now in a state. walter, suppose <u>you</u> tell me. i wrote the letter to you against all y's better judgement, when you sent it to stan and stan wrote me y began calling me names, and now she thinks that it would be much, much better for stan if i just ignored the whole thing and never saw him again. she says, in essence, that the poor guy never did anything bad enough to deserve me. she adds, my romantic little y, that this quarrel is the beginning of the end, and, that if we can display such temper and pride with one another, that one of us doesn't love the other enough, and she means me. if she is right . . . and of course she always is . . . 'tanley would be much better off. hell, though, i'm not being altruistic. i'm just as much afraid of being hurt anymore as i am of hurting him. i'm no martyr, but i won't go around being a chameleon just so stan can smile smugly at a "new shirley." do you suppose that if i were not to write, and to go on with this minor little matter of forgetting him that has occupied so much of my time for two weeks, that he would be miserable for about a week, and then start congratulating himself at having gotten out of it so easily? i don't really think, you see, that this deep devotion of his is going to last, and i'm practically sure that mine isn't, so wouldn't finishing it be better now than later?

yeah, i know. maybe i <u>have</u> talked myself into this attitude this last few days, when i thought everything was washed up. yeah, and if i had to do it, why didn't i do it a long time ago? but . . . well, you get the general idea. i'm not going to answer his letter for a while yet. besides, in a fit of girlish rage i tore up the last letter he wrote . . . the nasty one . . . and it was the only one with his address on it. so i'll have to ask you to send me his address, and i can't write him till you do. do you mind?

incidentally, this michael business is no lie. the only reason i didn't agree to marry michael this last week is that he thoughtlessly omitted to ask me. there were a couple of days when i was particularly unhappy, and i wanted somebody, and instead of stan, i was with michael. michael, i suspect, affords a nice comparison because michael doesn't care what or how i think, or act, and never even thinks to en-quire if i have defied my family yet today. i detest having to drag mi-chael into a disagreement between stan and me, but he is certainly becoming a contributing force to my attitude. it sounds as though i'm just giving all my troubles to you, gratis, walter, but god knows that you know stan much better than i, and you ought to know what i should do to make it alright for him.

i am in a somewhat deranged state anyway. they have taken me to the dentist, practically over my dead body. aforesaid dentist peered in an interested fashion at my pet wisdom tooth, said tch. seems tooth was not only wisdom, but impacted, abcessed, and buried vereeee deep indeed. so the dentist, knowing my father, gave me a water glass full of scotch, slammed novocaine into the region somewhat south of my right ear, and went at me with a chisel. he also told me i was a brave little girl, and he heard that i'd sunk a ten-foot putt for a birdie three on the sixteenth sunday; i certainly did take after my father, didn't i. upon which he poured me into the lap of a pale-faced y in the waiting room. the next day y came down with acute indigestion, which the doctor doesn't know yet whether it was appendicitis or not. now y has to take sedatives and i have to have an ice pack, and my golf game is ruined and y can't go to the library and read books on the inquisition anymore because she might have an attack. so we sit home and play chess. y read a book on chess and now she knows a gambit, which makes me very unhappy because i do not know a gambit. y says her gambit is called the queen's gambit, and it involves y's losing her king's rook, queen's bishop and both knights on the first four moves, which she says is awfully good strategy, but i think is silly, because it gets the board terribly mixed up, since she has to have her pawns in a roughly star-shaped formation, and they keep getting in my way. the fact that this gambit invariably ends in my getting mate without losing a man does not discourage y; she says that someday i will make a mistake and then she will have me, be-cause her gambit is absolutely infallible if i should make a mistake.

i have a new set of fortune telling cards; do you know where or what the occult review is? they put out the tarot pack . . . as i remember kabumpo peg amy* was of course the princess . . . i went to look, found that i did not have kabumpo, but that i did have the hungry-tiger†; have been reading same for the last hour . . . we tried to buy the chessmen in rochester's largest department store. thereby hangs a tale, and the newyorker ought to hear of it. we finally found them in sportinggoods, between a large canoe and an exhibition of shot-guns . . . honorable mama bought me miceandmen . . . WHICH RE-MINDS ME! . . . walter, i love stan so much; i wish i knew what to do . . . can't think about much else. it's all damn foolishness. hell with it . . . y, from her bed of pain, has only the strength to murmur a lov-ing message; no postscript.

    she has promised to write you, so be patient.

'bye

shirley

•   •   •

## [To Stanley Edgar Hyman]

wed. [August 3, 1938]

you go to hell, you. you're a masochist. and a deceiver of women. the truth of all this self-torture of yours is that (me miserable) i am afraid i do love you and the reason i sent that letter was because i thought it conveyed that idea. the letter you get wed. will further ex-plain, and i wish that if you do not believe me or do not care particu-larly (which it is obvious you don't) you would mention that fact and so stop me making a damn fool of myself. i refuse to be the victim of

---

* In *Kabumpo in Oz* by John R. Neill (1922). Kabumpo was the wise Elegant Elephant and Peg Amy was a living wooden doll who was revealed to be a long-lost princess in the Winkie country of Oz. Walter shared Shirley's passion for the Oz books.
† The tenderhearted tiger in another Oz book, *The Hungry Tiger of Oz* by Ruth Plumly Thompson (1926).

unrequited love. (i said the victim but i meant recipient as well!) and am tired of trying to lie to <u>everybody</u>, including stacia who won't believe me anyway. so sit back, take a deep breath, light yourself a cigarette and try and let this sink in. I LOVE YOU AS MUCH AS IF NOT MORE THAN I ALWAYS DID AND THAT LIE I TOLD YOU WAS ONE OF WHICH I CONVINCED MYSELF BECAUSE I WAS ANGRY AND HAD BEEN HURT AND IT SHALL NOT HAPPEN AGAIN IF YOU WILL TAKE ME BACK. (got it?) and now, my dope, if that has caused you to laugh, snort derisively (which you do very well, did i ever tell you?) or shrug and say etchapetchametcha, kindly sit down and write me a letter telling me so. if you are pleased and magnanimous, generous and forgiving, willing to TAKE ME BACK, tell me that too. but for god's sake believe me or i can't be answerable for the consequences. if some large lithuanian has captured your vagrant fancy, ok. if you've decided that Emerson Was Right, and you have no need of an unworthy object . . . i'm far too dignified to chase you, and much too proud to appeal to you, but i warn you i'll give you hell. but i wish that if you've stopped loving me you'd tell me so instead of writing me evasive letters, so that i can go into a decline and sit by the window and sigh over my embroidery. no, i do not weep large tears onto your picture. but i came near it yesterday when i got the lecture i deserved, (just because ernest has been bad and hurt that page i shan't write it over. hell, if i so much as <u>read</u> it over i'll probably tear it up!) from y (remember that sentence?). i am in a penitent mood, and shall undoubtedly stay that way until i hear from you about your reaction to this humbleness of mine. yeah, s. edgar, and i'm as humble as you've ever seen me. so please don't leave me in doubt. i'm in an awful state.

that is that. you know that i can't even be humble without parenthesis, or happy without side-comments, so i hope you grasp the essential soberness of that explanation. everything is there, without reserve.

you devoted your letter to saying things to make me writhe, didn't you? note: "if you haven't the decency to tell the truth . . . rather than indulging in these frenzied fabrications . . ." "oh, well, the guy can't see a thing until he's been told thirty-seven times, anyway," or: "you give the helen affair more importance than it deserves . . ." i commented briefly and kept my innermost thoughts where they belonged—in y's hands. my opinion of helen has not gone up. "don't expect any intellectually giant replies (from martha)." i've gotten out of the habit of expecting such from <u>anyone</u>, thanks. "everything is harlequin's fault but at least you can say for him that he never stays silly for more than a week at a time." that, knowing harlequin, i should say was an absolute lie. i refer you to duchartre, on the commedia, chapter on harlequin and his ancestors and he <u>did</u> go away. he went to the moon.* "i do not want stacia's love . . ." stacia is a sap but i can think of several esteemed gentlemen who would be glad to get what you scorn so carelessly. (that is a point to make you writhe and don't deceive yourself; i know your reaction.) furthermore i do not give a damn about your job and your being in your element with the women. i want to hear about you and that does not mean the books you are reading. and if you inquire thoughtfully in my next letter about the typographical errors in mine i shall refer your fate to ernest, who makes the errors. and you ought to know a lot about snakes.

as one i.s.p. to another, i think you're nice.

s.

•   •   •

[To Stanley Edgar Hyman]

monday [August 15, 1938]

adored one:

i am going to tell you about yesterday, partly because it will give you a new picture of these godparents† of mine whom you seem to loathe so,

* Merricat Blackwood will dream of "living on the moon" in Shirley's final completed novel, *We Have Always Lived in the Castle* (1962). Her mention of commedia dell'arte and Harlequin reveals a lifelong interest.
† These godparents are not named and their identity is unknown.

and partly because i was so happy. we went to their antique house at the lake. the house is at the bottom of a cliff . . . no, it's half-way down, and the cliff is of course steep, so that there is a precarious path down, and a road with a hairpin curve every ten feet, so that the only two people in the world who can drive it are my godfather and his hired man. you either wait to be called for by the car at the top . . . the car is as antique as the house or my godfather, and navigates those curves with what can only be forty years of familiarity . . . or you slide down the path. i always slide down the path, because it is dangerous especially since our recent rains and flood which washed most of it out, and you have to cling to trees all the way down. the house looks complacently off over the lake, which is still farther down the cliff, and reached by a worse path or more dangerous road, and is bluer than any lake has a right to be. millions of trees, of course, where pan might be living. trees that reach up to the house and look over the edge of the porch in an inquiring fashion. the house is filled with antiques because godmother's mother died and left it that way and godfather is far too polite to disturb the old lady's fondest possessions. we arrive, my honorable father chasing me down the path to effect an entrance, to be greeted by my godfather in an atrocity of a bathing suit that must have been condemned in 1906 as unsafe. he is, i think i have told you, the only intelligent man i have ever known. (he is a paleontologist!) my godmother has gone quietly to sleep somewhere and no one can find her, so we sit down to play some childish game that belongs to the two sons of the family. after godfather has beaten the pants off the three of us in this . . . some variety of tiddliwinks . . . more guests arrive, having come sedately down by the car. they are a prominent rochester business man and his wife. my godmother wakes up and appears in a pair of shorts which are most unbecoming (but too <u>damn</u> comfortable, my dear!). a delightful english doctor and his staid lady wife arrive, practically head-first down the path, and we are complete. in practically no time at all we are in bathing suits and being driven down to the lake. that is where i am happiest. godmother tells my mother briefly: "hell, girl, let the child swim without a cap. if she can appear in public in <u>that</u> bathing suit she can do anything. godchild, you're letting your legs get fat." so i swim without a cap. and sit on the raft and get myself sunburned because i am arguing with the doctor and honorable father about whether or not dinghies are better boats than snipes . . . the doctor holding out for snipes. race my father back to the shore, try to drown the doctor, get out of the water to my godmother's shrieks, to find that my suit, which is only a bra and shorts, has parted company definitely and finally, with most of me. thus breaking the ice.

dress hastily, with charming mother complaining mildly because i in my wet suit had sat on her girdle, thus making it more difficult to get on than ever, and don, sure of my godmother's defense, a dress with no back and practically no skirt, under which i am reluctantly permitted by charming mother, struggling with her girdle, to wear nothing. then cocktails, six or seven for me, and magnificent conversation with madame doctor re love, versus career. my godfather appeared long enough to advise me to take love, and vanished.

had a terrific appetite, up to then i had never eaten more than one steak at a time in my life. i had . . . i think . . . four, and two ears of corn, and watermelon and cake. conversation at the lunch table ought to have revised your opinion of my godmother at once. at the head of the table she was talking nonsense with honorable father. about cooking experiences, i believe. at the foot of the table godfather was holding mother and the rochester business man and his wife enthralled with a tale of anthills in germany, anthills containing four hundred million ants. he was discussing the possibility that the ants would destroy the germans before the germans could destroy the rest of the world. the doctor and i were chatting merrily about the harlequinade, racing happily through duchartre, winifred smith, and frank shay, to end up with a bang at karl marx. anyway the doctor started it by quoting swinburne. nothing, to me, is so fascinating as the several different topics at a table. godmother beamed at me, and for some obscure reason, said that she personally was very fond of the swissfamilyrobinson. which of course brought up alice in wonderland and the doormouse, and my godfather took a hand. this time it was necessary for godmother to drag us away. so i went to sleep, leaving a bitter bridge game in progress at one end of the porch, and my father teaching the ladies the tiddliwinks game at the other. i had a nice soft hammock overlooking the lake, which was blue, and a particularly nice rum collins, which was greenish, and lots of pillows. so i thought about lakes and rum and pillows and seh and such silly things for a few minutes and then, the collins having disappeared, fell asleep. to dream about lakes and rum and pillows and seh, and very nice it was, too. i was awakened by having a lighted cigarette fall on my sunburn. so we went swimming. and then we drank much more and then we ate much more and then we came home.

y and i have been trying to think of a nice cool way to commit suicide. between hay fever and heat, we think we are dying. it seems that the only things you can do in such a condition are nice quiet things, so we sit around and play chess, or do jig-saw puzzles . . . a nice occupation, requiring no brainwork . . . or go to the movies. god in heaven, seh, did you ever have hay fever? this is my third year of it, and every august i wish i were dead and every september i think that maybe i won't get it next year, but i do. the morning i wake up and see frost on the ground is the morning when my life will begin anew. so forgive; it is the hay fever.

write to me and be consoling. tell me it's not so bad, i'll be ok in september.

yeah. september. goddam. GODDAM.

goodnight, sugar. i'll be brave. i love you, hay fever or no hay fever.

s.

∙ ∙ ∙

"Stanley—a critic."

[To Stanley Edgar Hyman]

[August 18, 1938]

stanley,

i recall, with gnashing of teeth, that in an earlier letter you informed me that you had told your landlady that you were married and your wife was in rochester, expecting me to fall for that bait and come straight to your bed. that is merely a theory, of course, but i'm glad it boomeranged right into your face. you deserved it.

i wrote to robert and have already received an answer. robert and i have decided that castaway represents the struggle between the forces of good and evil for the soul of man. there seems to be some slight confusion in robert's letter, with his moustache inextricably tangled with ernest my typewriter of which he wants to know the sex and how one determines it. SHALL I TELL HIM? (you re-member ernest's erection, which is better'n yours. but robert might realize that i wasn't a lady.)

i haven't been doing any writing at all. i can't go near my beloved anthony, because (duck quick, more bitching) our own incomparable y has laughed at it for so long, and said so often that it is terrible that i have begun to regard it as definitely inferior, and worthless, and useless and not fit to go on with. worst of it is, i can see damn well myself that it's good, but this constant belittling has made me feel that perhaps i may be kidding myself. i wish she'd have the decency to shut up. is it fair for her to tell me over and over that i couldn't write a novel if i tried the rest of my life, that i'm making a dmn fl out of myself by trying, that no one really believes i can write, how-ever polite they may be, and that even if i could write i've never pro-duced anything to prove it? true as it might be, it doesn't help much. i'm so <u>tired</u> of being told what a fool i am! is she being fair, stan? is she telling the truth? is there anything in the world that can prove to her (and to me, now) that i <u>can</u> write? sure, i'm a sap for trying to write a novel, but the fact i can't get through her head is that it's a

<u>good</u> novel. you don't believe that either. no one does, damn their eyes. but no one's read it, either. and no one's going to read it ever, because i don't care a damn about showing little gods like you and y the nice piece of work i've done in private.

in my extreme boredom between trips to the dentist i have taken to reading the saturdayeveningpost. that, my sweet, is BOREDOM! i go to the dentist again this afternoon, but it's too hot to be scared.

look, my angel, re you. now it can be told. the day you wrote you were going on the machines* i put in several hours of sheer hell. please don't tell me until afterward next time. i was, frankly, scared to death, remember, all you told me of the machines was their danger, and all i knew was that right then you were probably getting yourself killed. I shouldn't like you half so much dead.

darling, don't let me lose you to dot and thy landlord's wife. i love you too much to shy away from killing two other women.

thy

mistress

• • •

[To Stanley Edgar Hyman]

[September 12, 1938]

dear,

will you forgive me for wanting to write to you even though by this time you are probably calling me names in the lexicon of seh? i want to talk to you. and just tell you all the things i've been saving up to tell you for so long, when i did not dare write to you, partly because you're not writing, and partly because i was trying to gather courage

---

* Stanley was spending the summer doing hard labor at a twenty-dollar-a-week job at a paper mill in Erving, Massachusetts. No one expected him to last at it, but he stayed, working for nearly two months.

to tell you The Truth. please, will you accept my position as it stands. and not try to change it? and will you not hate me?

so, carefully avoiding all mention of Us, i can tell you about this maze of weariness which encompasses me, and the reasons for it. i have seldom been so simply tired. blessed kay* stayed for a week, monday to monday, and, having led me to peace, departed. i had two days in which to resign myself to a glorious freedom, gratefully giving myself to the books i had been saving, abandoned myself to a comfortable chair and a pair of overalls, retired into oblivion. i had read a hundred pages of therainscame† when innes‡ called me last night to inform me that she would arrive today to stay until next monday.

kay and i drove rochester as nearly mad as rochester can be driven. we stole mother's car and drove twenty miles to ionia for hamburgers, coming home the "long way," or through naples, thus putting an extra hundred miles on the car. we saw a cow, much to my delight. there were also clouds which looked like elephants. altogether a splendid day. wednesday night we took mother and father at bridge to the tune of three rubbers. thursday morning my mother informed me that since it was necessary that i entertain kay somehow i was giving a dinner party that night. reluctantly, kay and i entertained at dinner. mother and dad left for new york shortly before our guests arrived, so cocktails were created by my brother under the weird influence of his girl's presence. aforesaid babe has the effect of making me feel horribly eccentric and somewhat lunatic. kay loathed her at sight, and y, tolerant and near-sighted, smiled politely, said "oh, really?" twice, and ignored de babe thereafter. barry adores the creature, god knows why. y arrived in dead black with her hair piled up on top of her head in hideous little curls. kay looked really charming in one of my favorite dresses, providing a welcome ice-breaker. informing me from across the room that she had spilled her cocktail, she gave me an opportunity to roar apprehensively: "what! on my dress?" much to the amusement of stepan, who had had four cock-

---

* Kay Turk, one of Shirley's Syracuse friends.
† *The Rains Came* (1937), a novel by Louis Bromfield.
‡ Innes is another Syracuse friend.

tails and was beginning to feel as though he might tackle even bridge
with equanimity. stepan had brought music for me, among them a
familiar fugue which made kay wince and which stepan played as
though knowing full well that every note he struck hit me like a ton
of thumbtacks. michael reclined, at ease behind his pipe, carrying on
a slow-paced conversation with y re modern novels, and bill* sat at
my feet and talked boats. alta had outdone herself, and dinner was
enough to cause even bill to sigh feebly and refuse to be moved. the
one high point of dinner was the sudden appearance of the
excitement-maddened babe at our table, where kay, bill, michael and
i sat comfortably discussing the superiority of pipes to cigarettes;
babe chose such a moment to lean confidentially on bill's shoulder
and scream peekaboo. the four-way look of disgust was enough to
bring my brother to his lady's side to drag her away. that finished de
babe. thereafter she sat in comparative quiet with her feet in barry's
lap, giggling. we played bridge. stepan played as though inspired by
the devil himself, and proceeded to show de babe, who prides herself
on her bridge, how we phi betes do it. significant is the fact that
babe, impressed not at all by stepan's phi bete key, fawned on him
when she knew he could swear in french. bridge was abandoned, and
the whole was divided into its parts. barry and de babe disappeared
to the amusement room to play ping-pong. y and stepan got confidential over the horrible mismanagement of the university's english
department. kay and bill quarreled violently over boats. michael and i
were talking about me, only somehow every time we talk about me
we end up talking about that goddam boat. finally, michael and bill
having taken their departure, barry and babe playing ping-pong remarkably silently, y and kay and i led stepan again to the piano. with
all the lights gone, except the one over the piano, with plenty of cigarettes at hand, with the clock pointing timidly to quarter past three,
stepan played for me. my request was for noise. he played liszt. my
request was for color. he played grieg. then he played for himself, and
for kay . . . strange old english songs, and the gavotte, and the only

* Bill is another Rochester friend.

two chopin numbers i like ... the chord prelude, and the polonaise. then, for y, brahms, and, for kay, the moonlight sonata ... by ear, damn him. and more beethoven fragments for me, and finally, as the clock was turning five, old songs ... and so kay and i sat up until eight, after they had gone, talking of strange things, such as sunrises on windy mornings, with dirty ashtrays on all the tables and birds calling outside.

so, after two hours sleep, we arose to take me to the dentist again. and i went to sleep while he was drilling, an experience certainly unique for me. and friday night we slept quickly and long, me with only a recollection of the little fugue in my head.

saturday the frustration girls were themselves again. seems michael and bill were racing the boat that afternoon, and, since it was a golden day with a long wind, we took the car and went to the lake. each with a notebook and a pencil we sat on the end of a long pier, trying to discourage the attentions of a young man who liked my hair and kay's voice. when a gorgeous smooth cruiser went by we stood up and waved, calling to be taken for a ride. much to our astonishment, the cruiser turned and came up to the pier, and the two gentlemen in possession said they would be delighted. kay looked at me and i looked at kay, and into the cruiser we went. our first intimation that the two gentlemen were not boyscouts came when they put us up in front and then headed into the waves, improving upon this opportunity to say that we certainly had gotten <u>wet</u>, hadn't we, and hadn't we better change our clothes. upon which they offered two sets of old pajamas and turned their backs. kay and i stayed wet, thanks. they said ok then we'd better have a drink. it was rum. we drank it. when they offered us scotch as a chaser and beer as a chaser for scotch, jackson and turk knew that they were in for another of their startling adventures. my whisky and beer went overboard and so, as i subsequently learned, did kay's. then, seeing the boats line up for the start of the race, we indicated politely that we'd like to go home now, thanks, but our offer was declined, since we were headed up the river. by the time we got a good distance up the river kay and i had consumed a good quart of rum between us. kay just had time to mutter aside to me: "keep your legs crossed old thing; we're off again!" when they anchored the boat and produced another drink. from that time on every drink they handed me went overboard. somehow, they got us down into the cabin. i expect we were lured. anyway, i didn't have the slightest trouble. i simply said no and doubled up my fist. the guy i had was the captain and owner of the boat, and you never saw a captain melt so fast on his own boat. you taught me well, seh. inside of five minutes i had the guy beating his head against the wall and crying. kay and hers wandered out into the woods somewhere, and from the look in kay's eyes when they returned i judged that hers had certainly never been a boyscout. by that time i was beginning to feel a little sorry for the captain, who was on his knees trying to appeal to my better nature . . . the dirty bastard, he ruined my dress . . . so i told him no, but i'd be on the end of the pier the next saturday if he was still interested. he was interested; he said he would wait on the pier for the rest of his life if he thought there was a chance of my coming. it was a smooth line, and the only trouble with it, i discovered later, was that he had meant it, and i had him. they didn't know our names, or anything about us, so i fed the captain an erroneous phone number, and had another drink on the house. when the captain came up into the light he had circles under his eyes and his face was all tear-stained, and he was dead white. his friend didn't quite look quite so bad, but he looked much more furious. kay beamed at me and i beamed at kay, and we said we'd like to go home now please. they took us back to our pier, and, silently we faded off into the night, leaving behind us the wrong phone number and a promise to be on the pier the next week. we got back home to discover that we had missed one of the best races of the year, and that michael and bill had come in second. this coming saturday is the day i promised i'd be on the pier. kay informed me afterward that she had learned the captain's identity; he is the dissolute, unmarried young scion of one of the richest families in town; his bank account runs, quite easily, into the millions. i was disgusted. somehow i always manage to miss my opportunities. wonder what would happen if i went back to that pier . . .

kay and i went back to the club on sunday, only to see our cruisers face to face. fortunately they didn't see us, and we ducked. that day we weren't interested, thanks. so we begged a drink off a triumphant michael and bill, and wandered around saying oh looka the pretty boats. and met the cruiser again, the captain was aboard, and saw me quite clearly. he also saw bill, who is big, and michael, who is power-ful. so the captain looked the other way. monday kay went home and i settled down, only to have seh start calling me. (incidentally, when you called sunday night, kay and i were drinking beer with bill and michael, all of us so tired we couldn't stand.) tuesday and wednesday i slept and went to the dentist, and today, just as i begin to feel sane again, innes is arriving. o god.

i discovered a book in my bookcase called fugue* which i am re-reading. it's a hideous barnes-sort of thing, and i derive much delight from writing nasty little notes in the margins. i shall give it to you so you can add some more nasty little notes. (or shall i give it to you? shall i have the chance? whether we are to see one another in syra-cuse this year is, you know, completely up to you.)

this week has taught me that michael is not for such as i, and he knows it. therefore what was previously a tense, strained, vaguely-misinterpreted emotion has now become an easy friendship, based on mutual devotion to boats and brahms. his mother, trying <u>her</u> damndest to make a match of it, and my mother, trying <u>her</u> damnd-est to make me happy, have given up so you had nothing to fear from michael, and, had i only thought to figure it out before, i imagine i might have spared you some bleakness. now, at last, i have returned to my former happy state of an emotion-less contentment.

please say that you will forget that i have been in love with you and be my friend next year in syracuse. i would be terribly lonely without you and, having loved you so much, i couldn't very well love anyone else until some far-off amnesia makes me forget you.

well?

s

* A novel called *Fugue* by Olive Moore (1932).

. . .

*Shirley has just turned twenty-two. She is at home in Rochester on winter break from Syracuse.*

[To Stanley Edgar Hyman]

Dec. 22, 1938

stanley,

you didn't write to me, did you? i decided i wanted to write to you anyway. it's christmas and there is an extraordinary combination of joy and madness in our house, as there always is around now. especially since my brother and i are both home, and my grandmother carries confusion with her like thurber's gardener had a thunderstorm. my mama clings to the hidden-package theory, having mysterious bundles round and about. i keep tripping over them.

i have been shopping, too, all alone, since y is working every day and every evening this week. i drop by and leer at her over customers' heads. christmas is incredibly horrible when seen from the jacksonian leaping-at-sudden-fears angle. for example, wandering happily along, in a daze of beatific peace-on-earthness, i found myself face to face with a windowful of monstrous bells tolling horribly right before my nose. to my mind there is something dreadful about large objects moving silently and somehow ominously, particularly when, like these, they were swinging slowly back and forth . . . and all the people watching were of course ghouls . . . something of the sort occurs somewhere in poe . . . pushing myself away from the window i ran square into an old apple of a hag who grabbed my arm and cackled: "something for others less fortunate, lady?" she had a large pot, regrettably empty, and she obviously expected me to take some definite action. i did. restraining the impulse to say bubblebubble-toilandtrouble i snarled: "don't be ironic" and fled. i walked down the street, flinching at santa clauses and their attendant charities, and met a friend to whom i did not send a christmas card. she seized me firmly by the arm, drew me off into a convenient doorway, and began to chat happily about wasn't it nice to be home. i was looking in the window, and it was the five and ten we were standing next to, the window was filled with ties, and they were practically solid on the back wall, and crowded all through the window until there wasn't room for anything else. i wish i could tell you the effect of crowdedness that the window gave; the worst of it was that the ties were almost all of a color—that peculiar deep maroon and hard mahogany brown, so that the feeling i got from the window was of dreariness and sheer ugliness trying to force its way out at me.

then when the girl was talking, she was dropping packages and picking them up and swearing at people who stepped on them, and one poor little old lady came by when my friend had dropped a lot of bundles, and my friend looked at the old lady and said why in hell don't you look where you're going, and the poor lady looked at my friend and looked at me and said i'm sorry and hurried away. i told my friend that the lady hadn't touched her and my friend said yes i know but i was so mad i had to blame somebody. (nice friends i've got) and then she started telling me how difficult it was to shop and she finished me by saying: "of course i like christmas, but i do wish everyone else didn't like it too; it makes it so hard for me to shop." then and there i suppose i should have socked her, but i didn't; i only left. i went to the library and stayed there until it was calm and nice outside and then i walked home through the snow and thought about how nice it would be if i could be in syracuse all by myself in the apartment reading.

mother and barry just arrived with the christmas tree. and we shall have mistletoe and on christmas day i am to put on a nice long dress and wear violets in my hair and receive guests who come to get drunk and by three in the afternoon my father and i will be very very drunk indeed and my father will say new york? of course you're going to new york. and my father's genial friends will kiss me under the mistletoe and my blessed godfather will take me off in a corner and say now then. what about this young man? will he like me? and has he got any brains? and i of course will say that this young man is very nice indeed. and michael will be here with joseph conrad on the brain and michael's mother with michael on the brain and me with a long dress and violets in my hair trying to think of something to say to them. oh i shall get so drunk. and i shall enjoy it too. because when the house is full of people christmas day doesn't get dreary and lonely and when you are very drunk you worry more about whether or not you can make the doorway than about whether there will be a welcome for you in new york.

alta asked me privately whether or not you got any of the chicken and i 'lowed as how you had and she smirked at me and said did you like it and i said you did and she said she'd send another soon. she also told me when pop wasn't looking that she had been going to communist meetings. she added that she still intended to teach me to cook.

i wish you'd write to me, just once. they are taking me to california next summer, in july. i want to go very much. but i would like to talk to you.

shirley

•   •   •

[To Stanley Edgar Hyman]

monday, june 5, 1939

I am not dumb you dope

paragraph by paragraph your letter: jay's hex is also responsible for the fact i suppose that i have had a nosebleed* since wednesday.

if jay would do two things for me i would be very happy. one is to tell me more about the blackmass and the other is to explain about

---

* Jay Williams was a friend of Stanley's, now also Shirley's. Jay later would become a film actor, writer of the Danny Dunn juvenile books series, and self-described wizard/ magician. He had given Shirley various charms to bring on her period during a time in spring 1939 when she had a number of pregnancy scares.

bubblebath and his pictures are wonderful and OH ESTANLIE
WOULD HE DRAW ME A BLACK MASS LIKE HE DID
FOR JUNE???

i have sent (that word is spent only ernest is sore about something) three days throwing away stuff because i have been cleaning
my desks. except yesterday when i played eight holes of golf and i
was SO BAD. i had two desks to go through and five packing boxes
full of stuff which is not surprising when you consider that i have
not thrown away anything i have written since i was six because i
hadn't the guts. y had the guts however and she sat and watched me
and said be ruthless. i am still not finished having two boxes still to
go but i found stuff from when i was about twelve and writing
lovely poetry only it wasn't love poetry but all about how i hated everything. i saved one or two as representative and maybe will show
them to you. there is one about how conceited people go around
boasting of how important they are and they set themselves up as
judges and say that some of them are better than others and what
are they anyway just a lot of dopes who don't know nuthing and are
only compensating for not being strong enough to keep on living
and do something that is important enough to justify living. that is
very complicated and i was surprised at how bitter it was and i
wrote it when i was twelve. then there are a lot of experiments in
fancy verse forms none very good and several starts of stories some
of which i will use later. one story interested me tremendously about
a man who was so afraid of dying that he killed himself—i swear
that's the story and it was very familiar indeed. then a couple of
years later i was writing lousy stories about harlequin and the come-
dia* which had just caught my fancy and i was also writing a novel
about a lot of people completely away from the world who were interesting because they were people and hated everyone else. the
characters were nice (about a hundred pages were written only i
couldn't read them all because i got tired) and it was the first time i
had used victor. there was the seven-year-old autobiographical original of cathie, my girl who was afraid people were going to talk to

* The commedia dell'arte and its elaborate costumes would remain a touchstone for
Shirley throughout her life.

her, no less than six separate accounts of the year with jeanne,* one quite good and the rest lousy, numerous letters from me to my-self . . . something i'll bet you never did . . . all pointing out errors in writing and action which are very sound and about which i obvi-ously did nothing because i still have the errors today. and there are a great many poems, going as far back as when i was around fifteen, about tomorrow and yesterday and today only when i was around fifteen the point in them was that things must be getting better and maybe tomorrow something (ANYTHING) would happen that would be nice. there are pictures of me that i wouldn't even show you, diaries that make me blush when i read them (incidentally, you never should have suggested that i had an unhappy childhood, be-cause from that angle most of this stuff is unhappy) and some of the diaries are miserable . . . and, as i have told you fifty times if i've told you once, you dope, it all stems from the fact that the only friend i had in the world was dot,† who flatly refused to read anything i had written and laughed at me when i did write and who wouldn't listen to any of "that trash" . . . there is an entry in a diary covering three pages on the theme "who cares for beauty; it is the mind which matters" and which, judging from the next seventy or eighty entries, did not convince me in the slightest. i also used to clip pictures of beautiful women out of magazines and write pages and pages about how i didn't have anyone to talk to and then talk to myself for lack of anyone else. for instance, i found an entry on my sixteenth birth-day: "i am now sixteen, and consequently very wise. and i'm not the slightest bit lonely, am i, shirley?" for about half an hour since i wrote that i have been lost back in 1932, reading about a gentleman named bud, no more, with whom i fancied i was madly in love and to whom i wrote long letters (unsent!) which i would not show to anyone if my life depended on it. even reading them now gives me a funny feeling on the back of my neck and they remind me much too vividly of high school and summertime and eucalyptus trees and keeping my desk locked because my grandmother was just waiting

* Jeanne Marie Bedel ("Jeannou"), an exchange student at Rochester, was a dear friend and confidante for a year.
† Dorothy Ayling, Shirley's early childhood friend in California.

to read what was in it. now, reading it over, i think it would probably have given the dear lady hysterics. and i must have been pretty desperate because some of the letters are even addressed to characters in my stories telling them all the things i wanted to ask people about and dot wouldn't listen to. (stuff about why didn't anyone else feel like i did and where could i go if i ran away?) jesus i wouldn't like to meet that shirley face to face.

i haven't come to anything more recent than when i was about seventeen yet but i hope it will be a little more respectable. as it is, i don't like to think about what i must have seemed like to my family and to dot . . . enough of that stuff. i am heartily ashamed of most of it, and a little in awe of myself. all of it is going to be burned . . . i am "being ruthless" . . . and when i think of what has been lying around loose all these years i turn pale.

you don't seem very real right now because i am back in 1932 and i am signing my name shirlie and i am very unhappy about bud whoever the hell he was and i am engaged in hating my family. you should thank god this stuff was burned before you ever saw it.

in spite of your not being real, i love you very much and want lots of letters from you.

cat

• • •

## [To Stanley Edgar Hyman]

thurs. [July 6, 1939]

my darling,

june* and i have found comfort at last. we have discovered that the basement is at least twenty degrees cooler than the rest of the house, and we are now happily settled, with me and a card table (exceed-

---

* June Mirken was a friend from Syracuse who became a very dear lifetime friend and, later, Laurie's godmother.

ingly difficult to type on) and ernest, and lots of cigarettes and completely surrounded with pillows and lamps and we have the Music
Box. june shares, surprisingly enough, my passion for the thing, so it
is now sitting on a table at june's elbow, singing softly to itself. june
also is singing. she has the thing fixed so it won't stop, and it goes
around and around and around. she is trying to make it be haunted
and it won't show off for her. embarrassing for me, since i have spent
all morning telling her about it.*

   i don't think june has been enjoying herself particularly . . . there is
of course nothing to do, and even june gets tired of that; i can amuse
myself indefinitely here because i can be happy all afternoon listening to the music box or cutting paper dolls, but june gets tired and
cannot read forever. she is anxious to get away, and plans to leave saturday. my young brother is sick . . . last night he developed symptoms
and this morning the doctor decided that he probably had the same
thing that kept him in the hospital for three weeks this spring. they
want to take him back to the hospital again today, only he won't
go . . . the doctor says it might prevent us from going to california.
mother is scared to death. i can't come to syracuse naturally. i can't
get the hell out when mother is wandering around not knowing
whether we're going to have to drag him off to the hospital any minute. i would like to have you come to rochester, only i don't know
about your coming this weekend . . . god in heaven, i want to see you
so much . . . could you, do you suppose, hitch up next weekend when
barry is better? i've GOT to see you before i go, if i go. if you don't
want to meet my father come any day but sunday. i think perhaps
you were wrong not to teach brown's† course; it would be a splendid
idea if you could teach from your own book, and it would help you
see better what's wrong with it. also, teaching a class like that would
do wonders for you if you ever decided you wanted to be a professor . . . your teaching the course would bring you closer to brown
which i gather is what you want . . . please tell me how the book is

---

* Shirley claimed for the rest of her life that the ancient music box was haunted,
and would turn itself on in the early hours of the night, usually favoring "Carnival in
Venice."
† Leonard Brown, their esteemed but controversial literature professor at Syracuse.

coming;* you never mention it and i am of course curious and interested . . . give my regards (seriously) to brown and marjorie . . . re fe-
lice† . . . june has been telling me about it; she is heartily opposed to
the idea. i've no opinions whatsoever, except that from what june tells
me it would be rather a messy business and would make rather a fool
of you. i don't give a damn if you marry felice, so long as you come
back to me and so long as you come back to me without having
made yourself ridiculous by messing around with a girl who doesn't
even know what you're talking about . . . but of course it's not my
business . . . you take care of these things yourself (that is not bitterness; it is a sudden realization that once again i have been meddling
and trying to tell you i don't like the girls you fuck . . . and i am not
supposed to do that. i'm sorry). i love you so completely and i am
trying very hard (and not too unsuccessfully) to think: stanley is
going to have another girl this summer and it doesn't matter; stanley
is going to have another girl this summer and it is none of my business; stanley is going to have another girl this summer and of course
he will come back to me . . . i won't be jealous, but he can't stop me
from worrying.

june can tell you all the things i can't . . . she met michael's mother;
she will probably meet michael. she also met barry's girl. my father
played accordion for june and bought her a drink on tuesday; my
mother took her to lunch and played bridge with her. knowing my
family, i would say that june is quite a success. they are all very fond
of her.

june and i were just talking to mother and i told mother you
thought you would come up this weekend and she said by all means
come. she said you must come for dinner saturday night . . . june says if
you do she will stay until sunday . . . unfortunately, we can't offer you a
place to stay that night, but you are certainly invited for dinner . . .
mother is not kidding; she is sincerely anxious to have you, and unless
barry has to go to the hospital i am very much in favor of it. please,
please come. darling, i want to see you! there are so many things i want

* Stanley is struggling to write a book of literary criticism, much later to become *The
Armed Vision* (1947).
† A woman Stanley is also seeing.

to talk to you about that i can't put into letters, and of course no letter is adequate for telling you how i love you . . . please come, stanley.

i love you so much so much so goddam MUCH!

cat

.   .   .

[To Stanley Edgar Hyman]

july 14, 1939

darling,

yes, your third chapter arrived okay and alta is waiting for you to come here so she can collect eight cents from you.

i read it six times and i think it is good. you have probably covered the subject as thoroughly as it is possible to cover any subject, and i think your outline-system makes it clearer. HOWEVER:

1. y desires me to state that she (having read it carefully and with much admiration) is hurt. in your section on identical rhyme you completely forget to say what to y is very important: that in chaucer's time and thereabouts identical rhyme was considered clever and technically superior. she points in breathless, gesturing horror to lines 17 and 18 of the prologue to the canterbury tales (which, in my copy, read "the holy blisful martir for to seke, that hem hath holpen, whan that they were seke . . .") she also makes nasty remarks about how you SHOULD know that the idea comes from the French. and concludes that my god has he really READ skelton's colyn cloute? i assured her that you had, that you knew all there was to know about identical rhymes and that you were the most wonderful man in the world.

2. what bothers me most in your section about slant rhyme is that my idiot savant mind remembers vividly that in class brown pointed out . . . in either this poem or another . . . that the alliteration completed the rhyme . . . that bullet-heads in line one was rhymed not only with the ds in lads but that the h in heads was carried over in

the hearts in line two, and the l of lads was repeated in bullet and in blind blunt . . . and so on . . . is this a peculiarity of this one poem or author or part of slant rhyme or am i crazy anyway?

3. yes, i was surprised. more than that, i was frankly dumbfounded. i realize, moreover, that, besides being one of the few contemporary poets using cross rhyme, i only used it once because you invented it and never wrote any yourself . . . thus that is undoubtedly the only example you could find of cross rhyme. darling, it's an astonishing and pleasant thing you have done to me, but of course i have an objection. i am sure that you have no intention of leaving it like that, so i am some reassured, but even in the copy you give brown i don't think it's very advisable. i think that brown, knowing me, would feel the whole book somewhat weakened by finding that you drew some of your examples from your friends.

i adore your example from ogden nash.

i am happy to see that you gave my friend lewis carroll a place among your immortals . . . along with me.

and i think you are unnecessarily nasty about swinburne.

but i think it is so good and i don't think i ever realized that it would be as good as it is. i'm awfully excited and proud and i shall go around with a copy of the book (dedicated to your father) under my arm showing it to people and y in a rather startled fashion gives you her wholehearted respect because she also thought it was so good.

and then this morning i get a discouraged letter from you saying what the hell you've finally run up against some work and please can you go out and drown yourself because you didn't really expect you'd have any trouble and anyway no one should have to work writing a book. you are quite right, darling. you SHOULD go out and drown yourself and no one SHOULD have to work writing a book especially if he wants it to be a good book. yeah, and the third chapter was so good and went so well that what the devil can be the matter with the fourth chapter? o fool. darling, i love you very dearly but i wish you had some sense. if you write ten hours a day on the same subject and only stop writing long enough to hear some guy lecture from what you have been writing (i can see you taking a book to meals) it's inevitable that sooner or later you should bog down and find that you've run out of words. you think you're a superhuman maybe? o darling come to rochester and we will play chess and alta has the look in her eye which sometimes means lemon pie. IF she gets her eight cents: otherwise, she states flatly, you will dine on sardines. mother says that if you come saturday we have a guest room if you want to make your own bed and wash dishes sunday morning.

as for me, i am still practicing the piano. i made a step in the right direction and am reading steinbeck's longvalley which i find interesting and any one of the stories worth three of minceandmen (that mince is ernest's idea of a joke god knows I didn't do it!). today is friday and i have to go to the dentist for the last time; a week from tomorrow we leave. barry is recovered so we only postponed our trip for about three days really. i went sailing with michael last night . . . the first time i have seen him in weeks . . . and the storm warnings were up meaning it was dangerous for small boats to go out on the lake and michael's is a VERY small boat. i know absolutely nothing about sailing, you know, and i had never been out in a wind like that. heaven help the poor people who aren't sailors. that goddamned boat went tearing around the lake on one corner with me unhappily clambering around the outside (and i swear it was the outside which is the side which should be in the water only it wasn't) taking down jibs and things. michael grew quite angry with me because i was all the crew he had and i kept starting to fall overboard and he would have to pull me back in and i got awfully wet and forgot about things like keeping the boat level and kept saying oooh looka the pretty sunset when i was supposed to be keeping the jib either in or out i forget. and i got the top of my head knocked off because something which michael said was the mnsl kept coming about when i didn't come about and michael would say hard alee and i would say what only he always meant i should duck and i didn't. and he kept doing funny things with sails and i would say what did you just do and he would say that is known as jibing it is impossible. and all the time that damn boat skimming happily along the water on one edge. i wouldn't tell michael for anything in the world but i was so scared i nearly cried when i got back on nice dry land and then people came around and said you shouldn't have gone out in that weather and michael would laugh lightly and say oh well she wanted to go, and i knew all the time that going was the LAST thing i wanted and then michael who had NO sense whatsoever fed me gin and then hot dogs and coca-cola and when i got home mother said i was probably starved so she gave me gingerbread and i don't know whether it is the after effects of acute terror or so much gin and coca-cola but i don't feel good but of course then there's the dentist coming up very shortly. oh yes, and michael kept saying he wished i weighed more because then there would be less chance of our going over which did not make me feel as good as it might have.

and y leaves tomorrow night having finished with the dentist and so she has come for dinner.

come quick so i can talk because i can talk more than ernest can write.

love,

cat

. . .

"What can I do, dear? my life is just one predatory
female after another—"

[To Stanley Edgar Hyman]

thurs. july 20, 1939

darling,

i had been waiting so long for your letter, and it was so good to get it; after you get this you must address your letters to me

    c/o l.h. jackson stecher-traung litho. co. 600 battery street san francisco, calif.

    it's a terrific address and practically impossible to remember; we leave early saturday morning, and actually got the trunks packed and sent off. this week is of course the hardest; people who have not spoken to me in three years call up and insist on giving luncheons for me before i leave (all of which i refuse: do you think i am a fool?) except yesterday when a friend of mother's who fascinates me took us to clubs and things with a lot of ladies and i sat in a corner and was appalled. there was a story in yesterday, but i was too overwrought to notice it. it was one of those ever-to-be-damned things where the hostess orders the lunch first. i ate six rolls and four cups of coffee and people kept looking at me and saying why you're not eating what IS the matter and mother would raise her eyebrows at me and i would dive into the lobster saying falsely oh i adore it i love it it's so GOOD really it is. i would have taken a firm stand and demanded something else only mother was enjoying watching me so much . . . when they put the lobster in front of me she took a look at my face and indulged in a fit of coughing which left her with a very red face and nearly crying. she took me out afterwards and bought me a sandwich, laughing still. but that's not what i started to tell you. it was about these women. the hostess was grace, who is a firm, masculine woman whose husband hasn't said a word in six years. she won't even let him drive the car ("now, fred, your NERVES, you know") and grace believes that the reason she exists is to help people, even if she has to stun them with a few well-aimed blows to do it. then there was her married daughter isabel, who has been married for ten years, and who theoretically lives in chicago, only has spent the last two years in rochester with her eight-year old son, trying to tell people she hasn't left her husband. isabel is a great believer in patent medicines, and her son takes iodine, cod liver oil, sun treatments, eats meat once a day, NO BREAD, and takes everything from midol to carter'slittleliverpills. she can't understand why he's spent most of his eight years in hospitals, so she gives him more medicines to cure him. once she took up christian science and he nearly died of pneumonia. then there was grace's sister petey, who is the most likeable person in the whole damn family. she married a man whom they say was "interested in racing" after knowing him for three weeks; for a year they lived off money borrowed from friends, and then he died in an accident; "he'd been drinking, you know," and petey has spent the rest of her life grinning over the look on her sister's face when jim borrowed two hundred bucks from grace. petey states flatly that now she is looking for a rich old man who will marry her and then die. petey i like. the last was corinne, a hysterical woman with a fondness for young men and a weakness for rye. she wears three diamond rings. one was her engagement ring, which was intended for her sister, only corinne stepped in and took the guy away from her sister and married him, and her sister moved in on them, turned into an invalid who might die any minute, and has lived with and on them ever since. the other two rings are because corinne caught her husband with a blonde in chicago, and once she caught him with a brunette in new york, and every time corinne wears a new ring people know that she has caught up with her husband again.

each of those women has a story i have tried to write and failed, and each of them represents a type of person i should like to see exterminated. i tell you about these people because i wanted you to see what they are like. they are ladies whom i have been taught to respect, even knowing about them, and i must respect them for the very false reason that they are older than i am. mother enjoys a dutiful friendship with them, and avoids them. the thing that was brought home to me so vividly yesterday was that these four, with mother and me, sat eating lobster at a fashionable club, all wearing broad-brimmed hats, all wearing the approved silk-dress-with-short-jacket which is considered correct for such occasions, all talking of husbands and children, clothes and other women, commenting in well-bred voices upon the ladies at the next table and tenderly modulating their voices so i (as the child) wouldn't hear some particularly shocking pieces of news . . . and, stanley, these women were <u>happy</u>. that i shall never be able to understand. this is their life, the height of joy is sitting at a table and talking and eating lobster. this was what they had spent all their lives working up to, this was the reason they had married and had children and earned money . . . to be able to sit at a table and talk. the climax of four lives! i asked mother afterwards and she said perhaps it was because they never knew their lives were so empty. and she grinned at me and said "but we'll go have a sandwich."

i read chapter four, don't think it as good as three, but i like it. from what i have seen, that book looks pretty good. the only fault with four that i could find was the fact that it seemed incomplete; i couldn't find just where, but in a few points it seemed that you had not said quite all that should be said, that you left out some trifling things which would have made it clearer. the only specific thing i can remember is in the quotation from tennyson about the bees; you did not say that the reason for the m-sound was to make it sound like the drowsy hum described; it is very unimportant to mention that, and yet it is such tiny things that give me the feeling of incompleteness. outside of that . . . which is of course only my delightful soul, looking always for something to pull apart . . . i think you're doing okay. please don't forget to send me the other chapters as you finish them. i have, incidentally, every confidence that the book will be published. it seems so exactly what they want, those stupid idiots who read, write, or regard poetry.

kiss burke* on both cheeks for me; i am proud of him, he has inspired in you a happier and more interested letter than i have had all summer. i suspect that he has re-awakened your somewhat slackened interest in life. kiss him on both cheeks AND on the end of the nose;

* Kenneth Burke, lifelong mentor of Stanley's, and his wife, Libbie, were dear friends of both Shirley and Stanley.

he has gotten you an invitation to brown's. and please tell me more of what he says. for reasons of my own, i love that man very dearly. reasons of my own being, o curious one, that he has made you seem happier. which is enough of a task for any man to call a good summer's work.

alta basks in what you said about her cooking; mother says the hell with the bread and butter letter; she thinks you're lying about having a good time but so long as you were comfortable it doesn't matter anyway. she's forgotten you already, and is more concerned with getting a credit card from the gas company. that has preoccupied her for three days and she sits around calling the gas company names because they want to know why the hell she wants a credit card. she doesn't know why she wants it pop told her to get it so she's trying.

i will write you every chance i get (i think that will be every night when we stop) and please answer, because the one thing that will get me through this next two weeks is knowing that there will be letters from you when i arrive in san francisco. i am finally getting interested in going, now that it is so close. hell, i wouldn't mind seeing yellowstone. so i go. and i love you and if you think i will not be counting the days until i get back you are crazy because i love you and i do not think it is a sound idea being away from you and i am in favor of never letting it happen again because i love you. jesus christ i do. in case you are interested there is a small fragment of a tear on the outside of the envelope; it is because i am going away from you and so far and i stopped to think about it and cried just very slightly on the envelope but mostly on the typewriter. it's going to be a hell of a long month but anyway you'll get a lot of work done, now, won't you dear.

all my love,

cat

•  •  •

[To Stanley Edgar Hyman, handwritten]

THE SENECHAL HOTEL, PHILIP, SOUTH DAKOTA

Tues. 4th day [July 25, 1939]

Darling—

Let's have a honeymoon and come to South Dakota on it—it consists solely of a million miles of nothing stretching a little vaguely in all directions—country which "used to be the farming country, only the farmers couldn't live, so the president (a fine man!) and his government took away the land and the farmers are being fed now—and if the government can put sidewalks in this city it can sure afford to feed a few farmers!" The quotes are from a little gas-station man whom Barry and I met tonight.

And all of Dakota—we're just outside the badlands now—looks like T.H. Benton's* paintings. Shadows and everything. We've spent all day in country inhabited solely by grasshoppers—they're a foot and a half long (like several things I can think of), with incredibly nasty dispositions (the comparison continues) and bright yellow in color. (the comparison ceases.) They get in the radiator and squash. They also get in the car and mother and I scream—and if you ever had a foot-long grasshopper caught in your hair, you'd scream too, my darling!

We can tell we're getting farther west because the people smile when they talk to you. I'd forgotten what it was like to sit in a gas-station for an hour and talk to other people driving through. Will be in Yellowstone by Thursday and in S.F. by either Monday or Tuesday, when you will get a respectable letter, typewritten. Is getting a letter from me worth enough to wade through this writing? Or do you just read one page?

I've seen lots of things I like, and am enjoying myself. If I can't be

---

* Thomas Hart Benton.

with you, I might as well be happy where I am. But I think of you oh, so much, and love you so terribly and so enormously. I miss you and need you and want you and love you—oh, <u>darling</u>, how I love you!

Please write.

I love you—

Cat

• • •

[To Stanley Edgar Hyman, handwritten]

STATE GAME LODGE, CUSTER STATE PARK, HERMOSA, S.D.

Wednesday, 5th day [July 26, 1939]

My dear—

You must forgive my writing (just this once!) on both sides of the paper—I have been religious about not doing it before—but tonight they gave me so little paper and there is so much to say.

First, I am happy. Very happy. I am sitting on a cool porch and, although there are a million moths which sit on the paper—and on me—it is very peaceful. Barry sits next to me, writing to Babe. He is very scornful because I jump when moths hit me in the face. He is turning out well, my brother. He has suddenly taken complete charge of mother and me, and handles hotel managers like a true man.

We didn't come very far today—I take back everything I said about South Dakota—it stinks—we started through the badlands at ten in the morning. It was so hot we couldn't get out of the car and we were halfway through and the car went mad—completely. The badlands are hideous. For about the first two hours they are interesting—those lovely rocks making castles and shadows and funny color—but after that they are dry and dusty and very very hot—I have never seen such desolation. perhaps it is because the heat got me down today for the first time in my life and I nearly died. I never knew what heat <u>was</u> before. Can you imagine hundreds of miles of prairie land where there are no trees and no growing things but cacti, and only that incredible heat? We drove through it for seven hours and saw no towns, only gas stations and here and there one of those ugly little red farms. I hate such things Stanley! And then, of course, the car broke down, and hell broke loose— things got a little strained, too, when Barry took the wrong road and we went forty miles out of our way. After today, I never want to come to the middle west again—it's hideous.

We finally reached a city—(around here, anything with more than two inhabitants is a town, and anything with a garage is a city) and got the car fixed and got into the Black Hills—we're in the hills now. We saw Mount Rushmore and the faces in the rock (I thought of Easter Island, and archeologists a million years from now, and the Easter Islanders driving up and saying "O, there's Mr. Lincoln—isn't it a good likeness though!") and we saw the places where there were supposed to be buffalo only there weren't any buffalo, and then we got into the mountains. Do you love mountains like I do, darling? They're so quiet and have pine trees and they are so quiet, with only the sounds of pine trees growing, and the mountains sit and think about how fine it is to be quiet. I love mountains so much that, as you know, I have been acutely homesick for them in the east, and now that I am in them again I just want to sit and look at them— I used to plan to have a little house with no walls at all, on top of a mountain, and live there all by myself and just sit and look—now, of course, my wants are somewhat expanded, but someday (and I prom- ised myself this tonight, and it is a sacred promise) I shall have a lit- tle house with no sides on top of a mountain. It must be a mountain with pine trees, and little streams and deer and even bees—I don't think I mind bees so much on a mountain. (a bee flew in the car today, and even Barry commended me on my behavior—mother will witness for you that I sat very still, turned very white, and never opened my mouth.) Oh but mountains! We stopped on top of one today, and I went far off by myself and sat and looked, and I didn't even think about you, my darling. I just remembered all the times at home—even with you—that I've wanted something and couldn't tell what it was. I think it's the absolute peace, and consciousness of age, and the silence which is in all trees, that I love so much—and after a long while, if you're very quiet, the trees begin to grow around you.

I have come inside now, because a moth flew in my eye—

I imagine that I have not managed in any way to convey that great comfortable feeling I have tonight. It is entirely apart from my homesickness for you and your arms, because that homesickness has not gone away at all, and I miss you dreadfully. But this is different. Way deep inside me all the restlessness has gone away, and I could stay here from now on, even without you. I wouldn't <u>want</u> to, but it wouldn't drive me crazy, or into that desolate, no-insides feeling I'd have anywhere else. I think that my restlessness and nervousness at home is an insane seeking for some overwhelming stability which I find here in this vast quiet. I know I don't love you any the less because I can take a deep breath at last.

You understand? Yes—surely. You always have.

So—goodnight, dearest, and love me and love me and write to me and miss me some.

Because I love you so.

your,

Cat

•  •  •

[To Stanley Edgar Hyman]

[August 2, 1939]

dear,

i'd forgotten, hadn't i? i mean, about fog and hills and oceans and things? because it's wonderful. i went to sleep last night with a foghorn going just outside the window, and the fog was coming in through the cracks. and we live on a hill. and the ocean's not far.

we got in about five yesterday ... i nearly disgraced myself by crying when i saw the city across the bridge. barry drove through town ... up and down sixty degree hills, and we found my grandmother, who had found an apartment for us. my grandmother is very practical, and was sure to get an apartment with a garage and a radio and a piano and lots of ashtrays, but she completely forgot about beds. she has been concentrating for two weeks on making mary baker eddy* and god think of a place for barry to sleep. last night he slept on the couch. there are only two beds, you see, and four of us. that had never occurred to my grandmother, who says in a sort of dazed fashion: "but she was such a lovely woman, and such a nice location and did you see that garage?" of course we're half way up a hill and we can't get the car into the garage ... but we have a radio. the wiring has barry and pop hysterical. there is one plug in the house and it serves four rooms. it is in the kitchen and the wires go right around the apartment to the living room and my room. in order to use the toaster we have to disconnect the livingroom lamps ... thus. we are in san francisco, we have a place to live (but no wastebaskets) and people are getting barry and me dates for saturday night.

thank god for your letters. it was so good to get them, even if they were little and inadequate for what i wanted. (uh-huh)

a collection of assorted uncles just arrived and barry and i must go shopping with them. we're to learn our way around the city, and unc' cliff is going to teach me to drive before i leave. that's a promise. i shall then do a very small bit of the driving back and take my license in rochester when i get home. i'll write you again tonight; i can mail this now if i stop. like yours, it isn't worth mailing, but i want to tell you i love you.

darling, darling, darling!

cat

•   •   •

* The founder of Christian Science.

[To Stanley Edgar Hyman]

thurs. [August 3, 1939]

darling auntie,

so now we are keeping house. mother is washing, happily and with
suds in her hair; i have washed the dishes, made the bed, and cleaned
the house. that last a bit inadequately, but i washed all the ashtrays. i
am feeling a little more like myself today; being in san francisco is
not quite so new as it was yesterday. i miss you dreadfully, as you
know, and i WISH you could see me keep house with mother.
mother is so happy now that she can cook and wash again. we got a
bed for barry and put it in the dining room, which is silly. and remind me never to renew old acquaintances again, won't you. because
i called up dot, my ancient friend (on a dial telephone with a party
line, which confused me) confident that she would be the same person she used to be. and instead she said "oh, shirley JACKSON! how
are you? i can see you on friday but i can only give you until one because i have an engagement EVERY day, really!" so i probably won't
see dot on friday. and i have nothing to do but go exploring and see
relatives. barry is happily getting himself dates and having a wonderful time getting new clothes from my father's tailor, and mother's
time is filled up from now on, and i have discovered that these
strange people who own this apartment have, hidden way back in the
bookcase behind seventeen zane grey books, something called
thebeginner'sbookofchess, and i have been reading all about castling.
     yesterday unc' cliff took barry and me out shopping and riding. we
went to fisherman's wharf and he took us around the city and up and
down hills, and he took us to chinatown. cliff, who has done a lot of
business down there, knows the cheapest places and the ones not for
tourists, and i told him i wanted a skull, so we went into a little shop
and a perfectly charming chinese gentleman listened carefully to me
and said well, only small ones, and he dug away in a corner and produced a skull the size of the ones on my charm bracelet but instead

of being just an approximation of a skull it was hand carved, and the most delicate and intricate little thing you have ever seen, and it was detailed enough to show all the little cavities and holes of the skull, and i screamed once and the chinese gentleman and i went into a discussion of skulls and where i could get a big one (he didn't know) and finally he grinned at clifford and barry, who were looking at lil statues, and said weren't the gentlemen going to buy the skull for me? and they bought it. for a quarter. i was madly in love with the chinese gentleman by that time, and he gave me his card and a map showing how to find his store, and then, just as i was leaving, he thought of something that might interest me. he wouldn't tell me what it was, but went digging away in the back and finally returned with . . . a set of ivory chessmen. i just sat and looked at them, and my chinese friend sat and looked at them and barry went away groaning. they were beautiful . . . he told me afterwards that they weren't ivory, but bone, chinese-carved, and they were about three inches high, and very delicate. and an inlaid board went with them. i nearly cried. clifford and barry came over and said why did the chinese play chess and i said didn't the game originate in asia and the chinese gentleman was proud of me. so he said i could have the set and the board for eight dollars. which isn't too cheap, considering that they are whalebone and not ivory. but neither barry nor clifford made a move to buy them. so i told the chinese gentleman that i would come back for the chess set and he said yes he supposed i would and said goodbye to me very fondly and i tore home as fast as i could go to cry on mother's shoulder. and she said no and i said but . . . and she said well, i was going to get you a new watch for your birthday and i said watch-smatch and she said well we'll go down and look at them and i said i wouldn't ask for a penny all the time i was in san francisco and wouldn't even send presents to my friends and she said well, we'll go down tomorrow and see. so we may go down today and i think the chessmen are mine . . . or, rather, yours. it means that i won't be able to send jupie or frannie or june or y or anyone anything from san francisco, but the hell with them i have a lovely chess set which i am going to save for stanley. i won't open the box. not until we can play with it.

oh, yes, and something else happened in chinatown. we were walking down the street and we came to one of these candy machines where you get little charms with the candy and barry put a penny in and clifford put a penny in, and a little chinese boy came up wanting to shine their shoes, and they said no, but he stayed, and then barry held out his hand full of the candy, because he didn't want the candy, he had only wanted the charms, and he said to the little chinese boy "take this instead." and the little boy (he was only about seven) hit barry's hand and knocked the candy all over the street and said "it's japanese" and turned around and ran away.*

there are a few japanese stores among the chinese ones in chinatown and clifford wouldn't let us go in there. he knew which were which but all the chinese merchants display signs in the windows saying WE ARE CHINESE. and we went into a chinese bar where they had incense and a dragon for a bar, and chinese cocktails (buddha's kiss, pagoda, etc.) and there was a nickel machine with elranchogrande on it. elranchogrande has been following me all across the country.

and pop met alec templeton† in the bohemian grove, because alec is also a member of the bohemian club, and pop heard alec and four other guys do a jam session in b-flat, which pop said was the most wonderful thing he had ever heard. and alec one night gave a private little concert and played his impressions of the grove and some of his comic things and pop is still raving. and, too, pop picked up the interesting little story that alec's family wanted him to be not afraid of his blindness, so they never told him he was blind, and alec didn't know until he was ten years old that he was not normal; he thought everyone was the same way he was. which is material for a story.

i am very anxious to get the next two chapters of your book. you

---

* This is two years after the Nanking Massacre, when Imperial Japanese troops committed murder and atrocities against citizens of Nanking, then the capital of China. San Franciscans are afraid such aggression could reach California, and are experiencing high anti-Japanese anxiety. The Chinese, however, are longtime California residents and workers and, as such, are considered welcome.

† Alec Templeton (1909–1963) was a Welsh-born American pianist and composer, with absolute pitch.

don't tell me enough about how it's coming on. and you don't write long letters. and you don't write often enough. and i love you.

cat

. . .

[To Stanley Edgar Hyman]

tues. [August 8, 1939]

my darling,

so this is what it's like to be lonesome! i haven't written for so long, and i've wanted to write and couldn't. i haven't heard from you either. i have the typewriter balanced on my knees and it's not too successful . . . there is no place in this house to type unless i use the kitchen table and mother is using that.

we're very comfortable and getting along very well. mother has engagements every day from now on, and barry and i (already heartily tired of this goddamn city and nothing to do) go to movies or just sit and read. and it's a shame, because i really love san francisco so much, except that being all alone in a city with nothing to do and no one to talk to is hard on one. of course it's cold, and the sun hasn't been out since we got here—it's always like that, with fog all day and occasionally rain, and never any warmth, always that damp awareness of the ocean so near, and we can see the fog coming in over the houses in the morning. our apartment overlooks the bay and the golden gate bridge . . . every morning barry and i race to the mailbox and there's nothing. barry hasn't heard from babe since we left, and he's getting irritable. we haven't seen the fair* yet, and we haven't gotten my chess set . . . i'm getting despairing. our grandmothers pursue us . . . mimi† is overfond of me and keeps trying to take me out to

---

* 1939 World's Fair.
† Geraldine's mother, Shirley's maternal grandmother.

dinner, and i won't go. we went to see my english grandmother* and
she is very ill. i adore that woman; she is so little and so frail and so
amused, and she sits there and says wicked little things in that delicate english voice of hers and everyone pretends that no one heard
her . . . uncles tomorrow, and my mad great aunt . . . i'm looking forward to THAT!

why don't you write to me? i haven't the energy to do anything but
wait for your letters. i am so goddamn lonesome. mother is having
such a good time that we can't do anything to spoil it for her. the son
of a friend of pop's . . . he goes to cornell and we've known him for
years . . . arranged a party for barry and me last saturday night; he got
barry a swell date, and for me he managed to secure my swedish
friend, rune, who i thought was in sweden. he wasn't. we went a hundred miles down the coast to a country club near del monte, and i
drank myself into a stupor. for good reasons. everyone got drunk, including rune, who had to drive home. he did, through the fog, and
nearly killed us all. we got home at five and barry discovered that the
evening (we were supposed to be guests!) had cost him eight bucks.
just the price of my chess set.

then the next day we went out to ross to see family friends. ross is
my favorite country. it's across the bay, and as soon as you get across
the fog disappears and it's warm and beautiful. my great aunt lives
around there and i remember going across in the train to see her
when i was about six. i remember the magic names that used to
mean little towns covered with flowers and warm and colorful and
gay. i loved that ride up there, and going past the towns again made
me very happy. the names! corte madera, larkspur, ross, san rafael, san
anselmo . . . mother and pop met in san anselmo and i spent the first
four years of my life there.

the day ended in one of the nastiest situations i have ever seen.
you see, i'm in the dog house with my father. as a matter of fact, he is
not angry, but just completely through with me. it's because of
grapesofwrath. i think i told you . . . he refused to let me read it and i
read it anyway and then he asked me what i thought of it and i said i

---

* Leslie's mother, Shirley's paternal grandmother.

liked it and he said why and i said because it was well written (my one valid excuse for my father) and he said it was communistic and i said so what and my father said california was full of the dirty reds and he thought it was terrible and i didn't say anything and he went on and i kept my mouth shut and he raved against the dirty reds and finally i couldn't stay quiet any longer so i said something mild about how the reds probably weren't as bad as he thought they were and he lost his temper completely and wouldn't talk to me. and there was nothing i could do. so that night in ross we had been drinking mint juleps all day and both my father and i had had too many drinks and then at dinner . . . there were about twenty people there . . . the people at my end of the table were singing and at pop's end they were discussing politics and i had had about seven glasses of wine and four or five glasses of champagne and so had pop and everyone was very gay and suddenly there was one of those silences and my father said from way down the table "my daughter's one of those reds" and everyone looked at me and the men on each side of me turned said oh, really, isn't that sort of silly and i just sat and looked at my father and he was a little drunk and he looked mad and sort of ashamed but very hurt. and i know he was ashamed of me and only trying to make it sound funny so it would be sort of a joke and everyone would laugh and he could think about it afterwards and think that maybe he did have a daughter who was a red but it was funny. he doesn't really think i'm a red but he does think i've got a lot of damn fool ideas. and the people who were singing yelled at me to sing the internationale and teach them some of "those damned red songs" and i looked at mother and she was laughing at me and barry was laughing at me and pop was being ashamed and the people all around me were waiting for me to sing the internationale and i said i was sorry i didn't know it and wasn't my father silly but it didn't make any difference they all kept after me and said sing the internationale are you really a red so i upset my champagne and everyone had to get up and clean it up and they forgot about me. except that my father doesn't speak to me any more and ignores me completely and just looks at me if i say anything to him. and i don't know what did it exactly . . . and i used to think such a lot of my father but then i think of just sitting there with him staring at me and looking so funny and his making everyone wait while he embarrassed me ... stanley, please help me.

we saw a lot of old friends ... not dot ... and they haven't changed and our old home hasn't changed and the eucalyptus trees are the same and burlingame is still nice but i want you. i love you so and i wish to hell i could come home to you and i'm afraid you'll have to marry me quick and take me away because i've got a hunch that if this keeps up much longer my father isn't going to let me come back to school and he is certainly going to get me the hell away from you. and of course i'm not going to let that happen so remember i warned you there's going to be trouble in the jackson family and i don't know whether it would be wiser to start it myself and get it over with or just let pop work up to it and let it be really good. they've started mentioning jokingly that wouldn't it be nice if shirley could stay in san francisco and work here instead of going back to school and wouldn't you like it shirley.

so for christ's sake are you prepared to help me.

cat

•   •   •

## [To Stanley Edgar Hyman]

saturday [August 13, 1939]

auntie darling,

disregard my last letter. everything is under control. no harsh words, no disagreeable scenes; poppa says how did you like the book meaning grapes of wrath and i said not so good so everything is nice on account of i lost my guts and figured i'd sort of like to go back to school in september and so he speaks to me now and even though he isn't overly cordial and still is in no mood to recognize me as his daughter and heir there will be no open warfare for a while yet and anyway he's leaving for home next week and there won't be any chance for trouble.

san francisco is nice only i am bored. i got my picture drawn and i saw a flea circus and i had lunch with relatives being one grandmother one great aunt one great uncle one uncle and it was hell because they all said how i changed and was i doing any writing and i wriggled and finally went off in a corner and read a book. and my great uncle wanted to talk politics and no one would listen to him only he got me into a corner and told me about Communism the Red Menace or How He Won the War. and he told me that i would be surprised about communism that he knew all about it and it was criminal and they ought to send those people back where they came from and some of his best friends were communists and they were undoubtedly misguided if they didn't like this country and he really knew some nice people were communists and i should look around and i might discover that there was one of those Menaces among my very friends. it is because of the bridges trial* of course and people always ask us new yorkers what they think back east. i have learned better than to argue now and yet it makes me so mad. if i only knew more. i went to a little lending library to see if i could get ulysses and she gave me instead a book called laborspy which she said was fascinating. so i took it out and it is one of those startling-expose-of-the-labor-racket-in-our-midst books, and two chapters of it made me sick so i went back to the chess book the people left in the bookcase here.

and we went down to burlingame again because one of mother's friends had decided to give a party for barry and me and she had invited twenty-three of the children we grew up with. since i was the oldest there (all my contemporaries have left town!) and the rest were from one to ten years younger than i, i had a howlingly good time. i also used to be able to beat the hell out of any and all attending only most of them are six feet high now and look down on the top of my head in an annoyingly condescending manner. i was about to go mad when a young man (of course neither barry nor i recognized anyone at all and had to be introduced) tapped me on the shoulder . . . he

* Conservatives tried to deport militant labor leader Harry Bridges in the 1930s and 1940s.

knew me because i was one of the guests of honor . . . and said hey
where the hell's the liquor. i embraced him as a brother and led him
to the liquor and he mixed each of us a good stiff drink and said he
needed that my god had i ever seen such a mob. i said no who was he
anyway and he said don't you remember me i lived across the street
for fourteen years my name is jim and i said hello have you got a cigarette and he said hey you turned out better than it seemed six years
ago do you know that you and i are the only two people here who
drink and smoke and i said no but in that case let's stick together. so
we stuck together and he has turned into a very nice man considering
that he never used to be able to hit a baseball and we made him
fielder all the time and he never had a chance to play much and he
told me who everyone was and we both decided that we belonged
somewhere else and we shot crap in a corner and he beat me only i
beat a funny little person who came along and said he used to swipe
my bicycle and he knew more good stories than anyone i have met
since my brother unburdened his soul to me the other night over dinner. so it turned into a rollicking evening and i had a wonderful time
at last and enjoyed myself more than any other time here.

    and unfortunately barry and i now have a fifty-foot yacht at our dis-
posal and we must do something with it. a friend lent it to us because
he never uses it and he says we MUST play with it only we are scared
because we don't know how to play with a yacht so mother said that
since it was going to be barry's birthday we must give a dinner party
on the yacht and invite all our little ex-playmates which means no
drinking and a jolly evening talking about old times and how lloyd
broke his arm trying to climb the walnut tree and how howard's dog
was poisoned by old mrs o'neill and what ever happened to peewee-
roberts anyway. and sooner or later someone will drag in the old scandal about how shirley was caught kissing the boy next door or about
how shirley and david got locked in the barn for two hours and they
didn't mind (we didn't either; i haven't had so much fun in years and i
was so goddamned dumb too) or how they used to play hide and seek
in the old pasture and shirley and ben . . . or shirley and alfie . . . the
hell of it is that david and alfie and ben and all the rest will be right
there . . . all except the boy next door who moved away and they DO

say that his mother married again and her new husband is the leader of the union somewhere and of course she was that type anyway and do you remember the time that she . . .

what a past. i swear i'd forgotten most of it until these people started telling me about it. there were only five girls in the neighborhood and three of them were always sore at me.

it hurts a little to think about it now, and i sort of wish i hadn't come back. i am constantly embarrassed . . . more at what i remember than at what people say, of course, but it was such a foolish life, and i'm glad as all hell to be out of it. i mean, that idiotic and constant terror of being noticed that i used to have and that used to lead me, of course, to do all those foolish things. gone? huh.

i must go to bed anyway, which spares me from a prolonged discussion of the jackson complexes. so, my darling, write me.

i love you,

cat

•   •   •

[To Stanley Edgar Hyman]

monday [Aug. 21, 1939]

dear o'hyman,

i'm so sorry i can't answer your last letter but i inadvertently tore it up and it fell in the fire. so sorry.

i'm happy to hear that you're enjoying yourself and not working too hard. and i hope you can arrange for your lovely new friends to give you some of their money. of course you can use it.

why didn't you sell the ring? a hundred and forty dollars would buy a lot of condoms.

did you ever think of marrying for money?

i'm afraid my activities wouldn't amuse you. of course there's the fair, and friends to see, and shopping and all the other stupid things we do, but probably the only news of interest would be that i have decided not to buy a chess set (after all, i couldn't afford it) and shall return to syracuse with an appropriate gift for my roommate.

i've met some nice people (not very rich, though), and i suppose i'm having a nice time.

i threw away the silly present i had for you; i'm afraid it's not luxurious enough.

the only thing that might interest you is that i met a gentleman the other night (a very wealthy man) who said he'd give me a job if i wanted to stay in the west. i don't know how serious he was, but i'm half inclined to take it. i'd make some money anyway.

barry and mother send their regards,

shirley

•  •  •

[To Stanley Edgar Hyman, handwritten]

tuesday night [August 22, 1939]

Stanley,

It's 12:30 and I've been sitting here for half an hour trying to write this. The family's asleep and I can't use the typewriter.

I'm sorry I wrote you such a nasty letter yesterday. It was unnecessary. I know, and stupid. I was just taking my bad temper out on you, and I hope you understand. Somehow your letter, with its visions of wealthy, (O, so wealthy!) lovelier girls, being with you when I couldn't—well, it made me miserable. It was a terrifically silly thing to do. And I _am_ sorry. And I was _jealous_, but now I'm trying to apologize and admit I acted like a fool. Is it ok? I didn't mean it, you must know, and especially about staying here—for a day I thought I would, but I guess I couldn't do it.

Can you really miss me when you're with those girls? do you go on loving me just the same, and, <u>really</u>, do you ever wish you were rid of me? I'm so far away, and maybe I read things into your letters when they aren't there—

And I miss you so, and every letter I open I'm afraid of what it's going to say—why shouldn't I be afraid, Stanley? They sound good, those girls.

I'll be home in less than three weeks—one more week in San Francisco. I'm very glad. My father had a letter from the university saying how proud he should be of me for my splendid academic standing—he was so pleased. he has a sort of feeling of at-last-she's-passed-something—it makes for harmony.

I want to come home to you, because I love you. And I won't be jealous again—God willing. Write me right away? (letters just don't <u>come</u> any more!)

Wednesday

I feel even worse this morning—got your letter. I feel all reassured and good. Except that that other letter will be waiting for you when you get back to Syracuse—there's no way I can get this one to you in time. So I feel terrible. Why do I do such things?

Anyway I love you tremendously and think it will be nice when I can tell you so again—and I mean <u>show</u> you—

S.

•  •  •

[To Stanley Edgar Hyman]

saturday, aug. 26, 1939

darling,

it's sort of silly, i admit, but i think i'm sick. i have been kept in bed for two days and am likely to spend several more here . . . i try to write with ernest balanced on my knees and it is not successful . . . of all the goddamned stupid things to do . . . mother is so upset, because barry got sick just before we left and now i get sick just before we go home and mother is beginning to feel that it is really more than she can stand. the only doctor we know in town is on his vacation and his substitute has been so busy that we can't find him and i swear i think i'll die before we find him. what have i got? barry swears i have just what he had, i think it's tonsilitis, but mother (dear mother!) is possessed by an uneasy suspicion that it is mumps. my throat is all swollen and uncomfortable and white and the only way i can look around is by turning all of me because my neck doesn't work, and i feel thoroughly stuffy and unpleasant and feverish and i wish to hell i'd stayed home where i belonged and had hay fever. i can't sleep. and i can't eat. and all i can smoke is what i sneak when mother is out, and it tastes terrible. by god, i wish i were dead. and guess what started it. you and your goddamned ideas. yeah. you thought it would be swell if i did these things. yeah. so what did i do? i went on a roller coaster.

we went on a yacht with many people and i was slightly drunk and so when we got to the fair i said something eager about merry-go-rounds and everyone said no roller coasters. and barry was there and that unpleasant little norman and a lot of strangers and norman was so scared of the roller coaster that i forgot myself and laughed lightly and said oh COME on norman i'll take care of you and the damned fool said ok so there was i holding norman's hand and people putting me in the roller coaster and i was thinking of how you would finally hear of it (new york girl killed in accident at fair; shirley jackson, 23,* of rochester new york was killed today when . . .) and on top of everything else i had made a last request and it was for a good stiff drink so i got three and jesus i don't know if you have even a rough idea of how i felt but it was certainly not good. and i had to sit in the roller coaster while we waited for it to start and i was so scared but i was so drunk that it never dawned on me that i didn't have to go and anyway norman was so scared that if i had gone away he would have

* Shirley will not be twenty-three for four months.

turned into a gibbering idiot. and i don't have the slightest recollection of what the roller coaster was like only that when it was over i opened one eye and said sure i'll go again and i had been in the last seat the first time and the second time they moved me to the front seat and i saw where i was going and i nearly fell out and when it was finally over i couldn't walk. and then people kept putting me on something and taking me off and buying me a drink and then putting me on something else and sometimes i was upside down and sometimes i was going around and sometimes i was being still and everything else was moving. and somewhere along in there norman got very sick and went home to die. by the time they got me back to the boat i was just as sick as norman only oddly enough it was different because when they got me home they discovered i had a temperature and i couldn't eat or anything and when i saw my throat on the inside it was all white and funny. somewhere along that afternoon i had twisted my neck which combined quite unpleasantly with the swelling. and i would most probably be a well woman today if i hadn't gotten myself so drunk and dizzy and upset and thoroughly jolted. and i was supposed to go to a very nice party indeed this afternoon and evening and i was supposed to go to burlingame tomorrow and to see the wizardofoz on monday and now i sit home and nurse my temperature.

and i took all yesterday afternoon to read your book because my mind doesn't work very well on account of my head being so big and stuffed with cotton so i can't hear and anyway i think the book sounds pretty good. i would like to wait and tell you how good i really think it is until i can rediscover the items which i liked so much . . . your examples i think are splendid . . . but i can't write it now.

i haven't heard from you in so long . . . darling i'm a sick woman write me at once. we leave on thursday so better not mail any letters later than tuesday morning. we leave, that is, if i am able. they're taking furniture out of this apartment on the first, so we leave here anyway . . . i love you . . . much.

cat.

. . .

[To Stanley Edgar Hyman]

tuesday [August 29, 1939]

dearest,

i am recovering. thank god. for a while i didn't give a good goddam
whether or not i ever saw the light of day again. i got your letter yesterday at just about the lowest point i had reached so far. i was in the
hospital and it didn't look like they were going to let me out and no
one knew what was wrong and mother came down to see me and
brought your letter. at the beginning i didn't write to you because i
felt bad and then i didn't write to you because they wouldn't send the
letter from the hospital without fumigating it first and after i was
home i didn't write you because i thought i was dying and so today i
am recovering and the sun came out (rose clear!) and so i am writing
to you a letter. i think i wrote you that mother thought i had
mumps . . . she called the doctor and he said make her eat a pickle
and i did and nothing happened except my temperature went up a
few degrees so the doctor came and looked at my throat and said
hm. and he went away after telling mother to give me a good laxative
(so she gave me an enema which is a different story altogether or
could i say thereby hangs a tale) and about twenty minutes after the
doctor left he called us and said bring shirley to the hospital right
away she has diphtheria. mother said my god no she hasn't we're
leaving town on thursday and the doctor laughed nastily and hung
up so there was i at the hospital and my god i hated it they all wore
masks and everyone was scared of me and i was so contagious and i
breathed in all their faces. i went to the hospital sunday morning and
it was monday afternoon that i left. and by that time they had decided it wasn't diphtheria so they decided to call it a throat infection
and they let me go home. and when i got home i had to perform
something called throat irrigation only mother didn't help right the

way the nurse told her to and i swallowed about a quart of something called hydrogen peroxide and then I knew I was going to die
because it is a very unpleasant drink indeed. so then i couldn't eat. i
hadn't been able to eat in the hospital because i couldn't swallow but
this was different. so mother gave me something she thought would
settle my stomach and then hell broke loose because it seems mother
made another mistake and gave me something the doctor didn't
think i should have and anyway i haven't had anything to eat
since . . . i think i have lost a great many pounds.

incidentally the doctor who took all the cultures of my throat in
the hospital was a chinese woman, dr li, and she was the only bright
spot in the whole time i spent in the hospital. she didn't speak english very well but she stayed around anyway and talked to me all the
first afternoon. she has only been in america for six weeks and left
china only because the japanese took over her hospital there and she
wasn't going to work for the japanese and she won't go back until
they're out of there . . . she's coming back east next year to spend a
year at cornell and then she thinks the war will be over and she can
go back to china. she says she can't be homesick because she keeps
remembering china the way she saw it last and no one could be
homesick for that.

all of which makes the fact that i miss you seem delirium. only it
isn't and the funny thing was that in that damned hospital i was
lying there half asleep and the door opened and i looked up and it
was you and then i knew i was sick and i got more scared only seeing you like that cheered me up at the same time only you wouldn't
stay . . . just closed the door and went away and i could hear your
footsteps going down the hall. and i never knew i loved you so
much.

there is a slight possibility that i may come home alone on the
train, but it is very slight. anyway we are coming home just as fast as
we can and so i'll be back in rochester in about two weeks. thank god
thank god thank god.

i'll see you soon and i love you more than i can say.

s.

. . .

[To Stanley Edgar Hyman]

saturday [September 2, 1939]

dearest auntie,

i am at last strong enough to write you a few lines; my fingers do not work too well, however, so forgive.

we are still in california; and i am afraid we will be here for at least another week. i have put on a fine show and driven everyone nearly insane, but at last i am on the road to recovery (meaning they let me have a cigarette yesterday). i now have three doctors working on me . . . someone finally called in a throat specialist who said the treatment they had been giving me was all wrong all wrong and so now everything starts anew except that i still take injections which of course do me much more harm than good because they knock me absolutely cold for a day and a half and i have to take one every other day. and the only thing the doctors agree on is that i positively MUST NOT DRIVE BACK TO THE EAST. they say if i want to drive back i must wait until i am completely cured which would mean two weeks more.

which makes for a very pretty combination of circumstances. every few hours i tell mother and barry with a catch in my voice that they must go on back without me and my doctors will see me off on the train when i am well ("go on, pal; i'm done for . . . save yourself and never mind about me . . .") but mother and barry say no. we were supposed to start home two days ago and my father in rochester knows nothing of all this except that mother sent him a telegram saying we were not leaving right away and now comes frantic telegrams from pop to the office saying what is wrong what is wrong. so finally the office took over and still without telling pop the head of the sf branch found us and brought us books and custard and a bottle of scotch which mother drank and this guy says well we will sell the car and you will all take the train back and we all said why that is a very good idea and then they went to see what they could sell the car for and it seems that they couldn't sell the car for very much so we will either take the terrific loss on the car and take the train home or mother and barry will drive and i will take the plane home alone. mother, who would worry herself into a stroke if she thought of me alone for five days on the train, can hardly worry over me alone for two days on the plane with a stop off in chicago where her friends will take care of me. that seems to be the most sensible solution and of course i am for it. things look pretty bleak. it will take at least four or five days for the infection to go away and then i must get back all the strength i have lost by not eating, and not sleeping, and being generally miserable. so it looks like a long hard winter.

the nicest part of now is that we left the apartment. we could have stayed a couple more days but the damned place was so dreary and the sun never shone and the curtains and the bedclothes and the furniture and the rugs all seemed damp and mouldy and it was so gloomy . . . so we left and came down to burlingame to a motor court, where it is lovely. it is run by such a nice lady who puts a chair out in the sun for me every morning and makes me sit there for an hour and she has two big black cats named tommy and jake and they sit on my bed and purr. and we are way out in the country and when i sit out in the sun in back there are cows walking around.

so i am tremendously comfortable and as soon as i can eat and talk and sleep i think i will be completely happy. i won't be really happy till i get home. please god!

oh, auntie, i miss you so! all i can do is write you long miserable letters about how bad i feel and i can't ever seem to make you realize how i need you and love you.

s.

•  •  •

## [To Stanley Edgar Hyman, handwritten]

thursday [September 7, 1939]

darling—

just wanted to tell you that we're on our way again—they decided i could drive and we're coming the shortest way home—skipping The Grand Canyon.

it's difficult to write because there is a cat playing with my pen—he is a nice grey cat and purrs when i rub his head. i don't know his name because he is a sort of transient—we're in a motor court and he came in and went to sleep on my face. i am put back to bed as soon as we stop anywhere, of course.

i haven't heard from you for so long that i haven't the faintest idea where you are or what you are doing. we stayed in Burlingame so much longer than we expected but we will be home only a couple of days later than we planned to be—approximately the 16th or so. we seem to be missing half the trip by coming home so fast, but we're all homesick and mother seems to feel that she must get me home as soon as possible.

i can eat now, and do, like a horse. instead of seeing me thin and wan and pale (as i am now, god help me!) you will see me sleek and fat.

we get very little news—the war, of course, which still seems un-real to me. nothing is quite real now, anyway, except getting home. thank god for the radio in the car—we get some news that way, enough to know what's going on.

i'll be with you soon. i think of you constantly. i love you, and o christ i want to see you—

cat

.  .  .

[To Stanley Edgar Hyman]

[Christmas vacation, 1939]

darling, i've been amusing myself (the long winter mornings) by
writing down my dream which has been following me. it followed
me right the hell out of a small nap yesterday afternoon into a prodigious nightmare last night. it would be such a perfect horror
story . . . i'll send it to you, to make a nice fat letter, and you will
write me back and say i am secretly in love with a crocodile, because that's what i think the animal was. funniest thing about it is a
very vivid sense (still) that i've done something wrong, and am
being punished. that's why it's so strange that i should be so convinced that it's imaginary; when i woke up i was reassuring myself
that the whole thing was in my mind; i hadn't done anything.
(whee.) the injury, imaginary, was to you; don't tell me i've a subconscious wish to kick you in the eye; that's not subconscious. no,
there was a guy and he was so goddam nice and i was so happy and
then you in the form of a rather greyish crocodile came up and
started to eat off my hand only i guess i drove you away when i insulted you and said i was sorry you were only a mirage. wish to hell
you'd been in bed when i woke up; i would have gotten even for
scaring me so. you goddam crocodile.
    and i was having such a nice time too before you came.
    hey. i'll be able to come on wednesday i think. well? you don't
seem to be writing to me, how the hell am i supposed to know?
and where would i stay? well, find out. i gotta get a letter from
you before i leave, though, because otherwise i won't know
whether you're expecting me and whether to come. WILL YOU
WRITE?
    it's terrible here. i don't want to come home any more. i like
shopping with my mother because she buys me things and i like
sleeping and i like reading and i like going places where they let me
have lots to drink but i don't like being home. there's my guilty

feeling, damn it. they're so nice to me too. but you're nicer and i love you just simply lots. only my mother writes to me. go thou and do likewise.

s. edgar

p.s. well?

*Shirley's dream*

was i afraid, was this it, was it fear? was this what it was like, fear coming to a deep garden of moss, coming into a garden and follow-ing me as i walked in the darkness and the quiet places of the gar-den? his hands on my head were the hands of fear, and when he smiled at me i was afraid.

could it have been, where was the need? could it not better have been regret, and longing to free myself from the garden where i walked and his hands on my head? when he smiled at me i wished myself away, and yet away with him, no longer in the garden.

the garden was dark, and the heavy moss hung from the trees and touched my head as i walked between the trees. there was a black pool in the garden and when i walked near the pool the water stirred and looked at me. trees had fallen into the pool and lay there, grey and rotting, and the moss from the trees moved with the pool, and stirred as i walked by the pool.

was it fear that came from the pool into me, so that i ran back to the comfort of the steps leading down into the garden? was it fear that drove me to the steps waiting there with no house beyond, and nothing but the steps and a low wall behind which to hide?

i cried and called to him and he came, touching me with his hands, and standing with me. and when the trees moved from the pool he was watching me and i pointed and he laughed. for the trees were moving and stirring and rising from the pool and rolling and stirring and creeping.

then it was fear and i watched, afraid. for he had seen and he was gone and i stood on the steps with no house beyond, watching the trees move from the pool to me.

and when the trees had crawled from the pool to the steps they waited and raised their heads to me and they watched me and i screamed, not calling to him, but to the trees which lay before me, watching me. "you are not real," i screamed. "you are not real. i have only thought of you. leave me alone; you are not real; you are from my mind; you are not real. oh, go back. it is only me, so go back; you are not real!"

• • •

*Shirley is spending spring vacation at home in Rochester.*

monday [March 25, 1940]

darling,

my family is really beating hell out of me on the california business. they have taken the attitude that of course it was to be your gradua-tion present and we were planning so many nice things for you but of course if you're so anxious to leave home it's all right with us we thought we had treated you pretty well but isn't it just a little un-grateful of you? and then they tell me how they can't see why i can't take three weeks off to go with them and anyway i'd meet all the guys my father wants me to get a job with—they'll all be at the con-vention. and i'm going crazy. i just walk out when they start. it's a lit-tle difficult except they have promised themselves that nobody's going to get mad every one keep his temper now and so they're very nice and very hurt and i'm practically out of my head. i just keep say-ing i'm not going i'm not going i'm not going and then i shut my eyes and hang on with both hands. so they figure they'll buy me lots of clothes, and mother picks out nice quiet patterns and says of course if you'll be working you will want something like this. and i suspect that i haven't convinced anyone, that in june they'll show up with a plane ticket for me expecting that I'll go with them.

it would be nice if vacation were all over with now and i could go home. i would even welcome getting to work on the fourth issue.* y's boss is reading thecosmologicaleye† and he says i should read it. y is going to give me tropicofcancer for a wedding present. could we use it? i told her she might better give me a bed. speaking of beds, i miss you rather. why don't we call this vacation business off and get back together? it's all awfully silly. and i love you lots. why don't you write me a small letter.

so, with love,

s. edgar h.

•   •   •

[To Stanley Edgar Hyman]

tuesday [March 26, 1940]

o darling,

i have come to the conclusion that my family is not so dumb. last night they dressed me all up with a red skirt like carmen and my hair done high and red red nails and expensive perfume and red carnations in my hair and silver sandals and a couple of drinks, and they took me to the opera. charles‡ drove us and called for us and my mother wore white satin and silver fox and diamonds, and we sat in the mezzanine among a lot of other women all looking perfectly beautiful, and we went out during intermission and met everyone my family knows and they all said to me shirley how wonderful that you're back for a while you're looking lovely will we see you in june?

---

* They would soon be working on a new issue of *Spectre,* the political "quarterly of the arts," co-edited by Jackson and Hyman at Syracuse.
† *The Cosmological Eye* by Henry Miller, a collection of short fiction published by New Directions (1939).
‡ Most likely a chauffeur hired by the family.

and then mother would say oh we're thinking of taking shirley to california with us in june she loves the coast so you know. and then of course the friends would say how perfectly wonderful shirley how lucky you are dear don't i wish i could go in your place. and then we would meet girls i used to go to high school with and they would all look so silly and i felt so tall and graceful with my high heeled shoes and two drinks in me.

see what i mean? i suspect that it's their next to last attempt, the last being a tearful plea on june 2nd. this attempt was unfortunately negated by the fact that my new shoes hurt like hell and my hair wouldn't stay up and anyway most of the people we met are people i hate the guts of. i kept giggling and mother kept saying be more sociable and kicking me and then turning around to smile at people. and i went to sleep in the second act and so did pop and mother was so mad at us both. the only nice thing was that i looked in the mirror before i went out and i was scared because i looked so nice and i just stood there looking, but that is not peculiar to rochester but peculiar to the dress and i shall bring it to syracuse and try it on for you to show you.

and of course the opera was terrible. i think that in order to enjoy wagner you must be either a native-born german or a native-born rochesterian. and the germans like him because they're patriotic and the rochesterians like him because good heavens! there's mrs. lee in the third row i didn't know she was still being seen with her husband! my girl brunnhilde was somewhat shrill and i was playing fourteen ways of looking at a valkyrie and kept myself amused. i mean, thinking i was wagner and my goodness i did leave the horn motif out of this scene didn't i or thinking i was the director who lost his place. i love the old norse legends better than almost anything else, and i was the only one there who knew how wotan lost his eye.

mo* frightens me, does he mean that or is he still thinking that it will all blow over? i think that we had better just go to south america QUICK. and oh, i love you rather, son, and it isn't really much longer.

* Reference to Moe Hyman, Stanley's father, who was vehemently against Stanley dating Shirley.

you crazy son of a bitch if you had any sense you'd marry the girl and stop all this fooling around.

s.

•   •   •

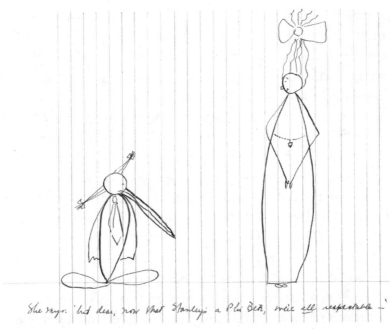

"She says: 'but dear, now that Stanley's a Phi Bete, we're <u>all</u> respectable.'"

## [To Stanley Edgar Hyman]

thurs. [March 28, 1940]

o stanul!

is nice. warm. sun.

i have discovered a refuge in rochester. yesterday i went down to see y at her bookshop and it was nice. so nice that i bought you a book. i have never been down there before, except to call for y, and i didn't know it was so refuge-like. y and i had lunch together and meadelux* came, with a red carnation. we were sitting in a booth with two eastman music students (recognizable by the triads in their buttonholes, the gracenotes in their hair) and one of them said to the other do you hear a music box? (y was holding meadelux under her coat) and the other said now you mention it i have been worrying about it for quite a while now and i believe it comes out of her, and he pointed at y who smiled reassuringly and said it does it does. then the music students bowed politely and took their departure. we went back to the bookshop and sterling, y's boss and my old pal, started an argument with me about how it was to the credit of rochester that he could sell more waldens than he could grapesofwrath, and lots of people came and argued with us. i had taken down a copy of spectre and sterling had been reading it and was distressed about your story. i told him the quotation of the title which my brother had taught me, and he said it wasn't a nice story. then a guy came in and met meadelux and me and sat down and said so you edit this magazine well well can you use any professional material? he said it was stuff submitted to him for publication. it seems he is the sole and rather unhappy owner of something called black fawn publishing co. mostly he is bringing out a volume of lorca translated by langston hughes. he says he is chasing lorca's brother around new york. he wants to bring out some of henry miller's work and kept telling me about DEAR henry, how difficult he was why i had a letter from him only yesterday . . . he also had a large sheaf of manuscripts of his own, which he wanted me to read. he says he is having a book of surrealist poetry published in the spring by the obelisk press in paris and these were some of the poems which were going to be in it. i waded through about fifteen pages of poetry and kept saying how interest-ing and he kept telling me about how he was the only american sur-realist and if he could only get to paris where they would Understand him, and i kept telling him he was about twenty years too late i asked him how he happened to write surrealist poetry and he said he just grew into it. every time he said that i would say o why don't you grow

* Shirley's cat, named after legendary boogie-woogie pianist Meade Lux Lewis.

out of it and he would say it is the only true art surrealism. he had illustrations for his book, which were lovely. much better than the poetry. by the way, his name is rae beamish* and i suppose he is
internationally famous as an excellent poet.

mother just came in to bother me about california again and then
she started about my going to new york in june and she says she will
give me fifty bucks and i must come home when it is gone only if i
SHOULD get a job my father wants to send me an allowance.

and i saw michael last night and he thinks he is going to marry
me in six months and when i said no he wasn't he laughed.

it's only thursday and friday and saturday and then i shall come
back sunday afternoon. y may come with me. and when will you be
back?

and i love you much.

s.

.   .   .

*Shirley is on a short Rochester vacation to please her mother.*

[To Stanley Edgar Hyman]

sunday [May 26, 1940]

darling,

it's gotten to be pretty hellish around here already. they were so nice
until they got me home and then they started in and it's still going
on. the trouble is my father was so damned nice and so decent that
there just wasn't anything to say. they have offered me a proposition.
they will do anything in the world, says my father, to prevent my
marrying you, even unto bribery and threats. if i marry you i can
clear out. they won't help me at all, won't give me any money to come

* Rae Beamish published *American Signatures: A Collection of Modern Letters* (Black Faun
Press, 1941) with contributions by William Saroyan and Henry Miller, among others.

to new york, and won't have you come here ever, although i can always come home. i finally got them to the point where, if i wait six months, until december, they will do all they can to help me, and won't open their mouths when we get married. my father is tremendously upset, and really knocked all to hell by the whole thing, and mother won't stop crying. my father is quite sure he can get me a job in new york, and will if i promise to wait.

so look. if it means a job for me would we be smart to wait? there won't be any trouble about my coming to new york, they won't ask me not to see you or anything, and they will go to california, which would be a great relief. i have been thinking that we could just live together and not tell them, is there some way we could work it like that? my father would come into new york on about the twentieth, take me around to these guys he knows, one of whom he says has practically promised me a job already, and then see me happily situated in new york and go away. he has been getting addresses of places where girls can live alone in new york and wants me to live in one of those places, but i think i could get out of that. by december i could hold them to their bargain, and they would have to let us go ahead and not say anything. darling, would you change your mind in six months? that is their main argument, of course, and it's one of the biggest reasons why i wouldn't wait unless we were living together. would you?

i don't know what to do. it's narrowed down to a quite simple choice between a job or no job. do you think it's worth it? living together anyway, i mean?

mother slipped last night and made a remark about something and my father quick tried to shut her up but it was too late and she had to tell me. some friends of theirs have organized a citizens' committee against unamericanism in rochester, and i don't know how far around, and are contemplating running all the communists out of town. my father said that there were similar committees in all the towns around here and all over the country, which didn't surprise me a lot, and then mother added practically over my father's dead body, that they had the names and addresses of all the communists around here and were really going to clean up on them. they are secret citizen committees—vigilantes, and they are only doing their duties. i suspect that my father is on one of them. he will be surprised when he has to run me out of syracuse. he tells me that they are all very secret and the members don't even know each other. very funny. he was insulted because i laughed, and he said i had no idea of the menace these communists were.

my brother took a crack at me this morning. he wasn't very nasty and, like my father, every time i showed signs of getting mad he shut up. he says he doesn't give a damn what i do, that he doesn't care whether i live or die, but he wishes i would stop making mother cry. so write me special and tell me you wouldn't stop loving me if we just lived together with a job for me instead of getting married with no job for me. i love you much and of course wouldn't stop whatever we did.

s.

•  •  •

[To Stanley Edgar Hyman]

tuesday [May 28, 1940]

darling,

apparently it didn't please you to answer my letter, although i made it as urgent as i could. is there any good reason why you should leave me not knowing how you feel or what you think? or am i supposed to guess? i'll be back in syracuse thursday morning, since i have a dentist appointment late wednesday afternoon. i had my wisdom tooth out yesterday and have to keep going back for treatments. it was pretty bad. i saved the tooth for you if you want it. it is the prettiest tooth i ever saw, and big.

i spoke to alta about records and this morning she showed up with four bessies* she had found in her attic. i think we have them all,

* Blues singer Bessie Smith's 78 rpm phonograph records, which Stanley was beginning to collect.

they're all columbias. the trouble is, alta has heard me talk about them so much, and knows they're worth more than a nickel, so mother is giving her fifty cents for each of them. i don't pay. also she is going around among her friends and telling them about the records. she doesn't want to sell them particularly, but is doing it as a favor to me. outside of my tooth which put me flat on my back, i have been shopping with mother, who has gone completely mad and is buying me everything she sees.

i went to a party with my father the other night and a great many people were there who knew about my wanting a job, and i had an actual serious offer of a job on field and stream* which my father declined saying that there were better jobs i could have. the field and stream guy wanted manuscripts rewritten and stuff. my father told him there was plenty of time for that later.

my father, you see, has assumed that i decided to take his offer. i left it up in the air, waiting for an answer from you, and then figured that your silence was either agreement or not caring to consider the problem at all, and so i let him think it was okay. right now i don't care. i was terribly worried about it when i wrote you, and wanted to hear from you right away. for a couple of days i waited insanely for a special from you, and i still think it's pretty damn lousy of you.

much love, and even when i'm so sore at you i miss you terribly,

s.

•  •  •

*No letters survive from the next two years, during which time Shirley and Stanley graduate, he magna cum laude, and move into a small apartment on Thirteenth Street in New York. They are married in a short, small civil ceremony on August 13, 1940, in a friend's apartment. Shirley's parents are greatly dismayed, and Stanley's father disowns and disinherits him. Stanley finds a job as editorial assistant at* The New Republic, *and Shirley takes many short-term jobs, including selling books at Macy's, secretarial work at an advertising agency, and writing copy for commercials at a radio*

* *Field & Stream* magazine, for hunters and fishermen.

*station. Stanley also contributes regularly to* The New Yorker's *"Talk of the Town" section. Meanwhile both work at their writing whenever they can make the time. In the fall they move to a rural cabin in New Hampshire to focus on writing; Stanley also collects reptiles and small snakes as a hobby, an interest of his since childhood. On December 22, 1941,* The New Republic *publishes "My Life with R. H. Macy," Shirley's first story published in a national magazine. In the winter the cold forces them to seek refuge in Syracuse. War is declared, and Stanley is 4-F due to poor eyesight, to his dismay. The following letter is to Louis Harap, editor of* The Jewish Survey *and close friend of both Stanley and Shirley.*

[To Louis Harap]

January 23, 1942

O Editor:

Now everything that once was youthful and sweet between us has perished, gone are the promptings of friendship, the easy sewing-on of buttons; there is left only, sad and perhaps a little bit pathetic, the editorial condescension, the artistic wistfulness. Here is your goddam story.

The story is, of course, better than you have ever printed in your magazine, better by far than I can expect you to recognize. The revisions, as you will see at first glance, are Stanley's. The art is mine. You will be kind enough to convey to chrstn std* the information that any inquiries or requests for assistance will be answered by Mr. Hyman himself, in his own handwriting. If her entreaties, or your own inadequacies, cause you to conclude that this work is not available for your magazine, your frankness will not be appreciated. Just send it along.

If you conclude that we are acceptable to you, I beg that you remember your former promise of illustrations, and contributor's note to read: Shirley Jackson is the wife of Stanley Edgar Hyman, himself

---

* Most likely a reference to another staff member at *The Jewish Survey.*

a writer of no small promise. Shirley Jackson claims to be a writer too, and has a beard to prove it.

Syracuse is wearing thin; you may see us before you expect. If you print this story, change one word of it and you will see us sooner. Leave out one line and you die. I charge you.

Writer,


Shirley Hyman

"Certainly he's in there. Why?"

*Two more years pass, for which we have located no surviving letters. Shirley and Stanley are well-established in the New York publishing and artists' circles. Stanley is on staff at* The New Yorker *(a position he will maintain for the rest of his life) and Shirley has recently published stories there, and in several other magazines. Laurence Jackson Hyman, their first child, is born October 3, 1942. They continue to write whenever they can. Their apartment, on Grove Street in the Village, is cluttered with books and papers, and becomes the site of frequent meals and raucous gatherings with their friends. It is a bohemian lifestyle filled with art, blues records, international foods, and intellectual debate over coffee and drinks. Shirley and Stanley love to give parties.*

[To Louis Harap]

[early 1944]

dear uncle louie—

i have really nothing to say in a letter, any letter, because i am saving up everything i know to get ten cents a word for, and it isn't every-body gets a letter from me these days either. however. i read, pains-takingly (why the hell don't you get a typewriter?) all your letters to stanley, and am very proud to find that you are now in a chazzical school learning to be a gwlyph. you must tell us all about it when you come back or when you learn to write. also stanley tells me that you are a private french chess (o you louie!) and have a frimbinch coming up. good for you, old man! i hope to god that when the army gets stanley and starts to make a man of him he will keep away from gwylphs, which i understand the army discourages anyway.

   stanley and laurence get along fine, by the way, except that i think stanley is going to get along better without the patter of tiny feet on his face.

   junie came back to town and is looking for a job. every time she comes over here laurence throws up on her and she has to stay for two days. the last time she came he decided to get teeth and she had to walk the floor with him because we couldn't wake stanley.

   now that we are making a lot of money we are living fine. we even saw a movie not long ago. i bought myself a fascinator, one of those head things.

   i do very little writing these days.

   by the way one of the things you most want to get a furlough for is to see stanley pushing a baby carriage around the block. laurence has the biggest and fanciest carriage on the block, with his initials in emeralds and a eunuch (we have to have a eunuch, he's such a <u>clever</u> baby) waving a peacock fan over his head. what did veblen call the stage of capitalism where you worry because the lady next door has four initials on her baby carriage and you only have three?

i lead such an active life these days, following laurence around and now and then finding time to answer the phone. i write at night, after the last feeding. i expect that by the time you get this the new yorker will have rejected at least three more stories.

stanley sends regards.

this is not a letter. this is a way of killing half an hour until stanley is finished reading the book i want to read. i will write you a proper letter soon.

s.

*postscript from stanley dictated to shirley:*

little i can add to shirley's magnificent social document . . . will put as many clippings as i can find in here and will keep sending them . . . news about your prospective furlough sounds fine . . . i think isidor was overly gentle with kazin. the reviews were uniformly favorable because kazin took care to lick the ass of every working reviewer. he left the nr* incidentally, because his book's success had made him too cocky to want to waste time in what he called "a menial clerical job" when he could be a great critic . . . i expect to hit the army about the middle of the summer.† write, we'll write, and come visit us.

yrs.

Stanley

*postscript from shirley:*

look, you should spend furloughs here when you are in new york. laurence doesn't howl at night and i could use your temporary ration book. house is always open to members of the armed forces.

s.

---

* *The New Republic.*
† Stanley is trying to enlist but having little luck.

. . .

[To Louis Harap]

[February 20, 1944]

dear louie—

it's been a long time since i wrote you, and i only do so now by default, i am afraid, since stanley wants me to write you and tell you he is going to write you.

stanley points out with some bitterness that he may see you before he writes you, he having just been reclassified 1A, and in some hope that the army will take him this time. i expect laurence is next. also my kid brother, who will no doubt direct a new invasion, from the way he talks!

we live quietly, writing books and being in a constant state of chilled horror at our son. he is tough, snarling, street cornerish. he leers, and talks back, and eats with his fingers and looks at his father and snorts contemptuously. he is already so strong that it is wiser to appeal to his good judgment than force.

i got tapped for the best short stories of 1944, and sold a couple more stories to magazines like the new yorker and mademoiselle. someday i am going to sell a story to colliers and then we can pay our income tax.

i have always wanted to see the places in england you take so casually. save them for me; i will exact a graphic description when we see you again.

love from all of us, and if you get a chance write soon.

love,

s.

. . .

"They get along fine."

[To Louis Harap]

[May 11, 1944]

dear louis—

laurence is a fine tough specimen of semi-animal personality, with a sort of deadly logic that confounds his father and a sense of parody that would do justice to harpo marx. he communicates almost entirely with the dogs upstairs who are fond of him in a patronizing sort of way.

did stanley tell you i am writing a novel? i decided that i might as well, just to keep stanley from sounding too superior about his old book. he wants me to tell you he is up to 1910. well, i am up to page fifty in my novel, and there isn't a critic in it.

i have been reading henry james and am having a hard time keep-

ing him out of everything i write, even letters. if i sort of drift off
into something like "it is with the deepest admiration and regret that
i find i must inform you that i am unable to bring myself to believe
that i could ever feel towards you as you were so kind as to indicate
that you could possibly have felt towards me, unworthy as i am of
such a gentlemanly and deeply human regard, although unwarranted
in my behavior, i trust, by the very graciousness of your tolerance
towards one who can only sign herself, believe me, my dear dear
friend, only, and no more, trust me, ever, your resigned and ever admiring . . ."

   i must stop writing letters and get to writing a novel. if you think
of any good scenes for a novel covering about forty pages send them
right along. i can use anything i can get. accept from all three of us
our undying devotion.

love,

Shirley

•   •   •

"Well, looks like we're going to win the war."

[To Louis Harap]

july 16, 1944

dear louis—

first of all, we are delighted to hear of your collection of promotions and transfers. i don't understand any of it very well, but it sounds terribly impressive.

you wanted to know how the invasion* news was received? it's hard to describe; i only saw what it was like in our neighborhood, and i think it was the most terrible day of my life. i went out to do my marketing in the morning and people kept stopping me on the street to take my paper out of my hands to look at the headlines, and the butcher looked at me when i asked for veal and finally picked up a handful of hamburger and put it in a bag and gave it to me, and the old lady who has the bakery was sitting behind the counter crying and when i muttered something embarrassed and sympathetic she wailed "they're going to raise my rent ten dollars a month," and then her daughter came in and told me she had four sons overseas. we got the news when the new york times came, and sat through breakfast with all the radios on.

stanley says he promised to send you copies of my stories; they'll be coming out soon. our collective books progress slowly; stanley reads more every day, and i write lots of stories, some of which sell. laurie is due to start writing his book any day; he has started getting out of his crib; we caught him one night and he had apparently been getting away with it for weeks; he hoists himself up and over the edge and lets himself down by his hands. like humphrey bogart going over a prison wall.

now he does it one-handed. so, until about ten o'clock at night when he gets really tired, he keeps getting out of bed and wandering into the living room and asking for a drink. consequently my usual

* The invasion of Normandy occurred in June and July 1944.

time for writing—the evening—has been curtailed, and i do even less. we still can't communicate with him so he goes blindly and happily on believing that this is the way people live, shoving elephants out of their way. he's got muscles in his back like joe louis. for god's sake come home and teach him to box, or tango, or ride a bicycle, or something. he's got too much energy for us. now, when he takes his nap we both go to sleep too.

we all send love, and are anxious to hear from you. s.

stanley wants me to add a postscript saying that kenneth burke, who has been teaching at bennington, let us know the other day that bennington is looking for young instructors and he mentioned stanley to them. if they should offer stanley a job it means i would be married to a college professor, doesn't it, unless i got wise in time? and can't you just see stanley teaching a seminar in a girl's college? whee.

• • •

"Yes. But why doesn't he learn to walk?"

[To Louis Harap]

december 29, 1944

dear louis—

we work hard and profit little. i sent my book* to the publishers, fifty-five thousand words of it, and stanley has completed ten thousand words of his first chapter.

stanley is making all ready, mentally, for the bennington harpies;† i am planning furniture and watching white sales in the paper. everything seems very cold and dismal, four days after christmas, with no stories selling at present and none being written. i am, however, enclosing a thing of mine from the new yorker; it was in a week or so ago. now that my book is finished i am looking again toward a novel; god send me a plot.

would you do me a favor someday if you have a chance? i had several years ago, a very dear friend whose home is in paris. naturally i haven't heard from her for quite a while, although i know indirectly that she is safe. if you ever get near there would you look her up? i think you would have many things in common. her name is mlle. jeanne-marie bedel. she and most of her family speak English. if you ever see her, will you show her one or two of my stories? she always thought i'd be a writer, and i never get into the overseas edition of the new yorker, so no one over there has heard of me but you, and you're a friend. i wouldn't ask you to do this if i didn't believe that you would be very favorably impressed with her; she is a terrific person.

i don't dare write any more since i want to enclose the story. love from all of us, including laurie.

love,

shirley

---

* *Elizabeth*, not finished and soon abandoned.
† Bennington College was a recently established, ultraprogressive school for women students interested in literature and the arts.

# TWO

. . .

## The House with Four Pillars: 1945–1949

i am having a fine time doing a novel with my left hand and
a long story—with as many levels as grand central station—
with my right hand, stirring chocolate pudding with a spoon
held in my teeth, and tuning the television with both feet.

—To Ralph Ellison, spring 1949

*In March 1945, Shirley, Stanley, and Laurie move to North Bennington,*
*Vermont, into the large Greek Revival house with four two-story Doric*
*pillars later pictured on the jacket of* Life Among the Savages. *It is a vil-*
*lage of less than a thousand residents in a rural farming and small manu-*
*facturing area in the southwest part of the state. Bennington College, an*
*ultraprogressive college for women, is only a mile from the Hymans' new*
*house. Less than two decades old, the college has about three hundred stu-*
*dents and a small faculty made up of well-known professional artists, writ-*
*ers, composers, painters, poets, and playwrights drawn to this remote small*
*center of learning because of its dedication to the educational philosophy of*
*John Dewey; students are expected to learn by doing, not just reading and*
*studying. Bennington College has a three-month winter non-resident work*
*term, when students take mostly volunteer jobs in the fields of their interest*
*and the faculty are free to pursue their own artistic and intellectual inter-*
*ests.*

[To Louis Harap]

april 1, 1945

dear louis,

we haven't done much reading or writing or even sitting down the
last week or so, which might account for our slowness in answering
your letters. we are fairly established in our new house now, but it's
been a fight. we were here a week yesterday, after a feverish week of
packing in new york, and a bewildering trip up here with laurie, who
had the time of his life.

due to some horrible inadequacy of housing possibilities, we have
a little nest of sixteen rooms, including a conservatory and two pan-

tries, and just mapping it out for the quickest route to the bathroom has been a problem. laurie knows every corner of it by heart, including the attics, of which there seem to be seven or eight, and the layer upon layer of cellars. he is also pleased to find that we are to have our friends the painters, paperers, electricians, plumbers, carpenters, and so on, with us for the next month or so; they are his joy and delight, and he keeps showing up for lunch with great streaks of white paint on his face. he has also met two little boys who live next door, who knocked him down and hit him over the head with a box, and he is completely captivated with them. except for the facts that stanley starts teaching next week and that tonight a neighbor made us a gift of a mother cat and four kittens, that is about all i have the strength to say about this house, except that it's lovely and sunny and dirty and agreeable and bigger than anything we've ever seen.

i am so happy you met jeannou and liked her; i was sure you would. i expect to receive a letter describing her meeting with you and giving her impressions of you.

not offended, i was more than a little irritated over your patronizing comments on my stories; i seem to recall that you turned down some of them for your magazine and then had to eat your words once before when they started selling. since i am probably no more tactful than you are, i can only say that i don't think you're any kind of judge of what i'm trying to do, and let it go at that. stanley believes you completely misread the review you commented on, and intends to write you to that effect, calling you to account for your further comments on his future career which, if not openly insulting, smacked nevertheless of that same misreading and deliberate judging by false standards. back to my stories again, i can only say that if you think a "full career as a writer" comes with the length of a novel you are more ambitious for me than i am for myself. there. now to something more pleasant.

as always when i get creative, i am creating more children. about october again; i can't seem to produce anything but libras; a little girl to be named joanne,* we believe. at any rate, we hope wildly that you

* Joanne Leslie Hyman was born November 8, 1945, at Putnam Memorial Hospital in Bennington.

might be here to wait around nervously those last few weeks, as before. i remember you hexed laurie into being two weeks later, just by wishing him to appear.

our new address is north bennington, vermont. i go every day to get our mail at the postoffice, and nod to the villagers. write soon. love from all of us,

s.

. . .

"What he needs is a baby sister."

[To Jim Bishop, Shirley's new literary agent at MCA]

August 16, 1946

Dear Mr. Bishop:

That is good news about the Yale Review. They are welcome to the story, and I hope you can hurry them about printing it. As for my life and work: I have been writing short stories for four years, published everywhere from The New Yorker to a high school textbook; I am married to a critic and have two small children, both critics; I am now working on a first novel; I live in North Bennington, Vermont, and am learning to play the guitar.

That is bad news about Covici,* the weasel, but I like your "they haven't laid a glove on us yet" attitude. Try to find another publisher for them, and you can bait them with the news that I am now working on a cheerful novel about a college girl,† suitable for serialization in anything printed on slick paper, which I will have in your lap, done up in red and green ribbon, by Christmas day. If they want to contract for both the book of stories and the novel, they are welcome to publish the novel first (as Covici isn't) but they must like the stories and want to publish them.

As for the stories, incidentally, I want to take the ten worst ones out and put in a few good new ones. Anyone who gives me a contract for a book of stories can have a say about which are the ten worst.

The other favor I would like to ask you is to needle Story‡ about when the hell they plan to print a story called Seven Types of Ambiguity they bought nine months ago.

I hope to see you in New York in a month or two and introduce you to my husband, who claims that you are his agent too.

Cordially,

Shirley Jackson Hyman

•   •   •

---

* Pat (Pascal) Covici, legendary editor at Viking Press.
† *Hangsaman.*
‡ *Story* magazine.

"Ex Libris: The Hymans"

*Two years have passed. We have no letters from between August 1946 and October 1948. Shirley's first novel,* The Road Through the Wall, *is published in February 1948 to few reviews and modest sales. The following is the earliest surviving letter that Shirley Jackson wrote to her parents (they begin saving her correspondence at this point). It is written four months after "The Lottery" was published in* The New Yorker *in June to huge acclaim, thrusting Shirley into the national eye. The mail she receives following the story's publication—mostly very negative and threatening—chills her. Shirley now awaits the birth of her third child, Sarah.*

[To Geraldine and Leslie Jackson]

thursday [mid-October 1948]

dearest mother and pop,

i have been postponing writing you, because i kept thinking that my next letter would be from the hospital.

first of all, there doesn't seem to be anything to worry about. i always seem to be late anyway—remember laurie?—and since i feel perfectly wonderful, and have no trouble getting around or anything, the doctor says just go on waiting. i go on briskly racing up and down stairs, and climbing the hill every day, and last weekend i raked all the leaves off the lawn, and so on, and no effects of any kind. i still haven't had a piece of candy, but stanley agrees with me that if the baby hasn't come by halloween i ought to be allowed to eat a marsh-mallow.

one reason i think everything is so delayed is that i keep trying to get just one more thing done before i leave, so i don't leave. first it was a story i wanted to finish, and get mailed off before i went to the hospital, and that's been gone nearly two weeks; then the proofs of my book of stories* arrived and i prayed for time to get them read—they went off a week ago. now i am debating doing another story. if i start it i'll want to finish it and it will keep me home longer; on the other hand, if i don't start it, and don't go to the hospital, i'll be awful mad. all the children's winter clothes are out and mended, the baby's stuff is ready, the only thing i haven't done is order my thanksgiving turkey.

stanley says he will send you a telegram the minute anything happens. who knows, it may beat this letter.

love to you and pop,

s.

•  •  •

The children seeing their parents as one

* *The Lottery and Other Stories.*

[To Geraldine and Leslie Jackson]

[November 18, 1948]

dearest mom and pop,

i have been wanting to write this letter for two weeks now, and of course each day i delay there is more i want to tell you, since with so many children now i find that i have about fifteen minutes at a time between meals and feedings and baths.

everything has been so pleasant, and sally* is such a good baby. she is on her own schedule, of course, and a very strange one it is, but she is fat and happy, and apparently very pleased to be here at last. laurie and jann are very fond of her, and jann can hold the bottle for her and will soon be able to change her. jann has begun an active social life, inviting guests for supper. and laurie has learned to read his whole school book, and is making such fast progress that it will not be long before he can read anything; he spends hours figuring out words in the paper, and writing lists of words on the typewriter.

laurie and jann have gone to school, and i have probably fifteen minutes before sally wants her bath and then i make beds and then laurie and jann come home for lunch, and then we all go to sleep, and then i wake up and go downstreet to do the shopping and then i make supper and then if something doesn't come up i may get back to the typewriter again. you can see how much work i do—make the beds and make supper—but it seems to fill up my day.

the only other thing which i didn't tell you over the phone was that two days after i got back from the hospital i got an attack of appendicitis, the first i've ever had and i hope the last. it was right at dinner time and stanley got the poor doctor over here from some fancy dinner he was attending; the poor man thought he was through with emergency calls from me, but he came over and said i definitely had appendicitis and for a little while it looked as though i

* Sarah Geraldine Hyman was born October 30, 1948, also at the Putnam Memorial Hospital.

was going back to the hospital again, but i got packed in ice overnight and the pain went away, so unless i get another attack i don't
need to worry about it. can you imagine <u>me</u> with appendicitis, like a
bennington student?

i haven't gotten back to writing yet, mostly because i am still trying to get the house going again. i have a story in the october mademoiselle, and one in the november harper's, and one in the december
hudson review, and one coming up in the february woman's home
companion, which is the one they bought over a year ago. also my
book of stories is due about february fifteenth, and i should have advance copies in a few weeks and will of course send you one. stanley
finally broke his contract with knopf because he simply couldn't get
along with them, and is now working on a contract for his new book
with a new publisher, and if that seems to work out i will probably
change to them too, since i don't much like the way farrar straus
doesn't sell or distribute books, even though they are the nicest people in the world.

the thought of having two beautiful daughters has both stanley
and me a little bewildered; we never really counted on another
daughter, and stanley says he is a little frightened of them. i went
to the local mother's club meeting the other night—i finally had to
go because they've been asking me for a year—and they were all
laughing at me because i suddenly realized that girls wear dresses,
that have to be washed and ironed. they had good chocolate cake at
the mother's club, though. no one mentions the fact that i also
write books, as though it were not polite to talk about. by the way i
lost twenty-five pounds, and no longer like candy. it was a dirty
trick, after all. stanley's mother sent me a box of chocolates and i
didn't like them and gave them to the kids. all my clothes are too
big. must stop. write me soon. lots and lots of love to both of you
from all five of us.

s.

•   •   •

[To Mary Rand, *Women's Home Companion*]

November 22, 1948

Dear Miss Rand:

I am enclosing a photograph, which I hope you will see is returned. If you need a glossier print, you can get one from the photographer, Erich Hartmann. If you do, please see that it is the same picture, since he also has one of me looking like Alexander Woollcott caricatured as an owl.

Here is all the information I can think of. I am twenty-nine,* married, the mother of three children (Laurence, 6; Joanne, 3; Sarah, 3 weeks). I was raised in California, came East when I was about sixteen, lived in Rochester until I was married, and since then have lived in New York, chiefly Greenwich Village, in the woods in New Hampshire, and now in this village near Bennington College, where my husband taught for a while several years ago. I like Vermont and this town very much, except in the winter, when I long for California. We have a large house, six thousand books (including my fairly sizable witchcraft library), two black cats, temporarily no dog, and permanently no car. My husband is a folklorist and critic named Stanley Edgar Hyman, and my son sings folk songs to my guitar-playing.

I have been writing professionally for about six years, and amateurly for as long as I can remember. I have sold a sizable number of stories to a wide variety of magazines. I have had a number of stories in anthologies, including a Foley Best Short Story in 1944. A volume of my stories entitled THE LOTTERY is being published early this spring by Farrar, Straus, including the "The Daemon Lover" in another form. Farrar, Straus also published my first novel, THE

---

* On her marriage certificate, Shirley changed her age to twenty-nine from thirty-one, and for the rest of her life, she will maintain that she was born on December 14, 1919, making her only six months older than Stanley.

ROAD THROUGH THE WALL, last spring. I am now working on another novel, and some long stories.

The only background information on this story I can give you is that the germ of it came from an anecdote someone told me at a PTA meeting. The story as it stands frightens me a little when I reread it. James Harris, in one form or another, occurs in a number of my stories, and I am inclined to believe he is the Devil. It would not be beyond his powers, certainly, to transform himself into a rat.

Shirley Jackson

. . .

[To Margaret Farrar, editor at Farrar,

Straus and Co., publishers]

[late 1948]

Dear Margaret:

Here are the corrected page proofs. The single big problem, as far as I am concerned, is the running of the stories together on the page, one beginning on the same page another ends, which I never imagined you would do. It seems to me to destroy any effect any of the endings might have, and I feel so strongly about it that I can think of no alternative to repaging the whole thing to begin each story on a new page.

Other problems are minor. I like the jacket design very much, but think the subtitle, with or without "or," complicates it unnecessarily. "The Lottery," which after all is the title of the book, would make a nice simple effective jacket with the black circle, while the James Harris line would just muddle perspective purchasers (ditto in the advertising—the subtitle seems to me to serve a purpose only on the title page). Can the subtitle still be taken off the jacket? If not, as a poor second best, can an "or" be put on the front and on the spine?

I have been thinking about the James Harris poem, and the inevitable place for it, it seems to me, is not at the beginning of the book, but at the end, after the last story, as an epigraph numbered "V," and just listed in the index as "V." I think this would give the reader a final jolt, and furnish the key to the stories where such a thing should come, after they have been read.

I hope you will let me see a proof of the jacket copy while it can still be changed, remembering the two bad errors in the Road copy.

I will be in town for a day or two next week, taking two-thirds of my children to see Santa Claus, and hope you will be able to talk to me about all this then. Most of them, although small things, seem quite important to me, and the repaging seems a big thing.

Shirley Jackson

•   •   •

[To Geraldine and Leslie Jackson]

saturday [December 18, 1948]

dearest mother and pop,

thank you so much for the card and letter, and for pop's nice birthday letter, and especially for the lovely robe. the robe will certainly come in handy—my old one was beginning to get a little drafty where the corduroy had worn off in patches, and wandering around this house at night is a mighty cold proposition.

i took both laurie and joanne to see santa claus in new york; we spent a day going around the stores. Bunny—my sister-in-law— came with us, fortunately, since that made two of us to carry the snow suits, presents from santa claus, half-finished lollipops, and so on. we started at ten in the morning, and rode on the merry-go-round at gimbel's, and jannie balked at speaking to santa claus. laurie was an old hand at it, and went up and sat on the old gentleman's knee and rattled off a list of approximately fifty items (including a camera, a typewriter, and a new electric train) but jannie saw only a

strange man trying to entice her to sit on his knee and she flatly refused. then we spent an hour or so riding up and down on the escala-
tors, in the christmas crowds, and the children loved it, and then we
walked around along with five thousand other people and saw the
window displays. then the children, who were running the occasion,
declared for lunch in the automat, and bunny and i doggedly
ploughed our way through the automat mobs, still carrying the snow
suits, etc., and since laurie and jannie must put their own nickels in,
bunny and i held off a crowd of people while the kids kneeled on the
counter and tried to decide whether they wanted a peanut butter
sandwich or a cheese sandwich, and apple pie or chocolate cake.
bunny and i each got a cup of coffee; i was too embarrassed to go
near the sandwich counter and bunny was trying to carry three trays;
laurie dropped his sandwich and the plate shattered and we all ran to
the other end of the room and pretended we hadn't noticed. after
that we got the children onto the top half of a fifth avenue bus and
rode them up and down fifth avenue for the rest of the afternoon,
counting santa clauses on the corners. when we got back to the hotel
we put the children to bed for a nap, and bunny and i took off our
shoes and ordered a lot of cocktails from downstairs; the children
thought it was the most wonderful day they had ever had.

that was my birthday, by the way, and stanley's father gave me a
birthday party that evening; in order to include the children, he arranged for dinner in the hotel room, with champagne and a birthday
cake, and the children both had champagne and felt very pleased
with themselves, and all of stanley's family was there, bringing me
fancy presents like bottles of perfume and nylon stockings. i felt like
a movie star being feted. thinking about that day now, i think it was
fun, but at the time i was pretty bewildered; the combination of the
cocktails bunny and i had had in the afternoon and the champagne
for dinner had both bunny and me giggling and mixing up our
words.

except for that one day, our whole trip was pretty discouraging. my
book of stories is all wrong; they set it in type all mixed up, and as a
result of fixing that, the book will be delayed until april; they put
through the copy for the jacket blurbs without consulting me, and

made two serious errors and a number of embarrassing statements about me, which i am trying to have taken out now, and which will probably delay the book still further, and their advertising campaign, which they told me about proudly, is so excruciating that i will never show my face out of vermont again. they are playing up lottery as the most terrifying piece of literature ever printed, which is bad enough, and they have a long statement from christopher morley saying that lottery scared him to death and will give ulcers to anyone who reads it, and they are working on things that say "do you dare read this book?" and except for lottery it's a harmless little book of short stories. i feel like a fool. and the two stories i had at the women's home companion and mademoiselle—they were both being considered, and looked very promising—both came back with glowing statements about how they were the best stories these people had ever read but of course they couldn't buy them. which leaves me high and dry till the stories get to another magazine. and stanley, who is marketing his new book, got offered a contract with a thousand dollar advance, by a fine publisher. the only catch is that they don't want to sign for six months or a year, until he's got more of it written. which leaves us high and dry again, and which also brings me to the uncomfortable part of my letter, which is your asking how we stood financially. i was going to answer you saying thank you and that we were doing fine, because stanley was getting his advance and i was selling at least one story, but now that everything has bounced at once things are a little grim, and i would like to ask you if you can lend us a couple of hundred dollars; we will be all clear again in the spring (those stories have got to sell somewhere, even to a literary magazine for fifty bucks; stanley is bound to get his advance sometime) and some money now would make it possible to clear everything up that can't be postponed, and would also enable us to keep mrs nadeau, who is our main luxury right now. we suddenly find ourselves living very bohemian-ly, something we haven't done in quite a while—i charged all my christmas presents at gimbel's and got out fast, stanley just barely managed to get money to the bank to cover the check we gave the hotel, and so on. we always manage to spend more than we've got, because money seems to come so easily, for stories and articles, and then suddenly something like this happens, and we realize that we live too well, and i think we both get scared. at any rate if you <u>can</u> find it possible, we'd be terribly grateful, and if not—just before christmas is a fine time, isn't it?—please don't worry about it. everything always manages to come out all right somehow.

i am writing frantically, partly to have enough stuff out so that <u>something</u> will sell, and partly because in the last six months i have been saving most of the stuff i wanted to write until after sally was born, so i am spending most of my time writing, and not doing much else.

i hope you have a lovely christmas. we will all be thinking of you and wishing you were with us. love from all of us.

s.

. . .

## [To Geraldine and Leslie Jackson]

january 7 [1949]

dearest mom and pop,

i may as well warn you right now; this letter is going to turn into a book before i'm through; i don't know why i can't write a short letter, but i don't seem to be able to, and so much is happening all the time that it's impossible for me to write less. i guess it's better than keeping a diary.

my first communication is a message from stanley to pop, which is that stanley wants to know what is the world's record for keeping those christmas tree lights going year after year because stanley thinks he has broken it. he says to tell pop that the light cord is entirely tire tape now; stanley won't give the lights up for anything in the world—he says they fill him with christmas spirit and good will toward men for the two days before christmas when he is putting them together.

our christmas started a day early, anyway. we had invited stanley's brother and sister-in-law and june and frank* (who hold an honorary position as laurie's godparents) for the christmas weekend, and they all arrived a day earlier than we expected them, so that the excitement which was due to start on christmas eve actually started the day before. with six grownups and three children in the house you can imagine how things were, and everyone trying to keep packages hidden, so that laurie and jannie were wild. on christmas eve our photographer was due to take pictures of the whole family, and that morning i discovered that the christmas tree we were supposed to get had been overlooked and we had no tree; finally, about five o'clock, the man arrived with two miserable little trees and said that was all he had left, and we should cut the branches off one and tie them on the other and it would be fine. you should have <u>seen</u> those bedraggled old things; the photographer came in one door as the christmas tree man went out the other, and then things started really hopping. the children were all dressed and i was too; i went up to get the baby and brought her down in her best dress only to find that jannie had not been able to stand it and had been sick on the couch and <u>her</u> best dress; everyone was running around except the photographer, who was calmly drinking martinis and setting up equipment. so just as i got the cover off the couch the laundry man arrived and i gave him the cover and made him wait while i stripped jannie and gave him everything she had on. as soon as i got her dressed she started again, and this time i had to change her <u>and</u> me. the third time she did it i had to change her and laurie. meanwhile the baby was getting handed around and admired and the photographer was drinking martinis and stanley and his brother had the christmas lights spread out on the floor where they had been working on them and it was like a scene from a marx brothers movie, with the photographer in the middle, surrounded by cameras and flash bulbs, drinking martinis. he must have put away about seven, because he was certainly feeling pretty gay. so we propped the photographer up and all lined up—our family, arthur and bunny, and no one wanted to sit next to

* June Mirken and Frank Orenstein were friends from Syracuse who remained close to the family for decades, often visiting for holidays.

joanne. then when the photographer plugged in his light, all the lights went out and stanley, who was looking grim and wildeyed by now, went down and changed the fuse, which promptly blew again; by this time the photographer was giggling and making faces at the children over the top of the camera; all the while we sat there in the dark while stanley changed the fuses. and june and frank, who were not in the picture, held flashlights for the rest of us. the photographer finally got half a dozen pictures, had a farewell drink, and went gleefully off carrying all his equipment, i put sally and jannie to bed, stanley made a new batch of martinis (we gave one to the laundryman, by the way; he needed it, too) and we went to work to set up our two christmas trees.

stanley and i both want to thank you, first of all for the lovely things you sent for us, and also for the checks. we are both very grateful; you were so kind to send the first check, and then, when the telegram and the <u>second</u> check arrived, we were a little stunned. thanks very <u>very</u> much. you know how much we needed it, and i only hope you know how much we appreciate it. stanley wants me to tell you, too, his additional thanks for the tie, on which he has not spilled anything yet, and i wore my blouse out to dinner, and also didn't spill anything on it.

after we got through christmas we figured things ought to quiet down a little, but they didn't. since last summer stanley has been waiting for the folklore and anthropology convention which was due to happen in toronto on december 27th, and consequently he took off for toronto, wearing his new tie, and the children and i settled down to a very quiet and relaxed week, to prepare for new year's weekend, when we expected six more guests. stanley was due back friday afternoon, and all our guests were also arriving friday afternoon, five from new york and one from upstate vermont. there was a big new year's eve party on campus to which we were to take all our guests, and on saturday we were having an open house with eggnog, as we do now every year, and had invited fifty people. anyway, apparently we planned too big. it rained all week and stanley called me thursday night from toronto to say he was leaving for montreal to get a train home on friday, and he had just been elected to the executive

council of the folklores, and on friday morning i called a taxi to go
into town to get whisky, and mr carver said "are you crazy?" and hung
up. and i called the bus station and they answered the phone and
yelled "no!" and hung up. then one of laurie's friends crashed through
the front door yelling "flood, flood." so that was how we found out
that we had a flood. i called the feeleys,* who were responsible for
the new year's eve party, and said were they going into bennington to
get whisky? and they said certainly, they'd be down in ten minutes to
pick me up. so, while the children stood around apprehensively, and
mrs nadeau wrung her hands, i put on high boots and an extra scarf,
slung my pocketbook over my shoulder, and started bravely out into
the flood, to get whisky.

do you remember the roads up here? the feeleys and i went
through the college, and there was a little water on the side of the
road, and a little more on 7 into bennington so paul elected to cut off
into a side road, which crosses a covered bridge and hits 7 again on
higher ground. anyway, we got a little way along it and realized suddenly that what we were trying to cross might have been a road a
while before but that now it was the walloomsac river. paul kept saying we'd be all right when we got to the covered bridge but then we
went round a turn and there wasn't any more covered bridge. so we
decided to go back, only the water had gone up six inches in the
meantime, and there was a big log across the road. helen and i got
out to move the log, and the water was up to our knees, and then we
tried to lift the log and it was attached to a fence lying across the
road. so helen and i walked back to the main road while paul followed us with the car, and the water was up to the running board
and had such a current that helen and i had to hang on to each other

* Paul and Helen Feeley and their two daughters, Gillian and Jennifer, were Bennington
neighbors who would become lifelong close family friends. Paul was a noted painter-
sculptor and fellow faculty member, and a prime mover in bringing New York art world
painters to Bennington, moving the college over the years into the international art
spotlight. He and Stanley were also founding members of the legendary Bennington
College Faculty Thursday night Poker Game, which grew over the decades to include
college presidents and deans, numerous artists, composers, writers, visiting dignitaries,
and many celebrities. Helen was a member of the college administration and edited the
alumnae quarterly magazine.

and it got higher while we walked—it was perfectly terrifying, to see the water coming higher and higher, so that one minute you'd be looking at a rock and the next minute it would be covered. we got back to the road all right, and helped some other people out, and they told us all the roads out of north bennington were flooded, and that all the people living between bennington and north bennington were being evacuated by boat. we watched our pretty little walloom-sac river for a while, and it was literally insane—charging along carrying trees and chicken houses and things—and then we came back to north bennington, without our whisky, and went to the post office and discovered that all train, bus, and phone service between north bennington and the rest of the world was suspended indefinitely. no one knew what was happening to the rest of the world. (a lot of the local people who own horses had farms or boarded their horses on farms along the road near the river, and many of the horses drowned; almost the whole town was talking about horses that morning and since no people were in danger everyone was trying to rescue horses.) the main bridge in bennington had broken and main street was a river, and all the stores in lower main street were full of water up to the counters. i asked the man in the post office what had happened to the montreal train and he said it was buried in a landslide somewhere near rutland. that cheered me immensely, as you can imagine. we went into powers store and he was standing in the doorway telling people to stock up, the north bennington dam (our little waterfall!) was going to pieces and might break and the electric current would be off, and the phone and other services were already gone. the poor man was in a panic, and so was almost everyone else downstreet, because of course if our little dam had broken everything in north bennington from our house down would be washed away into new york state. it was amazing; every few minutes the factory whistles would start blowing for anyone—anyone at all—to come and help pump; the polygraphic company is right on the river and they had tons of paper stored in their cellars, all of which they lost, of course, and everyone kept saying the water had gotten into the machines at the cushman company and the factory was going to blow up, and then someone would rush into the store and yell "gotta get the horses off the state line farm," and all the men would run out. and meanwhile helen feeley was buying food for her new year's eve party and i was buying food for my six guests and mr powers kept saying to stock up on bread and canned goods and candles. i figured that with food for six guests in the house i was all right, because by then i began to have a suspicion that they weren't going to make it. so the feeleys and i came back here, and it was about half past twelve and mrs nadeau was valiantly giving the children lunch; since i had not come back in an hour she had naturally assumed that i was drowned, and was carrying on bravely. i had one bottle of whisky in the house and helen and i flipped for it and i won, so i kept it, and we all had a drink and stood around the windows and wondered how long the dam could last. and then the feeleys left and mrs nadeau started wringing her hands and crying and saying she was sure stanley was still alive or i would have heard by now. so i threw her out, quite literally, so she went off down the street crying and i did things like mending the children's clothes and listening to the radio, which said we were having a flood. and paul feeley waded down from the college to see if i was all right and to get a drink out of my bottle which i wouldn't give him—the bottle, that is. i gave him the drink. and they started broadcasting a warning to boil all drinking water, so from then on we made our drinks with boiling water and whisky.

people kept dropping in to see if i was all right, probably because i had the only bottle of whisky in town, so about five o'clock when the phone was working again i was pretty cheerful, and then our guest who was due to arrive from upstate vermont phoned from rutland and said that rutland was flooded and there was no way to get to bennington. and he cheered me considerably more when he said the montreal train hadn't been caught in a landslide, that was the boston train, and they were bringing people from montreal into rutland by bus, and he would watch for stanley. stanley, i discovered later, had heard only that bennington and north bennington were the center of the flood area and everyone was being evacuated from both towns, and he was stuck between montreal and rutland with the conviction that the children and i were in a rowboat somewhere. he wasn't able to get any word to me till he got to rutland that night—by which time there was no more phone, so he left telegrams at each place he stopped, to be sent when it was possible, and they started arriving about tuesday and arrived all the following week. in rutland they sent him to troy, of all places, and he took a bus to troy and nearly drowned in the bus station, where water was up over the seats and ten feet deep in the railroad station. i finally got one telegram that night, saying he was all right, how was i? since i was all right i went to bed, and the next morning started getting telegrams from all the poor people who had been coming to visit us. every one of them took the eight o'clock train out of new york that morning, got to troy, and turned around and went back to new york.

tom paid a taxi driver some fantastic sum to tackle the trip down from rutland, and made it around noon on saturday, and since we were still due to have an eggnog party that afternoon he and i tried to make plans; we ended up with gallons of wine, which was all we could get in town, and about ten minutes before the guests were due to arrive stanley walked in; he and a couple of other people had hitchhiked from troy right through the center of the flood. he said there wasn't a thing left between here and williamstown, most of the houses crashed in by telegraph poles, and the road under the water most of the way; they spent most of their time driving across fields.

about twenty people came to our party, and we had a wonderful time. just having stanley home was enough to finish me, and i just sat in a corner and drank wine. and the cushman factory never blew up, after all, our little dam didn't break, although much of bennington has been badly damaged, and the people are still out of many of the houses.

anyway, life has been placid since, although we are probably due for a blizzard this weekend. stanley says i've been writing for two hours and have surely told you the story of my life by now. i caught my cold wading down the road, and everyone else caught it from me. i will not start a new page. write me as soon as you can—love and thanks from all of us.

s.

. . .

"I just like the binding, that's all."

[To Ralph Ellison]

thursday [spring 1949]

dear ralph,*

i told my older daughter last night that i was writing to you this morning about the pictures, and did she have a message for you? and she said, with a dignity and sense of propriety far beyond her years, "i

---

* Stanley likely started reading Ellison's work in the late 1930s, but they did not meet until the early 1940s, when a mutual literary friend introduced them. At the time, Ralph was editor of *Negro Quarterly, a Review of Negro Life and Culture.* He and his wife, Fanny, became lifelong friends and academic mentors to Shirley and Stanley, as Shirley and Stanley were to them.

would <u>never</u> send any message to <u>ralph</u>, but i will send one to his <u>wife</u>." so what was the message, i asked her, and she said, "please tell ralph's wife to tell ralph that my sister and i think the pictures are beautiful."

which they do; all three children pored over the pictures lovingly and admiringly, and laurie heartily regretted refusing to be photographed, because he thought that both girls came out handsomely. so do we. i still think you ought to go into the baby-photographing business. run a cute ad in the NYer. also you could do a baby book with the pictures you already have of sally. when do you people come up again? one of joanne's imaginary friends is named "fanny" and if that doesn't get you up here nothing can.

i realize—don't think i could ever forget—that i still owe you a batch of brownies. but i am having a fine time doing a novel with my left hand and a long story—with as many levels as grand central station—with my right hand, stirring chocolate pudding with a spoon held in my teeth, and tuning the television with both feet.

thanks again for the pictures. everybody sends their thanks and their love,

Shirley

•  •  •

[To Geraldine and Leslie Jackson]

monday [April 11, 1949]

dearest mother and pop,

although there are a million things i want to ask you—like how you are, for instance, and whether you are all recovered and feeling fine again—i am so excited by my book* that i've got to tell you about that even before anything else! you know, it comes out this wednes-

---

* *The Lottery and Other Stories.*

day, the thirteenth, and by now, two days before publication, they've sold more copies than they did of the novel,* and are talking seriously about passing any records so far for short story sales. they've had a second printing before publication, have two english publishers competing for the english rights, have featured reviews in the <u>times</u> and <u>tribune</u>, including an extra one in the <u>times</u>, daily as well as sunday, and an associated press review that says i am author of the week and that <u>lottery</u> is a work of genius and the publishing event of the year! there has been a lot of publicity about it, mainly because of the story <u>lottery</u>, so that featuring it in the book was probably very wise of them, although i opposed it. they've turned down three or four requests to reprint the story itself, because they are very optimistic about having the whole book reprinted as a pocketbook before the end of the year.

their publicity plan, which is smart although acutely embarrassing, got me down to new york for one day last week to be interviewed by a very nice man from associated press, who said that he understood i was a specialist in black magic and would i please tell him all about it. fortunately he had just bought me two drinks, so i was able to tell him, very fluently indeed, about black magic and incantations and the practical application of witchcraft in everyday life, most of which i remembered out of various mystery stories. he kept telling me i was the greatest writer in the world and i kept giving him this sick smile and saying thank you very much may i have another drink please. i kept thinking what a fool i was making of myself and then when he got up to go i said very politely that i hoped his newspaper would like the interview and he said if it worked out right it ought to hit about two hundred newspapers. all i can think of is some of my idiotic statements in two hundred newspapers.

also, the government—<u>don't</u> ask me why—has bought fifteen hundred copies to put in all the army and navy libraries.

joseph henry jackson† in san francisco, who is for some reason working his head off for me, is apparently holding bookstores up at the point of a gun and making them order thousands of copies. i

---

* *The Road Through the Wall.*
† Joseph Henry Jackson is an important literary critic in San Francisco.

think he thinks we're related. i have already passed the point in the sales where the advance is paid off, and all is gravy. from two thousand copies on i've been making money. they have six thousand in print now, with their two printings, and calmly expect to sell them all, although the novel only sold about three thousand. moreover, they expect to get rid of those odd thousands of copies of the novel now; they've had two requests from reviewers for copies of it, saying they missed it before and <u>lottery</u> has gotten them interested in it. the publishers haven't put a cent into it yet; all this is honest free publicity.

you can imagine how i feel, in the middle of all this. sort of small, and scared, and desperately anxious to go up and tap j.h. jackson on the shoulder and say listen, mister, the book is terrible, honest. because it is, of course. i read it a few days ago and it's flashy and sensational and all fixed up to sell. and every advance review we've seen is favorable, although they keep referring to saki, and truman capote, and john collier, none of them writers i admire particularly, as people of whom the stories are reminiscent. and they're all cashing in quite shamelessly on the press the devil has been getting recently, including half a dozen respectable books, mostly novels, which have come out in the last six months, and which use the devil as a character. also, there have been several odd witchcraft cases in the papers, and it all mounts up into a general interest in magic and such, which farrar and straus are exploiting, with me in the middle.

the thing that really sends cold chills up and down my back is the story that pyke johnson, publicity man at farrar and straus, is telling around as a great joke; it started with a joke of stanley's and mine, and i've been sorry for it ever since. when stanley was fighting with alfred a knopf, and the fight was at its worst, and everyone who knew alfred and knew what a rat he was, was urging stanley on and giving good advice, alfred took a weekend off and came up to vermont to go skiing, fell down the first day, and broke his leg. stanley and i made a joke about how it was obviously magic, and i did it, and we had to wait until alfred crossed over into vermont from new york because federal laws keep us from operating magic across a state line. it wasn't a very good joke either.

first thing we knew we started meeting our own joke everywhere we went, with all credit given me for breaking alfred's leg. and the first thing the AP man said to me was that he understood i had broken the leg of a certain publisher who shall be nameless, and would i please tell him all about it. and later pyke slaps me on the back and says boy, that story sure is going to sell copies of the book. i feel about those things exactly as though i had a very bad hangover and everyone was telling me the screamingly funny things i had done the night before.

if i really had a broomstick i would come to california and hide in the cellar of your house until about august.

i hope everything goes well with you now. and i assume from that that you're taking it easy and resting up. lots and lots of love from all of us.

s.

. . .

[To Geraldine and Leslie Jackson]

[June 13, 1949]

dearest mother and pop,

it has been so long since i've been near the typewriter that i've almost forgotten how to type, and i've <u>certainly</u> forgotten how to sit still. so much has happened.

the things that have been happening start with lottery's being quite a success; it's sold five thousand copies, which beats all books of short stories for just ever so long. i've been lined up for interviews and photographs in everything from <u>time</u> on—wasn't that picture a stinker, though? that was the one he wanted to take in the lobby of the algonquin hotel, and i balked. i've been interviewed by the times and the tribune and the associated press, and all the nonsense i told you about, that the publishers made up, is turning out to be wonderful stuff because the book is selling, so i have to tell people all this nonsense all over again, because the publicity man from the publishers is sitting over me and he corrects me if i say any of it wrong.

anyway on the strength of lottery i sold three stories in a row to good housekeeping and we paid all our bills including the income tax. and we bought a television set which was the silliest thing we ever did, and the children love it and so do all our friends. the reader's digest has picked up my third baby thing,* and something called omnibook† wants lottery, and the best short stories of 1949 does too. the agent turned down two people who wanted to make it into a play, and accepted the offer of an english publisher to bring it out in london this fall, followed, if there is any interest, by the novel next spring. if joseph henry jackson writes two more articles about it farrar and straus will put it into a third edition. the silliest thing of all is that my agent's ask-

---

* Shirley has begun writing lighthearted stories about the children after the success of "Charles."

† *Omnibook* magazine was published from 1938 until 1957 and ran authorized abridgments of bestsellers.

ing price is now a thousand bucks a story for me, and then she keeps me so busy with interviews i don't have time to write. except the new york times asked me very politely to review a book for them and i said sure. naturally i'm having a wonderful time being fussed over, and i love it, but i feel like an awful fool most of the time.

except for one other thing, that can wind up the literary news for today. surprisingly enough, stanley is not teaching but i am. stanley turned down the college offer of a job because they wanted him on a five year contract and he only wants to teach alternate years, and the next week there was a grand fight—completely unconnected—in the literature division and two of the faculty quit in the middle of the year. one of them was the short story man, and they asked me to fill in for him for a month, so again i said sure, and here i am teaching short story, and i love that, too. i have two classes a week and the girls and i talk very seriously about the art of writing and then they ask me very timidly where they can sell their stories and i tell them there's nothing to it. i took the job with two conditions—one, a hundred bucks a week, and the other, that the college president learn to square dance. if he doesn't learn by this coming saturday i quit.

aside from my being the belle of the ball this season, there is not much news. we acquired a dog, who is naturally the biggest dog in town. he is a three-year-old shepherd, named toby and is so big that when he stands on his hind legs he is a head taller than i. like most dogs that size, he's very gentle, and joanne rides on him. he is strictly the children's dog, although he condescends to come with me occasionally to my classes, and he has followed laurie to school three times. he wakes laurie up in the morning by putting his front feet on the top half of the double decker bed and licking laurie's face.

both stanley and i have been asked to lecture at the marlboro fiction conference this august; if we work it right the family gets a free vacation.

the only other thing is something i've delayed telling you for quite a while, for all sorts of reasons. it's about my teeth. right after sally was born the dentist announced that it was no longer possible to fill my teeth since the fillings fell out before i got downstairs, and he suggested i get what he called an artificial denture and what turned out to be false teeth, for the top teeth. after much family discussion i decided to do it, and i have spent all the time since being grateful for it. it was wonderful. i made four one-day trips to new york; the first one was to have six back teeth pulled, which i did at nine in the morning, and spent the rest of the day shopping and having four martinis for lunch to celebrate. and then i had another trip for a check-up, and then—the great moment, friday the thirteenth—the rest of the teeth out and the plate put in while i was still unconscious, so that i never saw myself without teeth and have not yet, thanks to will power. i've been to new york once more for a checkup, and the dentist said it was the most beautiful job he had ever seen, and i'm inclined to agree with him. the nicest thing is that it's really not noticeable; two days after having the plate put in i had to read lottery at a college assembly, and no one noticed it; i had no trouble talking or anything. since then, i've been lecturing to my classes and so on, with no trouble. i was very self-conscious for about two weeks, but no longer. i am just tremendously pleased with my appearance. i can eat almost anything, too. i tried a steak the other night and managed beautifully, almost without thinking about it. i look so much better, that i couldn't possibly regret anything but the necessity for it. also i grin in all the photographs.

this is a very confused and abrupt letter, mostly because i taught my class this afternoon sitting out in the sun, and got sunburned and so tired that when i came home stanley made a lot of martinis so i got tight before dinner. and then (probably because we were both tight) we went out after dinner and played baseball with laurie and his friends and i hit a home run. so by the time i got to this letter i was a little dopey anyway, but i didn't want to put off writing it just because i was dopey.

my class finishes in a week, so i shall be able to get to the things i want to do. we all send lots and lots of love, and are already excited about seeing you this winter.

love,

s.

. . .

[To Geraldine and Leslie Jackson]

august 23 [1949]

dearest mother and pop,

you must be wondering whether we are still possessed of a typewriter or a sheet of paper, after this long delay in writing. I wanted to get a letter to you in time to say happy birthday to mother.

we've been having a wild summer, and now i know how mother felt when she used to thank heaven that school was starting. two more weeks, and i think i can just make it. everything's been fine, but very hot and very lively. the children have had a wonderful time. laurie has learned how to ride his two-wheeled bike, although he still falls off when he stops, and he now does errands for me at the store, taking only a little bit longer than if he walked both ways. he has lost all his front teeth, now, and insists still on his crew cut and dirty sweat shirt and sneakers, and looks, in fact, like a typical north bennington subnormal farmer. his vermont accent is so flat and nasal he could pass for calvin coolidge. he has also taught himself to tap dance from watching the television.

and jannie is so much bigger; instead of being round and babyish now she's gotten taller and thinner so that she looks like laurie did a year or so ago. her hair is still all curls, and she's prettier than ever. she's turned very strange, though, in many ways. we've been watching her carefully this last month or so, because she is so different from both laurie and sally, and even though she spends a lot of time playing dolls with the other girls, she spends a lot more time all alone, playing mysterious games of her own, with songs and private dances. she is still so amiable and cheerful that it is a pleasure to be with her, but so very odd. no one ever knows what she is thinking about, or what she will do next.

and sally is nice, too. although she is just like laurie and so different from jannie—she is standing now, and trying to walk, and creeping all over. she eats crackers insatiably, and talks to herself, and her hair is curly like jan's, and she laughs all the time. i think it's true about how second and third children are more cheerful because they get worried about less, because both sally and jan are much more agreeable than laurie used to be, although laurie is so mature and self-controlled now that he isn't cross very much. altogether, the three of them have done so much changing this summer—they are all so <u>visibly</u> older, and have such distinctive personalities now.

i think the reason they all look so good to me right this minute is that we have visitors: red and minna* and their two boys, who are four and two, and the two boys are so wild and loud and badly-behaved, like company children always are, that my three look like angels, and they know it, too.

i can see butchie, the four-year-old, out in the driveway now, trying to wreck jannie's tricycle, and jannie standing calmly by eating a cookie and telling him coolly that she hopes he will get spanked. laurie is painting one of his masterpieces in his studio—he is a professional painter now, with all equipment and brushes neatly laid out by his easel, sally is walking around and around the inside of the playpen, and minna's younger, jerry, is systematically ripping apart the living room. stanley and i are cowering in the study.

on top of everything else i have a new girl, who arrived simultaneously with red and minna, and may not last as long as they do. her name is dorothy, and she is slow and not awfully bright, and spends all her spare time studying for a career as a missionary, but she does the work well. our career this summer with girls has been staggering. when i hired beulah early in the summer, we had decided to get a girl to live in and do all the cooking and so on, and after struggling with beulah for a couple of months i was about ready to go back and do it myself, because what beulah did was such a mess, that i was discouraged. so beulah left, and i put an ad in the paper and hired the first

* Red and Minna Sdolsky, friends from Shirley and Stanley's West Village days, remained close to the family and visited many times.

girl who answered; she moved in with us and seemed wonderful. her
name was virginia, and she was a little odd, but i figured anyone
moving into a strange house <u>would</u> be odd, so i overlooked it for the
week she was with us. she was a fine cook, but the children didn't like
her much, because she alternately scolded them and talked babytalk
to them. virginia had her first day off after she had been here a week,
borrowed my raincoat and ten dollars in addition to her pay, and disappeared, leaving all her clothes and things here. she hasn't been seen
since, but a nice lady dropped in to see me a few days later, announced that she was the women's parole officer for this county, and
asked if i knew where virginia was? it seems that virginia has been in
trouble with some man for about five years, was arrested and sent to
prison in new york state for a robbery she committed with him, and
had been paroled on condition she found a job and settled down
without ever seeing the man again. the parole officer asked me if i
wanted to prefer charges against virginia for the coat and the ten
dollars and i said certainly not, so i packed up virginia's things and
hired dorothy. since then the parole officer has called me several
times, to see if virginia has been here and finally to tell me that virginia has been located—wearing my coat!—and unless some miracle
happens, is on her way back to jail, because she has broken her parole
and is off with this guy again. i get my coat back, apparently, but
no ten.

add to all this the fact that we've been to two writers' conferences—
one at cummington, one at marlboro; at cummington i read stories
to the assembled gathering, answered idiotic questions ("where do
you get your ideas for stories?") and had a wonderful next-morning
playing water-witch; we all got out with forked apple twigs and
looked for water under the ground. turns out i can make it work, and
i wandered all over with my forked twig finding hidden springs. then
we went to marlboro, where i had one of the most shocking experiences of my life, read stories, answered idiotic questions ("would you
say that this story is symbolic?") and stanley gave a lecture on folklore and fiction, which started lots of arguments and went on an
hour and a half longer than scheduled because everyone had so much

to say. my shocking experience was meeting jack sheridan, who used to sit in back of me in the fourth grade at mckinley grammar school, and who was in my class until i left burlingame. he hadn't changed at all that i could see, and he says he has an old class picture in which i wore my hair in a dutch bob and looked awful. we spent a long time checking on old friends—he still lives in burlingame, and knew what happened to everyone—and stanley and i had a fine time being writers for two days.

jerry has just broken the television, i think.

i had better come out of the study and pick up the pieces. stanley says if i can finish this letter in two minutes he will mail it for me. so i will cut it short. all i wanted to say, anyway, was happy birthday. your usual birthday present has been renewed and should be coming along as usual, unless the new yorker's usual inefficiency holds it up.

lots and lots of love,

s.

•  •  •

[To Geraldine Jackson]

tuesday [September 1949]

dearest mother,

just a short note to say how happy I am that you're enjoying your trip, and happy birthday again. laurie is enchanted with the notion of you and pop wearing ropes of flowers around your necks. he has told his friends about it endlessly, and about your traveling in an airplane. it's given him great prestige.

his school started this morning, and i stood on the front porch and watched the procession of kids going sadly down the hill. laurie had on new pants—made of something resembling cast iron, which i hope will last for a month or so—and that was the only thing that cheered him. the boys say the second grade teacher is a horror; she pulls bad boys by the ear, and laurie is terrified. jannie's school starts next week.

stanley's in new york, at an anthropological convention; right now he is probably attending a most serious discussion of the American Indian. i am going down this weekend, although i do not plan to catch up with the American Indian. i want to buy some living room drapes and slip covers and some warm dresses for jannie and a stroller for sally. all this is possible because I have sold two stories this month, instead of one. laurie and jannie are now my two principal subjects for these light stories, so they get a cut every time i sell one—we went shopping a day or so ago, to get what are now known as "story presents." laurie got a cap gun and holster, and four boxes of caps; jannie got a big doll in a blue dress whose name is—heavens!—rosabelle. i, with the approval and assistance of both children, bought a bicycle for myself. now laurie and i go riding on our bicycles, and i have taken jannie for several rides on the back, and sally once in a basket. i am trying to work up to a position where i have sally in the basket, jannie on the back, and a picnic lunch hung around my neck. i rode for two hours the day i got the bike, went out to play bridge that night, and had to be accommodated with two pillows to sit on all evening, although i had wonderful cards.

our poor unfortunate virginia is back in the pen. i visited her in the local jail a couple of times, and got my coat back, although i'll never see my ten bucks again. she was very remorseful and unhappy, naturally, although I am convinced now, seeing her in what is by now her natural habitat, that she is not at all right in the head. I tried to persuade the authorities to send her to a mental institution instead of the pen, but my influence was not enough, and they seem to feel that unless she is actually homicidal, putting her into an institution is letting her off too easy. it was very sad, and made me mad with that sort of frustrated fury you get when you run head on into the sort of unimaginative, badly educated people who get into such official jobs. the parole officer has a daughter who wants to be a writer, and every time i mentioned virginia the parole officer insisted on talking about how i ought to meet her daughter. and the sheriff said it was not necessary for virginia to have any kind of psychological help because they would give her an intelligence test when she entered prison.

dorothy, virginia's successor, is working out very nicely. she is very fond of both jannie and sally, although laurie confuses her a little and i am very reluctant to leave her in charge of him. she is living in now, and until school started this morning i was living like a queen, getting up at about ten o'clock, and working in the study all day without worrying about meals or anything. now that school has started, of course, i have to get up to see laurie gets off on time.

dorothy and i have decided to do our own baking from now on, principally because the one bakery in bennington has apparently started using plaster of paris instead of flour. both of us turn out to be fairly good at following a recipe, and the house is suddenly full of nut cakes and brownies, sugar and tollhouse cookies, and apple pies. this is our season for good apples, and we have a bushel of macs which we all eat like candy. i spend my evenings with stanley away, sitting by the television eating apples and reading mysteries, with toby on my feet to keep them warm.

dorothy just remarked that my lunch was ready; i eat in solitary state without stanley, reading while i sit at the table, and while the children are roughhousing in the kitchen. pleasant days!

hope your trip continues to be as wonderful as it sounds. have a grand time, and write me if you get a chance.

lots of love,

s.

•   •   •

"Of course it is, dear—long as <u>anything</u>!"

## [To Geraldine and Leslie Jackson]

wednesday [October 12, 1949]

dearest mother and pop,

not much time to write letters these days, what with leaves to rake and birthday parties to give. this is mostly to say thank you for the nice presents, which arrived a couple of days ago and were received with great joy.

laurie's birthday is safely over, except for his party, which had to be postponed until this coming Sunday, because he wants his guests— twelve tough little boys—to see the hopalong cassidy movie on television. jan's birthday, coming up soon, includes a dainty luncheon for six young ladies from nursery school, and sally's, thank heaven, will be confined to the family and a cake with one candle. fortunately dorothy, who is still with us, although teetering on the edge, loves making cakes. laurie's main birthday present was a toy pool table, about half the size of a regular one, and just right for him and a shade small for stanley, who plays therefore at a handicap.

his main birthday present, after that, turned out to be one for all of us; his birthday was on monday, and that night stanley's father called up to say happy birthday, and invited both laurie and joanne down to see the rodeo that coming saturday. it's a great thing, at madison square garden, with thousands of cowboys and indians, and bucking broncos and gene autry and trick horses, and such. so laurie and jannie were hysterical, and then the old man gets on the phone with stanley and says "do you think you can bring the children down?" and stanley says he supposes so, and dad says "fine, you and shirley come along with the children; i have world series tickets for all of us." that was the thing that nearly finished me—you know, we've turned into ardent ball fans this summer—so i went upstairs and found a clean shirt for laurie and a clean dress for jannie and we left sally with dorothy and went off to new york on wednesday after-noon. we had tickets for the games on friday, saturday, and sunday, which turned out, unhappily, to be the last three. stanley's father had hotel reservations for us at st. george hotel in brooklyn, which has two dubious advantages: 1) it is directly across the street from the apartment where stanley's mother and father live. 2) it is here the brooklyn ball team stays when they are playing home games. it had a third real advantage this time, which was that stanley's brother and sister had flown down from maine for the games and had the room next door. we kept jannie in the hotel with us and laurie stayed across the street, and everyone took turns with the children in the morning, and stanley's mother had them in the afternoons while we all were at the games. every time brooklyn lost—which of course they did all three days—stanley's mother arranged to keep the children quietly out of sight until we had all cheered up again. laurie insisted on hav-ing a baseball suit, and she bought him one which turned out, most horribly, to say YANKEES in big letters across the back, and we ripped the letters off and got him a brooklyn insignia, and then every time he came into the hotel he had to run the gamut of unsober brooklyn supporters who were hanging around to see the ball team and who would stop him and say "you sure pitched a great game today, son" or "who's gonna win tomorrow, champ?" jannie got cov-ered with brooklyn ball caps and pins saying "i'm for the bums," by admirers. and every day at twelve o'clock all of us except stanley's mother and the children piled into dad's car and went out to ebbetts field and paid four bucks for parking, and sat there and watched brooklyn get beaten. we had wonderful seats, box seats right in center field, directly in back of dimaggio, and since we were all for brooklyn with the noisy bleachers in back of us we stood up and yelled "ahhhhhh, dimaggio, can't hit, you're gonna fall down, can't hit, dimaggio can't hit," which of course he didn't until the last game when he hit a home run almost into my lap. i suppose because he was mad at the names i had been calling him. we all got a nice sunburn anyway, and we're all hoarse. the children spent saturday afternoon at the rodeo, and came back with cowboy insignia on top of the baseball insignia, and laurie wore a cowboy hat with his baseball suit, and we all took the train home monday morning with so many souvenirs we could hardly carry them, although we required the children to suppress the brooklyn badges.

now the main subject of conversation around our dinner table is whether or not rickey is going to sell robinson and snider, and why he didn't pitch palica sooner.

enough of baseball. the season starts again next april, and by then brooklyn ought to have a winning team, and they will take the series next year and we will be sitting on the first base line where i can throw pop bottles at the umpire.

i quite agree with you about the recent stories. they are written simply for money, and the reason they sound so bad is that those magazines won't buy good ones, but deliberately seek out bad stuff because they say their audiences want it. i simply figure that at a thousand bucks a story, i can't afford to try to change the state of popular fiction today, and since they will buy as much of it as i write, i do one story a month, and spend the rest of the time working on my new novel or on other stories. stuff like the son and bully story turns out like that because i won't write love stories or junk about gay young married couples, and they won't take ordinary children stories, and this sort of thing is a compromise between their notions and mine, and is unusual enough so that i am the only person i know of who is doing it. that's why i can sell them. in addition, the fan mail on such stories is going up, and i am now getting long letters asking for advice on bringing up children, letters which i answer with the statement that if i knew enough to give advice my children would be better than they are. as a result, it's keeping a name for me, building up a following, opening new markets with plenty of money, and helping support us while i take my time with the novel. i haven't done much writing this summer—excluding one popular story a month—but am back at work on the novel now that the ball season is over. road through the wall comes out in a twenty-five cent edition in january, advertised, i am afraid, the way the reprint people are advertising all the legitimate novels they reprint—changing the name, putting a lurid cover on the book, and playing it up as some fantastic, love-among-the-haystacks routine. they expect a sale of seventy-five thousand, which seems fantastic. the stories you repudiate are selling at a furious rate abroad, two of the good housekeeping ones have turned up in england, and one other in sweden. none of this means much money now, of course, and the sixty pounds my english publisher still owes me has stopped looking like as much as it did, but still the things are building up to what will eventually be a regular reprint income.

it has suddenly seemed to us that north bennington has fewer advantages than ever before, for us. one or the other of us is constantly having to go to new york, the difficulties of making arrangements over the phone or by telegram are getting worse, and whatever business we have to do now requires that five-hour train trip, which is beginning to look like commuting to us. also, i am very much disturbed over laurie in school, since he is at the top of his class and is mostly bored because the work goes so slowly. i want very much to get him out of that school, and the result of all this is that we have begun to think seriously of moving nearer to new york, into a small community just outside commuting distance, where there are good schools and pleasant people. we have written to our friends who are scattered all over connecticut and upper new york, and are now getting opinions from all over. we are, naturally, trying to keep out of westchester, although we know many people around there, and stanley refuses to live in new jersey, for some obscure reason. we figure we can afford to pay a higher rent now, although most people want to sell instead of renting, but the condition of real estate in the places where we want to settle is so unstable—everyone thinks prices are going down fast—that we are trying not to have to buy, always allowing that we could if we wanted to.

the children are pleased with the notion of being somewhere where they have two television channels instead of one. i'd love to live in a house with two bathrooms and a town with at least one movie and a restaurant and an a and p. and the idea of being able to get into new york in a couple of hours instead of five intoxicates all of us. what do you think? wouldn't it be wonderful if we were living so near to new york that you could come and really visit us when you come east, without having to figure in that trip to vermont, and where we'd have enough room and bathrooms to be able to entertain you properly? we'd like to be out of here and into a new place by the end of the year, since we have nothing to keep us here. the nicest thing about being as free as we are is that we can do whatever we please; we could either of us get a job teaching in half a dozen colleges if we wanted to, or move into new york city and stanley could go to work in the new yorker office, or go to england, although we'd rather wait for that until the children are older. also, we must stay near new york for a while at least because until both of us have regular income channels with our writing we have to keep in touch with magazines and agents. in another couple of years there will not even be that compulsion to stay near new york, and then we'll come live in california for a while. so you can see why we keep writing for money. most of our money so far has gone into paying off ten years of accumulated debts, and into books.

dorothy has taken over the job of doing the shopping and getting the mail, so i have nothing now to do except sit at the typewriter and duck out of raking leaves. these long mornings have become my writing time. from the time when I send the children off to school at eight-thirty until dorothy calls us to lunch at twelve, i am trying to spend at my typewriter, except that i end up writing a long letter like this, instead of finishing the story which sits at my desk. it is much more pleasant to write about baseball and think about moving than it is to work.

write me soon, and keep your fingers crossed, that when you come in march you will visit us in a nicely located and fairly modern house, somewhere only five minutes from times square.

lots and lots of love,

s.

•   •   •

[To Geraldine and Leslie Jackson]

hallowe'en [October 31, 1949]

dearest mother and pop,

we are in such a state of high confusion that i don't know if i can write a coherent letter, but i'll try. stanley and i have just come back from (of all places in the world for us!) westport, connecticut, a nice fancy rich arty community which is apparently going to be our future home. we spend most of our time staring at each other saying "what are we <u>doing</u>?" and it's a good question.

i think i told you we were hoping to move. we wrote to friends asking for agent's names, trying to find out what was available. the best answers we got for our requirements came from westport, and so stanley and i went down and looked at the houses. so we found a beautiful one. we would have to rent this one with the understanding that we might buy it.

this house is almost perfect. it is two blocks from the station and a shopping district, is on the school bus line, and is at the same time almost isolated, or seems so, because it is on top of a hill with a lot of trees around it, and the other houses are similarly set back from the road, so although we have at least two next-door neighbors we can't see them. also, it has an acre of land, with a long rolling lawn in front

and plenty of trees, and a sort of wilderness effect behind. the house
has been empty for quite a while, because the owners hoped to sell
instead of rent, but they have finally given in and decided to rent,
and redecorated the house completely. it's fifty years old, and very
solid and nice, and the same sort of rambling victorian mansion as
the one we have now, but better made. it has a big cellar, paved
and very good for a playroom and—probably what sold us on it,
finally—an enormous porch going around two sides of the house, a
glass-enclosed porch in back, just outside the kitchen, and a little
second-floor balcony from which to pour boiling oil down on guests.
although it is not going to be very expensive in itself, westport is an
expensive town, and things like food and help are high, it makes up
for all this by being seventy minutes from new york, and the wonderful facts that we are at last in a town with restaurants and even a
movie, and decent stores. we are a five-minute bus ride from the
sound, where there is a town beach and yacht club. the exorbitant
rent for this gem is a hundred and seventy-five bucks a month,
which the agent thinks will boil down to one-fifty. when we consider
that we are paying fifty here, it sounds very dubious, but every time
we get worried, we look at laurie, who is getting rough and vulgar,
and who really ought to be gotten out of this town unless we want
him to be a farmer when he grows up. the same is beginning to be
true of jannie, although her school is all right. but she is beginning to
talk and act like the disagreeable little girls around here. i don't know
if the children in westport are any less disagreeable, but at least the
schools are better. and we all unite in disliking the vermont winter.
in addition to all this, we are no longer fond of the town. we will
probably not ever be farmers ourselves, and associating with people
who are gets tiresome. we tend to grow farther away from the college, as all our old friends are leaving, and there are now only a few
people we see up here. westport is full of people from the new
yorker, and advertising men, and writers, and minor editors—the
major editors live in westchester—and while they do not stack up
very well against an honest new england farmer, at least <u>we</u> will feel
more at home.

   our big problem, of course, is money, but i think we have that solved. on the basis of stanley's salary, and my writing income, we should be able to swing it if neither of our typewriters break.

right now i can't think or write of anything else; if there is good news from my agent in the next day or so we will probably take the house on the spot; if not, we will delay and worry.

just as i finished this, my agent called; she had the best news of our lives. good housekeeping wants to put me on a drawing account, against sales of stories. i send them eight stories a year, they pay me fifteen hundred every three months, plus extra on whatever they buy. my agent takes ten percent, and we take the house. this fixes the financial end of it, anyway. wow!

love,

s.

# THREE

. . .

## On Indian Hill Road: 1950–1952

Two articles recently [included] me among something called promising young writers, which is equivalent to being selected by the sports writers on their second-string all-American baseball team.

—To parents, January 13, 1950

*Stanley's book of literary criticism,* The Armed Vision, *is published in 1948, and in 1949 he resigns from teaching at Bennington to concentrate on his work at* The New Yorker. *Shirley's book* The Lottery and Other Stories, or, The Adventures of James Harris *is published in 1949 to enthusiastic reviews. The family has just moved to Indian Hill Road in Saugatuck, a beachfront suburb of Westport, Connecticut. New neighbors include the* New Yorker *writers J. D. Salinger and Peter De Vries, and many other publishing people. This is a very different lifestyle for the family; for Shirley and Stanley it is a wonderful convenience to have New York so accessible, most comfortably by a one-hour train ride, and to have friends from New York so frequently visiting.*

[To Geraldine and Leslie Jackson]

friday [January 13, 1950]

dearest mother and pop,

at last i have the chance to sit down and write you a letter, something i've been trying to do for exactly a month now.

our house is so pleasant now, and so comfortable. so far it has been a vast improvement over the other one; i find i enjoy getting up at seven into a warm room. we have the bookcases up and painted, taking every possible inch of wall space in the house, and most of the books in. that has been a two-week job, since the movers packed the books, and finding and organizing eight thousand mixed-up books is something i hope i never have to do again. there are still cartons of books around the house, blocking up the hallways, but they are going fast. naturally we have two thousand more books than we have bookcase space, but that has been true for the last five years, so we're not really surprised. unlike the other house, the study is now the main room, i suppose because the television set is in there, and almost everyone spends all their time there. it's a lovely room—one side, the one i am facing now, has four windows, and the other three sides are books. if that sounds like there are no doors, it's because the doors are sort of sneaked in behind bookcases.* fortunately it's a large enough room so that there is room for both desks, a small couch, and two chairs, with a coffee table, and makes a very comfortable place to shut the children into with the television while we have dinner.

joanne has not yet found anyone to play with, and spends all day at home with me, entertaining herself very well, but still very much alone . . . yesterday we were both invited out to luncheon, by a nice woman named katinka de vries, whose husband is on the new yorker,† and who has a five-year-old daughter whose name is jan, making a good deal of confusion. they came and picked us up at twelve, and we went to their house and had lunch, and joanne and jan played while katinka and i drank martinis—martinis in the middle of the day always give me a headache—and then we drove around the town to look at the beaches and such, and then came home. joanne was very pleased, and katinka and jan are coming to have lunch with us next week. i found it very difficult, on top of my headache, to spend a day with anyone named katinka, although she is a very nice person.

business also has gone back to normal, with my agent, who can call me now instead of writing, pestering me for stories and my publishers calling to say happy new year where's the new novel. someone wants to read lottery over the radio in boston, non-profit. an educational program put on by harvard, as if harvard didn't have enough money to pay reprint rights on lottery. also the fiction editor of colliers wants to take me to lunch next tuesday because he wants an old story of mine if i rewrite it. i told my agent the story was no good and she said fine, fine, talk him out of buying it, he wants to pay a thousand dollars and who needs a thousand dollars? so i quick sat

---

* The bookcases were built around doorways.
† Peter De Vries, editor, and author of twenty-three novels including *Blood of the Lamb*, *The Tunnel of Love*, and *Slouching Towards Kalamazoo*.

down and wrote a new story which is also no good but some better than the one he has and if the one he has is so much trouble to re-write i will slip him this one. my agent and i are also going to have cocktails at My Club—did i tell you i had A Club? it is called pen and brush, in new york, and is an association of terribly earnest young women who paint and write and do ceramics and have literary teas. mrs roosevelt is our honorary president, but i don't think she was the one who put me up for membership; it was most likely doro-thy canfield fisher,* who is very important down there, and patted me on the head the last time she visited bennington college. anyway it's sort of a good thing around Publishing Circles to belong to pen and brush, and it has a club steward, and stanley can't get in unless i take him. when you come to new york i will take you there. stanley doesn't belong to anything except the folklore society which doesn't have a bar.

i am glad that you and pop agree with me about the first prize in the short story collection. we also got another vote from one of the reviewers. and, which gives me great pride, two articles recently in-cluding me among something called promising young writers, which is equivalent to being selected by the sports writers on their second-string all-american baseball team. stanley is hard at work on his book, if you could call it hard at work when he goes into new york twice a week, is doing seventeen reviews, his paper for the folklores, and two long articles for the new yorker.

we have had guests almost every night, and weekends have been full up. the two senior members of the seven bookhunters, our find-ers of rare books, spent one weekend out here helping arrange, and one of them, who is a frenchman and a fine cook, deserted the books long enough to come out into the kitchen and advise me on making soup.† so i've been making onion soup and potato soup and leek soup

---

* Dorothy Canfield Fisher, prominent author and educationalist, lived near North Ben-nington, in Arlington, Vermont.
† Louis Scher, founding member of a rare book finding service called the Seven Bookhunters—although there were actually only three—became a dear family friend whose visits were a delight for the Hymans and their entire social circle. He was named Joanne's godfather.

and any other kind i can think of, ever since, and he is coming out again next weekend and says that he is bringing me a french soup kettle because the pot i have been using is not large enough. so when you come i will make you onion soup.

one very good thing about this house is the playroom in the cellar. we have the old music box down there, and joanne sometimes plays it as accompaniment for her dancing. laurie got a fencing set for christmas, from his crazy father, with real foils and masks, and they fence down there while joanne dances.

stanley and joanne are yelling for lunch so i must go and heat up some onion soup.

love from all of us, thanks again for the nice presents, and do write me soon.

love,

s.

• • •

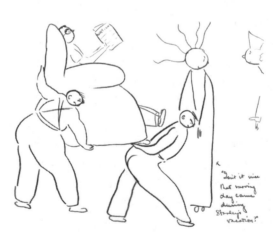

"Isn't it nice that moving day came during
Stanley's vacation?"

[To Geraldine Jackson]

friday [January 1950]

dear mother,

i only have time for a short note. joanne is waiting to go out for a
walk and shopping has to be done and we have a cleaning woman
named evelyn who is here today for the first time, and very competent she seems, too, and my agent is writing me nasty letters about
where are some stories, although why she should i don't know because i just finished one on request for colliers and the reader's digest
has just picked up charles and also the twenty-five cent edition of
lottery is out and when you see it for heaven's sake don't let anyone
know you know me because there is a picture of a disheveled redhead
on the cover and a caption to the effect that she had lost her demon
lover and is wickedly delicious and every time i think that someone
might know it's my book i shudder. i had lunch with the editor of
colliers last week, a fine lunch with three martinis and he said he
would buy my new story. and lottery is due out in england this
month.

   i started this to let you know that the lamp came safely, and is
beautiful, although it took us a week to figure it out. sally is walking
beautifully, and is starting to talk; she will be able to say grandma by
the time you come. it will be so good to see you, and will be so soon
now. jannie is planning to go back to california with you, i think.

love,

s.

· · ·

## [To Geraldine and Leslie Jackson]

monday [April 1950]

dearest mother and pop,

i have just come shuddering from the phone after learning that it
will cost us seven-fifty a week to have a man mow this lawn, and approximately thirty bucks to get apples off our apple trees; the man
said for heaven's sake what's the matter with everybody, later on in
the year you can get a bushel of apples from the grocer for about a
dollar and a half and all anyone thinks of is putting thirty dollars
into a tree to get a dozen apples a year. so i quick said never mind,
we'd plant some carrots out back instead and he said <u>Carrots,</u> why
does everyone think carrots are the thing to plant, because the weed-
ing you got to do with carrots will kill you, if you want to plant a
vegetable, plant tomatoes, you put them in and in two, three years
you got the prettiest little tomato patch you ever want to see, that
will cost you about seventy dollars. so i said tomatoes were seventeen
cents a pound at the store and he said lady, you said you wanted a
garden, didn't you?

our entire family has been taking to its beds sometimes all at
once and sometimes one at a time. television has proven itself
again: sick children on the study couch under blankets, watching
baseball games. sick daddy and sick mommy watching baseball
games. brooklyn has been doing fine, but so have the yankees.
giants, no.

perhaps what has saved our lives, is the greatest blessing which has
ever happened to us, named emma. emma arrived through a series of
coincidences and lucky breaks, and i keep knocking on wood she
should stay. she lives in, loves the kids and they love her—they all,
including baby, call her "emmy"—is a fine cook, and very sweet and
pretty and nice. she has taken over all meals, and almost complete
care of the children, particularly baby. when i come downstairs in the
morning there is hot coffee on the stove. we can go out any time, and

come back any time, and the children are perfectly happy. she's been here a week, and she still likes the children and us, and maybe she will stay. both stanley and i are making frantic efforts to write a lot so we can keep ahead of emma.

some television company bought <u>lottery</u> to make into a television play. i don't know how or when or who, but my agent says their money is good. also if this works out they may buy more stories.

stanley went on his ten-day book hunting trip and brought and sent home nearly a thousand books, which we have no room for. stanley's mother is still not at all well; every time they think she is doing all right she has a new attack and they have to start over. we are taking the children to see her this week, which will probably give her another attack . . . we have circus tickets for wednesday, and fig-ure to combine the circus and a visit to lulu,* just to round out the children's day.

emma can drive and says if we get a car she will a) drive it, and b) teach me.

stanley and i went to opening day at ebbetts field, and brooklyn won, and it was lovely. i almost caught a home run, except that it fi-nally landed two rows behind us, and we couldn't get to it. and we went out to dine with some very fancy writing people who live nearby and everyone there was a rich writer and had written a best-seller, except for one guy who turned out to be my editor at good housekeeping, and we were invited for seven, arrived at seven-thirty, and were the first ones there. we were served martinis made of pure gin with a drop of bitters, and drank these until everyone arrived, which was about nine. dinner was served at ten, after about eight rounds of those martinis. dinner turned out to be shrimp newburg, just the thing for stanley and me, and after dinner everyone sat in a circle on the floor and we played charades. everyone talked most in-sistently about lottery, and they were all surprised to find that we had not been in florida this winter. they all also commute to hollywood. stanley said it was the most awful evening he has ever spent in his life, and i think he was right. the only evening we could remember

* Stanley's mother, Louisa (Lulu) Marshak Hyman, married Moe (Moises) Hyman in 1915, four years before Stanley was born.

which was almost as bad was one we spent with four of stanley's aunts and uncles shortly after we were married. worse still, people we met at the dinner have now asked us on to <u>their</u> house, and probably the people we meet <u>there</u> will ask us, too, and heaven knows where it will end. they call it getting acquainted. i suppose it is very kind and very flattering of them, and they are certainly all very generous and pleasant—they all knew the name of <u>my</u> book, and of stanley's, and we didn't know any of theirs—but just the same they are very dull, and too shrimp newburg-y for us. no chips on the china, napkins for everybody, eighteen matched cocktail glasses, and so on . . . there's no doubt but what there's money in writing, if you work it right.

some maniac taught laurie to play dominoes, and no one is safe now except joanne, who can't add. i have promised him a championship match this afternoon because joanne has taken her first day out in a week and has gone to visit a school friend for the afternoon and supper. lots of love to you both, and write me soon.

s.

•   •   •

[To Geraldine and Leslie Jackson]

tuesday [June 1950]

dearest mother and pop,

i am glad you liked the orchid and even gladder that you are caught up in television; we find now that we are constantly defending it against people who say mean things about watching fights and ballgames all the time. i wish you could get our eastern programs—the ballgames are terrific, and brooklyn is in first place.

we have made our house into a perfect place to stay outdoors. we got a lot of picket fencing and stanley set it up for a big playpen for sally, where she is very happy. the playpen is located almost directly under laurie's treehouse in the apple tree, so he can drop cookies down on her head. (stanley just called my attention to a small brown rabbit directly outside the study window; it is eating buttercups.) next to sally's playpen, there are soon going to be a collection of chairs and tables, as yet unpainted and waiting for laurie to attack them with brush and shellac. we have a croquet set, which it turns out is definitely laurie's game, although joanne is still practicing golf swings with it, a barbecue thing which lives in the cellar and gets rolled outdoors when we want it, and we have taken all the junk off the back porch and moved the kitchen table out there, so that the children's dream has finally come true—they eat on the porch and have their food passed to them through the window. on weekends we look like a particularly second-rate summer resort, except the cuisine is superior.

i just told emma about the rabbit and she said if the mister had been quick enough we could have had rabbit stew for dinner; i think she had visions of stanley tackling the thing and strangling it with bare hands. diving through the study window.

i am to meet my english publisher next week. my new novel is almost finished and my agent is making a big fuss so we can ask for a larger advance. i met my publisher at a cocktail party last week and it seemed that i had had one too many cocktails because i laughed merrily and told him he was the biggest crook in town and i wanted twenty-five thousand dollars before i let him so much as know the title of the new book. he thought it was very funny and told my agent he probably couldn't go up to twenty-five thousand but was "very anxious for the book." this is my junior publisher, straus; john farrar would swoon if anyone asked him to pay that much for a book. roger straus and i have quarrelled ever since i signed with them but as long as he is amused when i call him a crook in front of half a dozen of his other authors i can't leave f and s.

emma just put lunch on the table. so goodbye.

love,

s.

•    •    •

[To Geraldine and Leslie Jackson]

[June–July 1950]

dearest mother and pop,

the dishes are still in the sink, stanley's pants are not sewn where he
ripped them, the animals are still unfed and so, in my usual fashion, i
sit down to write you a letter. i have had a rotten cold—as we all
have—and so have not felt much like writing until now.

emma is no longer with us. i thought it was too good to be true. it
was very odd, emma's leaving, and will make a splendid story for
good housekeeping: at four a.m. one morning i woke up to find
emma standing by my bed, whispering that she wanted to show me
something; i followed her downstairs and she informed me that
there was a little girl in her room playing with a bluebird. the little
girl, she said, had been sticking pins in her, and the Other People—
not specified—were all standing outside listening. i woke up very
fast, said "What? What?" and raced upstairs and shook stanley, who
opened one eye and said i was dreaming. so i went back downstairs
to see if i had been dreaming and there was emma; she said she was
looking for the little girl who had lost her jacket and anyway the little girl had no right to come into emma's bible class and ask silly
questions. i said she certainly did not, and raced upstairs again,
kicked stanley and said no, i had not been dreaming, and dragged
him out of bed and downstairs in his bathrobe. he marched bravely
up to emma (this still about four in the morning, pitch-dark, in the
kitchen) and said "now, now, what's all this?" so emma told him
about the little girl and then looked at him and giggled and said "i
bet you think i'm crazy!" so stanley said no, no, nothing of the sort, of
course not and went and hid in the study. we finally decided that we
had better get emma home to her mother, so i called her poor
mother and woke her up and said briefly that i was sending emma
home, but fast. i gave the poor woman no explanation, because emma
was listening and i couldn't think of how to say i thought she was

loony. so we put her into a taxi and sent her home, but only after i had spent about an hour patting her hand and telling her everything was fine. all three children were very fond of her, and so were we, but the whole performance was enough to make me feel very jittery for a few days afterwards. the one thing i was sure of, all the time she was talking, was that she was not feeling the least bit violent, but was as fond of all of us as ever, even though she was out of her mind. at any rate, right after emma left i called the woman who had sent her to me and described the whole scene quite vividly, and she nearly fainted, and said she had never heard of such a thing with emma, that emma was the most wonderful girl she had ever known, and was i <u>sure</u>? and i told her all about it, and she was terribly upset, and called emma's mother, who still works for her, and the result was that emma's husband had called her a few days before and said he was leaving her because he found someone younger and prettier, and he didn't want to hear from emma ever again, and emma (who had been home on her day off all the next day) had decided that the way to calm herself down was to polish off a bottle of whisky all alone; she had come back here late that night and had been drinking until she woke me about four. so that it was a combination of mental distress and drink and, aside from the scare it gave <u>me</u>, not very serious.

at any rate, that is the end of emma. so i've gone back temporarily to the housework, and don't mind it anywhere near so much as i did before. mostly that's because it's summer now, and there just isn't so much to do. i am feeling very ambitious about the cooking, and keep making cakes and such. i don't want to get anybody else at all, even for the cleaning, for a while, because the whole operation left me very nervous, and i haven't been able to bring myself to leave the kids with a baby minder; the two times i've been out since emma left, i've gotten stanley's aunt from new york to take care of things.

however, to prove in addition that i am still working, i sent off the first third of my new novel* to the publishers last week, and got an enthusiastic call from them yesterday, saying it was terrific, but not commenting on the additional information forwarded to them by

* *Hangsaman.*

my agent, that we expect a five thousand buck advance. we'll take four, we figure, and can be talked into three, but it will take a lot of talking . . . we had dinner in new york with a guy who is an independent movie producer in new york, who desperately wanted me to write movies for him. we are to get together again and see if it looks at all possible, although i am sure it will not, since i don't see myself writing movies, somehow.

lottery was on television last week, and pretty lousy it looked, too. i was horribly embarrassed; we were supposed to see it from the private viewing room at nbc, but decided not to at the last minute, and were so thankful that we had not. time magazine called me the next day to ask if i had written the television version and i told them no and they said then did i have a comment on it and i couldn't think of anything to say and mumbled something into the phone and they said thanks so much and heaven knows what they thought i said. so i have now been interviewed twice by time, and if i had a subscription i would cancel it. i can look forward to another time interview about next spring when with luck my new book would be published. also, i met my english publisher recently and had a wonderful time with him. he is a fine old man who says he reads all submitted manuscripts sitting on a haystack; he tried to talk me into giving him a fine old witchcraft book and made me what he said was an english martini, which was all vermouth and perfectly terrible. he says my book is due out in england this month. he wants the new book without even seeing it, which is very flattering.

stanley is working fiercely at a new yorker profile, which looks terrific. he has been at it for three months, and the end is finally in sight. he has another one to do after this one, and he has not been going into town very much. partly because i am very reluctant to be alone, and partly because it's been too hot. also the baseball season goes on nicely, and we spend literally two hours a day in front of the television set watching brooklyn win. or lose, which they did today. when we have company everyone gathers in the study while the sun shines beautifully outside, and everyone yells and jumps up and down, and hollers at the umpire. after the ballgame everyone goes outside and sits in the sun. the children, who are much smarter, play baseball instead of watching, and after a rough afternoon at the television set we can if we like go out and play a few innings on the front lawn. i turn out to be a fairly good hitter so far, but unable to catch the ball. laurie is a nice switch hitter so far, but can't pitch. stanley can both hit and pitch, but worries so about the relative positions of the bases that he has no time for anything else.

stanley figured out that if he put a pitcher of cocktails on the yellow table, and baby got in the playpen and laurie and jan in the tree house, and our guests stood over the charcoal cooker and watched the hamburgers, i would have nothing to do and could lie in the sun, and, for a wonder, it works out almost that way. we found that if you give guests enough to drink they don't mind cooking their own dinners. so we eat hamburgers and salad and then all play croquet and the children have a heavenly time toasting marshmallows. as a result of all this, we are inviting people lavishly for every weekend; they think they are being royally entertained, and we profit because they always bring gifts for the children, play baseball and croquet, and finally cook dinner for us. june, who is now fiction editor of charm magazine and buying all my stories she can get past the senior editor, comes up often.

laurie did get promoted, after all, and next year jannie will join him on the school bus. stanley took them to new york last week, to the dentist and to see charlie chaplin in city lights, and now they have a chaplin imitation, which they do with stanley's cane. laurie thought the chaplin movie was the funniest thing he had ever seen. joanne was dubious, since there was too much she couldn't understand. sally, who stays home in her playpen, has gotten to be a wonderful, happy baby. she plays with jan and laurie, and runs around the house wildly. toby is scared to death of her, because she sits on him without warning. the cats stay well out of her reach.

my dishes are still undone, stanley's pants still unmended, and now he wants me to read the first thirty pages of his profile. if i expect to get any sleep tonight i must finish this and get to work. write me soon, and lots of love,

s.

· · ·

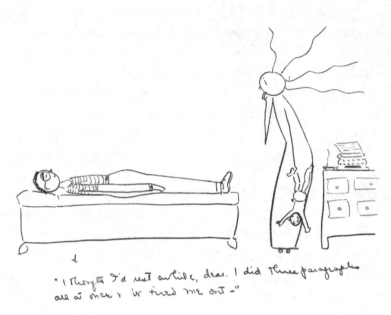

"I thought I'd rest awhile, dear. I did three paragraphs
all at once and it tired me out."

[To Geraldine and Leslie Jackson]

friday [July 1950]

dear mama and papa,

you will understand clearly from the fact that i am writing that i
ought to be in the kitchen making a cake for the weekend and that
there are several million words of novel due next week and that i
ought really to be feeding the baby and writing a story and washing
the breakfast dishes, if not in town doing the shopping. as a matter
of fact, it's not true at all: baby is still asleep, i ordered by phone, i am
not at all sure we should have a cake this weekend after all, and i am
nicely ahead on literature. i do have a mystery story i could be read-

ing, but that's all. my children are off bothering the neighbors and stanley is off somewhere in pennsylvania, and i haven't done any dishes since he left.

my only trouble is lack of energy. i spent all morning out in the sun, watching the children play in their new wading pool and wanting to get in myself. it is nine feet across and holds four hundred gallons of water, and is just deep enough for joanne to get her stomach up off the bottom and swim. i myself do quite nicely, since i wait till the children are through and then can spend a quiet few minutes lying up to my neck in water; the only problem is that someone always turns the hose on you. we also got the children a playhouse, where they now eat all their meals. it has chairs and table and will hold four children comfortably, sitting down to eat. emboldened by this, i have invited two fresh air children, a boy laurie's age and a girl jannie's age, to stay for two weeks. they come next wednesday and we are all very excited about it. with the whole place filled up with stuff to entertain children, it seemed so silly to confine it to our own two, and there are no neighborhood children the right age. i think if i had room i'd take a dozen.

sold two stories last week and got three thousand for my novel. there ought to be enough money there to feed five children for two weeks. even including lollipops. we'll probably be able to get our spinet now, at least, and the washing machine. perhaps even a cheap old car, one i could learn to drive without risking too much. one of the stories sold to the ladies' home journal, which has never bought one before, and they want more. also, my agent is now asking copies of my stories to be sent to hollywood. the television broadcast got them interested.

i got a real fancy doctor—he is what i would call a westport society doctor, and he was highly recommended to me. i went to him finally because i had a new siege with my familiar headache, and i wanted some dope for it—i've been taking codeine for five years, and it takes a prescription, of course, so i always have to go to the doctor and let him take a turn at curing the headache before i get my prescription. this guy went at it just like the rest (sinus? teeth? eyes? digestion?) and gave me a thorough examination, including trying to take a bloodtest, only i yelled so he didn't dare.

when he got all through, he said with pleasure that there wasn't a <u>thing</u> wrong with me. he was so pleased that i was a little bit surprised, and then he said happily that he was also an analyst on the side and while of course he did not ordinarily recommend a full analysis for a thing like this, still. so i said certainly not, i wasn't fool enough for that sort of thing. so he said well, i understood, didn't i, that my headache was psychological? and i said i understood it perfectly, and so since he couldn't cure it would he please give me a prescription for codeine? so then i got the westport matron technique. he said by the way, had i ever thought of wanting to lose weight? i said i didn't care one way or the other. he said well, it was obvious to him that losing weight was psychological just as the headaches were, so that it would be very easy for me to go on a diet, and through some mystic psychic about-face i would then lose my headaches. (i am apparently to relax nervous tension, which takes pounds off you, cures headaches, and probably lifts fallen arches.) i asked him very suspiciously what i had to stop eating and by the time he was through ("i can't ask you to stop liquor, because in this hot weather everyone wants cold drinks. and there's no sense giving up bread and potatoes, and depriving yourself of anything you want, because that would make you <u>more</u> nervous. if you get into the right state of mind, you won't <u>want</u> to eat.") i went home and checked on this baby's rates, which come to twenty-five bucks an hour. i am supposed to go back once a week, having eaten all i want, and he will give me an injection which will take it off me. at any rate, i must be the only person in the world paying twenty-five bucks an hour <u>not</u> to be analysed. at the risk of grave nervous tension i have stopped eating anything except salads, and i take the pills he gave me; my headache, by the way, disappeared as soon as i took some of the new codeine.

there is a wild baseball game going on out front. laurie saved his allowance laboriously and bought himself a dollar softball, which is now the treasure of his life. after the baseball game they will go swimming.

i am almost too lazy to move. i just went out and watched the
baseball game for a minute and nearly fell asleep.

lots and lots of love to you both. and write me soon.

s.

p.s. went to the doctor yesterday and discovered that i had lost seven
pounds in a week; he says it will keep up at about that rate. there's
something to this system, after all.

•   •   •

[To Geraldine Jackson]

thursday [July 1950]

dear mama,

thought you might be interested in a brief account of the most hysterical two days which ever happened in our ordinarily calm and
level-headed house.

laurie and jannie and i went to the station yesterday to meet our
fresh air kids, discovered with horror that jannie's girl had missed
the train and would not arrive until Saturday, and that, worse, since
we waited till all the children were gone, to find our girl, that there
was one miserable boy left over, unclaimed and unwanted. so of
course we came home to stanley, who was expecting us with a girl
five and a boy eight, with two boys nine. the chairman of the
thing, who made such a mess of it, has promised that our unwanted
boy will leave on saturday morning when the girl comes. our
two boys—i specified, by the way, that i would not have any
churchgoers—are both devout catholics, and want to go to mass
sunday. i said suppose they didn't and they said then it would be a
mortal sin and i told them in effect to get their faces set for a little

sinning, because sunday morning i sleep and i do not take kids to mass. they seemed unusually willing to forgo church, and not at all perturbed about missing the lord that morning, although one of them said uncertainly he guessed he better write the sisters about it and maybe they could fix it for him.

i nearly cried at the station, seeing these kids get off the train, all badly dressed and carrying paper packages of clothes and food, and all the girls wore dresses too big for them, and they all sort of looked around nervously and smiled at everybody. of our boys, larry has no mother and lives in a slum; his family is one of those sleep-three-in-a-bed propositions and when i asked him what he did at home he said play in the streets and go to church. he is the starving one, and eats everything he can find. he is the one who was sent out by mistake, and he is terribly nervous about where he is going next, and is afraid that he will be sent home. naturally, if it comes to that, i will keep him and heaven knows what stanley will say. bobbie is fat and cowardly, but unusually intelligent. he asks questions all the time, wants to do things right, and is always making compliments about everything, as though he had been primed to keep telling the people he liked everything or they wouldn't keep him. he lives in a housing project and flatly refuses to discuss his family, except for his baby sister, who is just sally's age, but not—he always adds hastily—anywhere <u>near</u> as smart. both boys jump when i tell them to do anything—again i suspect they have been schooled—and discipline is no trouble, except for the fact of course that my own laurie's nose is out of joint and he is making almost constant trouble, insisting upon special treatment. he likes both boys and is having a fine time, but he is very worried about stanley's and my favoring them.

at any rate, they are having a great time, eating like fools, and sleeping and enjoying the fresh air, which is after all, what they are here for. they were in our wading pool all day today, taking time out only for lunch and rest, and quitting only at dinner and television time. both larry and bobbie are fascinated by music, and the height of the day for them is to have me labor simple nursery rhymes on our old organ, so they can sing.

but, no, when i say confusion, i don't mean just <u>this</u>. this morning, completely unexpectedly, a girl whom i had interviewed as a
maid two weeks ago, and had told to keep in touch with me, arrived, needing a job at once. she had a friend with her who also
needed a job at once. i called someone i knew who wanted a girl,
we checked references, and tonight we both have maids. mine is
named elmira, a nice girl from the south, who reminds me of alta
in her manner—sort of deliberate and thoughtful. she is no cook,
heaven knows, but during the time today when both girls were
waiting here they cleaned the whole upstairs, and elmira seems very
competent in that department. she is nice to the children, and they
seem to like her. she was not at all disturbed at finding two more
children here, and treated them very nicely. i had taken the new
york boys aside and said that any remarks about her being colored
and i would whale them both—a familiar punishment, i discover—
and they were both excessively polite to her. anyway when i say
confusion i mean five children in all going different directions, my
agent calling up frantically every hour about a fight with the publishers about my new contract, them wanting half of second serial
rights, and two maids, one being broken in, the other keeping me
on the phone calling people to find her a spot. and stanley worrying about his shoes which were being soled and were not ready. and
the ball game on the radio. and the dog trying to hide under the
couch because there was thunder.

me, i went to bed and slept for two hours. elmira did the dishes,
stanley watched the kids, and the dodgers lost.

friday—8 days later

left this letter open because i wanted to add more to it, and have
finally gotten a breathing space to write a little. our life has settled
down considerably, and everything goes as smoothly as it could
under circumstances. elmira has been terrific, and is as kind and
sweet as anyone i ever knew. the children all love her. and larry got
offered a new place to visit, and went off on saturday morning very
pleased, and saturday afternoon a small blonde girl named kathy, just
jannie's age, arrived, and spent all saturday afternoon running away
and most of saturday night yelling mommy. i thought i was going to

have to send her back, and jannie was <u>so</u> worried, but on sunday she quieted down and by now she cries when we mention leaving. she and jannie adore each other. it has been amazing for jannie, and i have never seen her enjoy herself so much. laurie and bobbie are not completely happy together, but get along well enough, and bobbie is a little bit homesick. he is due to leave next wednesday, but kathy can stay longer if we want her, and i think we do. she and jannie are so little trouble—not half the trouble that jannie was alone—that i would really hate to see her go.

without elmira i could not have gotten through this week, particularly since on sunday a friend from bennington arrived with his three children—two girls fourteen and thirteen, and charlie, who is laurie's age, and they stayed for dinner and then he asked if we had room for the two girls overnight, since he had so much junk in the car he didn't think he could make it back to bennington with all three. so i said sure, and the overnight turned into five days, so we have had seven children in the house. elmira and i figured that we made twenty-five sandwiches every noon.

i have been working through it all—mostly late at night. the television broadcast of lottery stirred up a lot of talk, and they are thinking of doing another of my stories, and the script for the broadcast is being published, in a magazine article on something like the possibilities of television. which means that i have been getting more requests for reprints. someone is trying to make it into a ballet.

bobbie is playing chopsticks. the two little girls are dancing on the lawn. laurie is upstairs digging out his baseball suit. baby is asleep. elmira is sweeping. stanley is in his office. most wonderful of all, i am going into new york tonight to have dinner with him. elmira said sure, she could take care of things. it's my first time out since the kids got here, and i need it.

love, s.

•  •  •

"For $25.00 the least it could do is coast downhill."

[To Geraldine and Leslie Jackson]

thursday [August 1950]

dear mama and papa,

am writing because of news. a most amazing thing. i want you to
brace yourselves.

  this afternoon we got us a car, and tonight i had my second (professional) driving lesson and the school says i should get my license
next week. i am having a lesson every day until tuesday and then they
take me by the hand and take me into the examiner and he asks me
what seem to be a number of silly questions ("what is the brake used
for?") and i drive for him and then i have a license and i can drive my
nice new car, which stanley insisted upon having put into my name
since he is positive he will never learn to drive and it would be silly
having it in his name. so i have a car all my own. it is a 1940 buick,
two-tone green, and we bought it from friends and so have a reason-

able idea of its competence, although i have not as yet driven it. i have driven in it a number of times, to the beach and back with the people who used to own it. it is about the same style middle-aged family car that everyone else around here drives. so i will be taking stanley to the station and the children to the beach and the groceries home from market, just like everyone else.

anyway the man came tonight at seven-thirty and i drove until nine-thirty, through traffic and stop lights and past dogs and everything, the last hour in the dark, and did beautifully. i am just past the stage where i lean down to look on the floor to find out where the clutch is, but only just barely past.

when i went this afternoon to get the car registered in my name, and they handed me a set of license plates i was feeling exactly like the children when they got their new wading pool, and i have been proudly showing everyone my certificate that the car belongs to me. i never felt so odd. stanley says he expects i will not write for months because i will be too busy riding around in my car. i wouldn't be at all surprised.

love to you both,

s.

this is a week after the first letter, which i did not send because i wanted to send you further news of my masterful driving.

anyway, i have had a lesson nearly every day, but due to climatic conditions (thunderstorms every day just at my lesson time) and various crises, have not yet taken my test. i take it next tuesday and my teacher is confident that i will pass if i remember to let the clutch out EASY on a hill. today and yesterday we have spent going over and over the test area, doing everything he is likely to ask me, and except for the hill i am perfect, and do not get unduly nervous in traffic, although heaven knows what i will do without an instructor sitting next to me. i've been driving my own car, too, and i love it.

naturally there have been small difficulties. for instance, my attempting our driveway without estimating my speed, and crashing into the stone wall, while eric screamed "second, second," and i said

"What? What?" and the little girls sat on the front porch and laughed their heads off and wanted me to do it again. and the trifling affair when i was practicing u-turns for my test and forgot where the brake was and rolled back into a telephone pole and it will cost fifteen bucks to get the lock on the trunk fixed. all of which amuses stanley infinitely. i took all the children riding up and down our driveway and they seemed mildly impressed, but they all want to know when will i take them to the beach?

i <u>will</u> learn, you know, now i've started. for one thing, the people won't take the car back. keep your fingers crossed on tuesday. eric says pray that the tester doesn't have a hangover.

love,

s.

•   •   •

[To Geraldine and Leslie Jackson]

tuesday [August 1950]

dear mama and papa,

you must not be too shocked, nor must you decide that nothing is safe any more, because i promise you it will be a while before i get as far as california, but as a matter of pure fact—this is true, honestly—i went today and i passed my driving test and now, apparently, i know how to drive, at least that is what the man told me. i was so frightened that i didn't know at all what i was doing, and apparently did unconsciously all that i had been taught, because i made a u-turn and started on a hill, and parked magnificently, and when he told me i had passed i sat there with mouth open and said "what?"

everyone is so surprised, including me. this afternoon, after i got the license, i drove the kids to the store, and parked, and got my groceries and drove home, without hitting one single thing. and then

tonight i took stanley for a ride and he hung on to the window sill
the whole time but all he said was "oh" every now and then. the dog
is so positive that i cannot drive that he will not move from the
driveway when i come up. i nearly ran him over this afternoon and
stalled the car in the driveway. i also stalled it on the principal inter-
section here, but that was not because of the dog. one of the things
the driving school taught me was not to listen to people blowing
horns and yelling at me; these are of course inferior drivers who are
careless and must be forced to go slowly.

when the instructor this afternoon told me to park he waited until
the last minute and so i was going fast and i turned into the parking
space like a wild creature and brought up against the curb like duke
snider sliding into second. the instructor had his foot over on the
brake when i finally stopped, but i beat him to it and when he caught
his breath he said "my, you came fairly close," and i told him sweetly
that the official book said no further than twelve inches from the
curb. my teacher was standing across the street waiting for me and he
said i looked like barney oldfield making a fast turn. we took the
course almost cxactly backwards, so that the hill i have never been
able to start on i came to going down, and started without even
thinking on a strange hill. i made a left turn into traffic while the
tester's hair turned white, and very intelligently avoided hitting a little boy who ran out in front of me. i also got around a coal truck
without spilling a single coal. and now that i have the little paper
that says i can drive you should see me.

as i say, i am hesitant about driving to california for a few days yet.
however, if one of these days the nose of the two-toned green buick
pokes through your front door, glance at the license plate, and if it is
connecticut 470, it is me.

there is no news except my car. i have spent very little time on
anything else, in the evenings—i do not know how to turn on the car
lights, but the garage man promised to tell me—i have to stay home
and write. my novel is nearly done, but has taken an unexpected au-
tomotive turn. we still have two visiting children, and this afternoon
when i came home there were five children, stanley, and elmira, on
the front porch, all yelling "did you pass? did you <u>pass</u>?" i was com-

pletely unable, by the way, to drive home after the test. my teacher had to drive me.

anyway, i have a new toy. next time you write, send detailed instructions for backing up to a gas pump. i am beginning to run low.

love from all,

s.

•   •   •

*On October 1, 1950, Laurie rides his bicycle out of the driveway directly into the path of a car, and is thrown badly. Taken to the hospital by ambulance, he has suffered a severe concussion, broken thumb, and badly cut shoulder. It is his concussion that frightens the doctors and Shirley and Stanley so much, and the first hours and days are very stressful.*

[To Geraldine and Leslie Jackson]

wednesday [October 4, 1950]

dearest mother and pop,

just a short note—i didn't dare send a telegraph for fear it would frighten you—to say that laurie is substantially better, and the doctors are reasonably sure that he is out of danger. they let us visit him last night for half an hour, and we found him conscious and aware of the fact that he was in the hospital and hopping mad at the nurse, who gave him baby food for supper, and he nagged her into letting him have some ice cream. they have moved him out of the dark, absolutely silent room where they had him at first into another room with three other kids, where they felt he would feel more cheerful, which he does. that in itself is of course a sign of great improvement. he still cannot sit up or move around very much. the doctor said he could have one toy today, and so he is getting his birthday radio, and he has even gotten permission to listen to the world series.

there is still danger of some damage to his brain, but they are pretty sure by now that any bad effects would have shown already, and except for a splitting headache he seems to be in perfect possession of himself. last night he insisted on knowing how he got into the hospital, and when we told him he was hit by a car he would not believe us, and the story of coming to the hospital by ambulance struck him as terribly funny and he thought we were making it up. he does not remember one single thing that happened on sunday, and of course if he never remembers the accident that is perfectly all right with everyone. he is also very much annoyed at his broken thumb, which is horribly swollen and crooked because they won't set it for fear of further shock to the nervous system. they had to sew up his shoulder but did it while he was still unconscious and decided to let the thumb wait until it really bothered him. they are very reluctant to give him any kind of anaesthetic or sedative because of the head, but he is really quite good about the headache, which is the only bad pain he feels. he is being very brave about everything and the doctors and nurses all compliment him for that. he was mildly worried about his birthday and missing his party but we promised him a big party when he came home and that satisfied him. we are hoping that he will be able to come home sooner than the two or three weeks they first thought, but of course no one will say.

all our neighbors have gone over it so thoroughly to get the details and have made a point of checking to see if there was any blood on the street—there wasn't—and trying to get touching details like how does his dog feel, to which the only answer is that his dog feels terrible, which he does. the only thing is that it was completely his own fault; he came down the driveway on his bike without stopping at the road, and the poor old lady tried to stop fast and skidded into the bike. he was apparently not hit by the car itself, or not violently; all his injuries came from being thrown from the bike. there was fortunately a plain-clothes policeman nearby—we never did find out where he came from—and he took charge, calling the ambulance and forbidding anyone to move laurie, which it turned out was absolutely the wisest thing to do. we entertained laurie last night with the story of the ambulance tearing down the boston post road with the siren going and everything getting out of the way, and going through stop lights, and laurie was very sad that he didn't remember it. he was out of his head most of the time, and not in a coma until after he had been in the hospital for a couple of hours, which was apparently very cheering for a fractured skull because apparently an immediate coma is bad.

the phone rings every ten minutes and the doorbell rings every half hour and the neighbors have gotten together to get signs posted on our road to warn cars about children. joanne has been invited out every day for lunch and the afternoon and elmira and her mother, who are both still with us, of course, tiptoe around making special fancy dishes and have everything ready for laurie's beloved red-kidney-bean-sweet-potato-dumpling soup when he comes home. one little girl who regards him with special favor is making him a basket of presents, and one terribly thoughtful person sent us a bottle of scotch. my publisher called this morning and said there was no hurry about finishing my book, and the dentist allowed me to cancel my appointment. we get an almost daily apology from the people who walked in casually sunday afternoon; they were driving up from new york and stopped in to say hello, and came in the front door with the remark, "it's like a tomb in here."

must go. phone. love from us all.

s.

•  •  •

[To Geraldine and Leslie Jackson]

thursday [October 5, 1950]

dearest mother and pop,

i have been at the hospital most of the afternoon and evening, and both stanley and i are very happy at the way laurie seemed to be feel-ing. all his ailments are much less than they were, particularly his shoulder, which had begun to trouble him yesterday. the doctor took the stitches out yesterday, and they gave him an anaesthetic for it, which is itself good news. his thumb has not been set, and is very swollen but apparently does not bother him much, and the doctor said they would not set it until it hurt enough to justify the shock of setting it. his head, which is still the worrisome thing, does not trouble him as much as yesterday.

he has his radio, and was listening to the ballgame when we arrived today. he also has a lot of comic books which he is not usually allowed, and a set of cowboys on horses which annoy him because they won't stand up on the bed. he asked for a coloring book and crayons which i took him tonight and when we left him he was lying on his stomach coloring with the radio going, full of ice cream and not seeming at all sick. his two doctors still visit him every day but of course we can't get any word from them about when he can come home; they want to be absolutely sure about the head, of course. he remarked tonight that he expected he would have a scar on his shoulder, and seemed very pleased at the idea.

we were invited out for dinner last night, in bronxville, and stanley persuaded me to go. we went to the hospital first and then when they chased us out we headed for bronxville on the merritt parkway, and got halfway and had a flat tire. we sat on the parkway for an hour, starving and getting later and later, waiting for the garageman, who finally came and fixed the car; we arrived for dinner at ten o'clock and got a cold sandwich. everyone insisted it was too late for us to head home so we called elmira and told her we were staying over, and we came back early this morning. it was a good party and, except for having to stay over, probably what we both needed. most of the people were from the new yorker and knew laurie, and so we both spent most of the evening telling people he was fine. bill shawn,* stanley's boss at the magazine, is a highly neurotic and frightened little man, and he and his wife are both in constant fear of some horrible thing happening to their own children, and he was so afraid to ask about laurie that when he heard the news on monday morning

* William Shawn is still assistant editor at *The New Yorker*. He will soon replace Harold Ross and become the legendary editor of the magazine for thirty-five years.

he made someone else call first to ask how laurie was before he could call himself, and last night he came timidly up to me practically crying and reassured me for fifteen minutes about how everything was going to be all right before he dared ask how laurie was, and when i told him laurie was fine he went yelling off to find his wife and tell her because she had been afraid to ask. our hostess had obviously warned everyone not to talk about it because everyone kept starting to talk about it and then stopping and getting red and changing the subject. after a while everyone got tight and there was no more trouble. once i knew i didn't have to drive home i got tight too and so did stanley and i think it was better for us both than anything else.

in answer to your question about how we acted at the accident itself, we both apparently gave the impression that we were infinitely brave and calm, except that stanley used an unrepeatable word to the poor old woman who hit him, and i was completely unable to light a cigarette, although i looked up the doctor's number and dialed it correctly. i remembered to get joanne away and into the house before the ambulance came, and i clearly remember stanley telling the hospital clerk very solemnly that he worked for time magazine. when we came home from the hospital at about two o'clock stanley poured two water glasses full of whisky and we sat down quietly and polished them off before we did anything else. so you can see that we were both very possessed and level-headed. i really believe that until we got word monday night that he would be all right we were both in as much a state of shock as he was, and too dazed to know what was going on.

by the way, much the same thing happened to stanley when he was about twelve; he was hit by a car on a snowy night, and lay in the street for several hours before he was found, and even then he was found by some people who nearly ran over him, and they took him to the police station where no one realized that he had a concussion and they kept asking him where he lived and trying to make him tell them. his father finally showed up, trying to make the police go out and find him, and came in to find stanley sitting in a chair unable to talk and practically unconscious. he knocked policemen right and left and grabbed stanley and put him in the car and took him home, and of course has never forgotten it, and when he heard about laurie it sort of fused together in his mind and made the shock twice as bad for him. stanley remembers enough of his own accident to know exactly how laurie's head feels.

all that sunday at the hospital, too, i kept remembering the day barry broke his arm, and i remembered mother as being terribly calm and quiet about everything, and i kept telling myself that i must be just as calm, only i'm afraid i didn't do as well. i never remembered that day so clearly before, but in the hospital i even remembered details i didn't even know i'd ever noticed.

lots and lots of love to you both. i gave laurie your birthday telegram today and he was so pleased. he read it himself, of course. i had to explain every one of those odd little notes they put on a telegram.

love,

s.

• • •

[To Bernice Baumgarten, of Brandt & Brandt

Literary Agency]

November 6, 1950

Dear Miss Baumgarten,

I have just parted company with my agent, MCA Management. I am told that you are the best agent in the business. I will be in town Friday, November 10; may I telephone you and hope to see you?

Cordially,

Shirley Jackson

• • •

[To Geraldine Jackson]

thursday [late November 1950]

dear mother,

i have a bandage on my finger and cannot type very well, and as usual i have at least two splendid excuses for not writing sooner—one is the finger, which i managed to cut because we got a knife-sharpener, and the other is the fact that we were practically blown back into vermont this weekend, a performance which still has us jittery.

laurie started it; thanksgiving day he came to me with a dime and said what should he do with it, and i said why not give it to the nice old birch tree out front, so laurie said fine and went outside and came back and announced casually that he had given it to the tree and asked for a dime's worth of wind. so starting friday night his dime's worth of wind was delivered. all we could figure was that wind must be very cheap indeed for him to get that much for a dime.

laurie should have his head examined. nobody even dreamed we were going to have a hurricane. it was absolutely unexpected and apparently by the time the new york weather bureau got around to wondering if this wasn't maybe a little more wind than they had said, all their equipment had blown away. stanley and laurie went in to new york to the dentist early saturday morning, remarking cheerfully that they had better wear warm coats since it looked pretty windy outside, and elmira and her mother left on the same train, and sally and jannie and i went peacefully to work to clean the bookcases in the kids' rooms. about ten o'clock jannie remarked giggling that wasn't it funny, the playhouse up in the tree, and when i glanced out of the window it certainly was. while i was looking the top of the sandbox disengaged itself and floated off. i told jannie that my, it was windy and she said yes it was, wasn't it. i decided that maybe i'd better check the garage and make sure the doors were closed, since any good wind catches those doors and swings them open and we have about a thousand books in the garage. so i put on a coat and discovered that the only way i could get out to the garage was by hanging on to trees, found the garage doors open and was trying to close them when one blew out of my hands and landed about ten feet on the other side of the garage, scattering broken glass as it went. i figured there was no sense in going after it, so i threw blankets over the books and fought back into the house, toby being blown along beside me and very puzzled about it. and got back into the house to find all the electric current off and the upstairs porch door bending inwards and leaking. so i got towels and padded <u>them</u>, made an attempt to clean up the lake in the upstairs hall, watched the television aerial go by, and noticed sort of absent-mindedly, by then, that our neighbors' beautiful old pines—three of them—had come down in a heap in the middle of the street. which is where our electric wires were, too. it meant that we had no heat, no light, no stove, no phone, nothing. all we had was a cold turkey and laurie's battery radio. so i put the girls to bed with turkey sandwiches and the radio tuned into the ohio state football game, and there they stayed all afternoon. ohio state won, too.

about four o'clock my wonderful grocer ploughed his way up the hill, like the united states mail, with a haphazard grocery order i had phoned in hours before, and a half gallon of whisky. he had also put in a lot of candles. and shortly after that a taxi pulled up and our weekend guests arrived. i nearly fainted; it was an old friend of ours and her ten-year-old daughter; they had gotten to grand central on their way out to visit us and had turned around to go home again and the daughter was blown down on 42nd street so they decided it was safer to come out to connecticut, which it turned out it wasn't. stanley and laurie got nervous about the weather when their train into new york was an hour late, and began trying to get back right away, and made it at five in the afternoon. stanley said that once the wind caught laurie's raincoat and laurie was sailing off like a balloon except that stanley caught him in time. laurie loved every minute of it, including the store windows crashing in on either side of him and the cornices falling into the street; part of the new yorker building came down and squashed a couple of cars, and laurie and stanley had to walk home from the station, through the trees in the road and stepping gingerly over live wires. when they got here they found therese and me and the half gallon of whisky, with one candle and the battery radio, while therese's nora and jannie and sally played house with a flashlight. we gave the children all the cold turkey and pie they could hold and then put them all in bed, and then we went back to work on the half gallon of whisky. by about nine o'clock we couldn't think of anything to do except go to bed, because besides being dark it was getting colder without any furnace. sunday morning stanley brought the charcoal grill up from the basement, and we had a magnificent breakfast, with charcoal broiled bacon and, thank heaven, hot coffee. for some reason we cannot understand, our phone was on long enough for me to find out from a desperate man at the electric company that we would be lucky to get electricity in about three days. that meant we had to move out, because it meant mainly no furnace, so off we went to a hotel in norwalk, a horrible place; therese and nora went home, after finding out from neighbors that although a house a block away from theirs had collapsed, their block was okay.

half our town is gone. all of the beach and the beach houses are either submerged or on their way out to the sea, including a lot of cars, and many of the children in laurie's school, who lived in a development called saugatuck shores, a pleasant place on a point of land by the sound, are coming to school in borrowed clothes and telling wild stories of getting out of their homes in boats.

aside from our bit of weather, there isn't much news. i finished my novel and am delivering it tomorrow to the publishers; it will be published this spring if they can make it. i delayed it a month because of laurie's accident. i am trying to change agents, and have right now two of them working for me. they have divided me in half—the old agent gets everything up to and including the present novel, the new agent gets everything from now on, including the contracts for the <u>next</u> novel which she expects to negotiate as soon as this one is turned in. her plan is to contract for a year, at five hundred bucks a month, at the end of which time, she says blandly, i am to have an outline of a new novel for them. it sounds perfectly lovely, particularly since she is very firm about a clause in the contract saying i don't have to give the money back if i don't get the outline done in time. it looks like the book will be, actually, a collection and amplification of my stuff about children, which is a good investment for the publishers, since it is more apt to sell than anything else i might do for them. but i am so surrounded right now by contracts and legal language that i am dizzy. i have a contract with each agent, a clearance from one, <u>five</u> contracts with my publishers (none of these, the new agent points out hysterically, cancel any of the others, that being left out of all of them, so that somehow it comes out that i am committed for something like seventeen books all told), two contracts with my english publishers, an odd little contract with NBC about lottery on television, and—the big headache—an unwritten and unrecorded contract with good housekeeping by which i owe them a lot of money, although it was a verbal agreement and the new agent says not binding. i say not binding or not, i do really owe them the money, the old agent says well, we'll have to talk about it, the new agent says let them try and get it, and good housekeeping says that actually i don't owe them any money, but only four stories, which they are in no hurry for, and will buy whenever i feel like sending them along. this situation is the reason i got a new agent in the first place. but now that the novel is done i can give up the old agent altogether. also, ann harding* has arrived in new york, very much interested in this television series from my stories, and both agents are racing to find her to get the deal first. i am so happy that we have no phone.

laurie sends a request: i don't know if i told you about the coin collection he and stanley have started; they are trying to get a complete collection of american coins, without any emphasis on rare or valuable ones. one thing they cannot get is silver dollars, which i believe you can, can't you? laurie says if you will send him some silver dollars, as old as possible, he will repay you from his allowance. the repayment is a firm rule, of course, since he asks everyone for coins and can hardly do so without paying back an equal sum. the coin collec-

* Ann Harding was a well-known actress.

tion is growing daily, and laurie makes trips to the bank to get dollars changed into quarters and quarters changed into nickels and dimes. they carry on long learned conversations about straight standing liberties and mint marks. laurie is quite adept at it, and is fascinated and much better than stanley. i find that i now do all my shopping with discarded change, so that i go down to the grocery with fifteen dollars in quarters and dimes and have to count out my money to pay, much to the amusement of everyone around.

joanne, who was very much affected apparently by my story about her, has just arrived in the study with nine friends, all ellenoys,* who have come for lunch. they are all wearing corduroy hats and were all born in new jersey, to which place they return once a week on their ship, although some of them have rowboats which they use instead of the big ship. joanne is not in school again today because of her cough.

lunch time. some day i am going to take three days and really finish a letter; this time i got distracted by the hurricane. i've been waiting for a letter from you for quite a while and hope your not writing means you've been having a wild time in town.

lots of love from all of us; are you still coming in march?

love,

s.

•   •   •

[To Bernice Baumgarten]

December 11, 1950

Dear Ma'am,

Here is the original of A Visit, suitable for selling. It has been to Good Housekeeping, New Yorker, Holiday, and Harpers.

---

* Shirley wrote many short stories about Jannie's group of colorful imaginary friends, the Ellenoys, who gathered a considerable following among her readers.

Also a small story of the slight type I have been selling. I decided to get it off to you right away without waiting because unless I somehow make some money inside of the next couple of weeks I shall have to find myself a job writing jingles for greeting cards, or television commercials, or singing at Bar mitzvahs.

The title of the novel is now Hangsaman, and is taken from a nice old ballad about a girl who is going to be hanged unless her father or her mother comes through and pays her fine. The ballad will have to be quoted, of course. And I'm putting in some further explanation in the first section, to meet your objections there. They are going right to work on it, to get it ready for April publication.

Best,

Shirley Jackson

• • •

"No, I don't think I'd ever want to have another, dear.
It's too much of a strain for me."

[To Geraldine and Leslie Jackson]

january 2 [1951]

dearest mother and pop,

i hope you had a lovely trip, and a fine Christmas. it was so nice to
talk to you, and even to hear barry's voice, although he sounded completely unfamiliar.

i am typing under great difficulties; there is a power shovel going
in our back yard, digging a ditch which is now approximately ten
feet long and three feet deep, because some horrid internal function
of the plumbing gave way, and instead of calling a plumber like anyone else our landlord decided to dig up the cistern which would be
fine except they couldn't find it without looking, so the power shovel
is looking. makes it hard to think, this darn great munching away
about ten feet past the window.

the children were delighted with your presents, and many thanks
to both you and pop, for all the gifts and of course particularly for
the wonderful check, which we both appreciate more than i can say.

we had laurie's hand x-rayed by a bone specialist in new york, and
the doctor called us last thursday and said the pictures showed that
the thumb had never been set at all, but only sort of stuck together,
and that we had a choice: we could either let it go as it was, or we
could have it reset, and keep it in bandages for two weeks and a cast
for another month, but resulting, this guy guaranteed, in a straight
and perfectly normal thumb; the catch was that it had to be done at
once. laurie was out on his sled when the doc called so we went and
got laurie and told him the whole thing, and he was very upset and
we said he could decide which he wanted, either way okay. so after a
little while he sort of gritted his teeth and said he wanted it done. so
we took him into new york—one of those trips where you have half
an hour to get ready. and we put him in a horrible hospital and the
next morning they operated on him and i sat in the lobby downstairs

for five hours waiting to see him and at the end of the time the nurse said no, i couldn't see him because they didn't have visiting hours that day and i started to break up the hospital, slowly and methodically, so that finally, regarding the damage i was doing they said, well i could see him for two minutes, so i raced upstairs and said hello, laurie, and he opened his eyes and said hello, and then the nurse threw me out. so i made a sizzling scene in the lobby again, turning away patients by droves, until they promised to let him out the next morning because i think they were really afraid to keep him any longer because i might cut into the hospital's income. so we got him back, bandaged and theoretically patched.

laurie—that is, between christmas and hurting his hand again today, in case we should have had a dull moment—is now wanted by the police. it seems that in the fields next door a crew of men has been hired to uproot trees and generally lay the ground bare, and they have been using some great complicated piece of machinery, which is called simply "the works." and laurie and two juvenile delinquent friends, one of whom is thirteen and a full-fledged boy scout, sneaked over there and somehow all the red lanterns got broken and the works got started, so that the motor was going full blast when the foreman dropped over to inspect the works on sunday. he tracked the boys here to where they were playing cowboy, and all i knew was that i had stepped out onto the porch to persuade laurie in for lunch and this great tough man walked up to laurie who was standing on the lawn holding the pingpong gun you gave him and said "listen, you, i want to talk to you about that air rifle." laurie looked at the pingpong gun and then began to giggle, which was very wrong, since it subsequently developed that all the lanterns had been shot out with an air rifle. when the man began to yell at laurie i got sore and told him to get out and he said he was going to the police and then it turned out that the older of laurie's friends, who was by then hiding in the garage, had done the damage. i thought it was silly until half an hour later a police lieutenant dropped in on us and gave laurie a bad half hour because it seems that the boy scout had ratted and put all the blame on laurie. fortunately we were able to prove that first of all laurie had no air rifle but only a pingpong gun and second that with only one hand he could hardly have started the elaborate machine going and that third of all he was telling the truth when he said earnestly that he had thrown one rock but that when the older boy had starting firing the gun laurie had strolled away to admire scenery; the third delinquent confirmed this. so laurie got off with a good scare, but the other guys are in real trouble, since they not only wrecked the machine by starting it haphazardly, but also embarrassed the foreman, who could not turn it off himself and had to call charley back to turn it off for him. our son, the gangster. so perhaps the rest of your check will go for bail.

we are wondering these days about another child, since it seems to be the only sure way i can lose weight, and anyway sally is so old now she is no longer a baby. it would be fun to have another, and the kids are all for the idea. laurie wants twin boys and so do i. we haven't decided yet, but will have to soon, because sally broke the high chair and stanley says he will not bother to fix it again unless it will be used by a new baby. since laurie has a new carpentry set and is passionate about fixing things the vote will probably be yes. i have gone back on my diet anyway.

i must stop writing. i have a million stories to write. my book comes out april 10th, and i have signed a contract for the next. also, the one they paid for is nearly finished, and may even come out next fall.

so anyway it looks like a good year starting. many many thanks again from all of us for all the wonderful things you did, and lots and lots of love.

love, s.

•  •  •

## [To Geraldine and Leslie Jackson]

wednesday [February 1951]

dearest mother and pop,

we are having a blinding snowstorm which has been going on since early this morning. i had to send the kids to school in a taxi because i am nervous about driving in such snow and besides, although i can usually get down our hill without much trouble, getting up is something else again. i am now debating whether to have canned tunafish for dinner or to try to get down to the store.

joanne decided a few days ago that she wanted to start a scrapbook, and so i went out and got her a scrapbook and a jar of paste and half a dozen women's magazines. now joanne has gone crazy; she must have fancy little tea sandwiches for lunch, two-toned jello for supper, her breakfast cereal has got to have a face made out of marshmallow, and so on. her scrapbook is full of pictures of pretty little girls, and she is also setting up furniture, one page for the living room, one page for the kitchen, and so on. i sneaked one over on <u>her</u>, though; i suggested that as she finished each page she tell me the story of the things on that page, and i would write it down. so i have story material for months. all her little girls are ellenoys, of course, and i have had half a dozen requests for their further adventures. i had a letter from a lovely old lady who said that she and her husband had no children of their own, and were adopting jannie and her girls.

the reason you haven't seen any of my stories is i haven't written any. i spent most of my time until a month or so ago working on the book* but since then i have done four stories, none of which have so far sold, although that doesn't mean much in a month. however, about eight months ago, my old friend june was made fiction editor of charm, and the first thing she did was rush up here and go

* *Hangsaman*.

through my files and pick out a story she liked which no one would ever buy although we thought it was fairly good.* it was the first story she bought and last week it got tapped for the best short stories of 1950, making a great credit to me and a greater credit to june, whose editors are all very pleased at her eye for good fiction. charm has not gotten into the b.s.s. very often, and of course it's almost as important for the magazine's prestige as the author's. anyway, the result of it was that last friday i had to go into their offices and get introduced all around, particularly to the grand editor of the whole thing, and i had to sit in her office and chat gaily for half an hour; then june was allowed to take me out and buy me a drink on the expense account. after that we went to the opposite extreme and went down to the village where we met stanley and a pack of dissolute friends and we had a spanish dinner full of rice and clams and then went to the golden gloves. louis scher, our great friend and seventh bookhunter and subject of stanley's new yorker profile, is an ardent amateur fight fan, and he has insisted that this year we help him follow a young boxer named stoutmorriss through the finals of the golden gloves; we saw poor stoutmorriss get cleaned in the finals last year, but this year louis thinks he will make it. i like the golden gloves because up until the finals the fights are held in a small club in brooklyn and i can have a ringside seat. no one will pay fifteen dollars for me to have a ringside seat at madison square garden.

stanley is now pestering the life out of me to play bridge. the greatest mistake i ever made was teaching him. we can't seem to find anyone up here who likes to play, except for two couples neither of whom are very good and who will not, unlike stanley, come out on a bad night just to play bridge. i think however that it is mostly because right now he is doing his new yorker article on the brooklyn bridge, which has taken about six months of research. he is full of odd little facts about the bridge, and his desk is piled with big books and photostats of the new york times from the last century, and either bridge games or brooklyn bridges take up most of his time.

* "The Summer People."

stanley is really not a bad bridge player, just persistent. he has such an unfortunate mathematical and literal mind that once he is told a thing he believes it is always true, and it is like playing with a robot bridge player. until about two years ago he refused to play cards at all and then someone got him playing poker and that was the beginning of the end. once he learned poker and belote, bridge was inevitable, but i'm sorry i started it. until he learned poker there wasn't a deck of cards in the house.

both laurie and jannie are very excited over your coming to visit. jannie says she has trouble remembering you, you will find her very odd when you see her; perhaps you will know where she gets it. wasn't there an aunt maud who used to see things on the stairs?

it will be such fun to be together again. i will take you for a ride. lots of love to you both,

s.

•    •    •

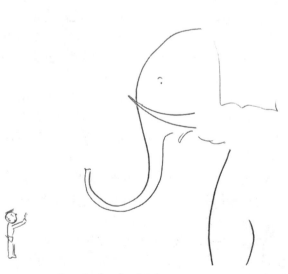

Laurie feeds elephant

[To Geraldine Jackson]

tuesday [spring 1951]

dear mother,

just wanted to send you the enclosed, which is (brace yourself) a
copy of my listing in (i <u>said</u> brace yourself) Who's Who in America;
a very flashy operation. i thought you'd be amused by the way it
sounds like a horse's pedigree; if they listed the number of races you
and pop won it would be perfect.

my publisher is lecturing in westport the end of this week and
we got stuck to lodge them while he and his wife are here. as a result we have to get invited along with them everywhere they go and
so we are tied up for drinks at something like fourteen different
places, all f and s authors who want to entertain the publisher, and
we are going to meet more people in two days than we have in two
years.

stanley and laurie put an ad in the paper about coins and a local
woman called us and said she had coins she had collected while she
was a navy wife before her husband was killed in the last war. so we
went over last night and she had spent many years in san francisco
and i dragged up all sorts of odd facts from my memories of california and she was so homesick that she tried to give the coins to
Stanley.

my agent just called to say that she thinks they may possibly
have reached an agreement so i must quick write something for the
movies.

love,

s.

•    •    •

[To Leslie Jackson]

friday [May 1951]

dear pop,

a praying mantis has just stepped out of the manuscript for my new novel; i put a strainer over it and will let laurie dispose of it when he comes home. i wish i knew what a praying mantis was doing in my book. hope you and mother are well. we're hoping to see barry and marylou in a week or so.

love,

s.

•   •   •

[To Geraldine and Leslie Jackson]

tuesday [May–June 1951]

dearest mother and pop,

when you called last night i was sniffling sadly over isadora duncan and stanley was weeping loudly over a double play which put the dodgers out in the ninth inning, and we were just debating taking a drink to cheer us up, but your phone call served nicely in addition, particularly since brooklyn came back to win in the tenth.

i also must have confused you very much with my wild stories of the movie world. what happened was that last week i got a telegram signed franchot tone, which had our local telegraph operator in a frenzy because it invited me to come to new york and discuss a movie project with him, and she kept saying "gee, you'll get to meet him, won't you?" so i called my agent and she made an appointment

for me to get together with franchot, and elmira <u>quickly</u> ironed my
one blouse and i raced out and bought a pair of stockings and i went
into new york and my agent and i sat down with franchot and a very
sharp operator named hakim, who is apparently the boy with the
money, and a flowery character named siodmak, who kissed my hand
and my agent's hand and kept jumping up to light people's cigarettes
and told me i was the greatest writer of the century and he had read
every beautiful word i ever wrote and that when he thought of doing
a movie on isadora duncan he thought immediately of me because i
was the only one, he knew right away, to capture her matchless personality because of my own matchless personality and he could see
the minute he met me that i was a person of insight and intelligence
and he flatly would not direct the movie unless i wrote it. none of
this, of course, is true. the idea of the movie was franchot's; he has
admired isadora for years and owns the movie rights to her autobiography, and siodmak hadn't even signed to direct it—the only part
that was remotely true was that he wants me to write it and had
made their considering me for the writer a condition of his signing.
except no one had a chance to consider anything because siodmak
wouldn't stop talking about himself. he kept asking me if i had seen
pictures he directed, and naming them, and it turned out that the
only ones i had seen, which i remembered lovingly, were the french
ones starring jean gabin, upon whom i had a crush on when i was
about sixteen, and that most of siodmak's american pictures, none of
which i had seen, had starred franchot tone, who got stiffer and
stiffer each time i said no, i hadn't seen <u>that</u> one. the funniest part of
the whole interview was when siodmak, practically with tears in his
eyes, lamented the fact that he was due to leave for italy the next day
to direct a movie for warner brothers and here he had only just met
bernice and me, and had to leave us right away. then he turns to me
and says "why should you not come to italy? you have seen capri, of
course? no? but my dear, my dear, you cannot live without seeing
capri—come with me?" i mumbled something about having to see
brooklyn finish out the season, and he says to bernice, "but no one
can write about isadora on a farm in america—we must do this
movie in italy—or paree—there is no culture in america." then to

franchot, "tell this girl she must come to italy—tell her we will take her to italy." so franchot, who is practically overwhelmed, like the rest of us, says meekly, "we will see that you get to italy." so bernice, who has been turning purple through all this, says very softly, "and miss jackson's husband? and her three children?" "we'll take them all," says franchot numbly. "and me?" says bernice, "i'm her agent, after all." "you, too," says franchot.

siodmak actually felt that he was talking me into writing a movie through the force of his personality, whereas actually bernice and i had decided ahead of time that if it looked like they'd pay enough we'd jump at it. the poor man was so proud of himself when bernice finally said well, we'd take a try at it, and everyone got up and shook hands with everyone else, and then they began making plans for getting me a copy of the autobiography and all the other books written about isadora, and i kept saying look, we have a copy of the autobiography at home on our shelves under D, and they kept saying, well, we can order it from brentano's, and franchot kept saying if i would come back to his hotel with him he could give me his copy and we could have a drink and he could tell me about the movies and siodmak kept saying well, why didn't i go back to <u>his</u> hotel and have a drink and talk about the movies and the character hakim who had sat there all the time wincing whenever money was mentioned, carefully refrained from of-fering <u>any</u>body a drink, so i said very quickly no, i had to catch a train home and i could get a drink there and anyway we <u>had</u> the book at home and franchot said well, then it was settled, they would mail me the book or send it up by messenger. bernice finally got them into the elevator and then she and i sat down and stared at each other and then she said by golly she wouldn't talk to those guys again or let me write one word for less than ten thousand bucks, nothing could pay for the hour she had just been through.

anyway i spent the weekend reading the life of isadora duncan who seems to have been quite a person, and bernice spent the week-end trying to get money out of hakim, and they finally came out of it with the following deal: they pay me two thousand dollars right now, and i do a twenty-page story, not a screen play about isadora, not bothering with dialogue or transitions or anything, but more an outline than anything else. concentrating on action, of course, rather than philosophy, of which she wrote plenty. then if they like the way i've outlined it, they pay me two thousand more. if they don't like my twenty pages, i can do them another twenty for another two thousand, or we can quit there; it comes to the length of a story and about three weeks' work. if they like my first twenty, and pay, then i do them a long novelette, sort of, a complete job, about a hundred pages including conversation and transitions, including characters rounded out, and so on—precisely a novelette. if they like <u>that</u> they pay again, another two thousand, before they can have it. i have then received six thousand, and again can quit. <u>then</u> (this was what finally broke hakim's nerve) if they decide to make it into a movie and put a screen writer to work on it (bernice specified that i should not have to do any screen treatment, since i have not the slightest idea how) and want me to work with the screen writer, supervising the characters and such from my own story, i get two thousand a month for as long as the screen writing continues and if you figure it as two months, which is average, i have gotten ten thousand altogether, although poor old hakim has only had to let two thousand at a time slip out of his clenched fist.

both bernice and i, and probably hakim, figure it will fold up after the first two thousand, since what they think they want and what will make a good movie are two widely different things, and most likely siodmak's dream of a story like "lottery" about isadora will hardly work out. which is why bernice is getting us paid in advance.

so anyway you can see how fantastic the whole thing is. none of us believe it, but we have been having a wonderful time telling everyone i am now writing for the movies. and if siodmak takes it into his head to do the picture in hollywood instead of capri i may find myself moved out to hollywood. and of course if this should work out i may get a chance to do another, although bernice says sweetly that if the first one is successful the second will of course cost more. the reason, by the way, that i switched to bernice for an agent is that she is commonly supposed to be the toughest agent in the business, and i think she really is. my last agent used to quit on any deal when it looked like she couldn't get as much as she wanted, and anyone could scare her, and she spent more time taking people out to lunch and asking me for news about the children than she ever did making money; but i don't think bernice has ever taken anyone out to lunch in her life and she has certainly never said two words to me about anything but business,* and there is nothing she likes better than getting someone like hakim by the throat. i wouldn't like to have her for a sister, but i do love doing business with her.

this fantastic dream has occupied us all, for almost a week. stanley and the grocer flatly refuse to believe that i was ever invited to italy at all, and joanne has somehow been persuaded that this movie actor wants me to marry him and i think stanley is making a secret list of movie actresses he intends to meet. i myself am planning on a new car, and it suddenly turns out that everybody needs new clothes. it has even caught up with elmira, who reflects that california is a nice warm climate. naturally we wouldn't dream of soiling our hands with the movies unless they guarantee us a twenty-room house with a swimming pool and a pair of dark glasses apiece so no one can recognize the classic writers who have lowered themselves for nothing more than money.

i took laurie and jannie to the circus and we had a lovely time, eating hot dogs and cotton candy and watching the high wire act. stanley's father got us wonderful seats in the third row and jannie was convinced that an elephant was going to land in her lap. i thought so myself, for a minute.

i went to the doctor yesterday, although i was positive anyway about the baby. he says i am in fine condition and recommended an obstetrician in bridgeport, which makes for a transportation difficulty, but the hospital there is immeasurably better.

by the way, yesterday i got a call from new york from elizabeth young[†]—remember her? she is visiting in new york this week, and wanted me to come in and see her, but i used my only blouse going to see franchot and so i persuaded her to come out here. she is coming tomorrow, for the day, and it will be nice to see her again. she al-

* Bernice's letters to Shirley are actually filled with complementary talk about the children, weather, food, travel, and many other subjects of common interest.
† The friend Shirley named "y" (pronounced "ee") when they lived in Rochester.

ways sounds so sad, and i suppose she has every right to be, living all alone and working and trying to bring up her little girl.

we all wish you would plan to come soon again. and i'm glad you liked the book.

we all send lots of love.

s.

. . .

[To Bernice Baumgarten]

Friday, June 1, 1951

Dear Bernice,

Hope these are OK. And that the treasures of Egypt are to be poured into our laps.

As I said yesterday on the phone, without this money I'd be in desperate financial trouble, but if there's any way to get it honestly, like from story sales, I'd love to go with you when you are able to tell Hakim in a few terse words what you think of his business deals.

The whole thing is entirely yours, and any decision you make is OK with me, particularly a decision to have H. eat these contracts word by word while you and I jump up and down on his stomach.

We entertained the Farrars yesterday with fancy dinners and whatnot, and Stanley says it ought to put at least another thousand on the next advance.

If I have my baby before these contracts are worked out I will name him Franchot.

Best,

S.

. . .

[Note: To Ann Harding, undated, but probably June 1951]

Dear Miss Harding,

Thank you for your kind and explanatory letter. Although I am very enthusiastic, and can see great possibilities in your plan, I still have a few questions.

1. To what extent would technical television knowledge be necessary on my part? As you know, I have no experience with television whatsoever, and know very little about any form of dramatic presentation.

2. Do you want to use those stories you mentioned (such as Daemon Lover; I should think you could do a marvelous job with that) as plays, adapted for television, or do you want, rather, new and original stories? I think that, on the whole, the stories already written might be better, particularly since you see several of them as "plays" already. The Tooth occurs to me, along with The Daemon Lover and one I should like to send you, as the most promising oncs to start work from. The one I should like to send you was not in the book, but appeared in the Woman's Home Companion last year; it is called The Magician (although they called it Kitchen Magician) and is a much lighter and gayer story than the others and would be, I think, valuable as a sort of comic relief, if it could be done at all.

3. As you know, I have a great interest in the almost-supernatural and the sort of dream-like plot; would you think that any such would work out? I think that television would be an amazing medium for such effects; what do you think? I am, as I say, excited by the whole idea and hope that we can work out something together.

The device of making thoughts audible seems like a good one (perhaps using a narrator?) but wouldn't it be possible, too, in a visual medium like television, to use as much action as possible in substitution for thoughts? That is, in Daemon Lover, for instance, a series of nervous maneuvers with the clock might be much more vivid than a series of heard statements about the time; a certain amount of the audible thought would be necessary, of course, but, if I understand your plans correctly, we ought to avoid the "arty" and "experimental" sort of thing as much as possible. I do not know the extent to which a camera may be manipulated in a television program (or in anything, for that matter; my work has always been directly with a typewriter and a sheet of paper) but it seems to me that imaginative camera work could do as much as anything to create the effects of indecision and fear. As far as other characters are concerned (I am thinking of The Tooth, for instance) they could be suggested rather than portrayed by a sort of stylized pattern—the dentist's office, say, is a familiar enough sight to everyone not to require any time spent introducing it, so that a very brief total-effect picture of a dentist's office, emphasizing mainly his ghastly tools, would be adequate to create a whole atmosphere of dentistry and would need then the dentist only as a voice, speaking in that horrible familiar tone dentists use.

These are, of course, only timid attempts to discover what possibilities there might be in a substitution of television for fiction. I see stories as in paragraphs and pages, and find it bewildering, but fascinating, to try to translate them into pictures.

Sincerely,

Shirley Jackson

•  •  •

[To Geraldine and Leslie Jackson]

june 22 [1951]

dearest mother and pop,

i've delayed a long time in writing because i've been trying to get some stuff done and maybe make some money. now that hangsaman is out i can hit the publishers for a new advance; no stories have sold since the first of this year, and the only excuse is that it's the worst year for fiction they have ever known; no books are selling, no maga-zines are selling, and so no one is buying anything to print. they blame it on television, of course. lottery is being done again on tele-vision, by the way, on cameo theatre, so keep an eye out for it. it is as atrocious a production as i have ever seen.

my movie career moves on slowly. turns out that franchot, who loves a dollar better than his right eye, finally brought himself to sign a contract saying that they would pay me two thousand dollars in two installments if they couldn't find any possible way of getting out of it. one thousand has already been paid, franchot doing everything but counting it out penny by penny, and arguing every minute (my agent said that up till the last minute she thought they were going to stop payment on the check, and that even after it had been deposited and mailed to me they were still calling her trying to get more con-cessions on the contract, and trying to make us pay for their lawyer) and the second payment is due on june 25th, if franchot doesn't shoot himself in despair over it. poor bernice, my agent, has put more energy into this contract than into anything else in years. both ber-nice and i were ready to quit the whole thing half a dozen times, but every time it sounded like we were ready to quit franchot would give in quick and we'd start all over. anyway, the first draft is done, and they seem to like it. we carefully fixed it, bernice and i, figuring that a little plotting on our part was indicated, so that although they own the first draft, no one can possibly enlarge it into a screen play except me. the whole thing is set up so that the characters have to be devel-oped exactly right in order to hold it together, and bernice made it perfectly clear to franchot that i had mountains of notes which would explain exactly how to do this, but of course this would cost money. franchot apparently turned pale and went off to lie down. but we paid part of our bank loan and our taxes, and if they come through with the rest we won't be in bad financial shape, particularly not if good old john farrar comes through with three thousand dol-lars advance for the new novel. bernice and i have now become the most mercenary pair alive, having learned from franchot. anyway, we've been having a fine time. hakim, the business manager, who read the script first, came to bernice with tears in his eyes and said that miss jackson was a really <u>sincere</u> author, one with true heart, and that for the first time isadora had become real to him. considering that i did the script in two evenings, i'm proud of getting that much heart in it.

hangsaman is selling as well as might be expected these days. the first edition is not quite sold out, and it doesn't look like there will be any second edition; again, they blame publishing conditions, since the reviews were almost all enthusiastic. i have been getting a good deal of fan mail on it, which of course is flattering, and several letters from college girls, saying that the same thing has happened to them. i have to answer them all, of course, and i have no idea what to say to the college girls, except that they'll probably outgrow it.

no day without some excitement. just had a phone call from a guy who said he was from the curtis publishing company, and that the ladies' home journal was running a story of mine this week; i said they were? not remembering that they bought the story a year ago and probably just got around to it. he said he had been searching indian hill road for a sign saying jackson and finally went down to our local drug store, where no one knew who i was (i am only in there seven times a day, and mr and mrs baer both know me perfectly well; they must have thought he was a bill collector.) until mrs baer caught my son and asked him what his mother's name was, and he thought she was crazy and said his mother's name was mrs hyman, of course, and they asked him if i wrote stories and he thought and thought and finally said yes, he believed i did. so they immediately called me and we got it straightened out; they wanted to see me about publicity, and i told them how to get here, so they just came. they have it all set i should appear on a connecticut radio show and a connecticut television show next week. stanley kept trying to keep a straight face, and i kept sort of saying weakly oh no not television, but it has been settled, and so next week, if it becomes final and definite, which it still please heaven may not, i got to go to new haven to be on a local television program on a channel we don't get, and then i got to go to bridgeport to be on a radio program at ten in the morning on a station i bet we don't get either. and when laurie comes home for lunch i am going to beat his head in.

we've been going to the beach nearly every day, and we are all nice and sunburned, except for joanne, who has her usual beautiful tan. joanne got promoted to the first grade, and laurie got promoted to the fourth. joanne of course did not get a report card, but laurie's card was exceptionally good; he has improved in everything, having lost so much ground after his accident, and in art has showed unusual progress. he is very proud of himself. he and stanley had an awful fight in the barber shop yesterday, because laurie got in ahead of stanley and told the barber he wanted his hair indian style, with a long ridge down the center and shaved off completely on the sides. the barber was reluctant, and checked with stanley, and stanley nearly lost his voice, although fortunately not entirely. laurie took the position that it was his head and he was going to do what he liked with it. stanley took the position, which i don't think was quite tenable under the circumstances, that so long as he paid for the haircut he could say what it would be like. stanley won, of course, but not by convincing anyone.

as i said, no day without excitement. since i wrote the last line, we have managed to pack the morning full. turns out that what laurie bought at the store was not gum, but marshmallows and matches (is mrs baer crazy, do you think, to sell matches to laurie and three of his small friends?) and the kids built a campfire in the field next to our house and began to roast marshmallows but of course the fire got out of control and they came screaming into the house and stanley had to go out with the fire extinguisher and put it out; he was so frightened he wasn't even mad at first, but after he got the fire out he sent laurie's friends home and then gave laurie what must be the worst whipping laurie has ever had and the way it stands now laurie is in bed for the day and probably for the rest of the summer. in the middle of laurie's whipping good old bernice called me to say that the way franchot is talking now they intend to go right into the screen play—more money for me, tra-la—and would i like to go to paris for three weeks? she said she told them i wouldn't go without my husband and they said they would talk it over among themselves. she also remarked that she had made a small sale—a magazine named woman's day has bought a story for seven hundred and fifty, which makes a substantial difference in everything. anyway laurie's punishment got much lighter when i came in and told stanley—instead of being shut up in his room for the whole summer he may be able to come out around the middle of july.

elmira and stanley are outside the window playing horseshoes. they play every afternoon, elmira because she wants to take a couple of inches off her waistline and stanley because he likes to play. it looks from here like elmira is winning; she just made a ringer.

i finally went to the doctor, who is in bridgeport and supposedly a very modern and excellent character; our doctor here recommended him. he turned out to be very nice, and made everything seem so simple and relaxed. i feel fine, have no trouble at all, and have his official permission to drive to canada july 5th; the doc says it's okay if i stop every couple of hours and have some light refreshment. i said i had never turned down a chance at light refreshment in my life.

almost time for the ballgame.

lots of love from all,

s.

•  •  •

"One thing you gotta have, dear, is exercise.
So rock me a little, will you?"

[To Geraldine Jackson]

[September 1951]

dear mother,

a small letter to let you know that i went to the doc today and everything is very odd indeed. i am in fine shape, but he is very perplexed
because according to all figuring the baby should not be due until
thanksgiving but according to position and heartbeat and stuff it
should be coming along any minute. actually, he said in about two
weeks, but then he got very cautious and backtracked; he says i
should count definitely on having the baby certainly by the end of
october, and probably sooner.*

naturally i find this wonderful. imagine saving that month . . . altogether the doc left me feeling that i could be ready to go to the hospital tonight or on hallowe'en, but it certainly explains why i've been
feeling so lousy for the last few weeks, if i have been much farther
along than i thought, and have been racing around as though it were
only about the sixth month. i had the baby stuff ready and my suitcase
packed in july. all i've got to do is convince stanley, who is nervously
figuring world series tickets; he had thought i would still be able to go
(that is, if brooklyn plays, which i suppose they will) but that was when
he thought i would have a clear month; i suppose laurie will get to go
in my place. he and laurie are going to the game on saturday.

i'll only be in the hospital five days—the bridgeport hospital. i have
five mystery stories in my suitcase, and my fancy nightgowns. the doc
asked if i was interested in this childbirth without fear stuff and i told
him certainly not. i told him to lay in an extra supply of soothing sedatives and he said take a stiff drink before you leave the house.

love,

s.

---

* Shirley is actually only six and a half months pregnant, and her fourth child will not be
born until late November.

. . .

[To Bernice Baumgarten]

September 17 [1951]

Dear Bernice,

The main thing that concerns me about Mayes* and the story he turned down is whether or not the story served to help convince him that my intentions were honest; do you think he found the story enough along their lines, although not quite right, so that he believes I am seriously trying to do one suitable for him? Because I really thought that that story was it, not having perceived the strong moral stand it might offend.

The Farrars, who are back from their trip, are planning to come up here on Friday, in theory to discuss Abigail,† but probably in fact to discuss the Yankees' chances, a subject upon which John and Stanley disagree violently. I have given some thought to the book, and have a couple of fine ideas for working on it to make everybody happy. If I didn't need the money so wildly—the price of babies has gone up faster than the price of beef—I'd set it aside for a while, but I hate to postpone a potentially satisfying book, and of course hate to throw away all that work.

I am still hovering between three and four children, and all my plans are tentative and uneasy. I am not allowed to do so many things that most of what I <u>do</u> do is sit at my desk and snarl, and if anyone crosses me I clutch my stomach and gasp. I'm enthusiastically tired of the whole project; it's <u>much</u> worse than having a book. And I still have no fourth baby plot.

Best,

Shirley

* Herbert Mayes was the mercurial editor of *Good Housekeeping*.
† *Abigail* is a fantasy novel Shirley is writing, but never finishes.

. . .

[To Bernice Baumgarten]

September 27 [1951]

Dear Bernice,

Thanks for The Lie, which looks dismayingly big. I'm afraid that the revisions, although I am anxious to get to them, will have to wait for a while; I find myself not able to concentrate for any length of time, and do things sort of an inch at a time.

I have gotten to the point where I am taking mystery stories out of my suitcase to read; this is the ultimate resignation.

Did you hear from the Farrars? They were most discouraging about Abigail, John going so far as to say it was dull, and convinced me that before trying to go on with it I ought to think much more about what I wanted to do with it. As with everything clse, I have put it off to solve later, and am meanwhile concentrating on the Savages book.* With any luck, you should see it in a couple of months.

The children no longer believe this nonsense about a new baby. They all sat and laughed when I brought out the old bassinet and washed it and set it up, and the girls figured it was for a doll bed. What has happened to faith?

Best,

S.

. . .

* *Life Among the Savages.*

[To Bernice Baumgarten]

Oct. 23, 1951

Dear Bernice,

That's wonderful news about the story in Harper's; I always figure that one of these smaller sales will inspire others, so that they invariably lead to good news very soon. I hope I'm right, anyway.

I have a three-horse parlay I'm waiting on: news that we have the Vermont house we want, the arrival of this reluctant baby, and a story sale to enable us to move; I'm certain they'll all happen within a few days of each other.

Since Life Among The Savages is moving along, and I'm working exclusively on that and gave up Abigail primarily at John's suggestion, do you think we could hit them for another fifteen hundred on it? On the grounds that I have given up the other book in favor of it, and it would be difficult to go on for the next few months working only on that without some money? I can't write the last story until I find out what sex the new baby is, but I should have the whole manuscript for them before the middle of next year—if I know the baby's sex by <u>then</u>.

I keep doing more stories because I keep figuring by the next story I'll be in the hospital.

Best,

S.

•  •  •

[To Geraldine and Leslie Jackson]

monday [November 12, 1951]

dearest mother and pop,

every time i talk to you on the phone i immediately sit down and write you a letter, because there's so much i forget to say. i intended to write you this morning in any case, though, because i have all sorts of funny news.

funniest of all is about the baby, of course. last friday i went to the doc and he said it looked as though i were ready to have the darn thing, so i should go home and buy a two-ounce bottle of castor oil, mix it with something i don't particularly like—because i'd never be able to touch it again—and take it at eleven at night, followed by an enema, and then go right to bed. he said i should have about four good hours of sleep before the castor oil hit me, and then i ought to begin having pains about two hours after <u>that</u>. so i was all excited, and came home to stanley with an enormous bottle of castor oil and a bottle of cream soda, which i detest, and everyone began to get excited and say things about how nice it was to be able to choose the day when the baby came. the children all asked to stay up and watch me take the castor oil, and stanley got all nervous, and shaved, and put on a clean shirt, and ralph ellison, who has been staying with us, writing and building some sort of a radio set down cellar and holding himself in readiness for a midnight dash to the hospital, got his car turned around ready to race out of the driveway, and i got the house full of food. we played bridge friday night with the olsens, and they promised to observe a moment of silence at eleven saturday night, and to be ready in case ralph's car wouldn't start or something, and in bridgeport the doctor was all set and everyone was going around telling everyone else that well, by this time tomorrow it would be all over. stanley and ralph and i had so many old-fashioneds before dinner, to get my courage established, that we were all still feeling fine by evening, and at eleven o'clock i got my castor

oil and put it in a glass, and it filled up about half the glass and
looked worse than anything i've ever seen. i've never taken it before,
you know, and the longer i looked at it the worse it seemed. i filled
the glass up with cream soda and it looked even worse, and stanley
and ralph, who were both a good deal more amused by it than i was,
insisted on stirring it until it got into a sort of oily bubbly state and
was perfectly dreadful looking. stanley sat on one side of me with a
glass of water and ralph sat on the other side with a couple of dry
cookies, that being the only thing i could think of that might coun-
teract the oil, and after about half an hour's discussion back and
forth, me maintaining that the doctor could never have intended for
me to drink this stuff, that it was obviously meant to pour into the
car radiator, and stanley and ralph taking the position that only a
coward would refuse to drink that teensy little bit of castor oil, i held
my nose and got it down, and stuffed my mouth with cookies and
stanley and ralph stared at me with real respect. i then had four
drinks one after another, good whisky this time with no cream soda,
and it turns out that i still feel the same way i always did about
cream soda, but i shall never eat another cookie as long as i live. so i
went through the rest of the unpleasant procedure, and then when it
came time to go to bed found that i was certainly not going to be
able to sleep. ralph went to bed on the theory that he was going to be
awakened early and he wanted to be alert to drive, elmira put her
head in the study door three or four times to ask how i felt, laurie
woke up sometime in the night and said "hospital?", stanley finally
fell asleep on the couch, and i sat in the study and watched television
until it went off, and then read a mystery. about three the castor oil
hit me, and when i tiptoed upstairs to the bathroom i heard elmira
leap out of bed and she opened her door and said "now?" and i said
no, and when i passed ralph's door he said was everything all right
and i said yes, and toby came to the door of laurie's room and
watched me sort of nervously, so i decided i'd go to bed and i did,
and about nine in the morning jannie came in and asked me tenderly
how i felt, and i woke up and realized i felt wonderful, better than i
have in months, with not the slightest sign of any kind of pain, and i
got dressed and came downstairs, and everyone looked at me with a

sort of icy stare, and virginia olsen was on the phone asking if i'd gotten to the hospital all right, and stanley had caught cold from sleeping on the couch all night, and everyone was sore at me, figuring that i'd obviously done something wrong. so i called the doctor and was sore at him, and he said oh, well, don't take any more castor oil, and i promised him i certainly would not.

stanley had a tragedy and is still in a nervous fever. he ordered two shipments of coins from germany, one of a hundred and fifty selected coins of the world, and the other of a hundred selected counterfeit coins of the world and the two shipments got mixed, so stanley got a package of two hundred and fifty coins of which a hundred were counterfeit. now whenever he has nothing better to do he takes out the box and works on it. at last report he had a hundred and three positively counterfeit coins.

we're definitely going back to vermont if we can, next year. i figure that after the baby is born (ha!) stanley and i will drive up and spend three or four days just looking at houses. stanley's been commissioned to do four new long articles for the new yorker, which makes living in vermont easier than if he is doing the kind of editorial work he has been doing here. of course there's no guarantee the new yorker will buy the pieces after they're done, and four of them are a year's work, but it's sure enough to make our financial situation look more cheerful. this time of year is always bad for stories, and we're both taking on whatever hack work we can get, like reviewing and writing on commission. i've been invited to lecture at the bread loaf writers' conference next summer, which is quite an honor, although they only pay a hundred dollars and expenses for two days there—it's in middlebury, vermont, and the most important writers' conference of the summer. i told them i'd read unpublished stuff, which means i have to write some before july. nicest thing is that eight years ago i was invited to attend bread loaf as a student, and pay for the honor, and was sorry to turn it down because laurie was too small to leave at the time; now i go as a lecturer and i'm glad i waited. if the baby is born by then, of course. these are all either writers or graduate students in english, and they attend the conference by invitation only, so i have to figure out something good. i was originally asked to discuss

the present state of american letters but the idea of my informing a
set of graduate english students about the state of american letters
reduced stanley to such a state that i wrote back and said i'd read instead.

a boy at the eastman school of music wants to do a doctor's thesis
setting Lottery to music, the greenwich connecticut high school is
presenting a pantomime performance of same for their high school
graduation play, and a man in oregon is on his third year of trying to
make it into a ballet. hangsaman has come out in england and the
one review i've seen remarks that it reads like a good british novel,
which seems to be high praise.

love to you both, see you soon.

s.

•   •   •

*Barry Edgar Hyman is born on November 21, 1951.*

[To Geraldine and Leslie Jackson]

sunday [January 1952]

dear mother and pop,

i sold a story to the companion, which with your check—for which
thank you again!—lifted us out of our financial hole, and they want
more stories the same, so things look substantially brighter; my agent
believes firmly that story sales come in threes, so she is now looking
for two more quick sales and i hope she's right. just finished a new
story, too. very cheerful.

we were house-hunting in bennington, and had bad luck except
for one house, in a real fancy old neighborhood. we went on from
bennington to northhampton, to smith college, stanley and laurie
and i, driving over those mountains on roads covered with ice, fifteen
miles an hour all the way, and me scared to death. laurie had a won-

derful time at northhampton, since we stayed with old friends of ours, who have no children and don't know what to do with visiting children, so after offering laurie all the books in the house they finally asked if he liked to paint? he said why yes, he did, and nancy immediately went to work and dug him up an easel, half a dozen pieces of cardboard, and a set of oil paints, which he has been wanting desperately. so laurie went right to work copying audubon birds from a set of dinner plates, and never moved from his easel again until we tore him away to go home.

we went seeing about this teaching job which they haven't offered me yet, and it turns out that Mary Ellen Chase—do you know her books?—has been teaching it for twenty-five years, using some of my stuff as texts, and wants very much to have me take over. so far she is the moving force in the deal, and since she is retiring she insists that she has the right to choose her successor, which is me. we were invited to have coffee with her the morning we were there, and went over to sit in her fancy georgian dining room, with three silver tea services on the sideboard, and drink coffee, and mary ellen, who is a fine funny old lady with a lot of great stories, described the course to me and asked if i thought i might like to teach it; she said flatly that she intended to have me do it, and asked if i would please consider it seriously. i never expected an open invitation from her to do it, and was a little bit staggered, and then really put the finish onto a wild morning by turning green and passing out cold on her dining room floor, the first time in my life i ever did such a thing. stanley was so stunned he said he just sat there and looked at me, and mary ellen chafed my wrists and slapped ammonia under my nose and everyone decided it was because she had invited me to teach her course, although i personally expect it was because i had done a lot of driving and perhaps a lot of drinking.

we then went (mary ellen insisted that i lie down for a while first, and she gave me a little bottle of ammonia to carry with me) to have lunch in state with the english faculty, and i couldn't eat and couldn't talk, so just sat there while everyone else talked, and i certainly made a fine impression. i thought <u>they</u> were a lot of stuffy old fools, as a matter of fact. they kept saying that since we lived so close to new york we must get to a lot of concerts, and we kept saying well, we went to ball games all the time anyway.

so we left smith unconvinced. heaven knows we wouldn't live there; if they offer me the job with enough money i'd live in bennington and commute; it's only one afternoon a week. since mary ellen practically runs the college, i imagine we'll be hearing from them, unless she feels I'm too fragile a type to take on a teaching job.

barry just woke up and said "bottle?" got to quit writing and feed him.

lots of love to you both, and many thanks for everything.

s.

glad i kept this letter open; the feeleys called last night that they have an even better house, definitely for rent, same neighborhood, but much more modern, and larger.

have been working on the book about the kids. nearly finished, thank heaven, except for the typing, which is a job of about a month. may get it to the publishers fairly soon, which means fall publication, which means an advance on a new book, already outlined. going to princeton tomorrow for a lecture on poetry (dearie me). did you see the story in harper's?

much love,

s.

•　•　•

[To Geraldine and Leslie Jackson]

april 21 [1952]

dear mother and pop,

terribly sorry to let all this time go by without writing, and sorry, too, to miss your call the other day.

up until the middle of last week we had no house to move into, although everything was set for us to move may first. all the houses we
wanted in bennington failed to work out for one reason or another—
and we were thinking of trying to get a new york apartment for the
summer, about our last hope, when the feeleys called us from bennington and said that we could rent the faculty house next door to
them until august fifteenth, so we did, and are moving up there may
first. it's a furnished house, beautifully located for us and the kids,
and it gives us a few months to look around. we have to put everything into storage, including the books, and last weekend stanley's
father sent two men and a truck and two hundred cartons, and they
started packing books. they got about half of them done, and are
coming back this week, so we have a hundred cartons of books sitting in the living room.

i am also within two pages of finishing my book, and am trying to
get that done between packings. the kids are delighted over the
whole thing, and can't wait to get going, particularly laurie, who will
be living right near all his old dear friends. we're in the part of campus called the orchard, where there are lots of kids.

love from all,

s.

•  •  •

[To Bernice Baumgarten]

April 25 [1952]

Dear Bernice,

Here is the baby; the first copy has gone to John Farrar. It's a final
draft, as I told you, except for two or three more stories I expect to
add. I am so glad to get it out of the way that I could scream.

We found a house for the summer last week and are moving next week, which is why I am a little bit hysterical—putting the children in storage, parking the books, dressing the furniture, and what not.

Am actually going to spend the summer on the new book. I feel ten years younger with a roof over my head.

Best,

S.

# FOUR

. . .

## Life Among the Villagers: 1952–1956

I have just gotten a running start into section four, going like
mad, pages piling up on all sides of the typewriter, and
Stanley says it scares him to death. He read section three
and was afraid to go to bed.

—To Bernice Baumgarten, December 31, 1953

*The family has moved for the summer to a faculty house in the Bennington College Orchard vacated for a time by music faculty member Paul Boepple and family. Ralph Ellison helps with the move by driving Laurie, some cartons of Hyman valuables, and Toby the dog separately in his car. The Orchard is a collection of ten small two-story cottages arranged in three rows, and surrounded by apple trees, located about half a mile from the college campus and separated by a long hay meadow and path alongside a seasonal pond. It is about a mile from the small village of North Bennington and the Hymans' previous house, and five miles from the much larger town of Bennington, Vermont. From the minute they arrive, the Hymans are surrounded by friends and colleagues: the Feeley family next door, writer Howard Nemerov and family, composer Lionel Nowak and family, and even their doctor, Oliver Durand, and his family live nearby in the Orchard.*

[To Geraldine and Leslie Jackson]

monday [May 1952]

dear mother and pop,

we've been here just a week, and we all think it was the smartest thing we ever did. we drove up from westport, and walked into a furnished house, with everything working, so that i gave barry a bottle as soon as he got in the door, and put him right to bed, while the neighbors were feeding the other children and, eventually, us. since we had so many friends up here the house was full by the time we had been here ten minutes, and we were supplied with milk and eggs and such, and the beds got made, and everything unpacked, and a bridge game going. as a result, moving was less of a jolt for all of us, and the three older kids settled down at once.

we live in the part of the campus called the orchard, because it is an orchard, with apple blossoms just beginning to come out all over. there are about ten houses in the orchard—one of them, conveniently, our doctor—and most of the families are old friends of ours, and all of them have children, so that there is a constant pack of kids all ages wandering around.

everything is so relaxed and quiet here, and so informal, that i find even housework is no problem. in addition to the furniture and dishes and stuff, the house also has a bendix, a dishwasher, and an electric mixer.

our next door neighbors are the feeleys, and we seem to play bridge with them every night. helen helps me with the washing machine, and we go shopping together. stanley and paul play horseshoes and poker and this weekend about ten gentlemen from the college are going to a camp on lake george for four days. stanley is going with them, mostly for the poker game.

we have several lines on old houses around here; our new hope is to buy an old place for very little cash, and get a mortgage to fix it up. we believe that we can manage that, and of course eventually we'd have a house just the way we want it. i sold a story just in time to pay our moving bills, and expect that they will take another one. i turned in my book, and so can get moving on the next one, if i can clear the guests out of the study long enough to work. the study, by the way, was the particular haven of the master of this house, a musician and composer, and is half full of an enormous grand piano, which we are supposed to treat with respect. a four-foot-high bronze bust of beethoven sits on the piano and cannot be budged. it's the most hideous work of art i've ever seen, and, worse, they have covered it with a plastic sort of cape, so that beethoven sits there, draped, and glares over my shoulder while i work. i wanted to use it to hold the oven door shut, but we couldn't get it into the kitchen. the house is very comfortable and convenient, although small for us, and since we'll be spending most of the summer outdoors anyway, we won't mind. there's a nice lawn, and of course the whole orchard in front, a pine woods on one side, and the college fields in back. we have a fine view of the nice old vermont hills, and not much privacy from the feeleys, which fortunately doesn't matter. we plan to sit outside during the summer and make very audible comments on each other's guests.

must go get sally at nursery school, so lots of love to both of you, and write soon.

love,

s.

. . .

[To Virginia Olsen, former Saugatuck neighbor and friend]

thursday [undated, 1952]

dear virginia,

my pen being irretrievably lost inside my typewriter somewhere, this letter may come out in royal blue ink. anyway it is such a pleasure to sit down, even at the typewriter, that i am ignoring the several thousand pressing obligations and doing you a letter instead. there is a lot to be said for being the famous writer sitting in meditation under the trees, as i am presumably doing, but then there is a lot to be said for a comfortable desk. my papers are blowing, and the chair is too low, so that my elbows rap against my knees. i would prefer to be a little less the under-the-trees type, but there is not a desk inside that will hold a typewriter except the one stanley has covered with coins.

things being the way they are, i cannot think or write coherently, so will try to describe our present situation incoherently, one of the basic tenets of good writing being that the style must be suited to the subject matter. the house, as everyone entering has most kindly pointed out, no longer resembles even slightly the elegant, gracious home the owners left behind, but has the unmistakable look of a somewhat more earthy occupancy. our arrival here was something like the entrance of cicero into rome. ralph beat us here by half an hour, having to stop once and let toby out (toby spent the entire journey sitting on ralph's lap) where we had to stop fifteen times and readjust barry, who kept slipping sideways. anyway, just outside of danbury, our grandpa shax had decided not to ride in his box anymore, and came easily over the top of the seat and settled down on stanley's lap with sally. we made a pleasant little family group, mother and dad with their children and their cat, riding along. shax slept on the front seat all the way, taking up more and more room, and stanley kept edging toward the door until he had to keep the window open to have someplace to keep his right arm. when we pulled up in front of our new home there were what seemed like a hundred children and a thousand dogs waiting for us. the kids poured out of the cars and disappeared while ralph and stanley and i began to unload. laurie showed up later in a tree nearby, and sally and jan said they had been out looking at cows, which subsequently turned out to be horses.

people kept coming in and out until about ten o'clock, when i went to bed, and left the merriment behind. stanley lasted until about one, and then <u>he</u> went to bed, and everyone downstairs continued drinking and playing cards and singing until about three, when ralph went to bed. the next morning the sun was shining and i got up at six and made ralph's breakfast before he went back, and around ten i woke stanley and he took care of barry, who was sleeping outside in his carriage, while i escorted laurie to school. i had the unforgettable experience of escorting him into the fourth grade, where everything stopped dead while laurie entered, and then everyone began to yell. all his old friends ran at him, and jumped up and down and shouted, and laurie, who had been scared to death of coming back to this school, just stood and grinned like a fool.

last night, helen came over to teach me how to run the bendix. i had so much laundry that it was beginning to pile up in corners, and stanley was back in westport, so helen and i brought out a bottle of whisky, and began putting wash into the bendix. by eleven o'clock helen and i had done so much wash that the floor was covered with an inch of water, from when i had forgotten to get the thing quite shut. in our girlish enthusiasm we inadvertently included two of barry's best wool blankets, which i discovered this morning looking like pancakes, and i think i used whisky instead of clorox in the last load.

we have fallen, actually, completely into a new way of life, completely public and unabashed, so that the kids run loose and so do the parents. i had forgotten, for instance, the vermont way of leaving your doors unlocked so that friends can wander in and borrow a cup of sugar, or the baker can leave the bread in the breadbox.

jannie said that if the olsens were here it would be perfect; i would also like bill to hear our train whistle, which is the only one in the world with a major key instead of a minor, and brought me, startled, out of bed the first night.

i can't find ways to express how grateful we are to you. i think we would not have been able to move at all without you, and, thinking about it, we would probably have left westport much sooner without you. the smartest thing i ever did in my life was stop by your house that afternoon and introduce myself; do you remember?

all of us send our best to all of you.

s.

· · ·

[To Virginia Olsen]

[summer 1952]

Dear Virginia,

It is eleven-thirty, Sally due home from nursery school in half an hour, lunch to be gotten and no beds made, so of course the only sensible thing for me to do is sit down and write to you. this is the first time I've been near the typewriter in days.

Our kids have settled down as though they'd been here all their lives, which in a sense they have. In these three weeks Laurie has changed so much that you would hardly recognize him. We had to get him a bike, and Jannie one also, and as a result we see Laurie only occasionally, and then only for very brief periods. Last night he was home for dinner, but left immediately afterward, and came home about eight with a live fish on a pole, saying that he had caught it, and tonight I am expected to cook it for Laurie's dinner. It's in the refrigerator and I only hope it's dead by now.

I managed to drop our coffeepot into the washing machine, so that all Barry's diapers came out full of dried coffee grounds. And the dishwasher chewed up one of our wine glasses and is full of ground glass, so I am gradually getting back to the old fashioned methods. We are having a housewarming party this weekend, to which we have invited seventy people, and all of them have accepted. We cannot of course fit seventy people into this small house, so I do hope they come in shifts. They usually do—first the librarians from the college, a little group of giggling middle-aged spinsters, who each take a drink and say something appropriate (like "hasn't the weather been <u>awful</u>, though?") and then the baby-minder set, who have to come early so they can get home early and take the baby-minder home; these people are terribly gay because they have to compress their whole evening into a short time. Then usually we get the earnest group, who have no children but have been attending an interesting lecture in town or else they have been sitting in on the orchestra rehearsal or directing a dance project; these people come in groups, sit with their groups, and talk to their groups about American values or dance or Palestrina. Finally we get the die-hards, who haven't been able to get away sooner because they've been having their own parties at home but are here now because they have run out of liquor; these people stay until morning and they are the ones, Stanley points out sadly, who will break our borrowed furniture. Some time during the evening our friends will come. We are obligated to have this large party, since it's the only way of getting rid of all favors in one fell swoop, and besides, a party of this kind does wonders for the college in the way of scandal. There is so much pent-up fury in a small place of this kind, that something is bound to happen every time these people get together and take a drink.

Every story I wrote before we left Westport has sold in these last three weeks except one. The book is due in the fall if they can swing it.

The house I always wanted—the first one we looked at up here—is for sale again, and if we can raise the down payment (hah) we will buy it. I've gotten sort of fatalistic about it. If we're meant to have it, somehow the money will turn up. A big advance on my new book, perhaps. Meanwhile, our little red house gets littler and littler.

Everyone individually sends love.

S.

. . .

[To Virginia Olsen]

September 16 [1952]

Dear Ginny,

I realize that you must by now suppose that we are all living in California or wandering vaguely southward in a covered wagon, or camping out ruggedly in the Vermont hills, and since I am not anxious to leave you in that undecided state, I feel that I must sneak in half an hour to let you know our present condition.

A chronicle of our adventures would astonish you; we left the campus house on August 15, with nowhere to go, and took up residence in a local inn (picturesque, ancient, expensive, catering largely to parents of college students and old ladies who want to spend two weeks sketching the covered bridges), where the children immediately settled down into a happy, well-behaved, mannerly life, dining in restaurants with obedience and charm. This unusual state of affairs continued for ten days, with the children literally enchanting everyone at the inn. Then—like I always said, it had to be a miracle—at breakfast one morning a friend of ours raced up the steps of the inn, yelling, and pushed and pulled us hysterically into a car and over a bridge and up a road and through a door, introduced us, and said "These people want to rent a house." "Fine," said a gentleman who looked a little like Santa Claus, at least at that moment. "Furnished?" "Yes," said Stanley, jaw hanging. "When you want to move in?" "Tomorrow?" said Stanley. "Right," said Santa Claus. "Here's the key. Electricity is turned on, water okay, grass needs cutting, and you'll want to pack up the books and clothes around the house and put them in the attic. Good luck." And our friend took us back to the inn, with Stanley hanging onto the key with both hands, and all of us speechless. And we moved in the next day.

The house belongs to Dr. Erich Fromm,* a psychoanalyst who taught at the college, and who built the house himself five years ago. He hadn't finished the house completely, but his wife was not well, and he took a leave of absence from the college and moved her down to Mexico, where she was better for a while, and then, this last spring, died very suddenly. As a result he decided he never wanted to see the house again, and had a friend come up to close the house; the friend had Fromm's power of attorney and decided on his own hook that the house should be rented so that someday, when Fromm has recovered, he can come back again.

His house is a dream. It's on a back road—disagreeably far out of town, requiring that the kids be driven to school and back—and is reached by crossing one of our famous covered bridges marked DANGER GO SLOW BRIDGE WEAK. It's set by itself in a field, with mountains all around and trees right now beginning to turn red. It's small for us, ranch style, knotty pine–finished throughout. All rooms on one floor, beautiful modern kitchen, large back porch, three bedrooms, and, at the very end of the house, what used to be Fromm's office, which we have made into a study-bedroom, with a huge picture window, private entrance, private phone. Three

---

* Erich Fromm (1900–1980), a German Jew who escaped the Nazis and moved to the United States, was a practicing psychoanalyst, social theorist, and philosopher, and the author of many books, including *The Art of Loving* and *Escape from Freedom*.

bathrooms. The upstairs, which is the part Fromm never finished, is one big room covering the whole house. One half of it is filled with the stuff Fromm left and the other half is an enormous playroom. The study is a lovely place to work, and my desk sits against the picture window, so that I spend most of my time looking out at the hills. Oddly, we are only just across the river from the college, although it's a long trip around by the bridge, and we can hear the college bells and see the commons building.

We all enjoyed your visit up here so much, except that it was inconveniently short—can you come soon again? Love from all to all.

s.

•   •   •

[To Bernice Baumgarten]

October 21, 1952

Dear Bernice,

I spoke with John Farrar about a week ago, and he asked that I get the revisions on Savages to him by the first of the year. Because of this, I've been concentrating on getting out some stories, and haven't done much concrete reworking yet on Savages. I can get to them right after I finish the story I am at present battering to pieces.

John said they had set June for publication, and I got a letter from a lady saying didn't I once write a letter about an election where one of the candidates got killed with a rock? Did I, do you think?

Best,

S.

•   •   •

[To Bernice Baumgarten]

[November 5, 1952]

Dear Bernice,

My typewriter broke down and I am using Stanley's, which is uncomfortable. This one has <u>got</u> to sell so I can get my typewriter fixed.

Shall work on the book with my right hand and do more stories with my left.

Best,

S.

. . .

[To Ralph Ellison]

Saturday [undated, 1952]

Dear Ralph,

A swift line on my way downstreet to say that those amazing pictures arrived and why do you keep on writing when you could set yourself up as a fashionable photographer? One of the ones who gets a thousand bucks for spending a day in your home, taking informal pictures of your children. Lunch thrown in.

We agree in thinking that the picture of Sally with the hand with six fingers is probably the best baby picture we have ever seen. Sell it to the Heinz baby food people. Laurie, who admires himself anyway, thinks your pictures are suitably flattering to him, and remembers having them taken. He is anxious to sit for you again, since you apparently did not show his tiepin to greatest advantage.

Stanley gave me a very halting explanation of the picture of him on the strange couch. After much thought, he said that he believed that his oculist had a couch much like that, and that you probably took his picture there.

We insist on paying for your materials; let us know how much. And you promised to send us pictures of your wife and self. And thank you very very much for some of the best pictures of the kids we've got.

As a matter of fact, <u>the</u> best!

Best,

S.

•  •  •

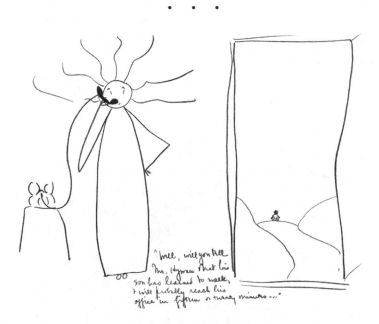

"Well, will you tell Mr. Hyman that his son has learned
to walk, and will probably reach his office in
fifteen or twenty minutes…"

[To Bernice Baumgarten]

Thursday, November 20 [1952]

Dear Bernice,

No one can say I don't work for a living; I sat up all night doing this. Worse, I spent the early part of the evening playing basketball, thirty-five screaming cub scouts vs. eleven gasping mothers; scouts, 21–19. I made two baskets, though, and got a terse word of praise from my son. Does the official boy scout magazine buy fiction? I got a whole new world of material, having been railroaded into being a den mother.

I have more stories almost ready. Stanley and I are sharing a typewriter while mine is being fixed, and he gets it today, so the stories are delayed.

Between basketball and your reassuring tone on the phone I manage to take heart somewhat. I wish I had gone into the lithography business, like my father wanted me to.

Best,

S.

•   •   •

[To Bernice Baumgarten]

January 19 [1953]

Dear Bernice,

This is for you. Whatever fee you think is best is okay with me.

Due to circumstances presumably within my control, I find work almost impossible right now. Every morning I plug away at doing

one whole page and every evening I throw it out. If I ever get together three or four un-thrown-out pages I shall send them to you.

Also I can't go outdoors because one of our strange cats has completely covered the doorstep with dead frogs.

Best,

S.

•   •   •

[To Geraldine and Leslie Jackson]

january 19 [1953]

dearest mother and pop,

i've been trying to get to writing you since i got pop's letter, but i'm
scared, because every time i write to you we have a blizzard the next
day. one morning the brakes were frozen, but fortunately they
thawed out before i got to a hill.

a couple of days ago there was a big cocktail party at the college,
given by a couple of students, with about fifty people asked. i spent
most of the party feeding coffee to our hostess in the ladies' room;
they had decided to make martinis, which they had never made before, and had gotten into a good deal of trouble with the proportions,
and had also done a good deal of sampling. the final result was probably the worst drink you have ever tasted, and of course the hostess
flat on her back. i choked down about half of one martini, which
turned out to be most fortunate; we left the party about nine, and
walked outdoors into a sleet storm, and i got quite a surprise when
we took the first corner, turned completely around, and ended up
sideways on the road. i came home two miles an hour, took the sitter
home at the same speed, nearly got cracked into by another car
which came around a corner the same way i had, and got home without trouble; we were supposed to have about twenty people coming

along to our house from the cocktail party, and only six got here. the general opinion was that if we had taken those dreadful martinis and sprayed them on the roads, the ice would have melted right off.

i suppose that once a vermonter gets to discussing the weather no other topic is possible. i can prove it, though, because in march when you come we will sit you down and make you look at color movies of the children playing in half an inch of snow. stanley's parents sent his brother and us each a home movie outfit—everything from camera and film to projector and screen, including something called a viewer and half a dozen parts we haven't fitted in yet. i got the camera end of it and stanley took on the projector, so we spent one evening studying the various books of directions and the first sunny day i went outdoors with the kids, and the dog and the cats, and took miles of pictures.

my own immediate idea was to forget about the kids altogether and make a small regular income in blackmail by taking movies of local parties, but stanley pointed out that once they find out you are going to bring your movie camera to parties they very shortly stop inviting you, and you find yourself socially isolated. i could have made a fortune at the cocktail party.

the kids are flourishing. right now the girls are making valentines, which makes spring seem not too far away. laurie is making marvelous things with his erector set, and is making timid experiments with his chemistry set, although i am in constant fear of an explosion from the cellar. jannie is very busy, either visiting or entertaining every afternoon after school. sally's nursery school is closed for the winter, so i'm trying to keep her busy with afternoon visits. her main occupation now is singing. we gave her a book of children's songs for christmas, and after a couple of evenings with everyone gathered around the piano singing them, she had learned them all. she has an amazing ear, and can pick up a tune accurately right away, and she has a fantastic memory. i use her all the time for grocery lists. jannie, who is our scholar, gets report cards which infuriate laurie, and it looks like all through school she will be the one who gets all a's. we gave <u>her</u> grimm's fairy tales for christmas, and i told her it was the book i learned to read on (i still re-member it; baba gave it to me, and i sat there until i had read it, and i can remember that triumph when it began to make sense!) and she is doggedly working at it. she has, somehow, taught sally to read and write the alphabet; she is a surprisingly patient and careful teacher, and was delighted when stanley sat there stunned while sally laboriously wrote the whole alphabet correctly. barry took his first step on christmas eve, landing with a flop on his big brother. the room which he shares with laurie now has thousands of blocks thrown around, making it very difficult to go in to cover them during the night, a brooklyn dodgers banner and a mounted butterfly tacked on one wall, a homemade indian tomahawk and a bird painting, both done by laurie, on another wall, and practically a full-size model of a jet plane hanging by string from the middle of the ceiling. i now refuse to make laurie's bed because i keep cracking my skull on the jet plane and i am convinced that while i am reeling around holding my head the tomahawk is going to fall down and cut off my foot.

i haven't done much writing since i turned in my book manuscript. a kind of reaction to the strain of getting the darn thing done. they are working on the jacket now, and are definitely using the picture of the kids, plus a lot of gooey sentences apparently written by the under-office boy. i cut the worst of it out, but it's still pretty bad.

stanley and i also want to thank you for the check, which was literally a godsend. we did certainly appreciate it very much, and thank you again.

our family doctor—much to the amusement of the children—had to go to the hospital for a minor operation yesterday, and stanley and a couple of the other grey ladies have gone off to visit him with a bottle of whisky and a deck of cards. i imagine that the doctor gets special privileges around the hospital, because it's twelve o'clock and they're not back yet. it's just possible, of course, that they could have stopped off somewhere with their provisions and never gotten to the hospital at all.

we're all waiting to see you in march; if we get a blizzard tonight i'll send you a telegram.

lots of love from all,

s.

•   •   •

[To Bernice Baumgarten]

Friday, March 20, 1953

Dear Bernice,

Many many thanks for the check, and for the thankless job I wished on you. I am deeply apologetic for having had to ask you to do it, and please believe that I wouldn't have if it hadn't been for extreme emergency. We were in one of those spots where the storage company was going to sell our furniture, and everybody else was on us, too. Ought I to write Roger?

Stanley has accepted an offer to teach again at Bennington, and begins in July. I think having an honest job after all these years of writing scares him a little, and I have quite forgotten the sober, self-effacing demeanor of the faculty wife, although I expect it will come back to me gradually. Stanley will have to find a suit, or at least a pair of pants and jacket that match. We will have to get our books out of storage; he is teaching Folklore. I am practicing up on the conversation which begins "And this is your first year at Bennington? How interesting; and what do you plan to study? Bird care? How interesting; and are you fond of college? How—"

I have been writing and writing and writing, but nothing seems to finish itself. With any luck I should have a story in a few days, though.

Again, many thanks for the check and the getting-blood-from-a-stone. Will send that story as soon as I can.

Best,

S.

•   •   •

[To Bernice Baumgarten]

March 26 [1953]

Dear Bernice,

The contract seems fine to me, and I'll be glad to sign. One of my closest friends up here is a notary, and it will give me a splendid excuse to run over and have a drink with her.

I am having a very rough time with the typewriter; although I have done halves of several stories, nothing comes out right, and I've thrown away almost everything for the last three months. I don't know why it is, and what it will come to, but of course it has happened before and no doubt will again, although why it always happens when we need the money worst, I don't know. I have a story which I think is inferior, which I'll send you as soon as it's typed; I could be wrong about it, considering my general view of stories these days. Our financial situation continues very rough indeed, since Stanley doesn't start teaching till July, and when no stories sell, bills accumulate. (Have you ever noticed bills accumulating?) Unless something else turns up, we will have to hit Roger again during April. I feel irresistibly like the dissolute young scion of a noble family who borrows from moneylenders against his inheritance.

My only cheerful item is that, unable to make any headway whatsoever with stories, I have kept doggedly at work on the new novel,* on the theory that what is no good in the novel can easily be cut. As a result I have thirty pages, solid, which Stanley has read and finds "remarkably good"; it's the scariest thing I've ever read. As soon as I have fifty or so pages I'll send them along to you and see what you think.

You think I ought to try writing poetry? Advertising jingles?

Best,

S.

* *The Bird's Nest.*

• • •

"And one typewriter ribbon, for a Royal Portable, and
a good typewriter mechanic if you have one."

[To Bernice Baumgarten]

March 31 [1953]

Dear Bernice,

The Landmark book* sounds like a wonderful idea, and I'd like very much to do it. Laurie, who reads Landmark books, is extremely pleased with me.

Salem witchcraft sounds like a fine topic, since I already have enough of a library on the subject to get the material easily, once our books are out of storage I can do preliminary work on the

* Random House's Landmark series of juvenile books was launched in 1950. They were published until 1970, producing a total of 180 books, all written by well-known writers rather than historians. Shirley was invited to write one on the witchcraft trials of Salem Village.

outline and generally drafting the book on the information I can find in the college library here. Would Random House object to a contract of, say, a year, allowing me enough time to get to my books?

If the witchcraft idea should prove too horrible for kids, would they let me switch to another subject?

But I'd enjoy doing it; I like the subject, and very much want, at present, something definite to work on. Many thanks, ma'am.

Best,

Shirley

• • •

[To Bernice Baumgarten]

Monday, April 6, 1953

Dear Bernice,

Sorry about the delay in the contract; had to cover Southern Vermont to find a notary, my friend having lapsed.

This thing which looks like a story is a story, and represents such a galvanizing of creative energy that it astonishes even me.

The trouble, I find, with writing and being absorbed in a book about dissociated personality is that after a while you begin to dissociate yourself. I am now worried about dissociating into a B3 personality which will finish the book to suit herself.

Best,

Shirley

• • •

[To Herbert Mayes, editor of *Good Housekeeping* magazine]

May 11, 1953

Dear Mr. Mayes,

I have always believed that you are a person of considerable sincerity and honesty, which is a good deal more than you apparently believe of me. Although for more than three years I have acknowledged and done my best to pay a debt to your organization, you refuse to recognize this, and view all my attempts with an air of suspicion and disbelief which surely indicates a strong doubt of my honesty, as well as my intelligence. I realize that one more protestation of my readiness to pay this debt by any means in my power can carry no more weight with you than my previous statements by letter and phone, but my own conviction, that you would if you realized the situation from my position do me more justice, argues that I should try once more.

I have only one source of income, and that is writing. I owe you a debt, which I have only two ways of paying. One of them is by means of stories, the method of payment originally and most reasonably intended, since it enables me to devote a certain number of stories to your magazine, which is of course what I always wanted to do. Although you have not found any of my stories satisfactory for your purposes, other editors have disagreed with you, and found them suitable and publishable. Failing to meet my obligation with stories, my only means of earning money, I have tried to arrange with you a plan whereby I may pay off my debt in the only way possible for a free-lance writer with an income derived solely from fiction sales, in small sums as it became possible for me to pay, irregularly by necessity, but with every intention of continuing payment until the debt was written off. I am sure you know as well as I do the impossibility of regular payments for such a writer, when sales are occasional rather than regular, and—in my case—barely enough to meet personal and household expenses.

My own preference in payment is, certainly, in favor of stories; naturally I feel a good deal more satisfaction and pride in seeing one of my stories in Good Housekeeping than I do, even, from paying off a part of my debt in cash. In spite of all my difficulties since with this debt, I have—as I know I have tried to tell you in every possible way—felt always that the arrangement with you which called for my sending you stories regularly as a generous and extraordinarily helpful offer on your part, made as much to assist an ambitious young writer as to have stories, and you know how deeply I regret that the arrangement I found so kind has become a source of worry and irritation to you, and that you have come to view me as a kind of dishonest, debt-dodging creature in whom you were unwise to put any trust.

I am sure that, since this situation has been largely forced upon you by the length of time gone by, and my own disagreeable financial position, any attempt to reinstate myself in your good graces is largely hopeless. I can only say again that I would like, more than anything I can think of, to be writing good stories and publishing them in Good Housekeeping; next to that I should like to pay off my debt to you as quickly as I can.

Sincerely,

Shirley Jackson

• • •

[To Bernice Baumgarten]

may 13 [1953]

dear bernice,

enclosed my newest document to mayes. my hair is curling. i got part of it, i believe, from an eighteenth-century letter-writer—it should end "until that day, i beg to remain, your most obedient humble servant," but i didn't have the nerve to put it in. first paragraph, indignation; second paragraph, justification; third paragraph, nostalgia; fourth paragraph, compliment. i have noted this down as a permanent form to follow. i have one further very secret line of defense; a charming girl i used to know confided in me once that mayes was always pinching her bottom at parties, and i am sure she is enough of a friend of mine to forbid him to pinch her any more if he sues me. i didn't like to put it in the letter, though.

one of the landmark books cerf* sent was written by maggie cousins, and a delightful one it is; i have not dared write her a note telling her how laurie and i enjoyed it. do you think i might send her a clandestine word? i have been reading and outlining for the landmark book, as i told you, and i wrote cerf to thank him for sending the books, and got a lovely letter back; i thought perhaps i should let him know occasionally what progress i am making.

i hope it will surprise you pleasantly to hear that i have a good (that is, good) hundred pages of my new book, titled at present "the elizabeth case," finished; the first two sections (of five) should be about a hundred and seventy five pages, and finished by the end of june and i'd like to send them to you then. nothing has gone so well in a long time; i know i've been talking about it for months but in the last few weeks it's gone tremendously. long book, too.

everything seems to have turned good after being so bad. you must have powerful magic.

s.

all this and money too! check arrived just now—thanks

•  •  •

---

* Bennett Cerf was a publisher and cofounder of Random House, as well as a lecturer and TV game show personality.

[To Geraldine and Leslie Jackson]

wednesday [May 1953]

dearest mother and pop,

i'm writing this, uneasily, because when you were here you said we
could call on you in a financial emergency, and i'm afraid we've got
one; it's not vital, but we need three hundred bucks, and if that is
more than you can spare temporarily, it's not such an emergency that
we will be turned starving into the streets!

our situation is a real freak. in january, 1954, we will be the richest
people in vermont; my book is already piling up money, with book
clubs and a condensation in the reader's digest in july, and all of this
money comes through the publisher, and reaches me with my next
royalty statement—january 15, 1954. as a result, although we will
have several thousand dollars next year, this year we are poorly. i sold
a story, and that landmark book, and stanley sold an article, so we
make going expenses, but—wouldn't you know it—my car has gone,
and couldn't hold out. it is in the stage of decay where every day
some new thing goes wrong, and i have spent the better part of the
last week parked awkwardly in the main street of bennington waiting
for the tow truck and trying to pretend i didn't see the crowds of kids
gathered around. i can get my new dodge any time, for the three
hundred down payment, and that is what we can't raise; stanley's salary at the college, which starts the end of july, will take care of the
payments until january, when we expect to be able to pay the whole
balance down.

we were going to trade the lincoln in through stanley's father, but
stanley's brother has recently been in very bad shape; he had two operations on his neck, and horrible x-ray treatments, and the probability of another operation by the end of the year; stanley's father is so
involved in that, financially as well as every other way, that we can
hardly expect him right now to work up much interest in whether
our car goes or not!

so, if you can help us, we would appreciate it very much, and if not—and believe me, we both realize that it's a good deal to be asking for, especially in our position of theoretical financial independence!—thank you anyway.

i have at least one story requested, which i have only to get done to sell, but again that is a matter of time, and time is what we don't have. also, yesterday, stanley, who was positive the mail would be full of bills, got three shocks one after another; the first—not really much of a shock, was a formal confirmation of his college appointment here; the second was an invitation to lecture at harvard this fall, all expenses paid for him and for me, and a hundred bucks besides, and the third, which finished him off completely, was an inquiry about whether or not he would be interested in being one of four american teachers who spend a month at salzburg, austria, lecturing on american literature to their university, all expenses paid. and since bennington is closed during the winter, which is when they want him at salzburg (if it should go through) he wired back that he was very much interested. it's run through the university of rochester, by the way. it's a tremendous boost academically, naturally, and of course by the time we were through thinking about it the kids and i were going along, and instead of a month we thought we had better take three, and see england and france and italy and maybe run over to Greece.

my new book is half-finished, and savages comes out on june 22; everyone thinks it will sell and we'll know pretty clearly by the end of a week or so. their first printing is 7500, and 10000 is regarded as a best-seller, so if they go into a second printing we are doing okay. right now, we know definitely that it will pay off everything we owe, and put us in a fairly comfortable position, with stanley's salary, so that we may be able to get a house this year and settle down for a while. like always, the future looks good; it's tomorrow and the day after that are rough.

if you saw the house we've been looking at, you'd know we were crazy. it's fifty years old, with two acres of land, a two-story barn, and sixteen rooms; within walking distance of the school, although a good hike from the college. two years ago (it was one of these old manor houses, with big high ceilings and infinities of space, big

arched doorways and lovely staircases) it was completely remodeled
into four apartments, and the owner wanted to remodel the barn
into four more. he died, and the property went to his wife, who says
she is far too old to manage an apartment house, and is so anxious to
sell that she is offering it at an extremely reasonable price. we both
love the house and if we could manage it when our ship comes in in
january, would be very tempted to buy it. it's also in a good neighborhood for the kids, with lots of other children, most of whom they
know already; it would be the first sidewalk we ever had, and jannie
could learn to roller skate at last. the grounds are tremendous, all
lovely lawn with shade trees. if we could buy it, the biggest problem,
of course, would be putting four families out, and she would take this
responsibility on herself. if we were willing to give two of the tenants,
who between them have ten rooms, a month's notice, they would
move without trouble, since both of them are fairly well off and can
find comparable places easily; the other two are the two little back
apartments, and would have more trouble; they would need more
time, but we could give them definite notice and move into the front
ten rooms; we would even keep them on for a while, since their combined rent would pay the mortgage payments.

  stanley got so virtuous about not drinking that i couldn't stand it,
and quit too, just to show him it wasn't so tough. now our house
looks like something out of the w.c.t.u.*—with stanley drinking
grape juice and me drinking ginger ale. i haven't paid much attention
to it, actually, since in this heat all i want anyway is something with
lots of ice cubes, but stanley still suffers. i suppose it is helpful,
though; he bought a suit last week in new york, in preparation for
teaching, and had to get two sizes smaller than his last suit. my
clothes are beginning to bag, too, and with the money i figure i've
saved not drinking i'm going to order me two summer dresses from
saks, which i saw in an ad. now i go into the liquor store about
once every two weeks and buy a bottle of whisky, which we keep to
serve guests, but we find that when we play bridge in the evening our
guests usually end up drinking ginger ale, too, and everyone always

* The Woman's Christian Temperance Union, founded in 1873.

says my, it's so much pleasanter not drinking, and why didn't they think of this before, and stanley goes into the other room and cries.

we've started using our porch again and we have all our meals out there. it's all screened, and wonderfully cool and pleasant, although kind of full of kittens right now. they're almost ready to give away. stanley—who takes the stand that six cats are too many, although he is outvoted five to one—was just sounding forth tonight on how we were all trying to kid him into thinking we were going to give away the kittens, and hoping he wouldn't notice that there were still six, when there came a meow at the door and laurie, answering, let in a completely strange, beautiful, half-grown three-colored cat, who was starving and wet from the thunderstorm, and very badly frightened. with stanley jumping up and down and screaming, laurie and i took the poor thing into the kitchen and fed it, and then shut it into the cellar to get warm and dry off. we told stanley we had turned it back out of doors, but i'm afraid he didn't believe us. I've always wanted a good three-colored cat.

i wish i could talk you into a visit here when the weather is good; artichokes here have come down to fifteen cents apiece, so you see we're getting civilized. also, our horseshoe court is set up and every day now, after lunch, i go out and let stanley beat me two games of horseshoes, and if you don't think iron horseshoe pitching in the hot sun is work, try it. i figure by the end of the summer i may be able to beat laurie; right now i tend to get the horseshoes around the branch of a tree, or through the front window of the house, but stanley says the walking i have to do to get them back is very good exercise for me.

well, as i started to say pages ago, we are not in any dire straits financially, so if it is inconvenient to you, we can certainly manage. if you can spare it, though, we'd be terribly grateful, and, in either case, thanks.

book for you this week, if all goes well. much much love from all of us.

s.

. . .

[To Bernice Baumgarten]

Wednesday, June 17 [1953]

Dear Bernice,

Momentous day, here it is. Elizabeth* herself.

Barry is much better, out of the oxygen tent for four hours today, very cheerful and happy.† He has been having everything from sulfa on, covering every medical discovery of the past ten years, and still gets injections regularly, to his vast annoyance. We have had cause to be very thankful for our small, modern, neighborly little hospital, where the head nurse in the children's wing is the nurse who was with me in the delivery room when Sally was born; she is a lady whom I never wanted to see again, but she feels a motherly interest in Barry.

So, at any rate, back to work again. I am very firm about Roger's giving me five thousand dollars to find out how Elizabeth comes out, and I hope he is happy enough over Savages to be agreeable.

I am most anxious to know what you think of Elizabeth. And I plan to relax and do some stories now. I wrote you once asking if you thought Mrs. Souvaine‡ still had the manuscript of Clothespin Dolls and if she might send it back to me. I figure I ought to have all that stuff in case someday Roger wants a Savages Revisited or The Son of the Savages Returns or some such.

Best,

S.

---

* Shirley playfully refers to *The Bird's Nest* by the name of its heroine.
† Barry had pneumonia, and was hospitalized and confined to an oxygen tent for days.
‡ Mabel Hill Souvaine was editor of *Woman's Day*, where "Clothespin Dolls" was published, from 1943 to 1947.

· · ·

[To Bernice Baumgarten]

June 23 [1953]

Dear Bernice,

I feel like the end of a soap opera. Life can be beautiful. And so Mother Shirley faces the future unafraid, with little Barry on his way to recovery, and every hope for her book's success . . .

We celebrated the great day* in our own peculiar fashions; I found a four-leaved clover, Laurie hid under a blanket in the back of the car going through the center of town, because the Times referred to him at one point as a girl, and Jannie fell into a pond containing an alligator. (She did; it was a baby alligator, but she ruined her sandals.) Carolyn Wolfe wants me to come to New York next week for M.M.McBride† and assorted interviews, and if I can find a pair of stockings I shall probably come, bringing my girls for protection.

Our copy of the book contract is of course in storage; can you discover the royalty rates and dates of payment? We are trying to figure out whether we can make the down payment on a house this summer. The bank people are thrilled about the reviews, but will not accept them as security.

I, too, am thrilled about the reviews, although the children snatch the papers away from me; they are all now literary critics.

I figured about six months to finish Elizabeth, perhaps a little longer. I think Doctor Wright can be livelier with a little emphasizing of the sensational nature of his discoveries, and I think I shall step up the old boy in the next draft. I'm glad you like it.

Best,

S.

* Publication of *Life Among the Savages.*
† Mary Margaret McBride was a popular national radio host in the 1940s and 1950s. Carolyn Wolfe was presumably her agent.

. . .

[To Geraldine and Leslie Jackson]

friday [July 1953]

dearest mother and pop,

this is the first time in about three weeks that i've been able to sit
down and write a real letter, and i'll bet something happens to interrupt me before i'm through. it's hot, and everyone is talking about
going swimming.

first of all, you haven't gotten the book you wanted because the
publishers haven't sent them to me yet. there's a big delay on filling
orders, and we think it may be because they're going to have a fourth
printing. so far, the last i heard, it had sold about fifteen thousand,
and last sunday it was sixteenth, or rock bottom, on the times nonfiction best-seller list. this week it could either be fifteenth or out of
sight. altogether it's doing beautifully, and we're so excited; it has already filled out our wildest expectations.

i've signed up with an english publisher. There's been all kinds of
nice publicity, and—for a wonder—even a few ads. fortunately the
kids have forgotten all about it, and no longer leap to see their pictures in the paper. i went down to new york for two days, and took
along sally and jannie; a publicity trip for which the publishers paid
all expenses, and it broke my heart to go to a fancy restaurant knowing that f and s would have to pick up the check, and hear sally order
a peanut butter sandwich. the girls had a wonderful time. our little
local train was on strike, so we had to take a taxi to albany, and consequently the train trip was practically painless.

they had gotten us a suite in a nice quiet hotel on park avenue,
which turned out to have television in the rooms, so the girls alter-
nated between the television set and the window. it was, naturally,
during the worst hot spell so far this summer, so it was hard for them
to get to sleep, and when it got too bad i just put them in the bath-

tub and let them play there as long as they liked. the newspaper interviews were in my half of the suite, so i sat and drank tom collinses with all these people and the girls splashed in the bathtub and came out once to have their pictures taken. then they would have their supper sent up and sit in front of the television set to eat it. we had only one day when we had to go out, and that was when i had to be on mary margaret mcbride's radio program. while i was on the program the girls went to the central park zoo with the f and s publicity director. i had a horrible time with m.m. mcbride, since she sat down with no rehearsal at all, announced that we were now on the air, and then informed me flatly that she had not read my book, or anything else i ever wrote, and so would i please tell her all about it? i found this highly offensive, since i was there by her invitation, and thought she might at least have read my book, so i said something to that effect, and this annoyed <u>her</u>. i found that there was nothing i could say to someone who had no idea of anything i had been doing for the past twelve years, and so didn't say anything. as a matter of fact, it's probably just as well; i was so mad that if i had tried to talk at all it would have been worse. stanley and laurie listened up here and said it was awful. i also refused to call her mary margaret, which hurt her feelings. she kept calling me shirley, which annoys me, so i kept calling her miss mcbride. she kept shaking her head at me and mouthing "mary margaret, mary margaret," and i went right on obstinately saying miss mcbride. i hope you never heard it; it was a real display of temper on both sides. mary margaret said afterwards that it was the first real failure she ever had, and then she tried to kiss me goodbye but i ducked.

i then went off with the girls and had a fine time at the cbs studios tape-recording another interview, but this time with a nice man who let the girls play with the microphone and talk to each other from different rooms, and then the girls got taken home and he and i sat down and talked for a long time and he said they'd cut the recording and use it the following day, but no one i know ever heard it, so i don't know how it came out. we came home the next day, to find that stanley and laurie had had a wonderful time taking care of barry; laurie had taught him to drink out of a glass and feed himself. that is going to be my only trip to new york for the next ten years, i hope.

last night we had a beauty of a storm, which i slept through until sally and jannie, operating as a committee of two, arrived in bed with me to say that the rain was coming in on them; not that they minded, because it was nice and cool, but their beds were getting wet. so i got up reluctantly and went and closed all the windows. nothing is any cooler this morning, however. my fingers stick to the typewriter keys and i am dripping wet.

stanley cannot say a word about my writing such a long letter; he usually protests that all these pages would make a story, but he has just figured out that savages is selling five hundred copies a day, making about three hundred dollars, and when i am making three hundred dollars a day just sitting around he can't open his mouth whatever i do. the book, by the way, went up to twelve on the bestseller list yesterday. reviews continue good. our little bennington bookshop has more orders than they can fill.

my car is still my dearest toy. it is so beautiful, and so fancy, and it is so wonderful to start out somewhere and know i'm going to get home again. the kids like to put the back seat down and just use the whole back as a kind of truck; the other day i had twelve kids in there, taking them swimming, plus one dog. we watch it all the time for the faintest scratch, of which our bad toby has already put three on the hood; he went crazy one day during a thunderstorm and tried to climb into the car.

in january—imagine this!—we pay for the car entire, plus paying every other debt we have, including, of course, our debt to mother and pop; we are then solvent, with a car, a house, a dishwasher and washing machine, and money in the bank, saved up for the day when we want to build. it doesn't seem possible, and all of it from savages. it may be bad luck to say it, but right now there doesn't seem to be anything more we need in the world; with barry well, a house in the offing, and the book a success, we are about as lucky as we can be. keep your fingers crossed, and knock on wood; there doesn't seem to be anything that <u>can</u> go wrong. plus the fact that f and s are enthusiastic about the manuscript for the new book, plus even the fact that the girls get a quart of blackberries a day from our own back meadow. the only fault stanley can find with the world is that milwaukee is only three games behind brooklyn, and moving up.

paul feeley, whose name is in the book four times, has figured out that, with a sale of approximately fifteen thousand, sixty thousand people have seen his name, and he is making book on where he will be in the best-seller list next week. there is a very small chance— good odds, though—that it will beat out the bible. can't see it touching polly adler,* though.

stanley says i may not start another page; he wants his lunch. so lots and lots of love from all of us.

s.

• • •

[To Bernice Baumgarten]

August 16 [1953]

Dear Bernice,

It is two in the morning; I just woke up out of a sound sleep and leaped out of bed to re-write the last page of this thing, having apparently dreamed up a better ending.

Stanley is in Canada with a group of book-buying blades, and he left the day after Laurie returned from camp, and the day after Stanley left, Laurie came down with mumps. So I have really been quite busy, mostly in the middle of the night. I have never had mumps, myself, and neither have Jannie or Sally or Barry, but luckily there is

* Polly Adler was a famous madam and author, best known for her work *A House Is Not a Home.*

a three week incubation period, so that none of us will develop them until around the first of September, which is of course the week we move. Laurie feels a strong sense of injustice about all this, since the girls will thus almost certainly be quarantined for the first two weeks of school, but Laurie will be perfectly free to attend.

I have also not had a chance to thank you for the monumental job of arrangement on the advance. By the time you are ready to put through a final deal on Elizabeth I should have more of it ready for Roger. John and Margaret came here for dinner a week or so ago, and John, who will as you know talk about any subject in the world except the immediate business at hand, was persuaded to admit that he liked Elizabeth but wanted the second section pepped up a little; I hope everyone will change opinions on that when they see the rest of the book, although naturally I expect to do some work on both first sections. By the way, I told John that we would have six bathrooms, four kitchens, and four telephones, all with different numbers, and he remarked evilly that he knew who would answer the four telephones—Elizabeth, Beth, Betsy and Bess, which scared the daylights out of me.

Anyway, I hope you like the story. Naturally, if you or anyone else cares to have it changed, I shall be happy to leap out of bed at two any morning to rewrite.

I hope you have had mumps, although I do not believe it can be communicated by the written word. Do you think you had better burn this?

Best,

S.

I am also sending, doubtfully, a small thing named Bulletin,* which may be the result of reading too much science fiction.

• • •

* *Fantasy and Science Fiction* will soon buy it.

[To Virginia Olsen]

september 2 [1953]

dear virginia,

it <u>was</u> fun to talk to you, although i was so sorry that we had only a few minutes to talk.

stanley wrote that westport transfer company, asking for our stuff on september first, and they wrote back was september third all right? and stanley wrote saying the third was fine, and so they said then definitely the third, and so today, the morning of the second, we get a telegram saying they are unable to get the vans, and hope to move our furniture "soon." i called them long distance, and pointed out very politely that either our stuff got here on schedule or i would come around to westport and smash up their warehouse, and that furthermore i supposed that they would pay our hotel bills up here while we were waiting for our furniture, and perhaps, now i thought of it, we would refuse to accept the furniture when it did come, out of spite, so he had better get it into a truck or a pushcart or a wheelbarrow and get it up here on schedule, see? and i still feel i said it very politely, although when i got off the phone i found stanley with his head on his typewriter and tears in his eyes and he said it was because he felt so sorry for the poor man at the transfer company because there was no way of answering an unreasonable angry woman. anyway, we are now waiting to hear from the man as to whether or not our stuff is coming tomorrow.

i can tell you all about the house, having spent long wistful hours there for the past week.

we have two magnificent rooms on one side which will be filled with bookcases, and make a lovely study, and a pleasant living room with a bay window, and a dining room and kitchen; upstairs, four bedrooms. off the kitchen is a splendid pantry and utility room, where i plan to put simply everything. we will have left-over furniture at first, before we take on the rest of the house, and this will

store nicely in the barn. expensive to heat because of the generous
ceilings and over-all largeness of the doorways and such, but poor
old mrs whitman, who wanted so badly to sell the house, confessed
to us right away that we would find heating bills high; "oh, dear,"
said mrs whitman mournfully, "it <u>does</u> get cold without heat,
doesn't it?"

it's the children's house, so fortunately they like it. savages paid for
it, in the form of a huge advance on sales from my publisher; he
didn't have to pay us a cent until next march, when royalties are due,
but he was so pleased with the book he agreed to hand over enough
for the down payment.

of course there's a flaw. mrs whitman (oh, dear me) didn't have a
clear title, so her lawyer and our lawyer are trying to determine
whether the thirty-year-old bill of sale was or was not signed by one
of the three heirs (that would be old laetetia hawkins, or it might be
hastings, who married one of the franklin boys and moved on into
north pownal, or didn't she go farther west, maybe into york state
even, or was that the watkins girl?) anyway it's the bank's worry. we're
moving in, and we haven't even paid our money.

we're having a lot of fun with it, anyway. no one cares whether
we stay in this house or not—what dr. fromm doesn't hear in mexico won't hurt him—and no one is waiting to move in here as yet,
so we can take our time. we sit around debating over what belongs
to us and what was here when we came. it breaks all our hearts to
think that the furniture and dishes and—particularly—books,
which belong in this house, will actually be either sold along with
the house, or rented out to people even more unscrupulous than
ourselves. the oddest thing is one carton of the doctor's professional
files on patients—he is a psychoanalyst you know—which was left
loose and open in a filing cabinet, and very discreetly packed away
unexplored by ourselves; whoever takes this house may, if they care,
rummage happily among these case histories and fairly intimate
facts; we have always thought of that one carton as dynamite, and
have taken care to keep it safely out of the way in the attic. good
blackmail material, particularly since many of his patients were
local people.

i have just been filling out my english income tax statement. it asks if i have been out of the united states in the last year, and i realize with a shock that i have not even been out of vermont; how do you like that for a country life?

ralph and fanny ellison were here for a weekend recently, and we were talking of our moving from westport and our last days with you people, and how we missed you; ralph said when i wrote i was to send you his best regards, which consider me as sending.

make your visit real soon, won't you? and love to all of you from all of us.

best,

s.

. . .

[To Geraldine and Leslie Jackson]

monday [September 1953]

dear mother and pop,

i have a million things i ought be doing, unpacking cartons and doing dishes and what not, but thought i would write you instead. i have four letters right here asking me to do articles, and a story i should finish, and curtains i should wash, and i am going to ignore all of them.

our new house is lovely, and stanley and i are almost as excited about it as the kids are. it's on the edge of town—as a matter of fact, we own the bennington-shaftsbury town line, and of course in north bennington the edge of town is two blocks from the store and the school and the post office. we're across the railroad tracks, and from his bedroom window barry can just see the little freight engine which pushes freight cars around once a day. we have two and a half acres of grounds, with nice old trees and a nice lawn, an enormous two-story barn full of pigeons, and a seventeen-room house, divided into four apartments. we live at present in the front two, totaling nine rooms and still have tenants in the two small back apartments; these have separate entrances and even a separate driveway. we plan to keep the tenants for at least the first few months, until we get over our first big expenses, and let their rent pay the bank. eventually we will take the whole house, mostly to keep books in.

the kids walk off to school every morning. they have to cross the tracks, but since we have one train a day i'm not very worried. they go with packs of other kids, and come home for lunch; laurie rides his bike. sally is in kindergarten, and goes off with the rest of them; with stanley teaching three days a week i'm going to be all alone. it's strange for me to settle down, after the hours of taxiing i did in the other house; instead of spending half an hour at breakfast time getting to school and back, i now wave goodbye to the kids and sit and finish my coffee. and instead of my driving four miles to get the baby-sitter, she walks up.

the barn is our greatest blessing. it's almost as big as the house, and the kids have the whole upstairs for a playroom. and the downstairs is a garage for me and one tenant and still has plenty of room for a pingpong table, all our bikes and wagons and stuff, all the things we want to store away (including two barrels of dishes), and a locked room, formerly a stall, where stanley keeps tools and things he wants kept away from the kids.

i will write again the next time i can make a path through to my desk. until then, you'd better keep your fingers crossed for brooklyn. they've got to do it this year.

lots of love,

s.

•  •  •

[To Bernice Baumgarten]

September 17 [1953]

Dear Bernice,

Do you know of any magazine that would like a sizzling article
on the criminal activities of storage-cum-moving men, naming
names?

I finally located my typewriter this morning and spent two hours
slamming away at a furious description of our treatment, and got it
out my system enough to use it for material later. I spoke on the
phone, just before, with a Mr. Morse, of the Westport Transfer
Company, and the plumber, who came softly in through the back
door while I was talking, said he stood there in admiration listening, because he never heard anything like it, even from his wife. Mr.
Morse said if I wanted to be treated like a lady, I better talk like a
lady; this was because I called him a liar and a crook, and he ob-
jected most emphatically to being called a liar. Mr. Morse chose ar-
bitrarily to leave one-third of our furniture in his warehouse, for
two weeks past the date it was to be delivered, because he "could
not get a van." The immediate result is that a hundred and sixty
cartons of books, weighing four tons, are placed strategically
around our house, located so as not to cave in floors. Mr. Morse
thinks our furniture might arrive "in a few weeks." Talk like a lady,
indeed.

Here are the contracts for Sweden. I never been published,
Swedish-like, before.

The house has gotten over its initial surprise with us, and has
begun to spread a little, and is, I think, relaxing. I hung two curtains
today.

Never in all my life felt more inclined to manufacture great stories.
I suppose it's because I can't find the yellow paper. Or it may be because of a feeling of fundamental security which is just beginning to

creep up on us. The kids felt it first, of course. Parents Magazine, here I come.

Imagine that liar calling me a lady?

Best,

S.

•  •  •

[To Bernice Baumgarten]

October 6 [1953]

Dear Bernice,

I am convulsed at Fantasy and Science Fiction; your letter made me laugh in the middle of the Brooklyn fiasco yesterday.* I have, as you know, been reading that magazine since its first issue, and even long ago wrote them a plug which they used for quite a while, and I think it is a real sweet tribute to my compliments and your stubbornness that they doubled the ante. Would you like to settle for a lifetime subscription for each of us?†

I have been reading Robert Caleff's journal on the Salem witch trials, and I think the main trouble will lie in making the book <u>not</u> a comment on the present day; the parallels are uncomfortably close.

I hope to get those stories out by the end of the week.

Best,

S.

•  •  •

* The Dodgers lose the 1953 World Series to the Yankees in Game 6 (4–3).
† The payment for "Bulletin" was a lifetime subscription.

[To Geraldine and Leslie Jackson]

november 9 [1953]

dear mother and pop,

it is always such fun to talk to you over the phone, except i can't ever think of any news. we are all excited about your trip. we just finished unpacking the books and pictures and records, which means the greatest part of the work is done. now all we have to do is plan for getting the floors sanded and the walls painted.

our downstairs tenant sneaked out in the middle of the night, owing a month's rent. We were mad at first, but then we thought of all the times we've been stuck to raise the rent, and even though we never sneaked out we often wished we could, so we figured we'd forget it. anyway we can rent the apartment any time we want. if no one wants it after a while we'll just open up the passageway through our kitchen and use it ourselves. i wish the lady upstairs would move; she and her children are getting to be a nuisance; partly it's the radio smack up against our bedroom wall which plays from seven in the morning until twelve at night, in spite of everything we say and partly it's the fact that she regards us as just a kind of convenience; she uses our phone all the time (although somewhat less since i took her up the phone bill to pay) and feels perfectly free to ask me to drive her around, into bennington or wherever she wants to go; she asked me if i would be a witness in her divorce case, and when i said no, she said that she and her husband had had an awful fight the night before and her husband had heard me through the wall saying that i was going to call the police. i didn't like to tell her that if they were having a fight i wouldn't dream of calling the police, i'd be right there with my ear pressed against the wall, so i simply explained that her husband was mistaken, and she asked if i'd keep an ear open the next time her husband came home, which is apparently seldom, since he has a girl in hoosick falls. i went up yesterday as courageously as i could, prepared to ask her if she would mind leaving at the end of the month, and she told me mournfully that she couldn't leave for six months, because she has to keep a residence in vermont to get her divorce. she hasn't paid the rent this month, either.

meanwhile, everything else continues to go well with us. savages has largely fallen off in sales, but the publishers wrote and asked me if i could get them the manuscript of the new book by january, since it is to be their big book for next summer. that means if i work constantly—and <u>really</u> constantly; no evenings off except possibly a saturday night bridge game once in a while, or a wild evening at the movies with the kids—i may be able to get it done. stanley is going crazy trying to keep up with his school work, because apparently the students work faster than he does, and in between times we try to unpack books. you can see why i don't get many letters written. also, barry has been off again on one of his colds, with croup and asthma, and they have decided to try and control it now with a kind of penicillin mixture he takes three times a day. oliver's* whole ambition is to get him through this winter with a minimum of discomfort, and he is sure that then by next winter it will no longer trouble him. he has taken to dropping over every afternoon for a drink, and to check up on barry. we no longer worry so about barry, particularly since instead of seeming thin and pale after the rough time he's had since june, he gets fatter and healthier and livelier every day. he's beginning to talk fairly well, and can communicate his wants perfectly. he torments stanley by stealing all the coasters in the house and hiding them, and stanley—who has, you know, this passionate kind of sense of order, and can't stand a table with an ashtray at each end, and only <u>one</u> coaster—gets almost tearful begging barry to give back his coasters. he also hides glasses of fruit juice and small toys and little pieces of cheese.

last night we had stanley's ten counselees down for a drink; i had not met any of them before, because i've ducked all student parties, and so i had a wild time trying to tell them apart. they all look alike and sound alike, and they all eat like pigs. i had spent the morning with sally and jannie making dozens of fancy little canapes, and

* Oliver Durand, MD, was the family's physician in North Bennington and a close family friend for decades.

every one of them disappeared in five minutes. conversation for the evening was largely about who liked cats and who liked dogs, and would mr hyman give cindy an extension on her paper until thursday? When stanley said he wouldn't talk shop, conversation largely died until i fortunately thought of asking the girl next to me whether she likes horses, and then we got a brisk conversation going again. the evening was finally enlivened by a fit of hysterics by one of his senior girls, who is convinced that she is losing her mind because she can't get all her papers written, the rest of them playing records. the girl was finally packed off home to bed, and the rest of us went back to discussing how we felt about snakes. they finally stayed till about two, and since they all had to be in class this morning, and so did stanley, they were able to have a pleasant little discussion about who would oversleep and be late for class. it was apparently a great success.

time for the kids to come home for lunch. lots and lots of love from all.

s.

• • •

[To Bernice Baumgarten]

November 11 [1953]

Dear Bernice,

I do not think that I can have Elizabeth by January first, but I should be able to get it done not long after that. I don't know how long, because, as I told you, it got jammed and I have been in the third section long enough to develop three dissociated personalities of my own. It begins to crack open a little, however, and I know that once I get it going it will move fast. I am very hopeful of not delaying very long. I would like, however, to know that it was signed up with Roger, if that is possible, for the whole five thousand (which must surely look safe to him by now) so that I can figure on that money for January and not think of stories and such for a while, but go all out on poor Lizzie. What do you think? Or are you getting dissociated too?

I have been invited to read the first section of Elizabeth to the next Bennington college literary seminar. The psychology teacher and our family doctor are going to sit in the front row and look incredulous. I am boning up on pre-Freudian catch-phrases.

June Mirken Mintz* was with me when I sent the apples, and she asked that her best regards be sent you. The poor girl is going to have her first baby next January in New Haven (because he teaches at Yale) and they expect her to have it Without Fear,† except she isn't going to; she has already got fear.

My letters to you are beginning to be as long as my letters to my mother. Except if I don't write her every three weeks I get a telephone call from San Francisco and she starts saying feverishly "Dear, are you all right?"

Best,

S.

•  •  •

[To Geraldine and Leslie Jackson]

december 30 [1953]

dearest mother and pop,

let me start by saying, generally, thank you very much from all of us, for all the wonderful things you've sent, and a particular thank you

---

* June Mirken attended grade school with Stanley in Brooklyn then also went to Syracuse, where she met and became close friends with Shirley. Shirley and Stanley appointed her godmother of their first child, Laurie. June has recently married Sid Mintz.
† Reference to *Childbirth Without Fear* (1942) by Grantly Dick-Read.

from me for the lovely birthday check, which went, with the christmas check, into our dishwasher fund. stanley feels that every minute
i am not doing housework is potential writing time (although i actually spend it sleeping), and so, many thanks for the new dishwasher,
which we expect to have in and operating by the time we see you.

we had a wonderful christmas, even better because it was our first
in our new house. stanley's brother and wife and child were here so
that the house was full of excitement. we trimmed the tree on christmas eve and all the ornaments survived the storage and moving, except stanley wants me to tell pop that although the lights are still
okay, they needed a little more tape this year, and new this year was
stanley's drinking eggnog from the children's supply, while arthur
and bunny and i, of course, had the reinforced variety.

the children and i combined this year, and got stanley just one
present, a tape recorder, which he has wanted for years. he finally
carefully recorded the children singing, but he cannot figure out how
to erase. i am loaded with scarves and gloves and two unbelievably
lovely indian miniature paintings, which are to go over my desk.

aside from playing with soldiers and trimming christmas trees, i
have been doing nothing but working on my book, which is suddenly due on march first. i feel that i ought to make some kind of an
effort on it, since they are paying me five thousand bucks on january
tenth, and have already sold the reprint rights. if i get it done, it will
be out in june; i'll send you a copy, of course, but i bet you won't like
it. it's had me walking in my sleep for the last month. the publishers
are advertising it as a psychological horror story, but of course it's
really more like moby dick, penetrating to the depth of the human
heart, and what not. i'm feeling very set up about it, as you can see,
because i got through twenty pages last night and ten more this
morning, which is real speed, considering that the plumber was putting in a shower upstairs at the same time and barry was steam-
rollering christmas candies into the rug. not to mention stanley, who
got the catalogue of king farouk's coin collection, being sold at auction, and was feverishly leafing through it looking for something he
could afford. savages is coming out in england this spring, i hope—

also germany and sweden and denmark and i think france—and i am very much taken with my new english publisher, who seems like a charming man; at any rate, he writes nice letters and sends nice christmas cards. i have a subscription to punch for christmas, so i can watch for reviews.

stanley and i were talking today about what a year this has been for us; i think it's the best year we've ever known. i think it's the house that makes it so wonderful, actually, because we've never had a place of our own before, and never lived anywhere we liked so well. i think you'll like it, too, when you see it, and now it's less than three months before you come. do you prefer a private apartment, or the guest room?

lots of love from all, and many thanks again.

s.

•  •  •

[To Bernice Baumgarten]

December 31 [1953]

Dear Bernice,

Can't let the old year go without telling you that I have just gotten a running start into section four, going like mad, pages piling up on all sides of the typewriter, and S. says it scares him to death. He read section three and was afraid to go to bed.

I took Christmas Eve off, though.

Best,

S.

•  •  •

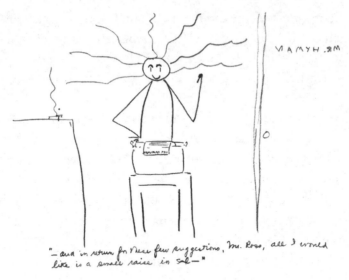

"—and in return for these few suggestions, Mr. Ross, all I would like is a small raise in sal—"

"—and in return for these few suggestions, Mr. Ross,
all I would like is a small raise in sal—"

[To Ralph Ellison]

January 8, 1954

Dear Ralph,

It was a tremendous success,* and he has been doggedly recording Sally singing "Away in a Manger" and Jannie reciting "The Night Before Christmas" and Laurie singing "What Shall We Do with the Drunken Sailor" and Barry saying "Wha? Gimme candy" and such priceless records of culture in our time; he refuses to believe that I was capable of unearthing your secret phone number. Also, now that I am able to discuss our conversations over the phone, I am unable to remember any of the news you told me, so you will positively have to write him and tell him yourself.

* The Revere reel-to-reel tape recorder given by Shirley and the children to Stanley for Christmas. Shirley had secretly called Ralph and asked for his help in choosing and buying it.

In any case, thanks again; it was wonderful of you. And when you coming up? Record a little something? Can you sing tenor?

Best to you and Fanny. Come soon.

S.

. . .

[To Bernice Baumgarten]

February 15 [1954]

Dear Bernice,

I'm scared to say anything about Elizabeth; except, of course, that you're going to be seeing her quite soon. What do you think of "The Others" for a title?

And I know how it comes out, too. Last person I would have suspected.

Best,

S.

. . .

[To Bernice Baumgarten]

March 1 [1954]

Dear Bernice,

It is with sorrow that I have to tell you that you will not see Elizabeth for another week or ten days; I thought she would be ready, but now it seems wiser to make several drastic corrections before sending it in, rather than trying to do them in proof, say. And I was so proud of my deadline!

Also, do you think that Mr. Cerf would give me a stay of execution? A couple of months, say? I have the book well sketched out, and could finish it fairly soon, but, to tell the truth, I am so limp from Lizzie that I lack the capacity to approach the new one with any energy, and I do want to do it well. If he says no, naturally I'll get right to work on it.

Now all of a sudden I am real timid and shy about Lizzie. I hope she remembers her company manners when I let her go out alone.

Best,

S.

P.S. I'm writing Roger about the delay. He no longer dares write me, probably for fear of shaking my delicate artistic balance. He writes to S.

• • •

[To Bernice Baumgarten]

May 17, 1954

Dear Bernice,

I have been working on a combination of McCarthy hearings by day, and witchcraft trials by night, a truly well-rounded life. The W. book moves on splendidly, and except for trying to play down the scary parts, I am going very well with it; I think I can say that it is going to be ready on time, although I hate to commit myself, since it always turns out that I want to rewrite pages 43-67.

At any rate, the great good feeling between me and Roger at present provokes me into thinking that he could be persuaded to put forth another two thousand advance on Elizabeth. I have been trying to do a couple of stories in between trials, but until they get themselves finished, we are going to have to hit Roger, although I hate to do it. He has been talking so enthusiastically about reprints and N. Book Awards, that I think he has enough confidence in the book to advance at least another thousand. As a matter of fact, he has promised to eat three copies in Macy's window if it doesn't get the N.B.A. He might be getting off better for two thousand. What do you think?

Did you know that six witches were at last exonerated by the Mass. legislature this year, after three hundred years? I cannot find out what would happen to their property, which was confiscated by the church when they were condemned; it would be, now, approximately in the middle of the Boston business district.

If Mr. Cerf wants a bibliography, I have a splendid one for him, nothing published later than 1720. I thought I'd put one in anyway, because I'm using some of the trial records, and he should know I didn't make them up, although there is a terrible temptation to improve on them.

Best,

Shirley

•  •  •


[To Bernice Baumgarten]

August 1 [1954]

Dear Bernice,

Here are the contracts. I think Mr. Joseph* is pleasant to deal with, and he certainly made Savages into a nice-looking book. I'm glad he likes this one.

* Michael Joseph was the English publisher of several of Jackson's books in the UK, including a 1954 edition of *Life Among the Savages*.

I am working on the witches, except that the devil background the lady asked for involves approximately four thousand years of theo-logical debate. (Were there, in 1860, really 6666 cohorts of demons, each including 666 companies? Is it true that the demon Asmodeous could not spell French?) I am enjoying it, however. Can you use a spell to drive away Lyars and Beggards?

Best,

Shirley

•   •   •

[To Bernice Baumgarten]

September 30 [1954]

Dear Bernice,

Naturally, whatever you decide about a Hollywood sale of Bird's Nest is all right with me, although the notion of Selling It To The Movies is intoxicating. Are you going to encourage them to improve the offer?

Just out of curiosity, do you think they would use four actresses, or one?

Best,

Shirley

•   •   •

[To Bernice Baumgarten]

October 11 [1954]

Dear Bernice,

Here are the additional sentences for Life; I have just worked them into the first paragraph of the story. I left out some such explanation as this originally because I thought the story was too long.

The royalty check staggered me. I was positive the decimal point was in the wrong place, but I am beginning to believe it now. As a result I now have the most beautiful refrigerator you've ever seen; the old one lasted long enough to show up in the Life story, and then went to pieces. It filled the house with some horrible choking gas, necessitating my rushing the children outdoors and down to the hamburg stand for lunch, providing me with material for a new story, if the market is not already overfull of refrigerator stories.

Do you want more stories? I never know whether to do more or not, when there are a couple out. I am afraid of overdoing it.

Best,

Shirley

•  •  •

[To Betty Pope, who has replaced Herbert

Mayes at *Good Housekeeping*]

[undated, probably fall 1954]

dear miss pope,

i think that a monthly series on home and children would be great fun and could actually be an original and provocative idea. it does seem to me that the first step ought to be getting away from the hackneyed, every-other-magazine type of article, the things that have been done to death and are simply not entertaining any more, and trying out instead a kind of off-beat (if you will forgive the word) series; the little odd things that haven't been used so often, the sudden unexpected views. i think of things like the children who are born losers of things and the ones who are born finders, the one child in the family who always gets the piece of shell in the scrambled egg or the bone in fish, the various small terrors and guilts of the mother every day and the shocks of finding out in many ways that one's children are real people. i don't propose these as necessarily subjects for articles, but as an idea of the kind of different ideas that should be used. also wonder about your aiming the articles at young mothers; in my experience the entire local p.t.a. reads good housekeeping, and the ages of their children cover a considerable range. i think there are a good many small funny articles that can be done about high school students and their parents, with a considerable audience for them; if nothing else, it would give the parents of smaller children a glimpse into the future.

i suppose that essentially what i am saying is that there is just so much fun and satisfaction in day-to-day life in a family that maybe it's time someone wrote about that, and shouted down the children-are-monsters people. some articles, perhaps, on the infuriating things, like bullies and outsiders and meanness, but always stressing the notion that things are fundamentally nice. i get many letters from women who feel that they are buried hopelessly under the endless problems of a family, and have found that just one humorous article has given them enough of a brief new glimpse so that they can dig in again and get the laundry done in half the time, or get through dinner one more night without screaming.

i admit it's a subject important to me. i'd like to know what you think.

Shirley Jackson

•   •   •

[To Geraldine and Leslie Jackson]

october 15 [1954]

dearest mother and pop,

it's been such a long time since i wrote, and i'm sorry. i've been feeling very tired and depressed for most of the summer—still working off my wild writing schedule last winter—and haven't had energy or spirit to write. things look a good deal better now, however, and i'm feeling more like getting to the typewriter.

life magazine decided that they wanted a new feature, a short humorous fiction piece; they were going to experiment with one issue and then decide whether it would work, and they asked me to do the first one. my agent, who is a great one for getting every nickel there is in such a deal, arranged that life should pay me two thousand dollars if they bought the story, and one thousand if they turned it down. i tried to make them agree to give me five hundred if i didn't write it at all, but they wouldn't go that far. anyway, they have the story, and can't make up their minds. the agent writes that they are afraid that the story may be too difficult for the average reader to understand. they asked if i would please write an additional paragraph making everything absolutely clear, which i did, and they are still worrying. we get the impression that changing the format of life is something like tearing down the new york skyline. in any case, once they opened the envelope they owed me a thousand bucks. also, if this should work out they may ask me to do more.

my crazy agent has also turned down a movie offer for bird's nest because it wasn't good enough. and she bounced a publishing company who wanted me to do a weekly newspaper feature column. every so often she calls and tells me about these things, and it's wonderful, because i get all the feeling of importance without having to do any work.

i believe laurie wrote you about your nice birthday present, and told you he dashed right out to the lumber yard—where he is a prized customer—to get plywood to make his train table. he has that big extra room, you know, and it is almost filled with the train setup. he takes carpentry shop in school, so the train table is quite well made. he also made barry a fine bookcase, which barry is very proud of, and he is working on some very important object in the barn which stanley and i are not permitted to see. this is the first year he has really liked school, and is doing much better than ever before. all three older children have started piano lessons, and seem to like it, although practicing is horrible. jannie is also in a drama class—her dearest desire—and once a week she goes off and, so far, paints scenery. sally has a dear friend, and they go back and forth to school together and tell each other the three words they have learned to read. it is so strange having all four of them gone.

i heard from my agent this morning that she had sold another story. it means i shall have to get to work; that was my last remaining unsold story; it went to mccalls, which has never bought anything before, but bernice says she is going to send them stuff regularly. i wonder if their recipes are better than the companion's?

i am reading at the college tomorrow night, selections from all my books. when i called stanley to tell him about the story sale, he said he would take me out to dinner to celebrate.

we are all very excited that you might be coming; i hope you will be able to. it would be so nice to see you, and laurie and i will beat pop at pingpong. we set our pingpong table up in the barn, and have been playing every day. at first stanley had to give me a fifteen point handicap, and now laurie and i can both beat him, but laurie can beat me. laurie had never played before, and it's amazing how fast he is. so pop will have to practice, or laurie will give <u>him</u> a handicap.

everyone sends lots of love. hope to see you very soon. love,

s.

•   •   •

[To Bernice Baumgarten]

November 18 [1954]

Dear Bernice,

I shall certainly try the piece House and Garden asks about, and I
have another half-finished story which I shall send soon. Mr. Whip-
ple, of Life, wrote me a very kind letter, apparently thinking that I
was terribly upset about their turning down the story, which of
course I was not, and saying he hoped I would keep them in mind
when next moved to do a similar article.

I am edging right now around a most delicate kind of story, which
I am afraid will turn out not well, partly because I would be writing
it out of a kind of nervous image-magic. We are in a kind of panic
up here; one of the music assistants at the college died of polio yesterday, after being sick for about four days. He taught classes, from
which students went to all parts of the college, including the nursery
school and practice teaching in the local schools. You can imagine
what is happening; the local paper of course gave great attention to
the whole business—day by day reports—and by this morning there
were only three children in the nursery school, instead of thirty, one
of them our valiant Barry. About fifty college students have fled.
What I was thinking about was a story on the spreading panic, like
the medieval plague; local shopkeepers do not yet hesitate to take
money from the hands of college faculty but it may very well come to
that. Do you think it is too touchy a subject?

I must also ask you for information regarding a play which I have
been doing, to be presented at the college. I am using the Salem
witchcraft material, although I will have to change all the names,
since I am not sticking to facts. The idea is that I write the play, a
faculty composer does the music, and the thing is produced by the
combined drama and dance departments. I'll send the manuscript to
you, of course, to deal with however you see fit, but what about the

music, which will be done specifically for the play? This is still in the future, of course—I've not quite finished the first act—but everyone is terribly serious about it, and it will be exciting if it works out the way it sounds now. How many tickets do you want for the opening night?

Best,

Shirley

•  •  •

[To Geraldine and Leslie Jackson]

december 21 [1954]

dearest mother and pop,

i know i owe you all kinds of apologies for not writing, and i can only excuse myself by saying that the last couple of months have been nothing but confusion and wildness. barry has not been out-doors since the week before his birthday. he caught a cold in the middle of november and he still has it, complete with wheezing. we were a little panicky at first, because there was a big polio scare at the college—two cases, one death, and students tearing off home in all directions. the kids at the nursery school had been indirectly exposed. the one good thing in all of it was that oliver ended up the school term with extra gamma globulin, and he says there is reason to be-lieve that g.g. injections will keep kids from catching cold. he is doing an experiment on barry and four other kids; if it works they should be cold-less for several months, and it may get barry through the winter more successfully than things look now.

all our cats vanished in the space of about a week, including my beloved old shax, which made me feel very unhappy. we decided that he was so old he just wandered off and died, which didn't cheer me much. the day we finally gave him up—when he hadn't been home for a week—a stray cat showed up, all black, very handsome, but only a kitten, obviously sent by shax as a substitute. he was starving and sick, so i took him to the vet, got him shot full of penicillin, and we kept him down cellar for a couple of days until he was well again. when we let him upstairs at last he marched past the whole family, straight to barry, and got onto barry's lap. we named him gato, and although he regards himself as barry's personal cat he has learned to like the rest of us. he's extremely intelligent, and has been a real blessing since barry's sickness. it is so nice to see barry working away with his cars and trains on the floor, and gato right there, or sitting in barry's lap purring while barry reads to him. when barry goes to bed and the cat is sure he is settled for the night he comes down and sleeps on the piano.

writing goes very badly, as i told you over the phone. thanks to a combination of a million things, partly barry and probably the kind of nervous tension i got involved in this summer, i haven't been able to do any writing at all. the witch book and the life story got done by a kind of dogged grinding out, and it took me two months to do the life story, when ordinarily i would have done it in a week. at that, they turned it down, but i got the half payment for it. bernice sold an old story to mccall's, and i got a whopper of a royalty check on savages, so we have been comparatively affluent without my doing any work at all. now, however, bernice is pestering me for a couple of new stories, some fool magazine wants an article, and here i sit. stanley says he is going to kill oliver for deciding that my jitters were due to overwork, because now i am all calm and collected again i still don't work, and he wants oliver to find something that he can diagnose as underwork. this letter is actually the first writing of any length i have done since midsummer so things may be looking up again.

it is maddening, too, because everything is so encouraging. bernice writes despairingly that she can sell anything she can get, and three or four publishers are very much interested in my doing a novel for them. also her hollywood agent is in a deal to sell bird's nest for a movie scenario, not on one of these big million-dollar things, but on speculation.

the witchcraft book is probably coming out in the spring. they like it very much. savages was translated into german and norwegian. i have a story in the bennett cerf humor anthology, and there is a woman in san francisco named elizabeth richmond who keeps writing me threatening to sue me for stealing her name in bird's nest. bernice won't let me answer her.

one of stanley's inspirations was singing lessons, which i start the first of the year. he has the idea that i must busy myself at interesting things, and not have any time idle to be depressed, so he has about three dozen brand new books lined up for me, lists of new things i am to decide about buying, and these darn singing lessons. the singing teacher at the college is an old friend and a real good teacher. but it will be a lot of fun and even if i don't come out singing i will enjoy it.

we will be thinking of all of you on christmas. lots and lots of love from all.

s.

. . .

[To Bernice Baumgarten]

January 29 [1955]

Dear Bernice,

Either Aunt Anna's* pink champagne, or talking to you, or mad carousing at the automat, has had an odd effect on my morale; these two stories are the product of the past week, and I have two more on hand to do. Whee.

I forgot to tell you that I had given up the story I wanted to do about the polio scare; it partook too much of my own dreary state at the time, and the material will fit much better into some other form, perhaps a scene in a novel.

* Stanley's aunt.

Obviously the sequel to Savages must be called On the Raising of Demons.

Best,

S.

•   •   •

[To Bernice Baumgarten]

February 21, 1955

Dear Bernice,

I hesitate about doing a piece for Vogue. Partly it's because what with one thing and another I haven't done the other one, on getting along with children, although I have pages of notes for it, and partly it's because I've never yet done anything for the editor but what she wanted it re-written and revised and changed and battered right into the ground, and the last time she asked if I'd mind throwing out all but the first paragraph and doing it over, I resolved never to tangle with her again. If you think better, however—and this was, of course, before I had your iron hand to defend me—I'll surely do it.

I am assuming, being a natural optimist, that the three stories you have, have all missed selling to the Companion or McCalls, and a plague on both their houses. I have the first vague notions of a new novel, and am anxious to get going on it, but I want to sell a couple of stories first.

The Michael Joseph Birds Nest is, I think, a lovely-looking book. I think the jacket is terribly funny. They left out the dedication to Stanley, and he is going to retaliate by adding the dedication to me to the other cuts in The Armed Vision; he is mournfully hacking his firstborn to pieces, putting in a page every time he takes out a paragraph; he will end up by taking out only the dedication.

Sally, the first day of her convalescence from flu, took up a Mother

Goose and discovered suddenly that instead of reciting the words she was following the text; we were electrified, downstairs, by a great triumphant cry of "I can read! I can read!" and without any more warning than that she set herself to reading every book in her bookcase; this morning she read us a paragraph from Birds Nest, remarking only that Mommy wrote pretty hard.

I believe I will be able to retire very soon now.

Best,

Shirley

•  •  •

[To Geraldine and Leslie Jackson]

march 7 [1955]

dearest mother and pop,

i can't imagine what you mean by our having cold weather; it's all of nine degrees this morning and only about eight inches of snow. you californians are superstitious about eastern winters, think it's cold all the time.

i nearly came part way out west to wave to you. the other morning i got a call from salt lake city, asking me to come out for two weeks this summer and teach a short story writing class at a writers conference. they paid all expenses, and five hundred dollars, and they pointed out sadly that of course they had no extra accommodations so i would have to leave my husband and children at home. for about an hour i was quite tempted at the idea of just going off all alone for two weeks, traveling by plane and visiting a city i didn't know, something i've never done before. stanley gave me some good pointers on teaching a class (like if your knees begin to shake sit down casually on the edge of the desk) and the children were all amazed. naturally when it really came down to going or not going i called the man

back and said no thanks. the next day i got invited—all expenses
again—to be on some panel quiz show on television in new york, an
offer which holds no temptations whatsoever. actually, since birds
nest was published i have made it a rule—officially on file at my
agents and my publishers—that i will involve myself in absolutely no
personal publicity under any circumstances, which includes everything from interviews and photographs to that cute biographical information ("she writes with a turkey feather dipped in rainwater")
everyone is so crazy about. i just refer everyone to who's who in
america, with great satisfaction.

the pocket edition of savages has come out; have you seen it? if
not, i can send you a copy. they are translating birds nest into french.
we couldn't get the danger program, but tom brockway saw it in
washington, and i found out that they took my poor harmless story
and put in a mad killer and a gun moll and a murder and a fight on a
racing train and a portable radio. i'm very glad i didn't see it. my
agent and i have just gotten the whole matter of re-writing settled
between us, because of this television program and the movie version
of birds nest; it came to a point where i either had to say no important changes in plot or character because i will defend my perfect
prose to the death, or simply say if you pay good money for it, it's
yours. neither the agent nor i felt any hesitation whatever, so i signed
the movie contracts.

we've been having a wild weekend. louis scher, the new york rare
book buyer, our great old friend, is here on one of his regular visits;
that means that he arrives saturday afternoon with quantities of good
corned beef from a new york delicatessen, presents for all children,
and a clean shirt, and from saturday afternoon until he leaves late
monday night we do nothing but play bridge, gin rummy, pingpong,
and eat. he is extremely popular with everyone up here, and everyone
wants to see him when he comes, so it means that we have three separate parties, one each night. saturday night was the social party, for
non-bridge-players, and everyone ended up playing pingpong, and
laurie stayed up until two in the morning beating everyone, very
pleased with himself at attending a real grown-up party. sunday
night was the night for serious bridge players, with two tables of

bridge which finally broke up at four this morning; tonight we have the non-serious bridge players, who will get sillier and sillier and finally all drive louis to the bus sometime around two. then stanley and i spend the rest of the week recovering, until stanley starts college again next week.

the kids are all well, sick of school and winter. laurie got the flu, very suddenly; then sally and jannie got it, but mildly, and barry got a slight cold, which was apparently from the same bug. laurie was out of school for two weeks, but the girls only missed a couple of days. then, after everyone else was all through, i got it, and spent two days in bed. the first morning the kids got my breakfast but it was so awful that after that i got out of bed and fixed my own toast and tea, and then the second evening stanley suggested that perhaps a little straight whisky might make me feel better, so i had some whisky and it nearly finished me off; i have never been so sick in my life. for about a week i couldn't stand the idea of taking a drink, and then one evening i was feeling fine and had a cocktail before dinner and by the end of dinner i had to go and lie down because i was deathly sick. i decided that since it was lent anyway i might just plan to give up drinking for a while, but stanley said it was all foolishness and imagination, so i tried it again, two nights ago; the feeleys were over and everyone laughed at me, so i took half of helen's drink, and couldn't get out of bed the next morning. so now i don't even dare have a glass of b and b after dinner, and when we play bridge, like last night, i drink ginger ale. it helps my bridge, and i feel fine the next day. stanley is not drinking either so we now have tea every afternoon. paul feeley says he is still shaking from the afternoon he wandered over for a drink and found me peacefully drinking tea, with a plate of homemade cookies, with the cat on my lap and stanley doing what paul swears was knitting, although he was actually untangling a string for barry.

jannie and laurie have been going to drama school, and had their big midyear performance last week. jannie was the star in her play, a princess, doing very well and looking perfectly beautiful in lipstick and a crown. laurie was the father in his play; he had gotten a special haircut to part his hair in the middle, and he wore a big black moustache which fell into his coffee cup in the approved manner, a cigar, and a derby hat which he absolutely adored; he is the biggest ham in the world.

sally is doing nothing but reading; i got her a few very easy books, and she went right through those, and is now reading fairly hard stuff. stanley says she reads as well as laurie, which is not as unjust as it sounds.

time to go to sleep. i got up this morning and saw the kids off to school, so stanley takes the afternoon shift. love from all of us.

s.

. . .

[To Geraldine and Leslie Jackson]

friday [April 1955]

dearest mother and pop,

since i have no car today it gives me time at last to sit down and write a letter. i have decided to be real bold and have the snow tires taken off, although it is only the end of april; we are having what is locally referred to as "spring" weather, which means cold, rain instead of snow, and mud.

we have been quite ambitious, had the lawn seeded and cleaned up, and gravel put down in the driveway. barry spent a wonderful day watching the dump truck bringing load after load of gravel, and then, best of all, they sent a road scraper to even the driveway, the driveway is supposed to get hard as a rock before summer. no more mud holes to get stuck in. and my raspberry bushes are actually getting a leaf here and there. stanley points out that sooner or later i will have to invent the trowel, since i cannot go on indefinitely gardening with a tablespoon. laurie planted a garden, mostly radishes and carrots, and he swears the radishes are coming up, although he is the only one who can see it. and we have one crocus. i have fallen into the hands of a lovely gentleman who comes around every two weeks or so with a beautiful catalogue showing pictures of marvelous flowering bushes and stately old trees, and every time he comes i fall for it and order something and so far nothing has come out looking like it does in the lovely catalogue, but i enjoy it and sooner or later something is going to grow, although probably not the grass seed, since half an hour after it was put on the entire pigeon population from our barn showed up for a great harvest banquet, and the kids and i, plus the dogs and cats, spent most of the day trying to herd pigeons off the lawn.

jannie spends all her allowance every week on books, and i have had to limit her to three books every second day from the library. she has read everything in the house except the psychology books. three afternoons a week she is engaged, with music lessons and drama classes and brownie scouts, and the other two afternoons after school she and carol* walk down to the library and apparently sit around and gossip with the librarian, because they stay all afternoon. as i keep pointing out to her, anyone who is too busy to make her own bed should really be too busy to pass the time of day with the librarian.

and now sally is begging to get a library card of her own; she is reading so amazingly that we can't keep up with her. her allowance isn't equal to buying books, so she spends her allowance on pencils and paper and writes her own books, and i have to buy the ones she reads. my agent has already offered to take sally on as a client, and i have no doubt but what she will publish—quite seriously—one of her books before long. last week was vacation, and sally had a fine time; she stayed up every night until eleven or so, reading and writing, and then slept till noon the next day, and flourished on the routine. all our children, as a matter of fact, like the kind of schedule stanley and i do, except they can do it; stanley had to teach the week of the kids' vacation, so every morning at eight o'clock stanley and i would have breakfast alone, and he would go off to school, and around ten or so the kids would begin to straggle down to the

---

* Carol Mackey's family lived nearby and she was one of Jannie's best friends.

kitchen. both sally and jannie are getting fine report cards and they are doing quite well in music lessons.

laurie, who still cannot read or write, turns out to be able to throw a pretty good curve; they have finally started a little league in this vicinity, taking in three small towns, and they have made up four teams, on one of which laurie is pitching; he is starting against south shaftsbury in the first game of a double header on memorial day. i had to get him a pair of official baseball shoes, with rubber spikes. he goes out to baseball practice at five, and then comes home around eight and makes his own dinner. aside from baseball, he is now interested in nothing but science, and is doing a regular series of chemical experiments in school, for extra credit, which he badly needs. he has been going to dances every friday night at the school, and taking a girl; the last dance i suggested that he invite three of his friends and their dates over for dinner and all go to the dance together, so he did, and i gave them a buffet supper which they ate on card tables in the living room; the girls were all very ladylike and the boys all had great trouble eating with ties and jackets on. laurie is still taking trumpet lessons, too, and expects to play in the school band next year.

jannie is going to camp this year, and laurie is not; laurie can't bear to leave the little league. jannie has been so anxious to go that we let her apply; i didn't want her to go, because i think she is too young—only nine—but stanley thought if she wanted to go that much she should be allowed to try it out.

i began singing lessons. the singing teacher here at the college, leslie chabay, a prominent giver-of-concerts and such, asked me if i would like to start taking lessons, and after stalling and sashaying around for a couple of months i finally went up for a lesson and loved it; i spent an hour and a half and thought it was about ten minutes. i go back the end of this week for another try at it.

later, it's now ten o'clock at night, stanley is out playing poker, the kids are asleep—all except laurie, off on a hay ride—and i can finish my letter.

stanley had a wonderful idea earlier this evening which has been charming me ever since; a new foreign car agency has opened in bennington, and he wants me to get one of these tiny foreign cars, keeping the station wagon for when the family goes, but using the tiny car for the million odds and ends of trips i make every day. he suggested that i could have a lot of fun with a fancy little car, find it easier driving and probably cheaper, and one story would just pay for it. i have been wanting to turn in the station wagon, because—this horrifies laurie, who is very prim—i am tired of the color. i want a pink one. laurie says he won't get into a pink one, but a pink one i intend to have. stanley says that since the car is entirely mine i can do as i please about color, but wouldn't i rather have something more modest, say a dark blue.

the companion bought a story just in time to pay the income tax, which i thought was nice of them. and they are talking of buying another, which is even nicer. no word on the great movie version of bird's nest; savages is turning up in translation all over the world, and i keep getting checks. stanley's armed vision is coming out this fall in an abridged edition as a knopf vintage book; stanley had to cut it by one-third, and it was just like getting barry's hair cut—howling and wailing and hanging on desperately. my publisher wrote me a lovely long letter, full of compliments and flattery; he had heard i was planning to find a new publisher and thought he had better get down to work; he had received a request from the university of california for my original manuscripts for the university archives, the university people pointed out that since i had been an undergraduate there and was always spoken of as one of their most illustrious alumna i might be interested in donating said manuscripts to my old alma mater. stanley and i decided they were thinking of helen hunt jackson, but i told them that the next time i cleaned my filing cabinet they were welcome to anything i found.

did i tell you that we had a new puppy? he was given to us about two months ago; his name is jack (or jackson); he is big and brown and will grow up to look exactly like our dog toby; he is silly and affectionate and fond of the children, just like toby; it's nice, too, to see barry and sally playing outdoors with two huge dogs guarding them, although heaven knows what would happen if any emergency came up—toby is well-known to be the biggest coward who ever lived. i think barry is actually better protected by his watchcat, gato, who never leaves him for a minute outdoors, and keeps an eye on him in-doors, too. the other night gato caught a mouse and took it up to barry's bed to share with barry, just as i was coming out of the shower with bare feet and nothing on but a bathrobe, and barry yell-ing to come get the mouse off his bed. what i did, of course, was run down the hall and into sally's room and slam the door and wait until stanley heard barry and came and made gato take the mouse—which was very lively—downstairs into the kitchen.

do you remember the fromm house, where we lived before we moved here? tonight just as i was making dinner, a woman knocked on the back door to say that she and her husband had just bought the house, and wondered if we could give them any advice about it, particularly about the electric pump, which was not working right. i told her what i could, and asked her how the house looked, and she said that the people who had rented it after us had left it in a terrible mess, and all the furniture just piled in the attic. i said i had always coveted some of the things in the house, and had actually been tempted to make off with the lovely little demitasse set and the elec-tric mixer and the good phonograph and she said she wondered what had happened; none of those things were in the house now. appar-ently the people who rented the house furnished after us just simply walked off with everything good, and left only the big furniture they probably couldn't carry. i'm really sorry i didn't take that demitasse set. fromm, a psychoanalyst, left all his files and notebooks lying around and we packed them all (not reading them; i'm sorry now) into one big filing cabinet and tied it up and put it into the attic; it is still there and apparently goes with the rest of the contents of the house. he had a number of famous patients, including a big holly-wood trade for a while, and i imagine all their case histories are still sitting up there in that attic. i'm sure the lady would give it to me if i asked her. think of the plots for novels.

stanley must have won thousands of dollars by now, so i think i will go to bed and read a mystery story.

lots and lots of love to all, from all of us.

s.

. . .

[To Bernice Baumgarten]

May 24 [1955]

Dear Bernice,

I am making little tentative stabs at getting some work done. I have
been thinking about that story, the Mice one; if another magazine or
so turns it down, I think I should try cutting the middle section
down. But actually I'm doubtful whether the middle can be cut without losing the sense of the story. I'll grit my teeth and read it, anyway.

Laurie is pitching the opening game of our new Little League
next week. If I don't get a story out of it I shall at least get a movie;
Laurie insists that I get three film magazines for the movie camera
and photograph the whole game. if only Laurie's curve is breaking
right we will be okay.

These are tense times; Howard Nemerov and I are racing; he is on
page six of a new novel; I have gone back to page one again. His
typewriter is broken, though.

Best,

Shirley

P.S. later. I have been talking to Mel Dinelli,* who was very excited
about the movie script of Bird's Nest; he says he is sending me a
rough draft to read, and wants to come up and talk about it, although
he suspects I may not want to see him after I've read it. He was full
of news items about people in Hollywood and New York who are, he
thinks, interested in the script, which I think is wonderful.

He said he was very fond of all my books, particularly "Life Among
the Natives," and just where <u>was</u> Vermont, and how did one reach it by

---

* Mel Dinelli was a screenwriter and writer, specializing in the suspense genre.

plane? I had to tell him that not only did we have no plane service, but there was no train, although we do have a bus of sorts. I suppose in Hollywood if there's no train they take a helicopter.

S.

. . .

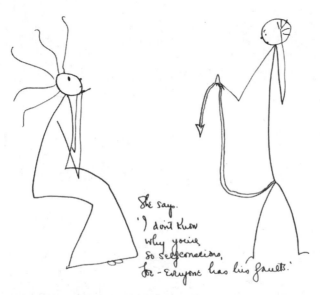

"She says 'I don't know why you're so self-conscious, for— everyone has his faults.'"

[To Mel Dinelli]

May 31, 1955

Dear Mr. Dinelli,

Many thanks for letting me see the dramatization of <u>Bird's Nest</u>. I found it exciting to read; characters I had always thought of as lying down flat on a page surprised me by standing up and walking around. It's impossible to describe the feeling of seeing this change from one medium into another. I realize, however, after reading the manuscript, that I could be of absolutely no use to you discussing it, since the translation is completely mystifying to me. I did like it, though, very much.

Sorry not to have met you, in any case. I hope that at some future time communication between Vermont and New York may be enough improved to enable us to get together. Perhaps jet transport through Schenectady?

Cordially,

Shirley Jackson

•   •   •

[To Geraldine and Leslie Jackson]

june 12 [1955]

dearest mother and pop,

just a short letter to say thanks for the beautiful wallet and pocket-book. and stanley wants me to add particular thanks for the fortune he found in his. he is delighted to have it, and most grateful. yesterday was his birthday so it was well timed, and what with the new cool shirt laurie picked out for him he will be the flashiest teacher on campus.

in honor of his birthday stanley went off the wagon; his school year is over in two weeks, so he figures he is entitled to a few drinks. we had some people over to play bridge last night and someone brought him a bottle of scotch, of which he consumed a large part. he won't get up this morning.

i don't know if you heard or read about bird's nest; m.g.m. bought it for production this august. stanley read the item in the

new york times one morning and came yelling out of the bathroom
to tell me about it, so i called my agent and she was amused, since
the official notice from hollywood had only just reached her, and
the sale was not at all official. it seems to be going through, however, only unfortunately no one is going to get much money. someone named eleanor parker will star in it; laurie seems to know who
that is, and assures me that the movie will win all kinds of oscars.
talk around the grocery has established that there used to be a
family of parkers in south shaftsbury and one of the boys moved
out west and raised a family, so eleanor is clearly almost a local
girl.

   i do not plan to see it, myself, but my agent proposes that they
have the grand premiere at the general stark theatre in bennington, if
they can get the bats out of the lobby.

   everyone around here was very excited for about a day, and then of
course lost interest when it turned out that no one was going to have
to fly to hollywood and no movie stars were going to be hanging
around upper main street in north bennington. stanley's students
treat me with a new note of respect, however. do you remember miriam marx, groucho's daughter, an old friend of mine? she is coming
up this weekend with her husband, and i hope to get information
from her about how they go about making movies and how to avoid
getting my name in the credits; i have read the screen play and it
sounds a little like ma and pa kettle. or abbott and costello meet a
multiple personality.

   everyone here is fine, weather warm, children lazy now that school
is out. stanley and barry have to go to school for two weeks more, but
barry likes it and stanley has no choice. laurie is banking about ten
dollars a week from his lawn mowing, although he says he is mighty
sick of grass.

                        love,


                        s.


·   ·   ·

[To Geraldine and Leslie Jackson]

wednesday [July 1955]

dearest mother and pop,

got pop's letter yesterday, and it was reassuring; i was a little worried, talking to you on the phone. pop's letter, though, makes everything seem fine, and your trip to south america sounds wonderful.

stanley finally got his students graduated, after three weeks of wild confusion. it happens every year, and we're never prepared for it; he gets stuck with late papers and last minute reports, and for the last three weeks of school it has become traditional for each student house, each organization, each department to give a separate party, so that—since you can't go to some and not others without being offensive—there is a cocktail party every afternoon and at least two parties every evening, usually ending in informal gatherings at faculty houses. none of the students seem to need any sleep, either. or any food. i found that a couple of times i had to gather up two or three of stanley's seniors and bring them down here and fill them full of scrambled eggs and black coffee. there were the usual number of seniors who ended up in the goldfish pond on campus in their best summer dresses. then the last two days everyone irons their dresses and finds their shoes and washes their faces and takes three aspirin and the parents arrive, and sit around on the lawn admiring the college and trying to get the real truth about their daughters out of the faculty.

after such a wild time it is wonderful to be free again. stanley put his one good suit away in the closet to stay until september, and there are no more white shirts in the laundry and we go swimming every day. the kids are having a wonderful time. after our long wet winter it's good to see the kids getting brown again. i got a terrific sunburn, of course, which is almost gone now. we do a lot of cooking and eating outdoors, and the kids make their own breakfasts and lunches, usually finishing breakfast before i'm up in the morning.

stanley went to new york last week, because the kids gave him
tickets to the brooklyn baseball game for father's day, and he took
jannie with him. jannie of course loves going shopping and to movies, which is apparently all she did. while they were gone laurie ran
the house, cooking dinners outdoors and seeing that the coffee was
hot by the time i got downstairs, and we spent our days playing miniature golf. after laurie had done the housework he usually went off
swimming at the lake with his friends, so sally and barry and i just
got into the wading pool and stayed there. i did some writing, not
very enthusiastically.

laurie is really enjoying himself this summer in the little league,
which has been started here. he is in it for this one summer, and will
be too old next year, so he's making the most of it. it has turned out,
coming as something of a shock to his cynical mother and father,
that he is a natural pitcher, and he has become something of a sensation locally. his team, the braves, is in first place. laurie's first full
game was a one-hit shutout, and his latest game, last monday, set a
record for local little leagues, since he was only two walks away from
a perfect game: of twenty batters in six innings, he walked two, got
two out with infield flies, and struck out sixteen. he also hit a double
and a triple. he got a tremendous write-up in the local paper. i took
him down to the barber shop yesterday and there were half a dozen
men around waiting, and all the conversation was about laurie's
pitching. stanley says that people point him out as laurie hyman's father. since we have been in despair all these years because he could
hardly read and write, it's nice to discover that he does have some
kind of talent.

our lives have been completely changed by this baseball, by the
way. the games are twice a week, one evening at six-thirty and sunday afternoon at three; it's amazing how the whole town, only a
thousand people, has reacted to the little league. everyone turns out
for the games, particularly since everyone has a boy on one team or
another, and feelings run pretty high in the bleachers. they built a
beautiful little field in about a week with volunteer labor. it's also
done what nothing else so far has been able to do completely,
which is finally break up the old feud between the college and the

town; some few college people, like us, who live in the town and know everyone, got along fine, but most of the college people were distant and did their shopping in bennington and never came near north bennington. now, though, the college people have started coming down for the games and getting to find their way around north bennington. we've been yelling for a long time about how the college people ought to come down off the hill and meet the townspeople.

peg wohnus and i go to all the games and sit in the bleachers behind home plate with mrs haynes, whose husband manages the braves and whose two boys are on the team, and stanley and fred wohnus keep far away from us and try to pretend they don't know us, because we make so much noise.* mrs haynes can't remember to call her younger boy rickey, and she calls him sweetheart, which is what she calls him at home, and when he comes to bat and she says "come on sweetheart" he turns pink and glares at her and once he came over and said "mother, <u>please</u>," and she tried to remember but in a minute she was calling him sweetheart again. stanley is concerned because when laurie is not pitching he plays second base and he stands too far out in the outfield and most of the time he is telling laurie to come in, come in. i have decided that if i sit directly in back of the umpire while laurie is pitching i can yell "no, you're blind, you're blind," whenever he calls the pitch wrong. the field is only two blocks from our house, so sally and jannie wander over whenever they please and come home if they get tired; they spend all their money at the refreshment stand and then go up on top of the hill and play tag with their friends. by a unanimous vote of the whole braves team, barry got elected mascot, and stanley's mother sent him a baseball suit saying braves, and now he sits in the dugout, very proud of himself.

well. if the braves stay in first place and brooklyn wins the pennant it will have been a very successful baseball season. the little league

---

* Fred and Peg Wohnus were dear family friends, and their son Willie was one of Laurie's best friends. Fred taught chemistry at the college and Peg was a pathologist at the local hospital. Mr. and Mrs. Haynes were town residents.

dodgers are the big threat for the braves, and poor stanley is hope-lessly confused.

   lots of love to you both, and to barry and marylou and butch.

love,

s.

i forgot to tell you about laurie's carpentry; it turns out he has two tal-ents. he has been taking shop in school this year and got very much in-terested, so stanley gave him all the tools around the house, and i opened a charge account at the lumber yard. whenever we want a bookcase or a shelf it is very handy to have laurie around. when stanley was out of town last week he decided to make a surprise for stanley. by the time stanley came home there was a handsome pine-panelled bar in the living room, beautifully made and finished, and solid.

   laurie reminds me very much of barry—my brother, i mean—sometimes, and i think there's a strong resemblance right now. maybe it's just because i always remember barry in a dirty t-shirt.

   got to go make dinner.

love,

s.

•   •   •

[To Geraldine and Leslie Jackson]

august 16 [1955]

dearest mother and pop,

my big problem is that, having signed a contract for a sequel to sav-ages, due next march, i now have to write it. it is to be called raising demons. they gave me an advance of five thousand of which half has been paid and the rest is to be paid "upon demand of the author," the notion that there is twenty-five hundred bucks sitting in the farrar straus offices that i can get just by hollering is almost too much for me. every time i run out of grocery money i get to thinking about it. i've been doing some stories, thinking now that if they don't sell they will at least go into the book; nothing has sold this summer, at least partly because it has been so hot and dry in new york; all my agent really wanted was rain, not stories. however, now they have had the tail end of two hurricanes, so new york is flooded and much cooler, and maybe the fiction editors will gather strength enough to get back to work.

jannie's letters tend to be two lines long and say "i went swimming" or "i had to write this to get in to dinner" or "please send me . . ." but she seems to be enjoying herself. she did remark that she had learned to eat beets, so her summer hasn't been wasted. she comes home next wednesday, and there are two surprises waiting for her. one of them is her room, which we have done over; she had a little room next to the playroom, and we cleared out the playroom and made it into a study for her, with her desk and a bookcase laurie made; she has been asking for more space and it is a very pretty suite now.

the other surprise is as much of a surprise to the rest of us, actually. the day we drove jannie to camp my car reached fifteen thousand miles, we had finished paying for it, and it was a little over two years old and stanley said no, certainly not, we could not get another one. so now i have a magnificent light blue brand new station wagon with a dashboard that looks like an airplane and all shiny and glittering. it just came yesterday and i am still trying to learn how to drive it.

sally and barry have been having a fine time while jannie is gone. sally suddenly discovered the oz books, and for the past few weeks has stayed up reading all night and has slept all day during the heat, which i suppose is as good a way to spend a vacation as any; she gets up in the early afternoon in time to have some fruit and go swimming. our friend bookhunter louis has been searching out books for jannie, which he sends in big batches; he finds them second-hand

and buys them for a nickel apiece, and it is such a pleasure for jannie
to get a big box of books. now sally is getting oz books, which are a
good deal rarer and harder to find, and there are now only two which
louis hasn't found for her; when he gets those she will have the oz
books complete.

louis got stanley in trouble, though; he was visiting here a couple
of weeks ago (one of the few weekend guests i could stand having
every week); and we took him to one of laurie's little league games,
when laurie was pitching. these games have gotten pretty exciting,
and we go to all of them; laurie's team won the first half of the season, and for the second half is rock bottom. his pitching was good
enough, but not the wonderful things he was doing with no-hit
games the first half of the season. at any rate, he hit a grand-slam
home run, the third over-the-fence home run of our little league, and
the first grand-slam. they got the ball back, and it will go into their
hall of fame, along with laurie's no-hit game ball. anyway we came
home from the game and laurie was sad about losing but pleased
about his home run, and louis remarked that such a fine hit ought to
be commemorated, and handed him ten dollars. laurie cheered up
considerably and then—as he does after every game—called stanley's
father to give him an account of it. when he told stanley's father
about the home run and the ten dollars the old man said he wasn't
going to be outdone by louis, and he'd add another ten and stanley
would be a piker if he didn't make it thirty. so laurie made thirty dollars and stanley was out twenty because he had to pay out his father's
ten. then he tried to borrow it back from laurie and couldn't, because
laurie had it all figured for lumber for his house. so stanley is broke
and laurie's house is nearly finished. besides lumber he bought two
windows and a door and a stack of shingles and tar paper for the
roof, which took care of his thirty dollars. now stanley is trying to get
a mortgage on the house; if he can't do that, he is going to sell laurie
the land it's on.

the house has been a whole summer's project for laurie and his
friend robert. robert's father is a carpenter, and both boys love carpentry, so they set out this summer to build themselves a house. they
earned all the money for the lumber themselves, robert with a paper

route and laurie cutting lawns. the house is beautifully built, solid and neat, with two windows and a door.

right now they are also excited about the idea of another dance in our barn this friday night; their committee has been at work with mops and brooms and we have set up our chaperone system again— five people here playing bridge, so that one is always free to step out to the barn every few minutes. there are twenty kids coming.

once jannie comes back school will be starting soon. stanley is working on class notes already. every time i say school shoes to stanley he turns pale. laurie will be in eighth grade, and expects to be in the school band with his trumpet. jannie will be a girl scout, sally will be a brownie scout, and a year from now barry will be in kindergarten and will have to walk to school with the other kids. one more year of taxi service and then i am free.

must go make lunch. since it's raining everyone wants something hot. bah. have a lovely trip, lots and lots of love from all of us.

s.

•  •  •

[To Bernice Baumgarten]

September 13 [1955]

Dear Bernice,

You talked me into it; I sat down last night and wrote this, typed it this morning, and here it is. So I will correct the witchcraft book and mail that tomorrow. The rest of the week I shall spend reading Dickens.

I told all the children to go out and find plots for me.

Best,

Shirley

. . .

[To Geraldine and Leslie Jackson]

wednesday [October 1955]

dearest mother and pop,

i guess the reason i always think i have written you is because i write the same material in stories; if i sent you the first drafts of all my stories you would have twice as many letters but i guess not as much true news. actually i have been working at the typewriter steadily, doing all kinds of things.

i have been working mostly on the witchcraft book; they send all those books to a historian for checking, and then back to the author for revision. the historian was very nice about the witches, since of course much of the stuff is hearsay and reported in half a dozen different manners. the historian was very upset over one paragraph in the book discussing the estimated numbers of demons working for the devil; i had two figures, both in the billions, and when the historian questioned them i could refer him to an ancient pamphlet in french, which i have naturally not read but didn't say so. of course the way to count the demons is to multiply the great pythagorean number by 666. that ought to hold bennett cerf for a while, i should think. the book was always scheduled for spring 1956, and they seem to be getting moving on it.

i am also working away at the sequel to savages, which is due march first, not that anyone thinks it will be done by then. and a new story for life magazine, a christmas story which it is very hard to do in october. and revising an old story for harper's. i got an unexpected check for five hundred dollars from the people who have the option on bird's nest for the movies; apparently they are keeping it for a while longer. i don't seriously think they will ever do anything with it, but as long as they keep sending me checks i am perfectly satisfied. also, i got a letter from someone named jerry wald at columbia pictures, a very respectful letter about how many distinguished writers tended to look down upon the cinema, but actually it was surprising how tenderly and thoughtfully the moving picture organizations dealt with really great literature; as a matter of fact, if i had any old manuscripts, even a narrative poem, he would be very pleased to consider them for movie production. since i happen to have a long narrative poem on the landing of the pilgrims which i wrote in high school, i suggested to my agent that she send it along to mr. wald, but i haven't heard any more about it. i want to keep the letter and frame it, because no one has ever written me such a respectful letter before. maybe hollywood is the place for us distinguished writers.

stanley is very busy at the college; he is acting head of the literature department this semester which means a lot of odds and ends of business. he is learning greek, too, because he always wanted to and now finds that he prefers to stagger through a greek play in the original and do his own translating for class. he is learning greek and jannie is learning to ride a bike and they go about it the same way, i think. one or the other of them is always complaining that it's too hard, it's impossible, no one could ever learn this. i'm so glad i don't have to learn anything.

stanley and laurie went down to new york for three of the world series games; they saw the three in ebbetts field which brooklyn won, and then came home to see the fine ending on television. i'm just as glad they got out of brooklyn before the end of the series; stanley's father said it wasn't safe to go out on the streets that week. they went to see pajama game, which laurie loved.

jannie is taking dancing lessons, this time tap dancing, with a pair of tap shoes she dearly loves. it looks as though she will have to get glasses for reading and schoolwork. she was unhappy until i told her we would send to new york for the fanciest, most jeweled, brightest pair of glasses we could find.

sally keeps on being a little crazy girl, as i told you, and spends her time reading, drawing, and sleeping. she is perfectly healthy and lively, but like a cricket. she is still reading anything she can get her hands on, and she and jannie are working through the entire stock of two libraries, north bennington and bennington.

barry will be writing you a letter one of these days; sally has taught him to make letters clearly and he can now copy half a dozen words so they can be read. he likes to copy messages on the kitchen blackboard, so that we come in and find a message, for instance, to call someone written in a strange straggling writing and barry swears that he answered the phone and took the message. he is very wise and quiet.

the predictions are for a heavy winter . . . maybe pop is right and we should live in california.

lots and lots of love to you both from all of us. laurie and i can play a duet, me on the piano and laurie on the trumpet. when you get here pop can make it a trio.

lots of love,

s.

•  •  •

[To Bernice Baumgarten]

January 2, 1956

Dear Bernice,

I am embarrassed to confess that before I could start this letter I had to blow an inch of dust off the typewriter. Most of the Christmas tinsel is off the floor, so perhaps things will get to be a little more simple in a day or so.

I confess I was a little saddened by Life's decision on the story, but hope that maybe they will give me a third chance; if I ran my household budget the way they run theirs Stanley would be cross, I think.

Through a series of necromantic deals with a series of British sorcerers Stanley got me a magic ring which has inspired a good deal of speculation around this house; I have been through all my magic books and can identify it only as a talisman controlling the liberal sciences and probably a demon named Gamygyn, who appears in the form of a donkey and can converse with the spirits of the drowned. Sally, who regards herself as an authority, says I may make three wishes a day on the ring, but I was scared, so she and Barry borrowed the ring and wished for a color television set. I am curious to know how old liberal-science Gamygyn copes with color television.

We got Laurie a trumpet for Christmas, not realizing that his friend Willie was getting a set of snare drums and his friend Ricky a clarinet. They call themselves the Sour Note Trio, which is perfectly accurate, and practice in our living room. I have been spending a lot of time out, just driving around and around in the car.

Now that the year has started itself off again, we can hit Farrar Straus and Cudahy for all that money waiting there. Can you ask them?

If Gamygyn produces the television set I am going to put him to work on the treasures of the earth, but until then I expect we will have to depend on the demon Straus. The manuscript may very well be ready by March 1.

I will honest get right to work. Barry is home from nursery school until March and the Sour Note Trio practices every afternoon, so I will either move my typewriter into the barn or find a little time in the late evening.

Best,

Shirley

•  •  •

[To Bernice Baumgarten]

February 21 [1956]

Dear Bernice,

With my well-known gift for making a damn fool of myself I have managed to involve myself once more in a mishmash. Are you ac-

quainted with a Vermont farmer named Tommy Foster? He lives in
Bennington, his wife teaches at the college, and Tommy himself, a
chicken-farmer and bird-watcher, has some semi-official connection
with Farrar and Straus. Many years ago when I had just finished
Road Through the Wall, he got in touch with Roger and suggested
they read it, and suggested to me that I have my then agent send it
to F and S, which she did and they took it and Tommy thus regards
himself as my literary discoverer although my own comparison,
which regards taxi drivers and brothels, Tommy views with Vermont
reserve.

I was taking tea and lemon puff cookies with Tommy's wife a
week ago, and Tommy joining us was talking about Demons, and remarked that in his official capacity he was much disturbed at rumors
that I was leaving F and S, and I told him that in his official capacity
as a friend of ours for the past eleven years I would tell him the main
reasons I wanted to leave—advertising, millions of petty irritations
like not knowing my correct address, and, primarily, the idea that I
knew no one there, had never done business with anyone but John,
and felt that my connection with them was largely non-professional,
so that my entire business association was on the level of fond little
notes from John and Margaret, with news of the family, and boxes of
licorice and books sent to the kids. I believe I have only seen Roger
three times in my life, not that I would regard that as a major catas-
trophe. it actually boils down to the feeling that so long as I am
going to call myself a professional writer I would rather not publish
in the general atmosphere of an indulgent old uncle who pats me on
the head.

So I told Tommy this, under the impression that I was having tea
with him and his wife. When I was leaving his house he said he
wanted to tell Roger and I said I would rather he didn't, and he said
Roger would want to know and I said it was silly, since all it would
do was hurt John's feelings, something I had been avoiding doing for
a number of years, and if I had ever thought Roger could do anything about it I would tell him myself, and Tommy said it was his job
to let Roger know things like this; if "his writers" were "dissatisfied"
Roger would want to know it. So I finally said I didn't care; I had

done enough general whining about this to suppose that Roger knew anyway.

I'm writing you about it because I don't actually know what Tommy finally said to Roger, except that Tommy called me yesterday to say that he Had Seen Roger and It Was Being Taken Care Of and Roger said I Was Not To Worry About It Any More. They are sending an editor up here care of Tommy, someone named Bad Sir Brian Botany, and it gives me some comfort to reflect that the Fosters are going to have to give a local party for him, Tommy as a chicken-farmer preferring to go to bed at nine-thirty. Although I would not for anything in the world cast any reflections upon the noble profession of chicken-farming, it does seem to be incompatible with politics. I did not even know that Tommy had discovered me, and I certainly did not know that he regarded his connection with F and S as official. And of course I would not have babbled so if I had suspected that he would regard it as his duty to tell Roger.

I don't suppose it's important, but I am always talking like a fool and then finding out that I have started something. So I thought I had better let you know about it. At least, I know enough to keep my mouth shut in New York, but wouldn't you think I'd be safe drinking tea on the Old Farm Road in Vermont?

Best,

Shirley

•  •  •

[To Bernice Baumgarten]

March 2 [1956]

Dear Bernice,

Enclosed is another story. I am gradually taking all my notes and putting them together to use for the book and in several cases, like this, end up with a finished story, so I figure the most sensible thing to do is send it along to you.

I have finished the second section of the book, but I don't like parts of it and intend to change it all over again. Shall I write Roger about not having the book until, say, the end of March? I have just about enough material for the third and fourth sections, but it will take some time to type and put them together sensibly.

One more thing. A good friend of mine up here* edits the Bennington Alumni Quarterly, a staid and altogether dull magazine which runs articles called "Suppose You Send Us Money," and "Support Your College" and she is most anxious to improve the general tone by having a story by me, to be called, perhaps, "The Life of a Faculty Wife," and of a character to lower the general stuffy tone of the magazine. The story is to be short, and she will illustrate it; I wanted some such material for my book, so I told her I'd do it. I did not think you would have any objections and I am more anxious to do it because Helen sews beautifully, and has guaranteed instead of payment to do all my fancy sewing (like the braid to go down the sides of Laurie's band uniform pants, and the wings on Sally's fairy dress, and so on) in exchange. I suggest that for your ten percent, by the way, you send up a basket of mending. Will there be any difficulty about using the article in the book?

Helen and I made rough plans for the story one evening, and it turned out there is a certain amount of bitterness in the heart of the faculty wife. Her husband and Stanley feel that this story must be very carefully censored, and that I must not use the—probably apocryphal—incident of the freshman who sneaked into their house one dawn and left a basket of fresh strawberries beside Paul's pillow.

I have been playing Authors with my girls every evening, to keep Sally and me in a literary mood. I want to compile a modern deck; Truman Capote <u>couldn't</u> be any funnier looking than John Greenleaf Whittier.

Best,

Shirley

* Helen Feeley.

. . .

[To Bernice Baumgarten]

March 22 [1956]

Dear Bernice,

The poor man got off the train right into the arms of Tommy Foster, who had—by the time they traveled from Albany to Bennington—initiated him thoroughly into the mysteries of banding birds. Tommy then abandoned him, without warning, on our doorstep, inadequately shod. I gave him half a dozen cups of nice hot tea and got the roses back into his cheeks, but I do not believe he will ever come to Vermont again. That was yesterday; today he spent the afternoon taking cocktails with the Literature Department of Bennington College and Dorothy Canfield Fisher, Tommy's other literary fad. Mrs. Fisher patted me on the arm, the way she always does, asked me what I was studying at the college this year, and left me with the admonition that Hard Work Accomplishes Many Things. Martinis, they had, but Tommy is of the put-enough-ice-in-and-it-will-go-around-twice school.

By a rare supernatural timing, I was on the next-to-the-last page of Demons, sitting here typing like a writer, when Mr. Giroux arrived. I finished it last night, and have only now to correct and change a few items; I have promised to have it in the mail next week. We spent most of our time trying to decide whether Roger has a yacht of his own or just belongs to a yacht-pool.

We both thought he was delightful, and are looking forward to seeing him again. He must be a very diplomatic man; he made me feel very set up at the notion of having an Editor, something I have never had before. Is he the one who changes all my "likes" to "As"? He talks of publishing the book in January, in hopes that the Christmas story will sell; but will no doubt discuss that with you. We spent quite a while praising you to each other, and I told him how you would not let me run away to Italy with Franchot Tone.

Best,

S.

.   .   .

[To Bernice Baumgarten]

April 2 [1956]

Dear Bernice,

Here is the baby, all fixed up and put together again. It is late by three days because my mother and father, whom we have not seen for two years, spent a week with us, and Pop helped with the corrections and Mother kept asking if it wasn't bad for my eyes, all this careful reading, and did the publishers really <u>care</u> if there were mistakes? Didn't they have people who did that kind of thing? And why did I let Stanley make all those changes? It is my book, isn't it? And are they paying you lots of money for it, dear?

I have two new plots. First, I want to do some stories <u>not</u> about kids; would anybody want them, do you think? The kind I used to write before I hit this lode, which I think is pretty well worked out now. Or has my name gotten itself so identified with this family stuff that a new kind of story would flop? I am all excited about doing a new book, a nasty little novel full of mean people who hate each other, although that may just be a reaction to the sweetness and light of Demons, and the new book might just have a silver lining; I could even let someone get married at the end, if that counts as a silver lining.

Anyway, I'm full of notes and ideas, and want to start right away.

And Mr. Giroux seemed so pleasant and nice that I suppose I would be foolish to look for another publisher, as I believe you always predicted, unless Roger is skimpy again on Demons. What is the biggest advance that yacht-owning pirate ever gave to any writer in his life? Because I want to top it by fifty cents.

Best,

Shirley

•  •  •

[To Bernice Baumgarten]

April 12 [1956]

Dear Bernice,

The first section of the new novel is finished, about forty pages. It looks very odd. Stanley likes it, but he is calling me Ivy Compton Jackson, which is I suppose as good a name as any. (Sample: "... I used to meet Miss Ogilvie coming out of his room." "Good heavens," said Miss Ogilvie, pale, "<u>that</u> could not be what she means by scandal.") I wrote a story which I fondly believed was some different from the family pieces, but it turns out to be in the same style, except that I have largely left out the children. I will keep trying.

I have been asked to read to the Creative Writing class at the college. They asked if I would bring something unfinished so the discussion could center around "putting a story into shape for publication." I went through my desk and found such a wealth of unfinished material I am embarrassed. So after the Creative Writing class gets some of them into shape for publication you can expect a great mass of stories. Stanley wants me to take them my novel and see if they can figure out an ending for it. I have been reading the Bible trying to find an inscription for a sundial; the book is tentatively called "The Sundial" and I think when I find a suitable inscription I will know what the book is about.

Best,

Shirley

# FIVE

. . .

## Writing Is Therapy: 1956–1959

The novel is getting sadder. I suppose it's because of a general melancholy, but a general air of disaster is slowly settling over Hill House. It's always such a strange feeling— I <u>know</u> something's going to happen, and those poor people in the book don't; they just go blithely on their ways.

—To Bernice Baumgarten, September 9, 1958

[To Geraldine and Leslie Jackson]

dearest mother and pop,

i figure you must be coming home along about now, and would like
to have this letter waiting for you. we thought of you on mothers day,
but it seemed pointless, somehow, to try to send flowers to south
america.

we took the whole family to new york for nearly a week, and had a
wonderful time. i drove down, and we went slowly, going down the
west side highway twenty miles an hour so the kids could see the
queen elizabeth, which was docked there, and taxi drivers yelling at
me from all directions. we stayed in the st. george hotel, across the
street from stanley's parents. laurie and jannie went to the theatre
twice, and jannie, who had not been to the theatre before, was as enthusiastic as laurie. now we have two theatre lunatics in the family.

stanley and i decided that laurie ought to hear some real jazz, so we
took him to four night clubs. we went to the metropole, which he
loved, because it was loud and noisy and had two alternating bands,
and then to jimmy ryan's which is small and very fancy, and where laurie went up and talked to the trumpet player, and would have been
perfectly happy to stay there all night, but we went on to nick's where
laurie asked if we could please sit near the band, so the manager put us
at the front table right under the band. stanley had one elbow on the
stage and kept having to duck his head because he was right under
the trombone and laurie was delighted, because he was about two feet
away from the trumpet player and presumably able to watch his

fingering. when they stopped playing stanley and i were both limp, but laurie was applauding wildly. we finished off at eddie condon's where at one in the morning we looked at laurie and he was sound asleep sitting up at the table, but we nearly had to drag him out to get him home. he kept asking to stay for just one more number.

those poor fellows are still trying to sell birdsnest to the movies. bridey murphy* has somehow merged in the movie producers' minds with multiple personality, so there are several movies cooking named things like "I led a secret life in 1712!" and "my multiple girl" and stark thinks he can somehow get birdsnest in under the line. he has renewed his option again. i cannot understand that man's optimism, but am not going to argue.

must stop. no more paper, no more time. lots of love from everyone, and write soon.

s.

. . .

[To Bernice Baumgarten]

June 12 [1956]

Dear Bernice,

My inability to communicate by telephone has clearly cost us several days; is there any way we can get an advance—in some haste—of five hundred or a thousand dollars? The State of Vermont without warning picked up the federal tax bill we owed and paid and announced that we consequently owed a whopping state tax, too.

The General Stark would be ideal for Lizzie's premiere; there is a

* Under hypnosis in 1952 in Colorado, Virginia Tighe "became" Bridey Murphy, a nineteenth-century Irish woman, and researchers apparently concluded it was the result of cryptomnesia. The case caused an international stir when it was published in a series of articles in 1954 in *The Denver Post*.

nest of bats in the outer lobby and these warm summer nights when they leave the doors open the bats going back and forth across the screen give an odd three-dimensional effect. I will personally see to it that they put towels in the ladies' room for the occasion.

Best,

Shirley

"The Dissociation of a Personality," by Morton Prince (credited in a footnote somewhere in Bird's Nest) is a real book by a real doctor about a real case. I used it as a foundation, although I strayed pretty far. There is a theory that Joyce wrote a good deal about it in Finnegans Wake, although of course how could you tell.

•    •    •

[To Bernice Baumgarten]

June 27 [1956]

Dear Bernice,

This is the last week of college and we have, since last Friday, been to fourteen parties. From five every afternoon until five every morning we are in the clutches of students and bourbon. They drop in at three in the morning, tearful and sentimental. It is very difficult to come home from a party and find six students sitting in the living room playing the piano and singing. This happens every year and every year we are prepared for it and every year it gets worse. At four o'clock every morning they start talking about the meaning of life and was education worth it. Last night we ran out of food on about the fourth visitation and I made everyone grate potatoes so I could make potato latkes and all of a sudden I was standing there by the stove making potato latkes and I thought what am I doing at twenty minutes after three in the morning standing here making potato latkes.

This is also the time of year when a certain type student asks me very confidentially if Stanley and I are really happily married. With a light in her eye. I usually pat them on the hand when I answer them. Gently, of course.

Tomorrow the parents start coming which means instead of bourbon we will drink a kind of gin punch most of the time and bourbon later after the parents have gone to bed. The fathers will ask Stanley if he has been taking good care of their little girls and the mothers will ask me if what they suspect about their little girls is true. In confidence. Stanley always says yes and I always say no.

Saturday they all go away. Sunday I sleep. Monday I go back to work.

Best,

S.

• • •

"You say that's a real snapping turtle, dear?"

[To Bernice Baumgarten]

July 17 [1956]

Dear Bernice,

First of all, many many thanks for the check. I am terribly grateful for your trouble in getting it, and feel like the world's prime nuisance.

Bob Giroux sent me a copy of the book jacket for Demons, and I think it is charming. I have a couple of small quarrels with it, and since of course it's too late to do anything about it, and would only cause disturbance to have me raising points now, I'll note them here, just to get them on the record, and not mention them to Bob.

First of all, of course, the house is clearly in Connecticut, not Vermont. That landscaping job belongs on Winton Road, Westport. So does the willow tree. In Vermont, a willow tree is effete. Ditto the fieldstone wall and lewis-and-conger standing lamp. It has been decided by the North Bennington postmaster, the milkman, and the barber that the tree in front is a New York maple, and the three tall ones in back probably elms. No respectable Old House in Vermont—or, I believe, anywhere in New England outside Connecticut—ever ever ever sat kitty-corner to the road. They all face front squarely, to keep a good eye on what's going on. The postmaster was amused by the mailbox, since he always thought that one of the reasons we moved was so's we could pick up our mail in the post office like everybody else.

These are all trifles, however. I do think the jacket is delightful, quite as good as Savages.

The Ivy novel, which was to be a long short story, got itself badly jammed in the middle and won't unwind. After working on one page for three days I put the whole thing tenderly into a filing folder, labelled it neatly, and set it in the center of my desk. In order to justify my existence I tried the first scene of the college novel, which came out fine, and which S. thinks should be set up as a short story. I shall type it and send it to you. I give you this dreary history just to let you know that I am not spending all my time hanging around the barber shop.

Best,

Shirley

. . .

[To Geraldine and Leslie Jackson]

august 8 [1956]

dearest mother and pop,

i have been extremely lazy about writing anything so far this summer, particularly letters, because the weather has been rainy and cold and depressing. it's started to warm up now, though, and i have gathered myself together and taken the cover off the typewriter.

i have also spent most of my working time signing things. between the movie and the new book i do nothing but sign documents and chase off to the college notary. i don't even try to read them; my agent passes them and says it's okay to sign. stanley says my signature is unreadable by now, but after writing my name about a thousand times on a thousand different things, i don't care what it looks like.

at any rate, things keep moving without my writing a word except my name. the landmark witchcraft book is announced for next month; demons is due january 2, although we will see copies sooner.

The kids are all fine, though we all have the feeling that we are kind of waiting for the summer to start. laurie and jannie, of course, go swimming whether the weather is good or not, and jannie is so tan it's amazing. she went to camp for a week, a 4H camp about twenty miles from here, and had a wonderful time; sally has not done anything all summer except lie in bed and read, and get up around noon and make herself something to eat; if it is raining she goes back to bed.

laurie has been playing baseball, with very little success. he is out of the little league and in a tri-town intermediate league. he can't pitch the longer distance, and can't hit the pitching, so he is quite depressed about it. he still loves jazz and his trumpet more than anything, and a couple of weeks ago we gave a party and he decided to come because one of our guests was a pianist who ordinarily plays respectable concert material, but can play jazz. he and laurie got to talking and the first thing we knew laurie had brought down his trumpet and they had a fine jam session, laurie playing considerably better than we thought he could. of course playing with someone who is good makes him surpass himself. since most of our guests were people with children laurie's age i felt really quite smug.

he has also gotten a break which i hope will work out. we are about sixty miles from tanglewood, the big music center around here. from tanglewood territory came, recently, a gentleman named barber, who had heard that stanley taught a course in folk music, using some jazz. barber runs a place called the music inn, about half a mile from tanglewood, and during july and august he runs a series of jazz concerts, so that music lovers can hear classical music in the afternoon and good jazz at night. barber has his own auditorium (open air, with a tent over it, and blessedly cool) and is really doing well with his concerts and the inn. he wanted stanley to come down for three lectures, each one to discuss jazz and folk music, and each one to be given in combination with an appropriate musician, who would perform in illustration. on one of the three stanley is to be on a panel with someone named the reverend kershaw,* who won the $64,000 question on jazz. stanley was interested, and last saturday barber called and said pack up the kids and our bathing suits and drive down to the music inn and look it over. they had someone named sarah vaughn (laurie says she is a far-out bop singer, too cool for him) giving a concert. so on sunday we drove down, having arranged

---

* Rev. Alvin Kershaw was an Episcopal priest (Emmanuel Church, Boston) and noted jazz expert. He became famous when he appeared on the popular TV quiz show *The $64,000 Question* and stopped the contest after winning $32,000. He later credited iconic gospel singer Mahalia Jackson for talking him out of continuing. Stanley and Rev. Kershaw hit it off immediately and became good friends.

to stay over and go back monday morning, and laurie got out of the car in front of the music inn and decided on the spot that this was where he planned to spend the rest of his life.

it's a fairly fancy place, college boys for waiters, a very informal arrangement for guests, and everything music, preferably jazz. the staff of the inn runs the concerts, too, so the waiters turn up at the concerts as ushers, and turn up on the beach as lifeguards, and play ping-pong with the guests, and sunday night after the concert the staff was all off in the auditorium having a jam session. the general handy man is a jazz pianist. he drives guests back and forth to the trains, announces the concerts, takes over the bar when necessary, and spends the evenings in the inn lounge playing boogie-woogie. barber plays the clarinet and his wife plays the guitar. nothing but music, everywhere, and laurie's eyes began to pop. we were the guests of the barbers, so we stayed in their house, and laurie then discovered that barber is a former stage manager, and had amused himself by setting up an incredible lighting system in his house, with a central board controlling a series of spotlights which will light any given spot in the room and a central skylight which holds a pink spot and can be raised or dimmed to give you any kind of sunlight effect you prefer. since laurie's other dear love is stage design, he and barber spent a wonderful hour playing with the spotlights.

the result of all this was that barber asked laurie if he would like a job at the inn next summer. he said that laurie could take the job of watching over the sports equipment. in the evenings he could help with the lighting in the auditorium for the concerts, and learn about stage lighting. he could then go to all the jazz concerts, live with the other boys at the inn, and sit in on jam sessions. laurie nearly fainted, and if it works out and barber is serious it would be the most wonderful summer possible for laurie.

jannie has had a kind of a job this summer. tom brockway's mother, who is over eighty, is staying with them this summer. she has been very sick and cannot be left alone, so one evening the brockways called here and asked if laurie would come and sit with her. laurie was out, so jannie volunteered, and was a great success. old mrs brockway was pleased with her because she liked to listen to mrs brockway's stories about when she was a girl; she was born in turkey and her family were missionaries, and of course jannie was fascinated. jannie has been on call for mrs brockway for the past month. she and old mrs brockway play scrabble, or talk, or read "little women" together, and have a fine time. the first time jannie went she was wearing shorts, and old mrs brockway asked her very politely if she would mind wearing a dress, since shorts were not proper for young ladies, so whenever jannie goes over now she puts on one of her best dresses and her best shoes, and marches off feeling like a lady. she has her heart set right now on being a nurse and she tiptoes around the brockways' house pretending to be nurse joanne.

stanley is writing his speech on the blues and jazz and folk music for the music inn, and very cross.

i can't believe that the summer is nearly over and school will start in a month. barry is going to kindergarten, and laurie will be in high school and taking latin. the evil day approaches when i must take everyone into bennington and buy them all shoes.

stanley says the temperature has gone up to eighty-three, so i will stop this and take the kids swimming.

love from all. write soon.

s.

•   •   •

[To Geraldine and Leslie Jackson]

october 4 [1956]

dearest mother and pop,

plenty of time before the world series game on television, so i can write a letter.

i sent you a copy of the witchcraft book, which finally arrived. i think the illustrations are terrible. i gave a copy to the local library, and so far one person has read it. i also, at jannie's urgent request, sent a copy to the sixth grade at the school, for their class library. also i discover from publishers weekly that i am in the best short stories of 1956, which came as something of a shock. the story was one i had written for (golly) fantasy and science fiction, for which i was paid by a lifetime subscription to the magazine. i am also in a science fiction anthology with a story i wrote for the companion many years ago.

my agent writes that a magazine called AUTO ANTICS OF 1957 is using three pages from lifeamongthesavages, which makes things even more confusing. i hope auto antics does not insist on giving me a lifetime subscription. i have a story in the current woman's day, by the way, and one in the companion. others due next month in mccalls and mademoiselle. and another in the companion. and a review in the new york times. savages has re-sold in england and the english publishers have taken demons for sometime next year. no word on the movie. when i add it all up it sounds like i have been working hard, but i haven't. spent all the money, too.

aside from this feverish literary activity, things are much as usual here. i am enjoying a small spiteful triumph. did i tell you about the article i did for the bennington alumnae magazine? helen feeley edits it, and she asked me to do an article on being a faculty wife. it turned out quite well, without too much venom, and apparently everyone liked it, until i found out, from about twelve well-meaning friends, that all copies of the magazine had been hidden for commencement weekend for fear some visiting parent might see the article. which made me very sore indeed. usually the alumnae magazines are kept displayed in the administration offices, and in the library, and around the college store, and all the other issues were, and are, neatly in place, but the one with my article is not in sight. i was mad enough to stay away from all the commencement activities which i was supposed to attend, and to make it clear that any literary connection between me and the college was ended. yesterday the admissions director called me; she said that she had just heard that i was annoyed at some fancied slight to my article, and she wanted me to know that there was nothing to be angry about; she personally had instructed that the article be kept out of the hands of visitors and prospective students because it mentioned student drinking and that was bad publicity for the college. i said the article mentioned drinking only once, and that was to say that the students served a punch made out of sweet vermouth, vodka, and cold cocoa. she said well it gave a bad impression of the college and she hoped i wouldn't think they had anything against the article or were trying to censor it or anything, but no copies of it would be displayed at the college at all. it was the middle of the second inning of the ballgame and i wanted to get back so i suppressed all the things i wanted to say and only told her as sweetly as i could that that was too bad, i was terribly sorry, and i hoped <u>she</u> wouldn't be angry, but i had given mademoiselle permission to reprint the article, and had even written in a few extra paragraphs for them. stanley says i was spiteful, which i guess i was. every college student in the country reads mademoiselle.

i just got the mail and there is a royalty statement from my publishers, with a three hundred dollar check. i like royalty statements because it is so nice to find that, for instance, hangsaman sold eleven copies in the last six months. birds nest sold twenty-two. and road through the wall, poor little stepchild, sold five. road has been reprinted again by the way and if you see it don't touch it. they changed the title, put a vivid series of untruths on the cover, and wrote me that their standards of good taste were very high, as high as they could be and still sell books.

laurie of course is at present in new york, attending the world series. stanley couldn't go this year, because of a combination of classes, a public lecture to be given on monday, and psychological larangytis, which he gets every year when brooklyn wins the pennant. laurie went down with his friend willie and they are apparently having a wild time. they have a suite at the st. george hotel, where the ballplayers stay, across the street from stanley's parents. they have breakfast with stanley's parents, go back to the hotel and go swimming in the hotel pool, take the subway to ebbetts field where they eat hot dogs for lunch, and see the game. then they have dinner with stanley's parents, which means one of the good steak restaurants in the neighborhood, and apparently stay up all night watching television.

stanley's father and his brooklyn friends are getting very superstitious about laurie; he has never yet seen a losing world series game—brooklyn losing, that is. whenever he goes, brooklyn wins. now, he is not going to saturday's game, and plans to come home on sunday. if brooklyn loses on saturday, there is no doubt whatever that stanley's father and his friends will knock themselves out getting laurie to sunday's game, and monday's and tuesday's too, if necessary.

worst of all, he is terribly ashamed of his mother and father. the day he left i stopped in at the record store and bought three rock and roll records for stanley, because stanley had run across a theory that rock and roll was perfect old-time blues speeded up which of course meant that in his folklore course he would have to demonstrate at least a dim knowledge of it. so we played the three records and (shh) we were both crazy about it. when we talked to laurie that night from new york i said by the way, this rock and roll stuff was really the most and laurie said <u>what</u>? i said we dig it, man, and laurie said MOTHER! and there was a long silence and then he said was it possible . . . did i <u>really</u> mean . . . had we heard any elvis presley? i said we certainly had and elvis was just the greatest. laurie said he was not ever coming home again. he was going to stay in new york forever. he would live with his grandparents in new york and we could send down his phonograph and his collection of duke ellington records.

jannie is starting ballroom dancing, which is being taught by a couple of college students. we figure it will be a great help to her to know how to dance well, because the local school has dances every week and by next year she will want to go. she is also back at piano lessons, and sally, for some reason, is mad to learn to play the clarinet. it is just like laurie with the trumpet; we had no idea he was the least bit interested, and yet when he made up his mind nothing would stop him; he is getting better every day.

we have three new cats, all black, all females and perfectly beautiful. they look exactly alike, and we can't name them because we can't tell them apart, so laurie named them, collectively, the blues. they are wonderful with the kids. there is one of them who is determined to civilize stanley, and spends hours every evening trying to get on stanley's lap. every time stanley puts him down the cat climbs back up

again, and stanley, who has never held a cat in his life, is beginning to
wear down a little. last night he let it sit on the arm of the chair for a
few minutes. naturally during the day they all sleep on his desk,
which maddens him, because they shove the ashtray a fraction of an
inch past its usual place, and maybe sometimes knock over a paper
clip or something and stanley can't settle down when he comes home
until he has straightened up his desk again. they torment the dogs
too. we have also had to remove all ashtrays, candy dishes, and ornaments from the living room and particularly the piano, since the cat
race course goes from the kitchen through the dining room—
preferably over the table—up and along the back of the living room
couch, full length down the piano, and back around the study to the
kitchen again. the race goes on every evening for about two hours.

barry is very mixed emotionally about kindergarten. i think he is
so used to being the baby of the family, and being the center of attention at nursery school that he can't settle down to being just one
more kid in a class. the kindergarten and the first and second grades
get out at eleven-thirty, and some of the bigger boys have been bothering him, so we sent his big brother out to take care of things, and
at least at present all is quiet. all our kids have had trouble fighting
going back and forth to school, and of course it makes me madder
than anything else. usually laurie can take care of kids who bother
sally and barry, provided they have no big brothers.

so they all keep busy. the schedule for each week ranges from sally's brownies to jannie's lessons to laurie's rehearsals, not to mention
the cats' appointment at the vets and stanley's getting to and from
the college. we have set up an iron rule about going out to dinner
privately every thursday night, just stanley and me—no children. so
we go have a lovely quiet fancy dinner in town; golly, how i look forward to thursday!

paul feeley is traveling in spain, painting, so helen is alone, and sold
their car for another which will not be delivered for a couple of
months. she has therefore no way to get into bennington to shop once
a week, so we arranged that every saturday we would go in together,
have lunch in a restaurant, a ladylike clubwoman lunch, with sometimes a cocktail first, and then do our shopping together. it's wonderful.

i am going to have to mail this letter in a story envelope. a regular envelope won't hold it. just reading it should take all morning. and it is time for the world series game to begin.

lots of love from all of us. write soon and let us know about your house. best of luck to you in it, and we hope to visit you there soon.

love,

s.

•  •  •

[To Bernice Baumgarten]

October 19 [1956]

Dear Bernice,

On the strength of your telephone call I called and told the man at the electric company that yes, he should bring over the new vacuum cleaner. I had not quite made up my mind but if I am going to have to get the house clean I had better have something to do it with.

Here is the letter from Mr. Margulies,* which I would be grateful for having back to show my grandchildren.

I would greatly enjoy doing a story for the NY Times Drama Section, and will even guarantee to like the movie enormously, which I am already prepared to do, since I like Mr. Dinelli's first draft. It would be exciting to come to New York (not Los Angeles, I think; my mother in San Francisco would be angry), for a showing of the movie.

You know as well as I do my singular gracelessness and idiot paralysis with regard to interviews, radio and—I have no doubt—TV. This I would think is absolutely out, categorically. I do not believe that I am photogenic, natty or self-possessed, and the children all have Vermont accents. On the other hand, I am extremely interested

---

* Leo Margulies was an editor and publisher of many paperback science fiction and fantasy anthologies. The contents of this obviously complimentary letter are unknown.

in the movie and everything about it, and anything I can do in writing I will be happy to do.

Incidentally, one of the contributing items in my fascinating ailment of the past few days was a brew of nervous tension and (reminiscent of my father!) high blood pressure. Result is a strict diet, no more cocktails before dinner (<u>that</u> was unkind) and a setup of what the doctor optimistically calls "tranquillizing" drugs. So I am changing my way of life. My future writing will be waspish, tending to dwell on descriptions of luscious foods, and at times hypnotically tranquil. I am enchanted. I will feel like Huysmans.*

Best,

S.

•  •  •

[To Geraldine and Leslie Jackson]

monday [November 1956]

dearest mother and pop,

i was very glad to get your letter and particularly your new address.

i am glad the apples arrived, and also glad you liked the witchcraft book. i have no idea how it is selling; they are not very thoughtful of their authors, and don't give out much information. will know next march when the royalties come in, i suppose. it should be on sale in all children's book departments, but again, the publishers are quite slow, and our local bookshop only got delivery a few days ago. there will be a story in the december companion, which should make pop homesick for the christmas tree lights; in january the companion is running a feature page on me and the kids, to correspond with the publication of demons, and they sent a photographer and an inter-

* Joris-Karl Huysmans, French Decadent novelist most famous for *À Rebours*.

viewer up here and the kids and i spent a pleasant morning being photographed and interviewed, except of course the photograph will be terrible. of me, anyway.

the movie will be released about march. the publicity department of the movie company wrote me asking what i could do to publicize it; would i be on the murrow person-to-person television show?* how about a series of radio and television appearances? or a feature article in the new york times drama section? would i come to a private showing in new york, or would i prefer los angeles? since they said nothing about paying expenses i said that i would come to a private showing in new york, and i would write them any articles they wanted, but would not under any circumstances consent to appear on any television or radio programs. the kids are all sore at me for turning down edward murrow. they are making some kind of arrangements for local publicity, which means that the entire thousand people in north bennington will probably go to the movie when it shows locally. he wanted me to write an article on whether it was possible to "go hollywood" in north bennington, but since i am not sure what going hollywood is i am very hesitant.

my own big news is that i have changed my way of life, or, rather, had it changed for me. i am having a wonderful time. about three weeks ago i had the flu and one evening was apparently very sick; stanley said i was raving wildly about not being able to go to bed until i had set the alarm clock, and it frightened him (i don't remember it at all, and i think he is making it up, but i know i felt just awful) and by the time he got the doctor over here i was not feeling well at all. i had a high fever and he gave me a shot that put me out cold and then went into the living room and told stanley that my blood pressure had gone way up and that i had always promised him that if i ever felt bad enough i would go to work on it, and he thought i finally felt bad enough, which i did. so he came the next day and we planned out my new way of life, which, as i said, i am enjoying enormously. i am on a very lenient diet, keeping track of everything i have to eat, and taking fancy pills; in the three weeks since i have lost four pounds and my

* Edward R. Murrow was a popular radio and TV reporter who later hosted interview programs on television. *Person to Person* ran from 1953 to 1959.

blood pressure is back to normal, but i am committed to keeping it up for a year. i have the whole kitchen wall covered with calorie listings. my big problem of course is liquor; i am trying hard to cut down on drinking but it is very hard, so i figure i will just have to get the food down to fewer calories to make room for the cocktails. oliver said definitely plan to include some drinks in each day's count, since the intention was to make me feel better, not worse. i have no trouble doing without desserts and sweets in general, but i do mind potatoes and bread. i am fascinated with all the calculating and figuring. my pills also include one of these relaxing dopes, which does take the edge off that jumpy feeling you get when everyone else is eating mashed potatoes. i can still go out with stanley for our weekly dinner at the fancy restaurant, and have steak, and out for lunch each saturday with helen and have a lamb chop or something. and everyone is watching me all the time. the waitress in the restaurant where helen and i go every saturday takes a deep interest in me, and suggests things like having lettuce and tomato instead of the cabbage salad, and she pointedly gives helen butter and leaves me out. stanley figured out that if i stopped drinking entirely i would have to eat an extra piece of bread and butter and a potato to bring my calories up to what oliver wants them to be.

i must go and make myself a cup of consome. fifty calories. write me soon again, and lots and lots of love from all of us.

s.

•  •  •

[To Geraldine and Leslie Jackson]

january 11 [1957]

dearest mother and pop,

the temperature is eleven below, so it seems like a good morning to stay indoors and write letters; my car has not started any morning this week, but who wants to go out?

i want to go out, i just decided. while i was writing those last words the furnace, which is directly under the study, started going boom boom boom like someone was pounding it with a hammer. i got to the phone so fast you couldn't have seen me move, and got the furnace people and i was so frightened i could hardly talk. i've never heard anything like it; i thought the furnace was going to blow up any minute and the furnace man said calmly that he didn't <u>think</u> anything would happen, they would send someone along later on, but it sounded like some of the pipes might be frozen so why didn't i call a plumber? i said i had barely been able to dial <u>his</u> number and why didn't <u>he</u> call a plumber and i would go and wait outside. then junior the taxi driver came up to drop off our morning papers and i said june you go down in the cellar and make that furnace stop going boom boom boom so june did. he didn't know what was wrong, but he fussed with it for a minute. so now i am still waiting for the furnace people but at least it has stopped going boom boom boom and i don't care if they think i am crazy if that thing goes boom once more i am going to go out to the barn and sit in my frozen car.

all this, you understand, with stanley peacefully asleep upstairs. he played poker last night and won ten dollars, which will just about pay the furnace man and the plumber. i figured if the furnace did blow up he was well out of the way of it, since he is asleep at the opposite end of the house and it might wake him although i doubt it.

i started originally to say thank you for the wonderful gifts you sent us for christmas; and of course thank you specially for the check, which we both appreciate so much. we cannot agree on what we want, so it is waiting in the bank. (the furnace just gave a little tiny boom. i don't know whether to run or not.) because as usual i do not have my brother's address, i would be grateful if you could send it to me again. they sent us a beautiful box of fruit which i would like to thank them for, and i would also like to send them a copy of demons. i hope you all had a wonderful christmas together; everybody but me drank your health in eggnog, but eggnog is 350 calories, so i used bourbon which may have as many calories but i don't want to know about it.

i am doing fine. i slipped a little over christmas but as of yesterday i have lost eighteen pounds and am actually enjoying myself. blood pressure is fine. tonight we are going out for dinner and i am going to have filet mignon, which you could hardly call starving. the only real trouble i have is not being able to drink at all; oliver said to plan on a couple of cocktails before dinner, just for morale, but if i have two cocktails before dinner now i almost pass out. one cocktail gets me high. it makes me very sad. i keep thinking that in a few months one sip of sherry will have me dancing on the table.

we had a fine christmas. laurie, who had spent a couple of months working away at some secret projects in his room, turned out to have made for stanley a breakfront, the most beautiful thing you have ever seen. it is to go in the dining room, and has cabinets below for all the junk stanley used to keep in the buffet, and shelves above for books. and he had made me a jigsaw puzzle table, invented by himself; it opens up and holds the puzzle in a kind of shallow well, so the top can close down and keep the puzzle safe when you're not working on it.

this is now monday, the 14th. it was twenty-five below when i came downstairs this morning, and of course my car will not start. it is supposed to go down around forty below tonight, which is cold even for vermont. barry cleverly pretended he had a cold this morning, so he wouldn't have to go out in it.

there was a bad fire around the corner last night, and we spent all evening watching the fire engines tear back and forth. i always feel so sorry for the volunteer firemen who have to get out of a warm bed in the middle of the night and go out in this weather. i dreamed about fires all night long, and consequently feel very jumpy today. on top of that two bad reviews of demons came in, both from texas, where they apparently don't like me (and i don't like them, come to think of it) and in spite of the fact that they are the only bad reviews out of about thirty i've seen, they still make me mad.

the book is doing very well indeed. the first printing was fifteen thousand, of which nine thousand sold before publication, so there should be a second printing by the end of this month, i hope. in spite of texas. ten thousand sales pay off the advance, so we should be making money by now. the little witchcraft book is selling well (and now i think of it, that one got a bad review in texas, too; what do they do down there, tear books up to feed the pigs?) and is getting reviewed in scientific american and such, and various school library journals have recommended it. the children were enchanted at finding their pictures in the new york times and tribune.

the local radio station gave demons a plug, and both local libraries have put it on reserve so anyone who wants to read it must either wait a long time or go and buy it. except the bookstore has run out of copies and the new ones have not come in. louis scher, to whom the book is dedicated, has already bought forty copies and has ordered more.

we are having a big publication party on saturday night, about seventy people coming, and louis insisted on being responsible for the food. he is coming up for it, and saturday morning we received from him a package of about fifty pounds of pastrami, corned beef, and salami, all great rareties up here, which should make the party quite a success. all i have to supply is mustard.

we are all excited because the people who run music inn have invited laurie to work there this summer. because he is only fourteen they have a kind of semi-fulltime job he can do; he will be caretaker of the sports equipment. he will be meeting people like armstrong and other great jazz musicians, and have a chance to sit in on jam sessions with the younger kids. he is getting very good on the trumpet; he still takes lessons from a teacher who tried hard to make him learn time and notes, but fell flat when laurie discovered that his teacher is a jazz clarinet player playing at nick's in the village during the summer; now they study jazz riffs and laurie can play anything on the trumpet and pick out any tune on the piano. he spends literally all his time listening to jazz, from the time he comes home from school (a waste of time, school; no jazz there) until he goes to bed at night.

stanley agreed to do an article on jazz for some magazine, which immediately sent him ten new books on jazz. he then wrote to one of the big jazz record companies explaining about the article and how he uses jazz in his course on folklore and got back a letter saying that of course they knew about him, and about me (i liked getting that plug; i didn't know jazz people could read) and would send him any of their records at two-thirds off. so he and laurie sat down with their catalogue one evening and they ended up by ordering about sixty l-p jazz records, and are now trying to play their way through them. barry and sally can sing any basic blues you name. jannie, who is a free-thinker, got her own record-player for her birthday, and records (chosen by me, because i kind of incline toward jannie's taste) for christmas, so she stays in <u>her</u> room and plays elvis presley and patience and prudence. she is very partial to bing crosby and harry belafonte. me, i actually like rock and roll, particularly a gentleman named fats domino, and every evening while i am making dinner and getting plastered on my one cocktail laurie puts on my fats domino records, and everyone else goes away and shuts all doors and tries to listen to armstrong or presley, but fats domino can drown out any of them.

as you can imagine, we live in the noisiest house in town; luckily mrs welling next door is stone deaf. by the way, on christmas eve the children took her over a copy of demons which they had all autographed and inside of twenty minutes we received two dozen roses with her thanks and best wishes. i understand from our mutual doctor that she is reading the book.

spring must be here. it's gone up to eight above. and my car is going.

stanley has been invited to lecture at brandeis college in march, which means that in addition to the three articles he meant to do this winter he must also write a speech. i'm in the middle of a new book but in no hurry to finish it, and now the companion has folded my only big magazine market is mccall's, and they have two stories of mine already. i keep counting the wealth i haven't got, coming in from the movie and the two books and planning to buy a new car. if i don't get rid of this one soon i will go batty. the one morning last week it started it had a flat tire.

we are planning to see you in march, and our house will be much quieter. thanks again from all, and lots of love.

s.

. . .

"Dear, as long as you're not busy, would you mind
lighting me a cigarette?"

[To Bernice Baumgarten]

January 25 [1957]

Dear Bernice,

I am very grateful to Miss Keegan for getting in touch with McCall's;
I wanted to get down to a few solid weeks' work on my lovely novel,*
and didn't want to stop to rewrite that piece so now I have done
about twenty more pages of the novel and it is really moving along
and I should have some few pages for you to look at soon. Did I tell
you that I got my sundial inscription from Dryden, finally? All that
Shakespeare wasted. I think the novel is about comparative realities.
But poor Essex is turning out a cad.

* *The Sundial.*

Bennington College is going to need a new president. Stanley and I want Leo Durocher,* but I think he is already employed.

Best,

Shirley

P.S. I have written six pages since the first half of this letter. Essex is still a cad but I have hopes of reforming him. May I dedicate the book to you or do you think you had better read it first?

•   •   •

[To Bernice Baumgarten]

February 20 [1957]

Dear Bernice,

Here is the first draft of the first seventy pages of Sundial. I have the rest of it sketched out and most of it written but not organized or typed to be readable. I am very anxious to know what you think of this, and whether you want to send it along to Roger. Also as I told you before, I'd like to dedicate it to you, but perhaps after you've read it you may regard that as a mixed compliment; it is certainly going to be an odd book.

I have had a letter from Arabel Porter[†] asking if Bird's Nest is a fictionalization of Three Faces of Eve. I am not going to answer her until I have cooled off some.

By the way, my sundial inscription still does not please me, and

* Leo Durocher (1905–1991) was a Major League Baseball player and legendary manager of both the New York Giants and the Brooklyn Dodgers.
[†] Arabel J. Porter was a well-known editor at New American Library.

will probably be changed again. If you think of any good ones let me know. And I still cannot decide when to end the world; what do you think of late August? To avoid another winter? Our wedding anniversary is August thirteenth, but Stanley feels it is unkind to end the world on that day.

Best,

Shirley

. . .

[To Bernice Baumgarten]

February 28 [1957]

Dear Bernice,

"Lizzie" just bowled me over. I had no idea it was going to be like that—my reactions, I mean; the movie itself I thought was extremely good, and enormously improved over the first script I saw. But <u>seeing</u> it was an amazing experience. I am still reeling. There were about twenty people there, but only a couple of my personal friends, who could be relied on to give a less formal, perhaps more honest opinion, and both of them found it a moving and exciting picture. I don't know if this is a usual reaction to seeing a book of your own made into a movie, but what I want to do is go over and over again. There were several places where I was just jealous at the things a camera can do and a book can't, particularly the last scene in the museum. What actually staggered me most, though, were the two Robins. As you must know, and Stanley is never tired of pointing out to me, I am an excessively prudish writer, and prefer to go two hundred pages around to avoid writing a scene like the one on the stairs. And yet it was so perfectly right that I have been given a kind of jolting new view of myself; clearly, it <u>was</u> in the book and I put it there and I am delighted; I shall be more daring. Essex, perhaps?

Gosh.

Shirley

• • •

[To Geraldine and Leslie Jackson]

monday [February 1957]

dearest mother and pop,

i was so glad to get pop's letter, and know that he is feeling all right now, even though we are all sorry that you won't be here for a visit this spring.

i haven't written sooner, although i've been trying to, because of the usual mess of complications that seem to gather around here all the time. first, barry got chicken pox, the day after i talked to mother on the phone. he came down to breakfast and said he had picked up a flea from the cats, who all sleep on his bed, and showed me six little spots on his stomach. by the time he had finished breakfast he was covered with spots; we just sat there and watched him get spottier and spottier. while he was in the thick of it some slick hollywood type called me from new york and said i must come down the following tuesday to meet the mgm people and have lunch and a cocktail party and see the private showing of this infernal movie, now called lizzie. i kept saying i would rather die than go to new york and meet a pack of movie people and he kept saying then we'll expect you for lunch on tuesday. so i told him all the children had chicken pox and he said he would see me on tuesday. a real hearty type. i finally got off the phone and made myself a stiff drink, and then called my agent and told her she must call this hollywood character and tell him i had discovered it wasn't chicken pox, but smallpox and of course i wouldn't come to new york. she called back later to say she had convinced him and she had convinced him so well that they had decided to send the movie to me. everything was now arranged for a private showing of the movie at the general stark theatre in bennington. then the manager of the general stark called me and he was terribly excited and upset because he couldn't think of any prominent people to invite to the showing, bennington being kind of short on mayors and movie stars and such, so i said invite the local librarians and the manager of the bookstore and i would bring my husband and my children and even though we wouldn't fill the theatre at least there would be <u>someone</u> there to see it.

the kids loved the movie, and stanley thought it was terrible. i actually don't remember a thing about it; i saw my name on the screen and then i think i closed my eyes and kept them closed. i think i was in a state of shock; i came home, made lunch, and slept till dinner, got up, made dinner, and went back to bed. about two days later i started remembering small things from the movie, but even now i couldn't tell you what it was like. i will have to see it again sometime. it is going to be released sometime this month, and the paperback edition of the book—now called lizzie, too—should be out about the same time. the funniest thing is this new book, three faces of eve, which is of course on exactly the same subject, but a much later case than the one i used. eve was bought for the movies a long time ago, but they were slow getting into production, and our movie was rushed through fast, so now it is being released just as eve is and mgm* is using very similar publicity, so everyone believes that they are all the same story, and we are not only getting the jump on them but building on their publicity.

anyway i hope you'll see lizzie. the ads are going to be very embarrassing but at least my name is in very tiny letters. they seem to think it will be successful. they are going to make a fuss about it in bennington; they are trying to arrange to have it open here, and the local paper runs stories about it. practically the only lines of mine they left

---

* MGM produced a similarly themed movie, *The Three Faces of Eve,* in the same time period as *Lizzie.* Shirley and others believed *Lizzie* could have been much more successful if it had not had the competition.

in are the ones for joan blondell, who is the old aunt; she sits there
with a fifth of bourbon and babbles. they must have used up twenty
cases of bourbon in the movie; there are shots of people carrying out
bushel baskets of empty bottles. stanley says it is because in hollywood they don't know anything about drinking because they all take
dope. they don't know much about psychology either. i did a good
deal of background reading before i wrote the book and one area of
hysterical behavior i know backward and forward is the dissociated
personality. they have made her into a lunatic, which she can't be, by
definition, and the doctor cures her with a very interesting combination of freudian analysis, pre-freudian hypnosis, jungian word-
association, and rorshak inkblots. not one of these systems gets along
with any of the others in real life, but i guess it is different in the
movies. i should think every analyst in the country would shoot himself, which of course might be a good idea too, except that then all
the bennington students who are being analysed would have to find
something else to do.

   stanley goes to boston tomorrow to give a lecture at brandeis college, and he is nervous. he got a new suit to wear and he has written
out a nice lecture and boston is one place you can get to from here,
since there is a train which goes there, although none going to new
york. he comes back on wednesday and then without doing more
than packing another clean shirt he goes off to new york.

   i figure that about next fall i will be able to get myself a whole new
wardrobe. i am so pleased; i have lost twenty-five pounds and people
keep commenting on it. i find i am much more agile, too, running up
and down stairs as i couldn't a few months ago. this diet has affected
my capacity for drinking; last night we were playing bridge and i had
two drinks and passed out cold. i am feeling very guilty and strange
this morning, although of course these days i cannot ever drink
enough to make me feel lousy the next morning. blood pressure is
fine, by the way.

   just got a call from my hollywood character in new york (he calls
me darling, he honestly does) to say that the movie opens at loews
state in new york on april 29th. he asked very politely about the
chicken pox, but he never waits for me to answer anyway. whatever i

say he just says "isn't that darling," and then "be talking to you again, darling." i said i thought the movie was wonderful and he said he'd "call the coast right away and let them know."

jannie and sally spent their school vacation cooking, and barry learned to make jello. jannie gave up her piano lessons because they bored her, and spends all her time reading. she is going to give another small dance in a couple of weeks; she and laurie alternate, and i am getting so i can handle a dozen teen-age dancers with no trouble. with laurie's parties stanley and i have to hide in the study, but with jannie's parties i have to hang around, because they get to giggling and get slightly hysterical.

sally has been very odd. sally has read through every child's book in the house and is now raiding our books. if you can imagine an eight-year-old girl reading adult novels. we try to steer her to the wholesome ones (if there are any) and i don't know what is going to happen. jannie gets books from the library, nice girl's books about nurses and boarding schools, but sally disdains them. we heard indirectly that she had made a scene in school, tearing up her language workbook because it was boring. at the same time her grades have gone way down, and she keeps trying to make excuses to stay home from school. i am going to have to go in and see her teacher, but i know it is at least partly the teacher's fault; laurie and jannie both had the same teacher, and they hated her. she uses incorrect grammar and teaches the children incorrect pronunciations. sally is far and away the brightest kid in the class, and is fairly stubborn about being right.

college starts on monday. poor stanley; he dreads it; he will have to get up at seven every morning. at least it means that the faculty will be coming back after the winter, and there will be a decent poker game, instead of the four lonely souls who sat around all winter.

barry just came home from school, which means that i have to make lunch. lots and lots of love to you both.

s.

. . .

[To Bernice Baumgarten]

March 18 [1957]

Dear Bernice,

A lady wrote me that her writing instructor made her copy out one of my stories word by word in longhand.

These are the writers of tomorrow.

I have really lost twenty-five pounds. Barry is enjoying an asthma-respiratory virus, and I am able to race up and down stairs carrying thermometers and trays in a fashion I could never have done six months ago. I am unbearably complacent about it, and yet I notice that in Sundial all they do is eat. Writing is therapy.

Anxious to hear the results of your negotiations with Roger. One of my greatest pleasures would be gone if I had to admit that he was a nice guy.

Best,

Shirley

•   •   •

[To Geraldine and Leslie Jackson]

thursday [early 1957]

dearest mother and pop,

it was so good to get your letter and to hear that pop is better and you are going to have a vacation. it will do you both a world of good to lie in the sun and soak up a lot of vitamins—it would do me good, as a matter of fact, since i seem to be enjoying one of those things they call a virus now (i always thought they were colds) and am running a temperature and feeling generally lousy.

i wanted to tell you about sally; i told you that she was not eating or sleeping, and was generally thin and pale and snapping at everybody. i took her to the doctor and he said there was nothing wrong with her, and i must try to find out if she was worried about something, or having some kind of trouble. so i spent hours talking to her, and trying to reassure her, and all she would say was that she had been having bad dreams, and that she was frightened, but she wouldn't say why. then i got a call from the mother of one of the kids in sally's class, asking if sally had ever mentioned the teacher and i said not particularly, and she said well, she had just taken <u>her</u> boy to the doctor because he was generally not well, and he had finally told her that the teacher had been bullying him, and that sally was another of her victims. then it all began to come out; i talked to sally and to other mothers, and i wish you could have heard the things that have been going on, with thirty children so terrified that they didn't dare tell. sally has been whipped with a yardstick, slapped in the face, had a clothespin fastened onto her ear, called a liar and a thief, and been made to stand up in front of the class to be publicly humiliated; one little boy had his head smashed against the iron radiator, another had red pepper poured inside his clothes, another had her face scrubbed with scouring powder, the class in general has been told they were fools and were all going to be sent back to the first grade to start all over, and any of them who answered back or tried to tell their parents were punished.

i went in to the teacher and told her flatly that if she ever touched sally again i would personally take the yardstick to <u>her</u>, and so for the past week sally has been reasonably safe; we had called an emergency meeting of the school board for last night so about twenty-five parents showed up at the school, and we told the school board all these things, and it got more and more horrible, because we kept hearing more that we did not know—she has been telling the kids nightmare stories (one about a mother murdering three little babies) to frighten them, and she keeps a baseball bat beside her desk to enforce order. for some reason, probably because i was madder than i think i have ever been, i did most of the talking, and said flatly that if the teacher was not removed at once i would withdraw my four children from the school and see that the whole affair got as much publicity as possible. i had a temperature of 102 and was probably a little more excited than usual. anyway this morning the school superintendent called to say that there was a new teacher in the third grade, and that the old sadist had been bounced. now all we have to do is get sally back to normal.

laurie is doing better and better with his trumpet; he and his friend tony, who plays the drums, put on a performance at the high school variety show; they were a sensation, and the result has been that they have been invited to join an adult band here, called the sage city six; their trumpet player left them and they had largely dissolved until they decided to take in laurie, but unfortunately they cannot accept any paying dates because laurie is too young. tony is eighteen, so he represents no problem, but poor laurie cannot even get a union card, so they can only play privately. they can, however, play for school programs and such, and they will play for the lions club minstrel show. as a result laurie is getting a lot of experience in playing in public, and is no longer as nervous as he was. he apparently cannot read music at all but has a fine ear and can pick up anything fast, and his trumpet teacher says his tone is as fine as anyone he has ever heard.

much love,

s.

•  •  •

[To Bernice Baumgarten]

April 29 [1957]

Dear Bernice,

Here is your second thrilling installment of Sundial. I am so generally despondent over stories, books, money, Sally and almost everything else that almost any kind word on it would be welcome.

Can you think of any way I can use the Sally incident as a story without being libelous? I am still so angry, but so is everyone else; our whole town got into the fight, and it just goes on and on, and the teacher is <u>still</u> teaching.

I can always comfort myself with Laurie, however; he is now playing with a small local band, all college boys, and the other night they played in Arlington and at two-thirty I was still sitting up waiting for Laurie and the door crashed open and he came weaving in; he had decided to be grownup like the college boys, and had been drinking beer all evening. For a minute I was shocked and then it struck me funny, and I sat on the stairs and howled while Laurie just grinned foolishly. I had to put him to bed, poor baby, and the next morning he was horribly sick, so I guess he has learned his lesson.

Partly I am despondent because I cannot use either Sally or Laurie for stories.

Anyway I'll be waiting anxiously for some word on this our Sundial.

Best,

Shirley

•  •  •

[To Bernice Baumgarten]

May 1 [1957]

Dear Bernice,

I have been reading an eighteenth-century moral tale about lying, by a lovely lady named Mrs. Amelia Opie.* She discusses various forms of "social" lying, like flattery, and instructing your footman to tell unwelcome guests that you are not at home (and so teaching the ser-

* Amelia Opie was an English author, poet, and abolitionist who wrote during the Romantic period in the early nineteenth century.

vant class to lie, you perceive) and pretending to acquaintance with the nobility when you are actually not received at their houses, and such. She illustrates each form of lying with an instructive little tale, showing how inheritances were lost and lovers betrayed by these little social lies.

Now I wonder if such an article is not possible now, either taking off from Mrs. Opie, (finding how her lies apply today, or, contrariwise, how hopelessly out of date they are in this age of professionals) or starting from scratch with two or three modern forms of lying, each illustrated by a little moral tale. In this case it might even be two or three different articles. They would have to be odd kinds of lying—her Lie of Benevolence, for instance, would hold that it is a kind lie to keep the news of impending death from a sufferer; Mrs. Opie points out that this is not justified, particularly if the sufferer has not made a will and you stand to inherit. She is absolutely serious, by the way.

I do not want to get tangled in this unless you think it has possibilities. I have actually found my niche in life, which is fighting with the school board. Because I was unable to think about anything else, I wrote the whole Sally business down, and so have complete notes for a story, someday.

Best,

Shirley

•  •  •

[To Geraldine and Leslie Jackson]

july 12 [1957]

dearest mother and pop,

i've been wanting to write for a long time, but have been wholly tied up with the new book of which, thank heaven, the first draft is now finished, except that i can't decide on which of four or five endings. also, we've been having our usual mid-summer rush of unexpected guests, and yesterday i sat in the study and worked while five different people arrived, spent a while, and left. it is really too much, particularly since one was here for lunch and three for dinner. in the evening after we got rid of everybody stanley read my manuscript and didn't like the ending i used and we squabbled about it (a very good subject to quarrel about, actually, since we were both sore at all the company and just pretended it was a literary difference) and stanley was so annoyed that he couldn't sleep which always happens to him, and sat up reading and snarling until about four-thirty and then tried to come to bed quietly and of course woke me and i remembered about the company and the ending of the book and couldn't get back to sleep, so now it is seven-thirty and stanley is sound asleep and i have been up since four-thirty and i refuse to change the ending of the book because why should he sleep and i can't?

we took laurie down to lenox, with about four tons of assorted equipment—tape recorders, record players and even a clean shirt. we didn't hear a word from him for a week, and then he called to say he had the fourth of july off, just one day, and if i could pick him up at nine (there is no bus or train) that morning and get him back by nine the following morning, he could come home. so of course i said i would, and i set the alarm for six, and went to bed at ten o'clock while stanley went out to play poker, and slept through the alarm, and stanley came home from the poker game at six-thirty and shook me and said "wake up and go get laurie; i won eighty-two dollars" so without ever quite waking up i gathered the eighty-two dollars and barry, who was awake because stanley had made considerable noise getting up the stairs, and barry and i headed for lenox, stopping on the way to have a very fine eighty-two dollar breakfast. laurie turned out to be wildly enthusiastic about the inn and excited about all that he was doing; all the rest of the boys are much older, in their twenties, but they have taken him in as an equal, largely i gather because of his trumpet playing. they work hard all day and play all night. laurie has been taking care of the athletic equipment and bell-hopping.

he says bop musicians only tip a quarter and every time someone comes in and insists on carrying one small suitcase and letting the bellhop take the others, you can figure the small suitcase has a bottle of whisky in it. he has also been running the lights at the concerts, and has managed to get free access to the potting shed by playing the bass fiddle, which he seems to have learned how to do. yesterday we got a long letter, very cheerful and happy, announcing that ethel waters'* manager had borrowed the mike to our tape recorder and wrecked it trying to change the wiring, and laurie had tried to catch a falling coke bottle, had cut the palm of his hand so badly that he had to be rushed into pittsfield where a doctor took three stitches. and he can only carry bags with one hand, which means two trips which means two tips. he doesn't say how he plays the bass one-handed.

jannie has been wandering over to the lake daily, getting browner and browner and spending most of her time, i gather, pushing boys off the raft. she looks so lovely with her tan; she is a very good swimmer. she looks wonderful and feels wonderful. she goes off to the first of her two camps next week, then comes home for a few days, and then goes off for the whole month of august. she will be about ten miles from laurie, which will make it easier to go and see both of them, and sally is finally learning to swim. stanley, who taught the two older kids, was ready to despair over sally, who suddenly this year made up her mind and is now actually swimming; the combination of such a triumph and a very quiet life, mostly reading and sleeping and playing outdoors with barry, has calmed her down a great deal, and she is almost our old sally again. i notice that she has gone back to writing stories, which i regard as a good sign. barry, of course, is getting bigger every day; he is on one of those growing binges. before he left laurie made the kids a treehouse, and sally and barry spend most of their time climbing up and down the tree, scaring me to death.

our new college president moves in next month, and they are planning a forty-eight hour poker game to celebrate the departure of

* Ethel Waters was a very popular Broadway and film actress, and touring blues singer.

the old president; they are making him give it, of course, and hope to win all his money before he leaves.

lizzie opened in london, and punch gave it an enthusiastic review. it is playing now here in third-rate theatres; laurie said it was advertised in pittsfield, and i think it is going to turn up at the bennington drive-in, but i am not going to see it again, thanks. i am going to syracuse to lecture the end of july. it has been hard to stay on the diet because of the general haphazard manner of summer meals, but i am still working on it and am still losing, although slowly. stanley has given up baseball. after the way the brooklyn players performed in the all-star game he refuses to listen to any more games.*

we are all looking forward to your next visit. we had such fun when you were here, and want to do it all again.

lots and lots of love,

s.

•   •   •

[1957]

dear martin,†

it troubles me very much to have to write you this, but i am afraid that i must ask that, in future, you telephone us before stopping off at our house, so that we can avoid further interruptions of our working days. as you must know, our house is as much an office as any you visit, and i especially have so little working time that i must protect myself against visitors to a large extent. we are both delighted to see

---

* The Dodgers and the Giants had just announced they were moving to Los Angeles and San Francisco, respectively; Stanley was furious and abandoned his lifelong team.
† Shirley and Stanley had an open-door household, common among the Bennington faculty, but they sometimes had to set limits so they could work; this is one of many uninvited and unannounced drop-in guests they had to contend with.

our friends at reasonable times, for reasonable times, and with reasonable warning and invitation, but i am afraid that i regard the six hours you spent with us yesterday as a wholly unreasonable intrusion, and i would prefer not to have it happen again. our house is not a hotel, a public telephone booth, or a country club, and i resent having it treated as such. because of the constant irritations yesterday my entire day's work was wasted and must be done over; i suggest that if you cannot find anyone in bennington with time as free as your own, you make your local headquarters in some professional establishment better equipped to cater to transients.

Shirley

•   •   •

[To Bernice Baumgarten]

July 14 [1957]

Dear Bernice,

Here it is. By golly, here it is. I have gone at it until I am wild-eyed, but here it is.

Now I am going to take a week off and go swimming.

Even though this is not the final draft will you hit Roger for the other thousand?

I am trying to rush it through because Bob was so anxious to have it ahead of schedule. I hope the ending drives him to tears. I wrote it six times six different ways.

Yippee.

Best,

Shirley

•   •   •

[To a complaining reader]

July 24 [1957]

Dear Mrs. White,

If you don't like my peaches, don't shake my tree.

Sincerely,

Shirley Jackson

. . .

[To Geraldine and Leslie Jackson]

friday night [August 1957]

dearest mother and pop,

for the past week barry and i have been here all alone and having a wonderful time. first, as you know, laurie is in lenox; joanne went to camp the first of august, and at the end of her first two weeks i went to visit her and the camp director said that they had a vacancy in joanne's cabin and if sally wanted to come for the last two weeks of camp they would be delighted. so we packed her suitcase full of clothes and off she went. she is having a marvelous time, is doing just what the other kids do, is eating enormously. the camp is very small, about fifty altogether, boys and girls, and very informal and relaxed. barry was charmed with the idea of being an only child for two weeks, and then stanley had to go to new york to the dentist and to the new yorker, so barry and i have been alone. the two big results of this have been first that i finished my book, and it is now ready for the typist and second that barry quite without any planning or intention fell into a group of neighborhood children and instead of being a small child who has to

be escorted to places to play has been wandering up the block daily to
visit his friends, and entertaining them down here.

i thought that since barry loves to travel in the car and stanley left
us some money we ought to take a couple of trips, so we drove the
forty miles to saratoga (only we made it nearer seventy, by going
quite a way in the wrong direction) but they wouldn't let barry into
the race track. they said if we wanted to come back for the trotting
races in the evening they could let him in, but not by day, so we went
exploring around the saratoga lake and then got lost again coming
home. nobody from north bennington has ever gotten lost on the
way to saratoga yet, although several have gotten lost coming home. i
told the school principal about it and she said she was having a bad
year; she had been down to the track four times and lost money
every time. the local priest, i hear, is way ahead for the season.

it has been such a busy summer that i can't remember half of it, i
think; like all summers, it has gone too fast.

stanley and sally and barry and i went to syracuse, where i gave my
little speech. they paid me three hundred dollars, on which we just
about broke even, since we insisted on staying in a hotel instead of
visiting someone (we hardly could, with two small children, we figured) and it was lovely; the room which barry and sally shared had a
television set right at the foot of their beds, also, the hotel was air-
conditioned, and it was ninety the day we got there, and hotter the
next day, so we were fine. i spoke to about sixty writing folk, read
part of the new novel, and answered millions of idiotic questions and
some embarrassing ones and then had individual conferences with a
selected fifteen of the students and then, the third day, sat there
while they asked me anything they could think of, and they thought
of all sorts of things i couldn't answer. this all took place in the room
where i flunked the final exam in spanish several years ago and also
our old friend and teacher, leonard brown, sat in the back of the
room and kept putting in questions like, "do you take neat notes now,
shirley, or do you still scribble on anything?" it was a lot of fun, and
apparently went well, because they invited me to come back next
year. the fellow who ran the writers' conference also runs a farm and
riding stable about thirty miles outside of syracuse, and we spent one

afternoon and evening there. sally and barry rode horseback and they went swimming while we drank vodka martinis and sally got into a fight with a rooster, which was a draw, although sally was armed with a broom, and then we met bix. these people had a magnificent great dane, and she had eleven puppies. the nicest of these eleven puppies was—is—bix. stanley argued and sally and barry were amused and so we drove the two hundred miles home from syracuse with bix in the back of the car. He is my own dog and he is going to be just slightly bigger than an elephant although now he is only six weeks old. he is already the neighborhood favorite and in the two weeks we have had him has outgrown two collars; i can still lift him, but barely.

on sunday morning we left barry with jennifer feeley, and two t-bone steaks, and drove to lenox, where stanley's mother and father were spending the weekend. we had lunch with laurie, who was wearing the dirtiest shirt i have ever seen, and then all drove over to visit the girls at their camp, and found sally actually fatter, and sunburned, and very happy, and joanne, of course, enjoying herself immensely; we watched her first dive. sally loves the food at camp, and had been horseback riding with joanne. after visiting the girls we went back to music inn, and sat on the lawn watching laurie work. he puts in a full day; he had dinner with us and then his real work began; it was a jazz concert of the wilbur de paris band, most of whom are friends of laurie's, and he had to take care of the lights, and help usher, and so on. he looked very busy and very officious, and made a good many trips back and forth across the stage before the concert, and around the auditorium, and looked very important. after the concert, he was off duty, and we all went off and ate enormous sandwiches and drank in the bar.

so all the children are well and happy, and none of them are looking forward to school. laurie in particular hates seeing summer end. his only consolation is that this winter he can go down to new york and get into night clubs because now he knows all the musicians. we met dizzy gillespie, who is certainly dizzy. and we met thousands of other jazz musicians and some old friends from last summer. laurie of course knows everybody, and has been taking time off to go to the jazz lectures they are giving.

my book has gone to the typist, stanley is preparing classes, and now all i have to do is get clothes ready for school. and practice getting up at seven in the morning. write soon, happy birthday, and lots of love from all of us.

s.

.  .  .

[To Bernice Baumgarten]

September 27 [1957]

Dear Bernice,

I know you've been waiting for this, and I'm extremely sorry for delaying it, but the Literature Department at the college asked me most urgently to give a reading from it last night, and even though I feel that I could recite large swatches of it I felt that I ought to have the manuscript in front of me.

I read the first twenty-odd pages, and was ready to stop, but there was such a clamor that I had to go on for the rest of the chapter. One of the students told me afterward that I had seventy-five sales assured through the reading.

It's odd—students who know me all year around, and treat me with that dull indifference they save for faculty wives, spend this one evening a year when I read publicly addressing me as Miss Jackson. This morning I am Mr. Hyman's wife again. My moment of glory.

Any publication date?

Best,

Shirley

.  .  .

[To Bernice Baumgarten]

October 1 [1957]

Dear Bernice,

I am most anxious to know what you think of Sundial. It may interest—and warn—you to know that I have twice had substantially the same nightmare about it, of trying to get into the big house and being driven away and pursued; I want desperately to turn around and tell them that they are nothing but a pack of cards, but never think of it until I wake up. This morning, fearful and clammy, I woke up with the clear statement in my mind that Mrs. Halloran* had told me the house was built in 1492, which probably means that it will be discovered by the Book Find Club.†

 Stanley says we need money. I am working on a story for you so off-beat it would draw puzzled looks from the editors of explorations.‡

Best,

Shirley

•  •  •

[To Bernice Baumgarten]

October 4 [1957]

Dear Bernice,

Now, no one could call <u>this</u> a family piece. Stanley says I may not start a new novel until after the first of the year, but must spend the next

---

* Mrs. Halloran is the self-appointed leader and head of household in *The Sundial.*
† The Book Find Club was an early book-of-the-month club.
‡ *Explorations* magazine was a short-lived intellectual journal of the day.

three months making a fortune from magazine pieces so we can get enough ahead so I can write a new novel which I already have partly outlined. I have also, at last, found someone to do housework and as long as I can keep her I can idle my days away at the typewriter.

My ex-English professor at Syracuse read Sundial and wrote me a learned letter about it, praising it and mentioning Mann, Chekhov, Meredith and James. Something very complicated about an "ironic central intelligence." My, I'm glad I'm through school.

Best,

Shirley

•   •   •

[To Farrar, Straus & Cudahy]

November 1 [1957]

Dear Bob,

I am extremely sorry, but I find the jacket copy wholly unsuitable.

First, although it is only a proof and I know can be corrected, I can see no reason why whoever wrote it should be so unfamiliar with my book as this. Orianna is misspelled throughout. The Captain's name is <u>not</u> Scarabombardon. Aunt Fanny's first vision is not in the maze.

Second, I mind the attempt at plot summary very much. Essentially, the only statement necessary is that the book is about the end of the world. Descriptions of the mirror reading and Aunt Fanny's visions are pointless.

Third, I object most violently to the one-adjective description of each character: "Senile Richard Halloran," "beautiful Gloria Desmond," "experienced Mrs. Willow," and so on.

I am sorry to quarrel so, but even leaving out the several additional and lesser objections I have, I think the carelessness alone is enough to rule it out. Since actually there is no way to summarize the plot, I would suggest that it be cut down to the following:

"The new novel by Shirley Jackson has the suspense of The Lottery, the psychological insight of Hangsaman and The Bird's Nest, and the cool humor of Life Among the Savages plus an irony and brilliance all its own. The twelve occupants of the Halloran mansion, set in the large walled estate outside the village, are awaiting the end of the world. It is their belief that they will be the only survivors of the general cataclysm. The little that can be known about the future, in advance, they now know. They can only wait for it; wondering what it is that they do not know . . ."

Since this would fill only one flap of the jacket, it would be my most optimistic hope that the other flap would be left completely blank. If you don't care for that idea, Bernice suggested that the other flap might list my other books.

I realize that this must sound like a childish temper tantrum, but it seems to me that Sundial is so precariously balanced on the edge of the ridiculous that any slip might send it in the wrong direction; I tried to keep it on that uneasy edge because I thought it made the book more exciting, but I wouldn't like to see anyone breathe on it too hard.

Best,

Shirley Jackson

•   •   •

[To Bernice Baumgarten]

November 13 [1957]

Dear Bernice,

Naturally, I am very much depressed by your letter; I can of course understand that Roger would be reluctant to advance any more money, but I cannot help feeling that I have never, after all, asked for any money from him in all these years which I was not prepared to earn. Perhaps it is because we are so desperate that I can't be altogether sympathetic toward his point of view. I cannot remember ever being so completely discouraged about everything.

However, I don't expect that whining will do me any good, so I have been studying the prospectus for SPECIAL DELIVERY; it does sound like a practical and pleasant gift book, and I'd like to do some of it. I think I could manage any of the sections he names, and would like to suggest one he seems to have overlooked. That is the other side of the excitement and pleasure of the new baby, the terrible feeling of anti-climax and being hopelessly trapped which seems to hit every new mother after about three weeks. I've never seen it discussed anywhere and yet every new mother I've ever known seems to catch it. It's a kind of horrible realization that you're in this business for life.

I have been working on a new kind of story, hoping that it might turn out to be practical. The one I am doing will be about thirty pages long; I like it, but wonder if anyone can buy it. The general state of mind I am in has me convinced that there's no use in finishing it and it is just a waste of time but I keep telling myself that that is not really a terribly constructive attitude and anyway I have nothing else to do.

I have just read this letter over and it does sound like a Bennington College freshman—the kind who either ends up in the infirmary with mononucleosis, or gets referred to the psychiatric counselor because of suicidal tendencies. I will be sure to let you know which I decide on.

Best,

Shirley

*Bernice announces her retirement, after seven years as Shirley's agent. She is replaced immediately by Carol Brandt, of Brandt & Brandt, Literary Agents.*

[To Bernice Baumgarten]

December 18 [1957]

Dear Bernice,

I am so very awkward over the phone at things like saying
goodbye—difficult to do, I find, in <u>any</u> form—that I can only write a
most inadequate note. I feel bereaved, as I suppose most of your
friends do, and tell myself resolutely that you <u>are</u> going to have
breakfast in bed every morning, you are, you are, and who could be
heartless enough to quarrel with your living blissfully in Virginia
raising racehorses or tobacco or whatever they do in Virginia, where
I will also go on believing it is warm all the time. But it is going to
be very strange getting along without you. I am also very awkward at
saying how deeply aware I am of all the generous help you have
given me during these years and the many kind things you have
done. "Thank you—goodbye" seems inadequate somehow.

   Now at least you can have all the kittens you want, and I will start
saving them for you. I hope you will keep in touch with us, and the
very best of everything to you.

Love,

Shirley

• • •

[To Carol Brandt, Brandt & Brandt Literary Agents]

January 8 [1958]

Dear Carol,

Many thanks for your letters and for returning LOUISA; I shall try
that beastly story once more (I don't know why she stayed with Paul;

I personally think the girl was feeble-minded but shall try to make her snap out of it and look alive) but I don't know when I can get to it. I am up to the neck in poltergeists right now, for the first book for Viking; did I tell you the title? THE HAUNTING. Poltergeists, I now know more about than anyone.

I am extremely distressed by receiving this morning a copy of a letter sent you by George deKay,* announcing that I was going to send them sample material for SPECIAL DELIVERY and then the agreement would go through; this was never my understanding and I would certainly not agree under any circumstances to doing the work before there was any contract, and am sure that this was Bernice's view too. What I did say was that after the agreement was made (and the money paid!) I would start the writing and send several pieces along to them to see if the general tone and style was what they wanted. If they want to hire me to do a job I will do it the way they like, but until they do hire me I don't work. This kind of thing always makes me uncomfortable because I am always such a dear innocent jerk listening to these guys talk and thinking how nice we are all going to do a book together and how exciting it all is, isn't it, and then I turn around and discover that they have gone off with the impression that I am a dear innocent jerk.

For Pat Covici,† on the other hand, I am anxious to write many many books; he was so sweet and so horrified at the idea that he might "edit" any book I wrote. I could not even bring him to promise to correct my grammar. Poor man; wait till he sees what I do with conjunctions.

It was such fun meeting you, and I came home full of enthusiastic ideas about writing all sorts of things.

Best,

Shirley

•   •   •

---

* George deKay was the cofounder of the M. Evans & Co. publishing house.
† Shirley's editor at Viking Press.

## [To Geraldine and Leslie Jackson]

january 14 [1958]

dearest mother and pop,

let me begin right off by asking a favor. do you remember the winchester house?* and can you, do you think, get me any information about it? or pictures and information (particularly pictures) of any other big old california gingerbread houses?

the reason for this is my new book; it is to be about a haunted house, and i can't seem to find anything around here; all the old new england houses are the kind of square, classical type which wouldn't be haunted in a million years. i have half a dozen sketches of california houses which look right, but remember the winchester house as a good type house for haunting.

i am all wound up in houses right now, and spent yesterday in the library reading old architecture books. it occurred to me that perhaps mother might have, somewhere, some of my grandfather's old books,† but i suppose it isn't very likely. it is so exciting; i may end up taking courses in architecture at the college.

we are finally beginning to settle down again after christmas. the children are back in school, without much enthusiasm, and we finally got some snow. stanley's school is closed until march, and he is trying to get some articles written and some plans made for writing his book, which he does next year during his sabbatical. and i am collecting houses.

i keep thinking that nothing ever happens, but then i realize that at least for me there have been great changes in the last few months;

* The Winchester "Mystery" House in San Jose, California, was built over many years by Sarah Winchester, widow of the gun magnate. It has long been believed to be haunted by the many ghosts of victims of Winchester firearms and is still very popular as a tourist attraction, with guided tours conducted daily.

† Shirley's grandfather Maxwell Bugbee was one of many famous architects in her family; he designed some of the most stylish "gingerbread" mansions in San Francisco. Some of the Bugbee houses are still standing, and are worth millions.

my whole professional environment has changed and it is like starting out all over again with a first book. first of all my agent, who is
the wife of j.g. cozzens, who wrote "by love possessed," decided that
since her husband had finally come into some money with his book,
it was time for her to retire, after nearly forty years. the head of the
agency died, and his wife and son took over, and i now find myself
with a new agent, although the same agency. also, one of the last
things bernice did was something she had been promising me for a
long time, which was to break my contract with farrar and straus and
sign me up with a new publisher, so I am now, after fifteen years,
signed up with viking with a fine contract paying me fifteen thousand dollars for my next three books. unfortunately, they won't give
me the money all at once—even bernice couldn't manage that—but
are going to dole it out to me over the next three years, during which
time i am supposed to write three books, although i told them i
won't. i am promising to write three books in the next five years, and
have started docilely on the haunted house.

january 16 (two days later)

the first copy of sundial arrived yesterday and one reason i left this
letter was to sit down and read it. only two mistakes, which is
pretty good, and neither of them serious. wait till you see the
jacket. it is wild.* more copies will be along in a day or so and i will
send one right off to you. i keep getting sad little letters from people around farrar and straus saying how they are so sorry i am leaving them, but adding bravely that they hope sundial will be an
enormous success, and i write sad little letters back which read like
lee's farewell to his troops although actually i am delighted to be
leaving them and i bet they are just as happy to see me go, since we
have been fighting for fifteen years. what happened was that we
needed money, and i asked bernice to ask roger straus for money,
which i have been doing with moderate success for a long time, and

* The original jacket featured large horizontal banners of orange and yellow, with the
title repeated four times in caps, alternating with banners of black featuring Shirley's
name.

roger said flatly no. demons did very poorly, he was unable to sell
the reprint rights for either demons or sundial, and the whole book
publishing business was gone to pieces, and he had no money. it
made me mad because i had been fighting with him over the advertising for demons, which he did very poorly, and one reason it
didn't sell was because of no ads. so bernice—one reason she was
the best agent in the business—said well, would he give us money
as an advance on a new book, as yet unwritten, and roger said no,
so bernice very slyly said if i wrote him an outline of a new book
and promised to deliver it by a certain time—since he knows i always have—would he give us some money <u>then</u>, and roger still said
no, and bernice said well, then, that automatically broke my contract with them under the clause she had carefully put in saying if
they declined to give me an advance on a new book the contract
was broken; she told me this in the morning and by afternoon had
gotten me an advance from viking. they told me at viking that
every time my option with roger came up on each new book they
had been asking bernice to see if i would consider switching to
them but there had never been a chance because each time roger
took the new book without any hesitation.

the result of all this was that on new year's day stanley and i with
laurie tagging along at the last minute packed up and went to new
york. we left the three younger kids with the two feeley girls, and had
four fine days. i went in and saw my new agent, whose name is carol
brandt, and who is one of those terribly well-dressed, self-possessed
women i always seem to tangle with in new york; they always decide
at once (which is very probably true) that i am altogether helpless,
completely unable to get across a street by myself, and they immediately settle down to make all my telephone calls for me, and see that
someone will watch over me until they can get me on the train home
again. carol arranged for me to have lunch with the viking people,
and witnessed my signature on the contract, and even called me afterward at the hotel to see if i had gotten back safely. the viking people took me to lunch in a fancy french restaurant and we talked
about san francisco and old houses. my editor there is named pat co-

vici, an old old man who is tremendously respected in publishing and has the fanciest office i ever saw. i met him once many years ago and he was old then.

i did a lot of shopping for a lot of stuff i didn't need, and was very pleased to find that all my charge accounts all over town are still open. we did a lot of eating and drinking too, and saw a lot of people and got back to find everyone had enjoyed themselves while we were gone. a most successful trip. my first vacation in a long time. and no diet.

laurie has been playing a lot, almost every friday and saturday night, at dances and sometimes at a couple of local roadhouses.* he is playing now with several different groups. since the bands he plays with are all professionals, laurie will soon have to join the union. also, his life at present is extremely complicated by jennifer feeley. after years of our saying why don't you ask that nice jennifer to the dance? he has suddenly discovered jennifer. We only knew that we never saw him any more; he would come home from school just in time for dinner and then go out again and come home late in the evening, and then one evening helen feeley informed me that we were going to have to tell laurie to stop coming over every night because jennifer wasn't getting any homework done. so we have put laurie on a curfew and the feeleys have put jennifer on a curfew and so now they can only spend afternoons together and weekend evenings, so they spend the rest of the time on the phone.

january 17 (another day later)

sally is doing fine. almost all of her difficulty from last year is gone; she loves her new teacher and is doing better in her work, although never as well as she did before last year. she has always been just as fiery and wild as joanne is gentle, so she still gets into wild fights,

---

* Laurie is now playing cornet in the house band at a nearby New York State roadhouse called The Merry-Go-Round, a very popular dance venue for Bennington College students. The band is led by George Van Burgen, a former tenor saxophone player in the Count Basie band.

particularly with some of the boys who walk up this way, but we have found a way out of that, which amuses everyone except the unfortunate boys involved. laurie and stanley have set up a murder incorporated organization, so he gets a quarter for telling off one of these boys, fifty cents for scaring him silly without actually hurting him, and a dollar for beating him up—although the dollar job has not yet turned up.

barry steams along in his own fashion. he is learning to read and write. he has learned just enough to be able to sound out almost anything. he went out the other day all by himself and made a snowman, in the odd way he does things, taking advice only from the gardener next door, who told barry about the snowmen he used to make. it also entertained old mrs. welling next door, who is, of course, unable to get outside in this weather and who relies a lot on our children's activities for something to watch, so she was watching from the window. his greatest playmate right now is bix, the great dane puppy, who is still a puppy but about four times the size of any other dog in the world. bix is extremely fond of barry and they make a very odd pair, because barry is still quite small. when bix goes out to meet him after school he is very apt to knock barry down and then barry, in a snowsuit, cannot get up again and someone has to go out and persuade bix to stop licking barry in the face and let barry get up.

two characters from new york came up to see me about a month ago, because they had worked out a theory that they should find a suitable audience and then get a book written for it, and they have decided that there was no light, cheerful book for mothers of new babies, particularly first babies. they want something which will be reassuring and yet not emphasize things which turn up in standard baby handbooks. half the book is to be anthology pieces and cartoons and such, and the other half—about fifteen thousand words— i write. i can do it in a week, actually. they wanted to put my name on the book, as author-editor, but viking raised such a howl, because the book is for another publisher, that i will only be in small letters somewhere inside, which is all right with me.

stanley wants to know if you keep my letters because someday you will have to publish them. it should be quite an editing job, with no dates on them.

everyone sends love, and please feel well so you can come east soon. lots and lots of love, and thanks again for all the fine presents.

s.

. . .

[To Carol Brandt]

February 5 [1958]

Dear Carol,

Due to a most unpleasant and enduring virus infection which I caught from my beastly children, I have been held up for the past week in work on the baby book. It is a little better than half done, however, so I truly hope it will not be long now.

Meditations upon the proper bringing up of children have been further interrupted by my Great Dane puppy, who is at eight months the size of a Volkswagen bus and who chose to enter the house hurriedly by way of the front window, causing a good deal of noise and shatter, and scaring the daylights out of Barry. the dog cut his foot badly, and fled in panic from room to room, pursued by Barry and by me, and leaving bloody footprints on all the floors and particularly on the light green rug. I do not know why I bother. I simply do not know why I bother. Barry was enormously entertained, Stanley stood by saying things like "well I certainly think you should train that dog not to come through windows; a dog who always comes through the window is—"

Local people tell me that there is a house in a little town about fifty miles away which is haunted. The people there see the ghost and talk to her. They do not ordinarily encourage visitors but everyone thinks that if I wrote them and told them I was doing a book they would invite me to come and meet their ghost. I am not going to do it because I am scared.

Best,

Shirley

•  •  •

[To Ralph Ellison]

[undated, probably winter 1958, handwritten]

Dear Ralph,

I have been trying to draw your house and cannot—Is there any possible way of getting photographs? Particularly the front—the ballroom—and the hall?
    Would be enormously grateful—
    Thanks again for a most pleasant visit & too much whisky.

Love,

Shirley

•  •  •

[To Carol Brandt]

February 26 [1958]

Dear Carol,

I gave up doing family pieces partly because the magazines seemed over-full on the subject—not to mention the book lists—and too many other people were working the same pitch; and partly because there just didn't seem to be any good ideas left any more. I have, on several occasions, however, done some particular pieces as definite assignments. If Mr. Fischer* is interested in making some definite suggestions I'd be glad to try my hand at it.

Would he like a short, semi-fictional, piece on ghosts? I think of nothing but haunted houses these days, and have gotten as far back as Freud, who says such nasty things about people who have psychic experiences that I think I shall not try to see any ghosts of my own.

Best,

Shirley

•  •  •

[To Carol Brandt]

February 26 [1958]

Dear Carol,

Although I had set March first as the starting point for the haunted house book so I would have time to do revisions on the baby book, I couldn't wait and sneaked off last night while Stanley was arranging coins and wrote the first ten pages. He was very much annoyed, because I was supposed to spend this two weeks making brownies and nut cake and potato pudding, and even doing a little cleaning around the house. I always prepare for a new book by reading all my old books over again, and he even sank so low as to hide <u>Hangsaman</u>.

Have you been following that poltergeist on Long Island? I am waiting to see how long they can hold out before they give up the house. You can't win against a poltergeist. And no one but me seems to understand the recent heavy snows; do you remember the billions of gallons of water that disappeared suddenly in New Jersey about a

* John Fischer was editor-in-chief at *Harper's Magazine*.

month ago? That was clearly poltergeist work, but when poltergeists steal something like that they always have to give it back sooner or later. Those people in New Jersey are extremely lucky that it was cold enough to freeze. It was unfair, though, to send it as far as Vermont.

I am very anxious for news of the baby book; I certainly hope they like it.

Best,

Shirley

• • •

[To Carol Brandt]

February 28 [1958]

Dear Carol,

I thought you should have my own highly-colored version of my telephone conversation with Mel Evans* last night:

(Assume the usual preliminaries: the phone has been answered by a small child, who says "Who? Who? Oh. Moooooooooooooooooom? Telephone. It's some man. Shall I tell him you're in the bathroom? What? Oh. Hello Mister? She's coming.")

Shirley: (snarling slightly) Yeah?

Mel: Shirley, this is Mel. Mel Evans.

Shirley: Hello. Did you send me a check?

Mel: I just wanted to tell you we thought the baby book was great. Simply great.

Shirley: I'm very glad to hear it. Now you can send me—

Mel: By far the best work you've ever done along these lines. Just great. I just got it yesterday and I read it last night and finished it this morning and I think it's—

---

* Mel Evans was cofounder of M. Evans & Co., publishers of *Special Delivery*.

Shirley: I'm very glad you like it. Will you—

Mel: You were wrong about the horoscope, though.

Shirley: I was WHAT?

Mel: August 21 is the sign of Leo. <u>My</u> birthday is August 21, and that's the sign of Leo.

Shirley: Well, if you want to be Leo you can, just so you send me—

Mel: I thought the work was just great. As a matter of fact, I thought the whole thing was just great. Just great.

Shirley: Listen, if we don't pay our bill they're going to shut off—

Mel: (tolerant amusement) Well, first I've got to raise the money, don't I? I'm so broke—

Shirley: <u>You're</u> broke? Listen, let me tell you what the man from the gas company—

Mel: And we all think it's great because we never expected to see the whole thing so soon, and to have it come out so well. Of course it'll be a couple of months before we get the rest of the material together, and settle about the name and so on—

Shirley: If you think I'm going to wait a couple of months for—

Mel: But we all think it's just great.

Shirley: I'll be glad to revise anything you like, but first—

Mel: Well, of course we haven't gotten to <u>that</u> yet. But it's just great.

Shirley: I'm very happy that you like it. So—

Mel: Well, I wanted to call you and let you know we think it's great.

Shirley: It was very nice of you to call. And—

Mel: We'll be talking to you, then. Goodbye, now.

Shirley: (hanging up reluctantly) Yeah. (Turns and goes into living room where Stanley is sitting drinking scotch and reading the Bible, Book of Luke) That was Mel.

Stanley: (anxiously) Did you ask him about the money?

Best,

Shirley

•  •  •

[To Carol Brandt]

March 3 [1958]

Dear Carol,

I am perplexed about the offer from CBS for SUMMER PEOPLE;
as you know, I would do a good deal for a thousand dollars and
would hate to turn it down. Can't some arrangement be made with
them? I know so little about television anyway that I have no idea
whether or not this offer is a good one, of course, but these days,
when I am not doing any stories, we get broker and broker faster and
faster.

Is writing a television script very difficult? It occurs to me that
some such thing might be my solution for that horrid LOUISA
story, since I am wholly unable to handle it the way it is, and they
taught me in college that Mann said an unmanageable story frequently works out in dramatic form. Also, I need the exercise; the
start of the new book sounds too much like the end of the last one.
What do you think?

That story is like a jigsaw puzzle anyway; it keeps bothering me
because there's a piece missing.

Best,

Shirley

•  •  •

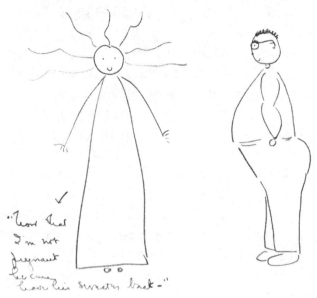

"Now that I'm not pregnant he can have his
sweater back."

[To Carol Brandt]

March 6 [1958]

Dear Carol,

I will now make a decision. It is perhaps my fourth decision in twenty-odd years, and it makes me very nervous. But I shall not shirk.

Three years with CBS is all right with me. I know it is longer than you like, but it seems enough better than seven years to warrant taking it, to my mind, and besides, CBS is the channel we get up here. This is only my decision, though—you still get the final vote.

I am extremely sorry that I can't manage Mr. Fischer's suggestion about the super-market. It is entirely outside my experience: we are, around here, still the farm women who come into town to visit together and gossip. We shop in a small-town grocery which we call The Store. When young Larry got out of the army and came back to help his father run The Store he brought a lot of fancy ideas he picked up in the city and he even talked old Mike into putting in a frozen-food case, but we're still a long way from a supermarket. You should hear some of the stories Larry can tell about the city.

I will try my hand at the ghost piece. I would avoid the Long Island poltergeist, I think, because very soon now it is going to turn out that the little boy is responsible; Stanley sometimes tosses me the Times when he is finished with it, and it does not sound as though the little boy can keep it up much longer. But there is a fine house in East Shaftsbury and I think I can put a ghost in it for Mr. Fischer.

Stanley's students will get their first look at his beard when they come back next week. Since Bennington girls are encouraged to speak their minds freely I think it will not be long before Stanley shaves. I have tried to tell him that a man who associates constantly with three hundred and fifty adolescent girls and thinks he can hold his own by growing a beard is clearly living in a fool's paradise but I am afraid it will take the students to point it out to him clearly.

Best,

Shirley

•  •  •

[To Carol Brandt]

April 8 [1958]

Dear Carol,

I am hard at work upon my ghostly book, a poltergeist story, and a sad little true little tale about my recent experiences with a gentleman calling himself Harold who gypped me out of two dollars worth of tin. Harold led me into one of my rare contacts with our local constabulary, and there have been few faces as radiant as my young

Barry's when he answered the phone and found that he was speaking to Police Chief Silver.

Best,

Shirley

•  •  •

[To Geraldine and Leslie Jackson]

april 10 [1958]

dearest mother and pop,

it is one of the loveliest spring mornings you can imagine, and i should really be outdoors planting bulbs or something, but ever since i planted the twelve blackberry bushes upside down the children have refused to let me into the garden and so i am forced to fall back on the typewriter.

since we've had two or three nice days in a row everyone is talking about summer. we didn't tap our maple trees this year because it was so rainy and cold and the sap wasn't much good, so we will have to use new york state syrup until next spring. last year we got enough syrup to last us through the summer.

our big surprise these days is barry. because all the other children take courses of one kind or another at the college, we decided to enter barry into a course in percussion instruments being given for the five to seven age group by one of the music assistants, and he has never had so much fun in his life. there are eight in the class, and they make enough noise for eighty. the woman who teaches the class has been concentrating, naturally, on time and rhythm rather than musical quality, and the first day she showed barry how his name sounded like two eighth notes, and showed him how to write them down on a piece of music paper. after a few classes, barry asked me if I would get him some music paper of his own so he could write his name in two eighth notes, so i got him a music copybook and he borrowed a pencil and went to work. this was on saturday, right after his class. by yesterday afternoon, when the class met again, he had filled up one book with written music and had started on a second. luckily, we had had weekend guests in the meantime, one of whom was a professional pianist, because barry was able to get some expert assistance when his music got to be too much for him. he insisted on being told about time differences, and then he started singing a little tune and writing it down. when we played it on the piano for him he discovered where he had gotten it wrong and corrected it. he took his music book to bed with him and sat there in bed composing, calling down every now and then to ask about things like triplets. when he handed his composition to his teacher yesterday i had to stand there and swear it was his own work, and explain that all we had done was answer his questions and when i had convinced her she went tearing out and found the chief composer at the college and showed it to <u>him</u>, and he came in and talked to barry, who was by then simply paralyzed with embarrassment, and said that if barry would copy out some of his music and give it to the composer he would set it for two or three instruments and they would play it at one of the college seminars. i daresay we will have to go one of these days and hear his first string quartet. pop will have a lot to answer for, if one of his grandsons is a jazz trumpet player and another a composer.

laurie continues to work fairly regularly every friday and saturday night; he is now playing with several bands, so never lacks for playing dates. he has been asked to come back to music inn again this summer and be a bellhop but he would rather see if he can play regularly with a band. we are quite unhappy because he has not been admitted to the putney school, where he very much wanted to go. he simply has to get out of north bennington next year; it's getting worse and worse, and even playing once or twice a week doesn't make up for the general miserable quality of the teaching in the high school and the fact that literally the only entertainment for the kids around here is hitch-hiking to the bennington movie. his only friends—aside from jennifer feeley—are the boys in the bands he plays with, and they are mostly williams college students, so that he

is too young to associate with them unless they are playing. he still
has the same problem of playing in places he couldn't get into otherwise because of his age. jennifer is leaving next fall, to spend two
years with helen's sister, and so laurie will be all alone. by the way, did
you get the clipping i sent you about the play he and jennifer were
in? they went on to win that state contest, and were finally elimi-
nated in the southern new england contest, beaten by a new york
state high school. we drove up to middlebury with the feeleys to see
the southern finals, and it was wonderful—practically the entire
north bennington high school showed up; miss corcoran, the high
school principal, was there, and everyone swears she took a drink in
the inn before the play. we were the four most nervous parents you
ever saw, and i think it was a relief to all of us when they got beaten.
the north bennington high school has never gotten into regional finals before; this is the first time they have gotten past the first contest.

joanne is riding high these days. she spends more time putting on
lipstick and nail polish and curling her hair than she does hanging
up her clothes, and most of her planning seems to settle around a
young man named oliver durand, oldest son of our doctor, who is a
year ahead of her in school and consequently a very desirable catch.
he takes her to all the school dances. the durands live on the college
campus near the college pond, which is actually a kind of swamp
about a foot deep, fine for ice-skating in winter, but usually dried up
by summer. the kids have made boats, because the pond is unusually
deep this year, and oliver's boat is easily the finest; it is a raft with a
pink sail and two people can ride on it, although i discover that it
tips over easily. joanne's greatest triumph is that oliver's boat is
named "joey" after joanne, and she is the only person besides oliver
who is allowed to sail the boat. everyone is very jealous of her.

sally is growing at last. she can no longer wear barry's clothes,
which is a great relief, and she is looking forward to camp this summer. she is still studying french, and is still keeping her book order
with her new york book dealer, who sent her another package a few
days ago. tonight is the school spring gym program, when the
smaller grades perform for their parents. if i can get through the un-

bearable excitement tonight, i must gather myself together to attend the lions club minstrel show on saturday night, to hear laurie play in the band. and next week joanne's class does a polka for the p.t.a. you can see how busy things are. stanley refuses to go to most of these things because he says the chairs in the school auditorium are too hard.

sundial is still selling well, and has just about run through the second printing. it's getting some fine reviews, and a particularly crazy set of reviews in the catholic magazines, which have taken it up as an issue. we got a furious review from a current catholic magazine saying that sundial was an outright attack on the catholic church, that the halloran house was actually heaven and mrs. halloran was the anti-christ and the other characters were dissenting protestant sects and true catholics everywhere should rise to defend themselves against this defamation. oh, yes—the first mr. Halloran was god and the poor old man in the wheelchair, kept prisoner by the heretics, was actually the true religion. considering that my information about the catholic church is extremely slight, i am very pleased to know that i managed to get so much of it in.

   lots and lots of love to both of you, and come soon.


     s.


• • •


[To Carol Brandt]

April 29 [1958]

Dear Carol,

How nice to be in Portuguese at last. Here are the contracts.

  Pat Covici wrote asking if I would possibly dare to commit myself on whether or not I ever planned to get a manuscript for him (that is not nice of me; his letter was so polite and kind) and I have just written him saying that I will send him a novel by spring 1959. Now all I have to do is write one. I also said I would try to get some pages to him in a month or so to see if he likes it.

I have also been called upon by James Thurber* to report, for his book on Harold Ross,† the reactions of Harold Ross to "The Lottery." That was even harder, because so far as I know or ever heard the only reaction Ross ever had toward "Lottery" was a kind of mild irritation.

I have a kind of story about ghosts to send you, but all my life, from ghosts to Harold Ross, has been infuriatingly complicated by my new unconscious device for avoiding work, which the doctor, patting me gently on the wrist, calls "a kind of arthritis," although I am sure he does not know any more about the devious kinds of arthritis than I do. At any rate, for days now I have been nursing a bad finger and musing gleefully upon his further statements that I have "a typical malformation of the fingers" and may "expect further difficulty." In other words, if I can swing it, I need look no farther for excuses not to work. I flatly refused to go over to the hospital and stick my finger into one of those frightful machines they have over there, so he makes me keep soaking it in oil of wintergreen and not even the dogs will come near me.

I can't keep it up very long, though. I'll get the story out to you in a day or so, and then settle down, snarling, to writing a book for Pat.

Best,

Shirley

•  •  •

---

* James Thurber, an internationally popular humorist, novelist, cartoonist, and writer and editor at *The New Yorker*, would have known both Stanley and Shirley.
† Harold Ross was the founding editor of *The New Yorker*.

[To Carol Brandt]

June 3 [1958]

Dear Queen Midas,

I am so excited over the way the novel is going that I keep sneaking back to it, during lunch, or late at night, to add just one more page. What I will do is get as far as I can before mailing it to you, and hope to get it to a point where something happens. As I tried to explain yesterday over the phone it has to start slowly because it is going to get so crazy so fast, and because the people and the house must be fairly well known before the ghosts show up. I have a note for later on which reads "Hand beckoning? Dog in fits? Moan?"

Looking forward to seeing you.

Best,

Shirley

•  •  •

[To Carol Brandt]

June 4 [1958]

Dear Carol,

I am most almighty pleased with myself. I hit the bottom of page 66 at four this morning and decided to quit for the night; this morning, reading it over, it seemed like a good place to stop temporarily and a good amount of manuscript to send to Pat Covici. I do not think I will write any more ghost scenes alone in the house at night, however.

I am also annoyed at having chosen the name Theodora, which I seemingly cannot spell, any more than I can spell verandah.

Stanley points out that at the rate of twenty-five pages a day, or night, I could finish the book before we come to New York. He says Voltaire did, but of course, that was in French.

I am lightheaded. I have a rough idea of what is going to happen to poor Erica* and if she had any sense she would pack up and leave on page 66.

Best,

Shirley

. . .

[To James Thurber]

[summer 1958]

dear mr thurber,

i am sorry to have to tell you that i have almost no information regarding mr ross' reaction to my story, the lottery. i never met mr ross, and all my dealings over the story were with gus lobrano;† i do know that when gus called me to say that they were buying the story he asked—"for our own information"—if i cared to take any stand on the meaning of the story. i could not—having concentrated only on the important fact he had mentioned, which was that they were buying the story—and he asked if i thought the story meant that superstition was ignorance; if the story could be called an allegory which made its point by an ironic juxtaposition of ancient superstition and modern setting, and i said sure, that would be fine. he said "good;

* "Erica" will soon become "Eleanor."
† Gus Lobrano was fiction editor at *The New Yorker* under Harold Ross from 1938 to 1956.

that's what mr ross thought it meant." since at that time none of us, i
believe, had any idea that the story would raise any kind of fuss, i
have always assumed that mr ross and gus <u>were</u> only asking to make
sure that their interpretation was a reasonable one; this "meaning" for
the story was afterward the official one that kip orr* used in answering the letters that came in.

mr ross had all the letters sent to me, including the ones which
were addressed to him or to "dear ed" or to the magazine in general.
because i am sentimental i put them in a scrap book, and it is now
almost impossible to get them out again. i find, however, that i have
the one note mr ross wrote about the story, and even that was not to
me, but to someone else instructing that the letters be given to my
husband to give to me, since farrar and straus might find them useful
as publicity for my book of short stories, which was due to be published, and which—naturally—featured "the lottery." since i cannot
get the note out of the scrapbook, i will copy it for you and enclose it.

if the scrapbook itself is of any slightest use to you, i will gladly
send it on. it has, as i say, the letters which came directly to the new
yorker and the letters which were forwarded to me, and the newspaper clippings and such. i have not bothered to keep it up since, although i still get letters fairly often asking me what that confounded
story means.

i wish i had more information to give you. since we were here in
vermont during the entire tempest, i knew nothing except what was
written to me; perhaps i am just as well off, not having had a chance
to hear what mr ross had to say about it all.

all best wishes,

Shirley Jackson

•  •  •

---

* Kip Orr was a features writer at *The New Yorker* who also dealt with letters to the editor and the unexpected volume of correspondence sent by readers in the aftermath of
the publication of "The Lottery."

[To Carol Brandt]

June 9 [1958]

Dear Carol,

Here is the children's play; the delay in sending it has been my son's fault, because I have been waiting and hoping that he would write down the music, but he has just taken to his bed with a virus which seems to be half caused by too much trumpet playing in drafty road-houses.

Stanley says that if I can write and sell six stories this summer he will let me get a grey convertible with pale blue upholstery next fall; since the car always belongs entirely to me I like to let my gaudy tastes run wild, but it also means that I have to work for it. Conse-quently I am feverishly working away at another story, along with the book.

About the book. I am glad you like the beginning; it is misleading, however, because due to the mishmash they are all going to get into later the present picture of Theodora and Luke is altogether mislead-ing. (Misleading, misleading; you'd think I was running a paper chase.) Luke is not at all the sugary romantic character he seems to be now, but an exceedingly unpleasant young man, and Theo is an ass. The doctor is married; his wife, Erica's sister and brother-in-law, and Luke's mother will be among the occasional visitors, I think. Also, I have to find out what Erica is always feeling so damn guilty about; she must have been rotten to her mother.

I am extremely sorry to have to say that we will not be able to get down on the 19th. I do regret it, because we were looking forward to seeing you, but an unexpected vista has opened up. Laurie goes off to work, the two girls go to camp, and my blessed sister-in-law has in-vited young Barry to visit them for two weeks at the end of July. That means that for the first time in sixteen years Stanley and I will be ALONE, in a kind of beautiful golden silence. So we think we will spend some of that time in New York and some at the Saratoga track.

Have a nice trip to Italy.

Best,

Shirley

•   •   •

[To Geraldine and Leslie Jackson]

june 16 [1958]

dearest mother and pop,

in the past three weeks i have written

1 children's play, 3 stories, ⅓ of a novel, no letters and feel that it is time i quit everything else and wrote you. i had to get to work because my new publisher wrote me a very polite, very wary letter about how they would certainly like to know if i ever intended to send them a book, so i had to write them one. once i got to work on that it seemed reasonable to write up the stories that have been sitting around in notes, and the children's play.

we are just coming into the wildest part of the year, when all the kids are out of school and stanley still has to go, and the college is in a fever of term papers and final productions; from now on until the end of june we will be knee-deep in cocktail parties.

we are all well and very excited with plans for the summer, although everything will happen at once—june 28 is the college commencement, the day laurie leaves for lenox, and the day the girls go to camp, not to mention the final faculty party in the evening; for some incredible reason, i am the chairman of an organization known as THE FACULTY WIVES COMMITTEE, a group which apparently exists for the purpose of making cheese dip for cocktail parties. now we have a president's wife who delights in entertaining, so our little committee is not really much use; my first suggestion, on being elected, was that we disband, but they said it was not fair because i was just trying to get out of the dirty work, which i was. anyway i have the job of planning and running the final faculty party.

i am feeling very important right now, anyway; last week bill fels, the new president, invited us over for a drink, and of course (we knew it ahead of time) what he wanted was to invite me to teach at the college; the literature faculty is going to be one short next year because howard nemerov is taking a leave of absence, and they badly need someone to teach his classes, or similar classes. at any rate, bill finally asked me and i was finally able to say no positively, but it was flattering to be asked. i did offer, at stanley's suggestion, to help out in counseling next year, which would lessen the department's work to some extent; it means that i meet half a dozen students one hour a week each, and listen to them talk. they are supposed to bring their college problems, work and such, to the counselor, and the counselor then channels the problems off to the people who can deal with them. all i have to do is listen, and there are two or three girls who are interested in writing and i can read their stories and steal their plots.

stanley's mother, father, brother with wife, and scott, spent memorial day weekend with us, and we had a great time. they always arrive with a car full of food and presents, and this time bunny completely captivated joanne by walking into the house in a flaming orange chemise dress—even laurie liked it—and bunny spent the entire weekend helping joanne put up her hair, and fixing the hem of a skirt, and such, and arthur spent the weekend listening to laurie's tales of woe about girls. arthur and bunny drive a brand new convertible, and were perfectly willing to drive the kids around town so they could wave at their friends. altogether, a most enchanting aunt and uncle. i am kind of surprised, you know, that bunny had the nerve to wear that dress in public.

the girls are going to the same camp as last summer; the camp is only half an hour's drive from here, and it is small and informal, with a lovely lake. the people who run it are comfortable, easy-going types who have four children of their own. last summer i used to make the grand circle, from bennington to camp to laurie at lenox and back to bennington, in about two hours. laurie is pleased at going back to lenox; he is getting to be quite a well-known figure locally, and sits in with various bands in various un-savory places every weekend. we hear of people running into him in roadhouses as far away as troy [New York]. he is making a good deal of money, and thank heaven, putting most of it into the bank. we are rather worried about him in general, because all he wants to do right now is play the trumpet and date the college girls and drink beer. it's an odd problem, because all his difficulties seem to be reasonable ones for his age, but the one upsetting thing is the trumpet playing, which gets him into association with people much older, and perhaps sometimes not altogether suitable, and lets him into places like roadhouses where kids of his age don't usually go. he seems very much older, by the way, and is certainly self-possessed and poised enough for a boy much older. stanley hears from his students that laurie "really took the place apart" when he was playing at a local roadhouse, and that's all we know. if we ask him he tells us where he was, but it's hard to keep track of him. he dates only college girls with cars, you understand; we wonder sometimes what excuse he gives for not having a car, since stanley hears everywhere that his son is eighteen years old, that being lau-rie's story, of course laurie gets older every year but the college freshmen stay the same age. he entertained a young lady here last night, a very nice girl who is in stanley's freshman class. they stayed in the music room playing records while we played bridge in the living room, and the minute i brought out food they showed up, both starved. unfortunately we were playing bridge with paul feeley, and laurie and jennifer feeley quarrelled in a most spectacular fash-ion about three weeks ago, and i am sure that paul went home and told jennifer about laurie's date. everyone got involved in the laurie-jennifer business, and i wish i could write it as a story. laurie did a really splendid job of offending everyone including his mother and father. he and jennifer were supposed to be going steady (horrible phrase) and laurie disregarded the rules by going

out with another girl—actually, <u>three</u> other girls—and then got
sore at jennifer when she did the same thing. there was one high
point when he walked into the local soda shop and there, scattered
around the tables, were the girl he had a date with, the girl he had
broken a date with, the girl he had <u>forgotten</u> a date with, and jennifer. how he got out and sneaked home i do not know. the story has
a happy ending, though. a few days later an old friend of helen's
called her, said she was up for the summer with her son, who
wanted to meet some nice young people, and would jennifer be interested in introducing him around? it turns out the son is eighteen, in dartmouth, has a car, and was immediately taken with
jennifer, and laurie is furious. she apparently had the good sense to
wave at laurie when she drove past with her young man.

we took the whole crew of them last night to a special college
production, which was the most wonderful thing i have ever seen;
the drama staff chose a harlequinade from sixteenth-century italian
drama, and did it with fantastic sets and a lot of acrobatics and
slapping people with wooden swords, and they opened it with the
entire cast of fantastic creatures parading down the center aisle of
the theatre banging a drum, and they run up onto the stage and put
up their set, banging into each other and standing on each other's
shoulders to put up the curtain, and so on. stanley and i went to see
it the first night, and were so delighted that we wanted to go again
with the kids, and then found that we couldn't get tickets. we got in
touch with the head of the drama department, and told him our
sad story, and he reserved the first four seats in the front row for us,
so we had the best seats of all. at one point in the play this guy—
who is a kind of stage janitor, doing a clown act with a mop and
pail, and delighting the children—comes to the front of the stage
and pretends to throw the water from the pail into the audience,
only it is confetti, and is supposed to scatter over the front few
rows; this was done right at our side of the stage, and we were
looking forward to the moment, because it always raised great
shrieks in the front rows; of course, we hadn't told the children. unhappily, last night, instead of throwing the confetti his hand slipped
and he threw the pail too, and it went sailing past joanne's ear and

smacked a little boy in the row behind. so they were surprised, all right; sally and barry thought it was part of the play and were very pleased. the little boy wasn't hurt. then a little later in the big duelling scene, a wooden sword got out of control and sailed into sally's lap, which she again thought was part of the play and laughed happily until we made her give back the sword. i had previously put in a request for pantaloon's ornamental mask, which was a beautiful piece of work, and at the end of the play it was formally delivered to me. as a result we all feel very much as though we had actually participated in a sixteenth-century theatrical performance, and all four of the children have a sudden vivid feeling about the commedia del' arte. pantaloon's mask is hanging in the living room. i am particularly delighted since the next thing they do at the college, next fall, may very well be my play.

it was joanne's fault. some of the college faculty kids got together with a drama student who wanted them to do a play. they did a haphazard informal play, mostly ad lib, and sally and joanne had prominent parts. the play was presented to a small audience, and was extremely well received. as a result they immediately wanted to do another, and were all enthusiastic until they got to the library and found that there were simply no one-act plays for children that were anywhere near their abilities. so, foolishly, i said sure, i'd write them a little play. i decided on a re-write of hansel and gretel, with the children as the villainous characters, always mean and quarrelling, and the witch won't keep them and the parents won't take them back. i wrote it in one evening, and the kids loved it. i called it "The bad children; a play for bad children," and then laurie offered to write music for it if i would put in some little songs, which i did, including one called "mean old wizard blues," to which he wrote a fine blues tune. unfortunately so far it is the only one written down; he can play and sing the rest but is too lazy to record them. the play got itself finished and sally sneaked a copy off to school and passed it around the fourth grade. it turned out to be too late this year to put it on, so they planned it for the fall, however, in the meantime i got a call from a school in williamstown saying that they heard i had a one-act play suitable for children to act, so could they possibly put it on next spring? i was still trying to digest this when our school called to say could <u>they</u> put it on? i had already sent over a copy to bill alton, who is the college drama head, asking him if he could give me some advice about technical things in it, since i had never written a play before and bill called back and said would this possibly be available for the college students?

the result is that the play is now at my agent's being copyrighted; it will be sold to one of the companies which publishes children's plays, and i will collect royalties on it. i also put laurie's name on it as the composer of the music, which may provoke him into getting the music written down, although maybe mean old wizard blues (it starts "i want a rich witch, baby . . .") may not be just the thing for everybody's high school. he's also doing an incantation boogie.

the college people love to do big stage productions, with odd effects and wild sets and lighting, and one reason this play appeals to them is the scene where the witch and the wizard set up a magic incantation, with a wild dance—laurie's incantation boogie. i would love to see them do it.

stanley had set ten o'clock last night as the absolute deadline for his class papers to be turned in, and was apparently very emphatic about it, because at five minutes to ten he asked me if i would run up to his college mailbox and collect the papers that were there, and when I walked into commons at five minutes after ten there was a great cheer; about fifteen of his students had waited to see if he meant it and planned to pick up the papers. i explained that the extra five minutes was my doing because i wanted to give them a little more time.

i hope you read this letter in installments, like a book. it is so much easier, actually, for me to write long long letters telling you about everything than it is to write short letters leaving half of it out. i suppose that is the penalty you have to pay for having a writer in the family. there are so many letters on my desk waiting to be answered; it makes stanley angrier than anything else to see unanswered letters. he says that i wait until there are so many letters they cover the desk and then start a novel so i won't have time to answer them.

we are going to michigan this summer, where i am supposed to lecture. they pay my expenses, which means that if i go by myself i will fly out for two days, but we are trying to arrange for all of us— that is, stanley, barry and me—to go, and the idea of going by air-plane thrills barry. i am also lecturing at a writers' conference in connecticut, where you lecture one evening and then sit in on discus-sions for the next two days, and they offered me expenses and a hun-dred and fifty dollars which is about average unless you are james gould cozzens. i wrote them and said to make arrangements at the hotel for three of us, my husband and one child were coming with me, and the next thing we know is that they have printed their offi-cial announcement saying that i am lecturing and stanley is joining the seminars as a visiting critic. stanley wrote them a sizzling letter saying that he was not accustomed to making his lecture dates through his wife, and that they had no authority to use his name on the program without dealing with him directly, particularly about payment, since the money they paid me did not include him as an assistant. we are waiting to hear from them saying they don't want either of us, which would be fine. we keep running into this difficulty because when i go with stanley sooner or later they ask me to sit in on something, or give a brief impromptu talk to a few of the stu-dents, and of course it is expected that i am doing this out of pure goodness, since it was stanley they hired, and then someone else turns around and does the same thing to stanley when they hire me. the solution is to go alone, but we like going together and making a vacation of it.

lots of love to all from all. keep well, write soon.

love,

s.

•   •   •

[To Carol Brandt]

July 9 [1958]

Dear Carol,

My most earnest thanks are due to all of you; to your son for seeing that that check went out, to yourself, for the wonderful candy, and to some extent, I believe, to McCall's for buying me my convertible. It is a tiny black Morris Minor with a red top and whitewall tires, and children stare at me as I zip by. I go up to the parking lot at the college and do figure eights.

I enjoyed lunch with you and Pat enormously, and am seriously grateful for his readers' comments. I think Pat knew perfectly well that I wouldn't pay any attention to the ones I didn't find helpful. It was a lot easier talking to Pat with you there, and far pleasanter, although two cocktails before lunch is an indulgence we in Vermont find dissipating; I went off and bought five dresses.

No, I have not been working. I have been riding around in my car. But I promise that as soon as some of the shininess wears off I will write thousands of pages, starting with the little story I have waiting here. We fly to Michigan next Wednesday, a project far more terrifying and complex than your flying to Italy, and I must give a lecture out there, which I must also write between now and Wednesday.

I am so excited about those two stories selling so fast.

I am going out and ride around some more.

Best,

Shirley

· · ·

*"oh, no, we haven't got company — just a few friends of Stanley's dropped in."*

"Oh, no, we haven't got company—just a few friends
of Stanley's dropped in."

[To Carol Brandt]

September 9 [1958]

Dear Carol,

Here is the new story, SUMMER AFTERNOON, and three carbons
of old ones. I am sorry to send the carbons rather than clippings from
magazines but I prefer these versions to the ones that were printed.

The novel is getting sadder. I suppose it's because of a general melancholy, leaves turning red and a frost last night, but a general air of
disaster is slowly settling over Hill House. It's always such a strange
feeling—I <u>know</u> something's going to happen, and those poor people
in the book don't; they just go blithely on their ways.

Best,

Shirley

•  •  •

## [To Geraldine and Leslie Jackson]

october 27 [1958]

dearest mother and pop,

i was feeling so nostalgic this morning; i was making mimi's nut cake—i have to make it often because everyone loves it—and i was wondering how she would have liked making it with the walnuts already shelled in a can, and an electric mixer.

i hope your trip was wonderful; we've loved getting your postcards, and none of the children believe there really is a place called fiji.

i might as well give you the bad news first: laurie was bounced out of prep school after three weeks. it was all his own fault; he apparently couldn't go from the fairly free life he was living here; the first week he was in school he was warned for smoking and the second week he heard that his band was playing a date in troy, and figured if he asked the headmaster if he could go he would not get permission, so he left without permission; the headmaster called us and we tracked him down and got him back to the school, and then the third week (what an idiot he is!) he walked into a bar in the small town near the school with half a dozen other kids and they all ordered drinks. the others were suspended but laurie's record couldn't stand another crime, so he was bounced. the headmaster was very nice about it, and a good deal more understanding than we were; he thought that all three offenses were so open; and so obvious that any person doing them would expect to be caught. he said why not keep laurie at home for the rest of this semester, and then re-enter him in january, if he seems to have learned any sense. he hates being back in north bennington high school, but is trying to do his best, because he still wants to go to college, and he is back playing weekend nights with his band. if it has done nothing else it has at least taught laurie a lesson in discipline i hope he will never forget.

all four children this fall seem happier and more settled than usual; barry is no longer a baby, and doesn't have to be watched or entertained all the time. barry is also reading; he was just like sally, and discovered all at once that he could pick up a book and read. when he finally found a book he could read all the way through he wouldn't give it up, but went back to the beginning and started over. sally has been feeding him carefully chosen books, and he is now on his third, reading each one at least twice. sally is odder than ever, of course. almost all the nervousness and irritability left over from that frightful teacher is gone; camp did wonders for her, but she still does not have any particular friends and nothing interests her but drawing and writing. we are giving her oil paints for her birthday, and a good phonograph hoping to interest her in music. sally is quick and careful and remembers everything she is told.

joanne is closest to driving us crazy of any of them, right now. it takes her an hour to get dressed in the morning, and one morning she is starved and eats six pancakes and the next morning she has gone on a diet again and will take only a dish of prunes. she has to change her clothes three times before school. she is an extremely good dancer, and with all her giggling and general unbearable vanity, very popular. the phone rings for her all day long and she is always invited to the dances well in advance, and her days are as full of plots and counterplots as a spy movie.

as for the rest of us: stanley, me, cats, dogs, and such, we try to bear up. my great dane is bigger than my car (which is still my dearest toy) and we have five new kittens. every now and then stanley says "when are we going to get rid of the kittens?" and the rest of us kind of turn away and pretend to be doing something else.

stanley has accepted an offer to teach for six weeks this summer in the columbia university graduate summer school. it is quite an honor, and pays well for not much work. the girls and barry will be in camp, and laurie has several playing jobs lined up already, so i could go if i wanted to, but i can't see finishing my book in a small, hot city apartment. stanley alone could live at the faculty club. i may spend part of the time there, but i am committed to a writers conference again in connecticut, and probably another trip to michigan, so we will be all over the map.

we have started giving dinner parties once a week, and it's quite a lot of fun; for a long time it was difficult to entertain in the early evening with children around but now they are always upstairs reading. joanne earns a good wage for waiting on tables and i have a new cleaning woman who gets the house looking decent, so it is practically painless, except for cooking the dinner. there are so many people up here we never get to see except at general parties, and a lot of people we owe dinners to, so it looks like quite a social season.

write me soon all about your trip, and all our love from all of us.

love again,

s.

. . .

[To Carol Brandt]

December 3 [1958]

Dear Carol,

I am so surprised and happy about the Post that I can't think what to say; I will try to work them out a biography. And many thanks to you for sending on the check which, as you knew, we sorely needed.

Sorely is the word for me, too, right now; I walked out of a cocktail party on Monday in high heeled shoes onto an icy path and landed flat on my back. As a result, I can hardly walk and sit very poorly indeed, but, not being able to move around, I put a cushion on my typing chair and finished off the present draft of Hill House, which means that I am running about a month ahead of my schedule. Stanley read it last night and likes it. Now I get a new typewriter ribbon, and type the manuscript once more, incorporating all my notes and putting in what I left out of the plot. I am very set up about it, because I think it came out nicely.

The only really comfortable position I can find is lying down. Either I must move to a warmer climate, or give up high-heeled shoes. Or cocktail parties.

Best,

Shirley

.  .  .

[To Geraldine and Leslie Jackson]

december 15, 1958

dearest mother and pop,

first of all, thank you so much for the magnificent bag; it is perfectly beautiful and i needed it badly. my little car will not fit in it, but it will only just fit in my little car. i had a lovely birthday, and it started off so nicely by being able to talk to you. everything went perfectly—my football team beat stanley's in the last three minutes, and i won a dime, and then it turned out that there was a conspiracy on hand which decorated the dinner table and provided a beautiful cake.

we are all well, looking forward to christmas, and keeping busy. this is the last week of school, and this morning we have six inches of snow, and it's still coming down. my little car goes through, though, much better than the big one; it has one great advantage—because it doesn't have much power, it stops immediately when you take your foot off the gas, which means you don't have to use the brakes and so of course do a lot less skidding. this morning, though, when i took stanley to the college and went up the big hill i had a rough time. the lowest gear on these little foreign cars will get you up the side of a house, they tell me, and the little cars were getting up the hill and the american ones weren't. we went up kind of sideways, but we got to the top, and then of course when i came back down again it was very lively, trying to duck the american cars stalled on both sides of the road.

my poor cleaning woman, who lives fifteen miles upstate, couldn't get her car out at all this morning. mrs wright is really very nice, and a most pleasant person. she comes three afternoons a week. because i never know where to tell anyone to start cleaning, she took it on herself to plan out what she did; one day I was struggling to sew a button on my coat and she took it away from me and did it, and now does all our mending. and she feels very sorry for me because i am so helpless. every now and then i tell her kind of timidly that i _can_ write stories and she smiles at me and says not to worry. she is very much amused at seeing me sit at the typewriter all morning, and cannot understand why i want to waste my time at such a crazy occupation. her daughter, who is joanne's age, got one of my books out of the library and the whole family read it and mrs wright thought it was very nice. but mrs wright cannot somehow make any connection between the book she read and my working every day. she loves to gossip and knows every disaster or scandal that has ever happened in vermont, and every now and then i can get some notes for a story from her.

laurie seems to have adjusted extremely well. his school work has been poor, because he got so fouled up between schools, but in all other respects he is far better than he was. we have kind of given up hope for his education, since he is slowly building up a career, or at least a job, for himself in music. he is now in the union, which means that his pay has gone up to union scale, and has been invited to go to bermuda at easter time, for two weeks with all expenses paid, to play in a hotel there; also the manager of the roadhouse where he works weekends has offered him a contract job; laurie is to get together a band, and be responsible for them for friday and saturday nights all year round. the pay on this would be considerable; but of course we are not altogether in favor of it, since he is far too young to take on that kind of responsibility. just getting a band to be all together in one place is a major operation. we will not let him drive, and we will not let him drink anything except beer. he wants to smoke, and we compromised on a pipe, which he likes very much and i think he believes he looks very sophisticated with his pipe. whatever he earns goes directly to stanley and into the bank. he thinks it's terribly funny to come downstairs in the morning and pay over what he calls stanley's allowance.

i have been keeping busy. one reason it is so hard to stay at the typewriter is that everyone is so excited and wild that there is really no chance to think. last night the children had their christmas pageant at the school, joanne singing in the girls' choir and sally and barry singing with their classes. after that i brought my three home, put them to bed, and went off to the college to meet stanley and go to three student parties, where we met laurie off and on. there was a program given by the students of the social science division, kidding the faculty, and it was one of the funniest things i have ever seen. they did a parody of the faculty poker game, with paul feeley in a pink shirt and red tie and stanley, who was identifiable by his beard and his chain smoking, and it was incredible to realize how much the students know about the faculty—and they had emphasized a lot of little eccentricities no one would ever think of noticing. they were very cruel about one of the historians who never lets anyone forget that he graduated from harvard, and one of them who is inclined to be a little bit stingy will never, i think, dare mention money again.

each of the student houses has a christmas party this last week and the parties tend to be very different, although usually loud and wild. we keep meeting laurie from time to time, always with a can of beer in his hand; he loves these parties, of course, and seems to know more students than stanley does. one party had hired laurie and his band, and that was great fun; we don't get a chance to hear him very often and he was really good, full of spirit and enthusiasm and i guess beer.

for christmas joanne's present is a private phone, although that may be a big mistake. we are giving laurie a typewriter and sally a bike, and barry has finally gotten old enough for a phonograph, so it ought to be a gay noisy christmas.

i told you that i sold a story to the saturday evening post, but didn't tell you—because we didn't know yet—that stanley has also

sold them an article, one of that egghead series they have been running, on literature. It means that one of these days you will open your
post and run into one of those full-page pictures of stanley. i have
stories waiting at the journal and mccalls, and two small articles from
the book i did on babies will be in redbook. i am selling every story i
write but simply have not enough time to do many; i will have to
spend january working on some because we are going to need the
money. the first draft of my book is finished, and by march it should
be finally done, thank heaven. i have put it away for a while before
going to work on it again; I need about a month to forget it and then
start fresh. it should be published next fall.

for six years the editor of good housekeeping, named herbert
mayes, has been feuding with me in a crazy kind of fashion. no one
can find out what he ever had against me, but he hated my former
agent and seems to have picked up grudges against many of her clients, for there are a lot of us in the same boat, artists, writers, and so
on. mayes closed down the entire hearst organization, about six magazines, to all of us, and i have heard that he kept a file of names of
people whose material was never to be put on his desk, but returned
at once. the result was that my stories never went to him, and my
present agent built up a market for me with mccalls and the journal,
and then mccalls turns around and fires its entire editorial staff, including all my friends, and hires mayes away from good housekeeping with <u>his</u> staff and his file of enemies. for a couple of weeks it
looked awful; if mayes kept up his feud and I was still blacklisted at
the hearst offices there literally wasn't a magazine i could sell to, and
i was kind of discouraged, and it wasn't any comfort to know that
there were a lot of others feeling the same way. finally my agent persuaded him that he should give up his old feuds, presumably to start
new ones, and he said he would run my story and would keep
mccalls open as a market for me. she did get the hearst magazines
open to me again, though, and this sale to redbook is a good omen.
also the post is interested in more stuff, so i feel a good deal better.

i have become fascinated by the idea of writing a play, and may
very well try it next fall. i have two one-act plays, one for the kids
which is off in new york being copyrighted, and one for the benning-

ton drama department which they are putting on next spring. I have no trouble writing the dialogue but cannot understand how to move people around on a stage, and bill alton of the drama department here is trying to teach me. he says if i do a long three-act play suitable for professional production he will let me try it out with bennington actors to get it right before sending it along to my agent; the agent would turn it over to the theatrical agent and there would be a chance of getting it produced for real. it is all very vague, though, because i may be in the middle of another novel by then. what i could do is write the novel in dialogue and then see which way to finish it—as a book or a play. also i don't know how it will feel to see the thing on a stage, and maybe once i hear them saying my lines out loud i will never try again. sooner or later someone always suggests doing something for television, and i get the creeps when i think of it; one of the playhouse things bought an old story of mine and it has simply been buried, no sign of its ever being used, and the Schlitz people asked me for three stories, old ones, to be re-written for television, and i have never heard a word about those, either. my agent says that it is like doing business with a flock of birds—they have to get ten or twelve people to agree on everything, and no one seems to know quite what is going on; you can never count on them until the money is in the bank. even then, by the time they have finished taking out everything controversial or odd in the story, it turns out to be exactly like everything else they put on, with no more individuality than the commercials. i hate the whole business.

jay williams' new kid's book, coming out this spring, is dedicated to sally. she doesn't know it yet. she corresponds with him regularly, very strange letters about an imaginary country they both believe in. she has written three little books for barry which are extraordinary. stanley told her once as a joke that he would not allow her to publish until she was twelve, so she has set that age for her first professional book. walt kelly* sent her a pogo picture, of a pogo offering a bouquet to a sally; we met him in a bar in new york and he was charmed

---

* Walt Kelly was a syndicated cartoonist and creator of the popular Pogo series that ran daily from 1948 to 1975, featuring Pogo the friendly Possum and the brash Albert Alligator, among many others.

by our description of sally; he also made me a kind of shocking picture of albert alligator chasing a lady alligator, which is framed over
my desk.

i wish we could be with you for christmas, and we will be thinking
of you. all our love to all of you.

s.

.   .   .

[To Libbie Burke]

Thursday [February 19, 1959]

Dear Lib,

Just a note on time stolen from my book to say thanks thanks for the
wonderful letters about your house and the pictures which have gone
into my house-scrapbook. We are considering remodelling our present house to look like yours and are starting with a fireplace which
the man is coming today to put in, digging through the wall about
four feet northwest of my typewriter.

Stanley works steadily, persistently, doggedly, hysterically. Great
piles of manuscript accumulate on his desk. Perhaps he will have a
book before this wears off.

I had already anticipated one aspect of your house—doors leading
out of the kitchen in every direction; mine was so you could get out
fast when something came at you from a corner.

Looking forward to seeing you soon. I will show you my scrapbook when you come back.

Love,

S.

.   .   .

[To Carol Brandt]

March 30 [1959]

Dear Carol,

I am too embarrassed, or too proud, to write this to Pat Covici, but
for the record I want you to know. After all my promises about getting the book to him by April 1, I found myself last Wednesday,
going fine, on the beginning of the last chapter. Here, I swear, is what
has happened since:

1. Every child in our family, one after another, came down with
flu. Now Stanley has it. I will go mad if I have to open another can
of chicken soup.

2. Our senior cat, not to be outdone, has picked up an infection,
requiring visits to the vet, and medication; have you ever tried to feed
sulfa pills to a large and still strong cat?

3. Sally, recovering from the flu, stepped on a rusty nail. She must
go today to the doctor for a tetanus booster.

4. Some vital piece of pipe fell out of the furnace in the middle of
the night. No heat for flu patients until we can get three men to replace it. Emergency situation, of course.

5. The entire plumbing system backed up, from a clogged septic
tank. Water is seeping through the cellar wall. Emergency situation.
Six men with bulldozer, because the ground is frozen too hard to
allow hand digging. Two plumbers. No water. It is refreshing to see
me washing dishes in a dishpan which I empty off the back porch.
We are allowed to brush our teeth if we do it fast. No baths, of
course. Barry has invented a system of washing with a water pistol,
outside.

6. I forgot to get the dog licenses.

Last night after I got everyone to bed, grimy and snarling, I managed to do a couple of pages. But I am still substantially where I was
last Wednesday. I like to pride myself on getting things in on time

and I thought I had this one made. I am not writing you this, by the way, so you will pass it on to Pat; I would rather you didn't. As a matter of fact, I am feeling kind of heroic. If I can work all day and all night today and tomorrow I can still get it to him the first week in April. A splendid demonstration of how great art is only achieved through suffering.

Here comes the bulldozer. On to chapter 7.

Best,

Shirley

The plumber just remarked amiably that on the whole it would have been cheaper to take the whole family to Florida for a few weeks until the ground unfreezes.

. . .

[To Geraldine and Leslie Jackson]

friday [May 1959]

dearest mother and pop,

sorry not to have written sooner, but it has been literally impossible. i was working eight hours a day at the typewriter to get my book finished, then on the publisher's revisions, then on the articles for good housekeeping, and still have at least two more articles to go. the first will appear in august, by the way, and my story will be in the may 30 issue of the saturday evening post, stanley's article in the june 13 issue. they are publishing my new book this fall, which means everything has to be done at top speed.

on top of the various literary pressures things have been generally upset; stanley's father had what they called a "fairly mild" coronary attack last week, and is in the hospital, not allowed to move or lift a finger for at least three weeks and then three more at home. we thought we would have to go to new york but he cannot see visitors until he goes home, so all we can do is call every night; stanley's brother is there, and luckily, because of course stanley's mother has taken it very hard.

also, we are having a heat wave. the temperature has been above ninety every day for a week, and stays in the eighties at night. the children love it, of course, but it is almighty hard to work. stanley has been having a rough time, since he was behind schedule already on his book, and between the heat and his book going badly and worrying about his father I genuinely believe that he is going to be sick himself if i can't make him calm down. we are going june first to a kind of literary convention at a resort in the poconos, and it will be four days of comparative rest for him, so i just hope he can hold out that long. he can't sleep, and sits up reading most nights. the only time he was really cheerful was when the government sent him a refund on his income tax.

anyway, things are not all a tale of woe. the kids are fine, nearly crazy with spring at last, and the leaves and the lawn green and strawberries growing wild in the fields. all the kids have changed, even in the short time since you were here. laurie came back from bermuda with a nice tan and great ambitions; he had met a girl from a college in virginia and they were so taken with each other that she invited him down for their spring weekend and dance, and laurie took most of his money out of the bank and flew to virginia for a weekend. he had his first encounter with segregation, and it shocked him horribly. he came back saying he would never go south again, even to see his young lady. he passed his driver's test without any difficulty at all, and has taken over the station wagon, which is practically on its last legs but still goes. he now can take jobs in cities relatively far away, and has more work than he can handle. he made a hundred dollars last weekend, which just about pays for his virginia trip. this weekend he plays in boston and next weekend in pittsburgh. he has also been invited to go with a college band to europe next summer, and will be playing with them in new york city over this coming winter. he has to rent a tux for the job in pittsburgh. in the meantime he is still supposed to be painting our back apartment, but we can't compete with the wage scale for union musicians. he was chosen king of the junior prom, by the way.

joanne, only in junior high, was not allowed to go to the prom, but was among several junior high girls chosen to do menial jobs like taking coats and serving punch, which of course turned out to be very exciting and important, and to require a semi-formal dress, something i had not expected to deal with for a while. we spent two days shopping, bennington being very limited in this area.

sally, who changes while you look at her, is an entirely different person these days. she is strictly a summer child anyway, and kind of freezes up during the winter and then blossoms with the first flowers. she rides her bike and goes on long walks by herself. she has stopped quarrelling with everyone, and suddenly has friends dropping by nearly every day.

barry is so busy these days he never has time to talk to any of us, and falls asleep the minute he gets into bed. he and a group of buddies have suddenly become able, this spring, to walk to one another's houses—they all live within a certain radius of the school.

stanley, after two more sleepless nights, has finally agreed to let me call the doc, thank heaven. (he keeps putting it off even now, though; and he gets so irritated when i try to argue with him about it; i am sure there is nothing wrong with him except the strain of all these things at once, but he will only listen if the doctor tells him.) right now he is afraid that something will prevent our going away next week, and he kind of suggested that maybe it might be a good idea to wait on the doctor till we came back but i said i wouldn't go unless he saw the doctor first.

stanley has sublet a two-room apartment at columbia for the time he will be teaching there. new york in july and august is not fit for human habitation, and i cannot imagine how silly i would have to be to leave nice cool vermont and sit around in the city. stanley is very amused, and a little jealous, because i quite seriously plan to drive myself down to the race track at saratoga—about forty miles—and spend a day at the races; i love the place, and he never has the time to go, and so this is my chance. what i am most afraid of is all the good people around here who will think "poor shirley, all alone for the summer." this is my chance to get a lot of work done and some exploring—i want to go to several new england towns and see old houses—and the idea that everyone is going to want to take care of me worries me. i can't make anyone understand that after twenty years of always tagging along after stanley or the kids i now enjoy going places alone. i drove down to middletown connecticut, where i gave a lecture at wesleyan, and had a wonderful time all by myself; i found myself a nice old inn where i stayed and i got lost of course, but not seriously. also i like to stop and talk to people and look at houses and i can never do that if i am with someone else. it has occurred to me that i might even do an article or two on new england towns but i won't know that until i see what i can find to write about. saratoga during the summer is like a suburb of north bennington; no matter when you go you meet half a dozen people from home. our entire town lives around that track. every morning in the store you hear who hit the daily double and how louise dalton has been playing the two numbers of her age for years now, and every year she gets older and last year's age wins.

now, though, i must go to work to earn enough money to lose at the track. i am still doing the good housekeeping articles, but no word yet about whether they want a contract for a monthly one. keep your fingers crossed.

joanne hopes to come sometime early in july; is that all right with you? also, what kind of clothes should she have if she goes into san francisco with you? in new york she would wear summer clothes, but dressy, is it the same there? she will have to look like a lady on the plane. i can't tell you how excited and happy she is to be coming.

i <u>must</u> stop now, and go make lunch. i can hear barry and his friends coming up the hill. lots and lots of love from all.

s.

.   .   .

[To Carol Brandt]

May 18 [1959]

Dear Carol,

Pat has very kindly sent me the first copy of HILL HOUSE,* for their catalogue, and since I am most anxious to be agreeable and ladylike I am only asking them to change one word, although I am concerned to find that their general tone seems to emphasize the "readers who like ghost stories" angle rather than the idea—mine—that this is a serious novel. I tried to say this politely to Pat, but of course realize that their publicity is none of my business anyway and I don't know what will or will not sell books. What I did balk at was the statement that there is many a chuckle in this book.

I have a clean new filing folder with one small note therein, for a new book.

Best,

Shirley

•  •  •

[Letter to a fan]

wednesday [summer 1959]

dear mrs ramsey,

that was an unkind cut of yours about having almost finished my cup of coffee, unkinder than you knew, since for two weeks i have

* Publicity copy.

been indulging in a frightful and probably contagious (burn this letter) intestinal disease, and greet myself in the morning with a teaspoonful of paregoric and a bracing cup of cocoa. i thought for a while that my husband was feeding me small regular doses of arsenic and went at once and changed my will but he says no, he is essentially a kind-hearted man and could not bear to see any living thing suffer the way i suffer when i watch him drink his morning coffee.

i do not answer fan letters (jay williams—do you know his charming books for children?—got a letter once from a little girl saying "every time i write to an author it turns out he is dead. if you are alive will you answer this please?") but sometimes they are like yours, from somebody it would be fun to talk to so i do. i am also taking the liberty of sending you something of mine i bet you haven't read. parts of it are better not read at all but it was written for fun and my older son made his first theatrical appearance as the enchanter, blowing his lines only twice.

what is an adult education writing class? i mean, which is the operative word? not education, surely?

most of hillhouse was written when i was alone in the house, yes. with six black cats lying around. it was easier when i was actually writing than when i stopped and wondered what was going to happen next. i am not able to get started on a new book because all i really want to write is another ghost story and you simply can't write two. i am toying lightly with the idea of a murder story but suspect i lack the courage to kill anyone. my husband is wholeheartedly afraid of ghosts and absolutely refuses to read hillhouse even though i offered to mark scary passages so he could skip; he did give me the greek and hebrew words and most of what we were calling the lucan devices (particularly that delicious book the father made for his daughter; there actually was a book somewhat like that advertised in an english auction catalogue, although i enlarged and detailed it considerably; we bid a hundred pounds for the book but missed it; some other ghoul got there first).

do write again if you feel like it. it was nice having your letter; i won't say that you made that damn cocoa more palatable, but you helped.

cordially,

shirley jackson

•   •   •

[To Barry, Sally, and Joanne]

Monday [July 20, 1959]

Dear Barry/Sally/Joanne,

This is to be a very long letter full of adventures, so I am making a carbon copy and sending that to Joanne and the other to the camp for Sally and Barry. First of all, I want to tell all of you how glad I was to get your letters. It is nice to know that all of you are enjoying yourselves.

(Joanne: Sally caught two sunfish. Barry painted a rock. Barry has learned to swim a little. Sally got her cheek cut because some fool boy was swinging a stick, but she was not seriously hurt.) Laurie and I are enjoying ourselves, too; Laurie has been going down to jazz concerts at Lenox, and he met Count Basie. The only one who is <u>not</u> enjoying himself is poor Dad. I have been with him this weekend and he says it has been terribly hot in New York and even though his apartment is cool and his office is air-conditioned, by the time he gets from one to the other he is worn out. He can't sleep because it is noisy, and the only really good thing is that because his apartment is on the tenth floor there are no flies. He bought himself a lot of clothes, thank heaven, and now has enough socks to last him for a while. Also, he tried to buy a tube of toothpaste and couldn't remember the name of the kind we used, so he made the man in the store take out every kind until he found the one he recognized. (Barry, Sally: speaking of clothes, Joanne writes that her cousin Barry is choosing her clothes for her; she says he helped her buy a skirt covered with pictures of old railroad trains.)

Dad had to go to Newport, Rhode Island, this past weekend for a folklore festival. He had to give a short speech, and it sounded like a nice weekend, so he asked if I would like to meet him there. He drove up from New York with some friends, and I started from here, leaving Laurie to feed the animals. Newport is a very strange place; it is an island and you can only get there by going across a long bridge and then on a ferry boat. The bridge was very long indeed, and very slippery, and Morris was simply terrified, sliding around over that ocean. On the ferry boat I was almost homesick for the ferries we used to take when I was a little girl in San Francisco; if they still have them I hope Grandma will take Joanne on one. Newport itself is a fairly small island, about three miles wide, so there was not much trouble finding the way around. I met Dad in the hotel and it was so nice to see him again. We were both so hot and tired we just sat around the hotel room having a drink and taking cold showers. It was a lovely hotel, very big, and we were in a kind of annex, where they were putting all the people who came for the folklore junk. The next morning we took the top off Morris and drove all over the island. About fifty years ago many very very _very_ rich people from New York owned most of Newport, and used it for summer vacations, and it was the fashion to build enormous, very elaborate houses along the edge of the ocean, some of them as big as the French chateaux I have in pictures, and many of them very strange architecturally. There is at least one castle. Most of the big houses have about a hundred rooms, and big beautiful gardens which reach down to the edge of the ocean, with big stone walls for the ocean waves to crash against, so you can stand on top of the wall and look down on the waves. By now most of the rich people have given up the houses, because these days it is simply too expensive to run such a house for the summer (it took forty servants, for instance, just to keep the house going, and twenty gardeners to take care of the grounds) and most of the houses have been closed up, because of course no one will buy them. We drove along the ocean drive, and it is sad and strange to see these great huge houses standing there, one after another, as though they were sailing along against the sky, and all boarded up, with the windows shuttered and sometimes chimneys falling down. Two or three of them have been bought by a group of people who want to preserve them as kind of museums of the way people used to live in Newport, and one of them, "The Breakers," was open when we were there, so Dad and I went on the tour through it. It made me want to cry, because all the furniture has been kept, and it is so lovely, with no one ever going to live there again. Most of the ocean front of the house is balconies, where they used to have breakfast looking out over the ocean, and the other three sides are gardens. Inside there is one room all gold and silver, with a little gold piano with pearl keys, and marble mantlepieces from Italy in all the rooms. (Sally: I just talked to Mrs. Wohnus and she said they had seen you at the Williamstown theatre at "Auntie Mame" and you had a beauty of a black eye.) As far as the folk festival was concerned, I have never seen so many guitars in all my life. This was the first time they had tried it (although they have a jazz festival every year) and they were surprised because so many people came. It went on for two days. In the evenings they had two programs of various performers, one after another, of different sorts. (We only went to the first evening program, which was quite enough, I can tell you; it lasted for five hours.)

Cynthia Gooding* was there, and sends her love to all of you, as do Willis James and Langston Hughes and Marshall Stearns,† all of whom you met at Lenox. Langston says, Sally, that Sammy Price is playing now in a nightclub in New York, and Dad is going to see him and will give him your love. We had dinner one evening with

---

* Cynthia Gooding was an American folk singer known for her recordings of traditional songs from many cultures for Electra and Riverside. She toured nationally and in the early 1950s performed at Bennington College, where she met Stanley and soon became good friends with the entire Hyman family, sometimes staying for days as a houseguest and even performing in the living room, accompanied by various Hyman children.

† Langston Hughes was a poet, social activist, playwright, and novelist, known as a leader of the Harlem Renaissance. Willis James and Marshall Stearns were folklore and jazz writers and scholars. All were participants, along with Stanley, in the Lenox folklore and jazz Symposium, and all became family friends.

Willis and Langston, and all they could talk about was Lenox and you kids. Cynthia was on the program the evening we went; it was held in the open in a kind of stadium, and there were over three thousand people there. Unfortunately Cynthia had chosen to wear a purple chiffon dress with a long scarf, and sitting up there on the stage with the wind blowing she had more trouble managing her clothes than she did with her guitar. There were some wonderful bands, and a man named Memphis Slim, who played and sang very much like Sammy Price,* and a new fine singer named Odetta, and the Kingston Trio arrived just as we were getting ready to leave. Cynthia wanted me to meet them so I could write Joanne all about them, but all we had been hearing all weekend was how disagreeable they had become since they've been famous so I thought there would be nothing good to write Joanne about them. After the outdoor program the performers (of whom Dad was supposed to be one) came back to the hotel for a big party, and since the program hadn't ended until two the party went on until about four, and then a group of awful amateurs in the hotel got into a room, and sang until six in the morning. No one got any sleep, and no one could quiet them. The next morning they were singing again at breakfast and a lot of us were going to catch them and strangle them, but we had to go hear Dad give his lecture, which he did very nicely, considering that he hadn't had any sleep. We didn't want to stay on for any more because we were sure they were going to sing all night again and we were sleepy, so Dad and Cynthia headed back for New York and I started home about three in the afternoon. I got about halfway, as far as Springfield, Massachusetts, and found that I was falling asleep while I was driving, so I went to a hotel and got a room with a television set and had my dinner sent upstairs and watched television while I had my dinner and then went to bed and came home yesterday.

I am supposed to be doing a Good Housekeeping story about Christmas, but it is very hard to think of Christmas right now. I

---

* Sammy Price was a well-known boogie-woogie and barrelhouse pianist, singer, and bandleader. He was the house pianist the first year the Hymans visited The Music Inn, when he invited Laurie to sit in with his band, which included legendary trumpet player Herman Autrey. Sammy became a Hyman family friend.

never wrote to the man with the haunted houses because I have been
so busy I haven't had time. Dad is having dinner tonight with Jackie
Robinson. He used to be a great baseball player in Brooklyn, and
Dad is doing a New Yorker article on him.

I got a telegram saying that my new book is being considered by
The Book of the Month Club, which means absolutely nothing. They
consider every new book that comes out, but if they should take it as
one of their selections we would make a lot of money. New stove.
We'll hear the end of July. Everyone keep your fingers crossed.

Now I really must stop and write about Christmas. Lots and lots
of love to all of you; and write soon. Joanne give our love and thanks
to Grandma and Pop.

Love,

Mom

· · ·

[To Geraldine and Leslie Jackson]

november 2 [1959]

dearest mother and pop,

for the first time in almost four months the pile of work on my desk
is down to manageable proportions; that is, i have only about three
things to write, and twenty letters. i am very sorry not to have written for so long, but so much has been happening, and i have had
deadlines following me around all the time.

we are having our first really nasty weather, cold and rainy and
windy, and of course everyone is sniffling. barry always gets just a
trace of his old asthma when he starts to cough, and has to stay in
bed; he has been down for a couple of days but seems fine today. everyone always has a cold on monday morning anyway.

most of the news here is good, and some of it is simply wonderful.

let me start with HILL HOUSE. it has gone into a second printing, is selling well, got good reviews all over, including a rave review from orville prescott of the newyorktimes, and has been taken by the reader's digest for their condensed book in april. when my publisher called to tell me about the digest he said that by the way their minimum guarantee was thirty-five thousand dollars, to be divided between him and me, and for about two days i went around thinking he had said thirty-five hundred and feeling terribly pleased. stanley finally explained it to me. it means a good deal to pat covici, my editor at viking, because when i left farrar and straus two years ago he had enough faith in me to persuade viking to take me on with a big advance and not bother me until i had finished the book; now, of course, they will be more than paid back.

it also means that for a while i can choose what and when i want to write and no starting a new book until i feel like it.

most of all it meant that the day the news came i went out and bought a hillman station wagon, turning in the dodge with considerable joy. i get the new car this week; it is lovely, grey and white with red upholstery. it's considerably bigger than the morris, but still not the size of the american small cars, and quite a lot fancier. laurie will now drive the morris, which pleases him, and the hillman—which is a four-door station wagon—will hold the whole family.

i have also just signed the contracts for english publication; they like this better than any of my other books, i suppose because it is actually—and is intended to be, in spite of what <u>time</u> said—just an old-fashioned ghost story. <u>time</u> is usually nasty to me, which is odd considering that the book section is run by an old friend, but he always liked <u>hangsaman</u> and thinks i have never done another good book since, and ever since <u>bird's nest</u> he has been convinced that i am actually a secret psychoanalyst, which is pretty silly when you come to think of it because i have never read more than ten pages of freud.

oh, there is lots more news. we are going to europe, stanley and i, in the summer of 1961. by invitation. they wanted us to go in 1960 but stanley has to finish his book. it is because of jackie robinson, whose profile stanley is just finishing; jackie was invited by an organization called "cultural tours" to take a group of people on a sports tour of europe; they ask various people to lead tours in their field, set their own itinerary, and generally act as names to attract customers. the people met stanley through jackie, and wrote asking if we would be interested in leading a literary tour, so stanley said yes. jackie is taking his tour to the olympics. i want to see the great houses of france, and am busy trying to think of literary associations for them. of course england is easy; i will also finally meet my english publisher, who keeps writing me asking me to come for dinner.

my new great interest right now has turned out to be english kings (richard III did <u>not</u> kill the princes in the tower) and of course all I really want is a couple of weeks at the tower of london and hatfield and bosworth, all probably housing developments by now. stanley has gotten me stacks of books on the tudors and the wars of the roses and i go around muttering dates to myself and considering writing letters to the london times.

oh, yes. i am making a record. a firm called folkwaysrecords which puts out records of writers reading their own works has asked me to do a record of lottery and one other story, and since i will not go to new york to do it i have to try to get it done on the college recording equipment here.

as you can see most of our news is actually HILL HOUSE because it is all happening so fast, but even otherwise things are going on. laurie is doing exceptionally well in his school work, sitting in on an english class at the college and piling up credit for his going to college next year (we hope). laurie still gets two or three letters a week from his girl, and they are meeting in new york at thanksgiving time, when he also has an audition with a williams college band on the chance that they may get a job on a boat next summer. he is also playing with the bennington college orchestra in a brass concerto; they will give at a concert next spring. he is <u>also</u> starring in the high school senior class play (which i wrote. and i will now see the world premiere of my first dramatic creation). joanne is directing her class play. she tried out for a local summer playhouse, and banked very heavily on getting in with them next summer. luckily the weekend she went to try out we had as house guests the two people who run the compass players in new york, and they said if she was turned down (which of course she was) to plan on spending a week or so in new york with them this fall and getting a look at off-broadway plays and maybe even get a chance on a future job in the compass theatre. this means painting scenery, of course, but she would love it. she may change her mind, though; her girl scout troop is taking a training course at the hospital in being nurse's aids, making beds and entertaining patients, and she loves <u>that</u>; we may have her turning into a nurse.

sally is so changed no one knows her. she came back from camp much less of a wild tomboy, and much more grownup. she is getting interested in clothes, and goes off to school each morning looking unbelievably neat and ladylike. she is in a dancing class at the college, and last year she was nothing but a pest, always rough-housing and wild, and this year she is the best in the class. this year she has a man teacher for the first time and he has awed her, so she is doing very well at her work and is generally altogether different.

barry plays the clarinet, goes doggedly off to his lessons, is learning to play football, and brings home an endless series of young gents to climb in the treehouse. i can't tell one from another but the other children point out that i can't tell <u>their</u> friends apart either.

we expect stanley's father at thanksgiving; his father is much better and goes back to his office now, but cannot climb stairs and must be careful on his diet. he will eat turkey when he is here, though. fred wohnus had a coronary last month and is almost recovered, although still being very cautious. it is certainly the thing to have this year; i think there have been a dozen around and it seems that we are always sending off flowers to the hospital. everyone is giving up smoking and drinking, and living on cottage cheese.

please write. i hope you can come east some time not in march, and get a look at some decent weather. everyone sends lots of love.

love,

s.

•   •   •

[To Leslie Jackson]

wednesday [late December 1959]

dear pop,

i can't tell you how upset and unhappy i was when i got your letter. can mother really think for a minute that i would dream of ignoring her on christmas? i can't understand how she could believe such a thing, and why she doesn't just assume that nothing came from me because it was held up in the mail or some such thing. actually, i ordered her a crazy little perfume gadget that i thought she would like, from altman's three weeks ago, and it should have been there long before now. but mother should know that we love her and think of her on christmas and drink your health every year when the old christmas tree ornaments are taken out and stanley and laurie put more tire tape on the light strings.

   i am just terribly sorry that the gift was delayed, and that mother was unhappy; it just seems so incredible to me that she would think i had forgotten.

   will write again later. love to you both.

s.

•  •  •

[To Jeanne Beatty, a fan]

December 29 [1959]

Dear Mrs. Beatty,

Many many thanks. You have done us a great service. We knew Moomin*only in the big picture book, and never dreamed there was

* A series of beloved children's books written by the Finnish author Tove Jansson.

any kind of "real" <u>Moomin</u> book; we have now the publisher and such, and are ordering. Your Moomin was read with joy around our family.

I have looked forward to writing you, and had promised myself a pleasant morning dwelling on dear books (<u>do</u> you know <u>Unknown Magazine?</u>*) and of course find myself with half an hour, a sick type-writer ribbon, and twelve thank-you letters waiting. I have promised absolutely to begin a new book next Monday morning, after the children have gone back to school; that means that I must lock myself up in my cave for four dogged hours a day, and sneak a minute or so here and there for writing letters and making lunch ("You will eat vegetable soup again today and like it; Mommy's beginning chapter three") so if I do not write now I never can.

Yours was the only kind letter I received. I am less than pleased with the unkind letters, which all come from librarians, and ask how we are ever going to beat the Russians to the moon if our kids read all this fantasy stuff ("There was a copy of that book about Oz in our library but of course our children could never manage to get through the first chapter.") and recommend stern measures for my children, who are clearly never going to be able to cope with the modern world, and will clearly fall into all kinds of psychological pitfalls.

I spent Christmas afternoon with an old friend who believes that the changes in the geography of Oz were due to the fact that Baum never intended to write a second book and kind of started fresh, as it were, with almost a new country and certainly a new illustrator. (Do you know the <u>Narnia</u> books, C.S. Lewis? If you don't, don't read the last one, where the children involved discover that they have all been killed in a railway accident and, being dead, may now stay in Narnia forever; we all found this a blasphemy and an outrage.) We gave our Sally the complete works (eighteen volumes) of E. Nesbit for Christmas, and are waiting in line for her to finish each one. Sally also asks how old your Shannon is, and does she like to write letters? Sally is a joyful correspondent, far more reliable than her mother. (Jay Wil-

* *Unknown* magazine was an American pulp fantasy magazine published from 1939 to 1943.

liams' <u>Magic Gate</u>? Or the <u>Danny Dunn</u>* series? He is a dear friend of ours, and particularly of Sally's; the new Danny Dunn book is dedicated to her, and will be published on her birthday as a surprise; she and Jay share a strange world with their own calendar, in which Jay-Hey-Day is a feast day, and Salli's Eve a magic ceremony; no one else knows anything about it.) I am enclosing with your books a piece of nonsense I wrote for my kids, which they have never let me live down; I do indeed regret the children's song, which Laurie set to music and which I hear day and night.

Again, many thanks. Best wishes to all of you for a wonderful new year.

Most cordially,

Shirley Jackson

* Raymond Abrashkin wrote and directed *The Little Fugitive* and collaborated with Jay Williams on the Danny Dunn book series.

# SIX

. . .

## Castles and Hauntings: 1960–1961

i talk out loud when i am writing and yell and swear and
laugh and sometimes cry, and it makes stanley nervous,
particularly when he knows i am writing about something
that will scare him.

—To Jeanne Beatty, February 5, 1960

*The Haunting of Hill House is published by Viking Press in 1959 to superb reviews and great success, and film rights are quickly purchased by producer-director Robert Wise. In 1960,* Special Delivery, a Useful Book for Brand-New Mothers, *a collection of humorous short pieces by several writers in addition to Jackson, is finally published by Little, Brown to Shirley's great embarrassment; despite the publisher's promises to keep her name in "very small type," it is instead trumpeted on the cover, on the title page, and in advertising. Shirley begins work on her next novel.*

[To Carol Brandt]

January 19 [1960]

Dear Carol,

I am slow-witted when people start using phrases like twenty thousand dollars; it was not until I got off the phone the other day that I realized concretely that you had really sold SUNDIAL for a movie. Or probably, anyway. It has always been my favorite, you know, and I have always thought it would lend itself perfectly to dramatization. At any rate, it is wonderful news.*

Now. The new book is named, tentatively, WE HAVE ALWAYS LIVED IN THE CASTLE. I like the title, but my Sally believes that there is already a book—perhaps a fairy tale—with that title. Anyway I am using that title for now. The book is completely outlined, although of course I may always go off on some tangent, and is, at present, about a murder, although of course not a mystery story. (Although I may write a mystery story yet.) I am not very pleased

* This did not happen, and *The Sundial* has yet to be adapted for film.

with the way it is set up now, so I will not decide finally what it is about until I have part of it fully written.

I will be happy to talk to the gentlemen about SUNDIAL whenever they are interested.

Best,

Shirley

. . .

[To Carol Brandt]

January 26 [1960]

Dear Carol,

Please <u>please</u> do not let Pat go on thinking that I will have a finished book for him in six months; in six months I will have something to show him, perhaps the finished first section, but I will not commit myself to a complete book for at least a year. The poor miserable thing only exists in outline and notes right now. When I said six months hard writing I actually meant six months without doing anything else; I hate to rush this kind of thing because then I always want to rewrite it after it is published.

Barry has been experimenting with electro-magnets and has somehow magnetized my desk scissors so they stick to the typewriter. There are hazards in this profession, many more than the reviewers realize.

The only reason I am particularly anxious to see SUNDIAL in a movie is my own partiality for the book; I would love to see someone do it.

Best,

Shirley

. . .

[To Jeanne Beatty]

monday [February 1960]

oh golly i don't know. you mean like Books That Have Changed Our Lives? i assume it wouldn't be WAR AND PEACE or DON QUIXOTE or LITTLE WOMEN although i still get all overwrought over JANE EYRE. and i always took PRIDE AND PREJUDICE to the hospital to have babies with. do you know sylvia townsend warner's LOLLY WILLOWES (why on earth did i start putting these damn titles in caps?) and all the josephine tey books particularly THE FRANCHISE AFFAIR and THE DAUGHTER OF TIME and anything at all about elizabeth 1 or as a matter of fact any of the tudors. none of these has made me a Better Person of course. and i think i am probably the only person around these days who reads samuel richardson for pleasure; SIR CHARLES GRANDISON is perhaps my dearest book. i don't recommend it however unless you are in jail or somewhere else where you have plenty of time. mystery stories i read all the time and stanley gets furious because he is always reading something like ULYSSES which i frankly regard as a great bore. i have downstairs to read tonight a great huge biography of cardinal wolsey and an eighteenth century novel with long s's about a lovely accomplished modest universally beloved young heiress whose family is forcing her to marry an aged reprobate because he has a title. it's very nice. upstairs here in my study i have a ngaio marsh mystery and my own SUNDIAL which i confess shamelessly i have been re-reading. it is the only one i ever re-read.

odd that you should have thought of voodoo because of course that is what it was. laurie was building me a bookcase (he builds very good bookcases which never wobble) and when i came in to check on it i found on my desk a length of rawhide tied into nine knots and i asked laurie how it got there and he said he found it on the floor in the corner where the bookcase was supposed to go and he thought it might be something i wanted so he put it on my desk. well i guess anyone knows what that means so i took the thing

downstairs very gingerly and put it into a box of magic names i have
in order to neutralize it but i guess some of it got out. we finally decided that i had better untie the knots and see if that helped any and
it did. i mean i have kicked the paregoric habit and this morning i
had a cup of coffee and a slice of tomato (i do not ordinarily have tomatoes for breakfast but i was feeling bold) and shall probably be extremely ill later today but i have a little white pill to take.

my husband is an english teacher too, at bennington college (don't
you find english teachers get a little stuffy about MOBY DICK after a
while?) and is just finishing writing a book which i am almighty glad
of. for four years he has spent his free days writing and all his evenings
reading so that our social life has been confined to perhaps one evening a month and that grudging. if anyone drops in (and there are
great droppers-in around here although we have discouraged all but a
few) i sit in the living room and talk and stanley shuts himself in the
study and works. gee. we used to play bridge and give cocktail parties
and have people over for dinner; it used to be great. now that the book
is nearly finished i am getting stage fright at the idea of seeing people
again. he was nice about summers, though; all our children go away all
summer, sally and barry and joanne to camp, all together, joanne as a
counselor and laurie off on some business of his own—one summer he
had a job as bellhop at a jazz resort and last summer he went to europe
with a band and this summer he may go to europe again or he may
take a job playing in a roadhouse (i have gotten used to the idea of my
little boy playing the trumpet in a roadhouse particularly since he
brings home some very odd friends particularly jazz musicians and
there are jam sessions in the living room, while stanley who loves jazz
sits in the study and works). anyway, the children are all gone all summer so stanley says it is pointless for me to cook dinners when we live
in a state with some of the best country inns around, so all summer
long we dine out, wandering forty or fifty miles away and getting back
early enough so stanley can go in the study and work.

what kind of things do you write? jay williams is an old family
friend of ours; we knew him when he was an actor. can't stand his
wife. he is a particular friend of our sally's, and sends her the danny
dunn books; they write incredible letters to one another, both being

mildly batty. (jay reminds me of the Tolkien RING trilogy; do you know that? or THE HOBBIT? i can't get the kids to read THE HOBBIT although i love it.) do you really make dresses for your girls? joanne has tried to teach me to sew but i can't. because my mother used to make me lovely things and i hated them. she made me an evening dress to wear to my first formal party and i was absolutely sick with embarrassment. what is facing?

i should be working because my new book was due at the publisher's a year ago may fifteenth but i have spent the greater part of the morning composing verse. and cursing sally. we have contests around this house; every so often a notice will appear scotch-taped to the front of the refrigerator announcing CONTEST ABSOLUTELY NEW CONTEST and it will be something frightful and we will all dutifully enter. sally has a contest going now, ending at dinner tonight, for the best poem fifty words or less, in honor of our cat (senior cat of six) toro. it is very hard indeed to find a rhyme for toro. particularly since he is an evil baleful snarly old tyrant. toro is the judge. prizes will be given. stanley did his entry yesterday and spent all evening bragging about it and all i have is a last line ("with teetotal toro as tutor") and nothing to do with it. wait. i just thought of scooter.

*it might seem absurd*
*that a beer-drinking bird*
*would endeavor to ride on a scooter*
*with teetotal toro as tutor*

oh, well. it won't win anyway.

you should not write such pleasant letters because they encourage me to these interminable replies. it's because i would rather write than do anything else i suppose. anything else meaning particularly this morning getting yesterday's laundry out of the dryer.

best,

shirley

. . .

[To Jeanne Beatty]

friday [February 5, 1960]

dear jeanne,

i will so write ten pages if i like. you just don't have to read them, is all. i was feeling very silly because i thought you were not going to answer my childish letter, which i so much enjoyed writing, because it was childish, and it was so good to get your letter today. do you find it crazy, kind of, sending a letter out into the blue and then just wondering where it got to finally and how it was received and whether someone said goodlordlook at the length of this and then used it to light cigars with? but i feel that about stories too, although i defy the nonfiction editor of good housekeeping to light a cigar with my current article which she is busily rewriting at this very moment. anyway i do not believe that you went down into the cellar by yourself even the next day. i do not believe it. i'm sorry, it's just not the kind of thing you can believe—i know, i know, but i just don't, and i'm sorry and all that, but you have to think of human nature and all. (unless of course you are one of those intrepid english spinster types who venture out into the sahara with a baedeker and a hip bath; do you know frank baker's thoroughly delightful MISS HARGREAVES? if not, let me know and i will send it to you.) but the cellar no. for one thing it might have been a real ghost and not just some mad killer intent upon his vicious pursuits. or it might have been a rat or something, you know. or something real bad like a loose horse. (loose horses are the worst. they wear their hair in dyed tangled mops, and paint their nails and put red on their cheeks and dance can cans and generally bring a bad name upon womankind in general.)

i had to promise myself that i would not come back to this letter until i had done my good housekeeping stint since naturally i would rather be writing you a letter than doggedly pursuing an un-

rewarding idea through pages of heavy handed prose. i am so consumed with guilt about good housekeeping that it is almost
impossible for me to write anything for them (stanley accused me
of stealing the h from his typewriter but now i think he has come
and stolen it back) because last year when we were very broke indeed they (i have to go back over heveryone of those hs) offered me
a column spot to run about eight times a year and of course it was
wonderful but then hill house sold to hollywood and we don't need
the money but they were so nice to me i got to keep doing the col-
umns and the woman editor there thinks she is making them clev-
erer when she takes out my exquisitely formed phrases and
substitutes madison avenue slang. she calls me darling over the
phone too. one reason i never go to new york is because my agent is
that kind of lady too (eight feet tall with lots of gold bracelets
studded with rubies and enormous hairdos and the right shade of
lipstick and a kind of little tolerant laugh) and i am scared of them.
i always upset the martini onto their perfect grey suits. or fall down
so the headwaiter will have to come pick me up. she goes to the
hairdresser every morning, my agent. stanley has just left for new
york because he is on some odd committee concerned with the future of bennington college.

   it is so quiet without stanley's typewriter going downstairs. he
has a downstairs study, see, and i have an <u>upstairs</u> study because if
you must know the disagreeable truth he kicked me out of the
downstairs study because my desk was a mess and i never covered
my typewriter and he bribed laurie to repaint the guest room and
they moved my desk up there and planked the typewriter down on
it and said there. so i raided the house for everything i liked best
and brought it all up to my study and shut the door and i live in
here. stanley will not come past the door because not only are my
books <u>not in alphabetical order</u> if you can conceive of such a thing,
but one of the shades is always pulled up crooked and i put my pictures anywhere i like them and they are not level. stanley asked me
why my study was so much lighter than his and i said because i was
in it and so one afternoon he came up and sat down for a few min-

utes breathing heavily and cowering and finally with a wild shriek he leaped up and straightened a picture and fled. each evening sally and barry come in with their game of clue and we play three solemn games, me losing. through some mysterious architectural alchemy one of my windows regards one of laurie's windows and in the summer time he sits in his window and plays the haydn horn concerto for me. i wrote hill house in the dining room though. i talk out loud when i am writing and yell and swear and laugh and sometimes cry, and it makes stanley nervous, particularly when he knows i am writing about something that will scare him; he said that one morning i was making such a racket in the dining room that if he could read the book he could pick out which scene i was working on. (i know which scene it was, too; it was the scene near the end where luke is jeering at eleanor and i was trying to get the right edge to luke, to indicate exactly that light evil tone, which i never did get actually the way i wanted it; stanley says i was yelling, "look alive you idiot.")

i was going to say some awfully profound things about the hobbit because of course that is (i think) the essential of all fantasy; clearly it is not written to satisfy the reader but began years ago when the author lay in bed at night telling himself stories to make up for the spanking or the fact that the other kids wouldn't let him play second base; the non-important things are the ones not important to the author's ego. (why do any of us write, come to that?) i think more of islandia,* which is revolting in a sense, full of adolescent prurience (for two hundred pages his hero—a harvard graduate, no less—tries to bring himself to a pitch of boldness so he can put his arm around the heroine, but of course once that first deadly step is taken things move on apace, but still very much of the sixth grade) and yet the book stands as the work of a grown man. and i think that the queen of the elves is exactly what leaped to tolkien's mind when he thought women; of course, english dons are easily distinguished from errol flynns, and i daresay tolkien's whole

* Utopian novel by Austin Tappan Wright (1942).

knowledge of women might have been early concretized by terror of his headmaster's wife. in any case it is only one step removed from boy's life and you know what they thought of girls there. funny, you don't notice the lack of females in robinson crusoe; i wonder if it isn't because dafoe never felt called upon to explain that he simply couldn't care less. i am not very coherent; what i am trying to say is that the idea of women as a particularly irritating mystery is very close to tolkien and the islandia man and consequently they get very stiff and sophomoric about the reverence due to queens and princesses and you only know they are not actually the captain of the cricket team or the president of the senior class by the fact that they are insistently referred to as she. i cannot read the second volume of the ring anymore because i think it falls apart, as though as a child he had gone over and over lovingly the fellowship and the good comrades who set out with him ("i will take the ring, although i do not know the way.") on his grail-journey and then found himself, grown-up, without the boy fancy which would continue the story, and had to fall back upon learning and logic to complete it. (surely when he was a boy the book ended with his becoming king of all the countries and on very good terms with his adored mother, the queen of the elves.)

 i have a morris minor convertible, black, with red wheels. for heavens sake you don't need to know how to drive. i have had the morris for a year and it giggles when i drive it and on the ice you only need to head it toward the nearest snowbank and it stops, giggling helplessly. stanley does not drive either but he likes me to drive fancy cars which are of course always registered in my name (i have two cars now like two heads) and he makes sure they are heavily insured. i was so delighted with the morris that I went out and bought a hillman station wagon but it doesn't giggle so now laurie drives the hillman and i go along madly with the morris. last summer i had my ultimate vacation: i was alone. on the fifth of july i found myself alone in the house, but alone. it was the first time in my remembered life that i had been completely alone for any length of time. first thing was, no cooking. i went out for lunch.

(for lunch!) i went out for dinner. i did make myself breakfast because i was ashamed to go out for coffee. it took me four days to fill
the dishwasher (because i ran out of coffeecups). i slept. the phone
rang and i said sleepily that i was sorry, i was really too busy to go
anywhere for dinner. after a while i packed a suitcase (new; i
bought it specially) and morris and i took off. it was great. we
stayed at inns and told people fantastic stories and wandered. morris wanders beautifully ("there's a road; let's take that") and we did
get home in time.

   if my typing seems erratic it is because laurie (erratice? escarole?)
is playing one of those stereo test-records just downstairs and the air
in my room is full of airplanes flying just overhead and dive-
bombing into the typewriter; every time i stop to light a cigarette i
duck. engine trouble. you can't send a mere boy out there, lieutenant.
it's not right, i tell you, it's not right; that crate hasn't been up in fifteen years.

   our stereo is new, of course. i gather from the way you toss around
words like "momaural" (one-eared mother!) that you are old hands at
this kind of thing. ours was set up last week by a friend (ralph ellison;
do you know his great book <u>invisible man</u>? because it was written in
our house with sally sitting on his typewriter tormenting and he
would really rather set up electronic equipment than write) with barry's help ("barry, hold this wire") and of course they won't let me run
it but i like to sit and drown in it. someone turns it on for me. whenever i turn it on the television set lights up or all the cats get blasted
off the couch. jerry's pretty close, sir. better get the women under
cover. oh lord, clue is coming. ("mommy please try to pay attention.
it's mrs green in the conservatory and that's just laurie's record.") my
god they're bombing the village.

                    best, best,


                    s.


                 •   •   •

"No, I'm sorry, we can't come tonight. Stanley is
cleaning his filing cabinet."

[To Jeanne Beatty]

friday [February 12, 1960]

dear jeanne

ha. you have caught me. you knew I was just sitting here at the
typewriter pretending to work. longing for a letter from jeanne so i
could answer it. feeling generally irritable and sharly (snarly shirley
that is) because barry is sniffling and home from school and cannot
go to his valentine party even though i made millions of valentine
cookies (my ha has not come back. the typewriter man says he can
put it back but he must keep the typewriter for three days and
wouldn't i look like a fool pretending to work <u>without</u> a typewriter?) and laurie for some unspeakable reason is lunching at the
rotary club and joanne is lunching at school and if i had been smart
enough i could have let sally take her lunch and shared a small cup

of chicken soup with barry but now i must Make Something. longing for a letter from jeanne so i could read it, i do mean. your letters
are wonderful fun and i won't do without them. besides you can't
afford not to write because stanley in a fury figured out that considered in terms of pure writing time my letters are worth forty
dollars a page if only you could find someone to buy them. he has
come upon the grisly notion of editing my letters after my death
and has made me write my mother—to whom i write about twenty
pages every few months—and tell her never to throw away anything i have written her so the poor woman will really have to get
an attic built onto their one-story ranch style california house to
store my letters. if i locate anyone who will cough up forty dollars a
page i will let you know. (he also figured once that the brownies i
made were worth six dollars a brownie. this is because he grudges
every minute i do not spend writing although he is very fond of
brownies.) he was thinking about death because he had to fly to
detroit last tuesday. he will be there for four weeks with perhaps a
quick trip home in the middle (home home in the middle) and he
will give four lectures at wayne university on Poetry and Criticism
and i read them and they are very nice. the first was last wednesday
night and according to a small family tradition we all stopped
whatever we were doing at eight-fifteen and said bon chance papa.
we must tell laurie bon chance in two weeks; he is the enchanter in
the bad children and the high school is doing it in the district play
contest although they put my particular hate of a girl in as gretel
and consequently i will not go and see it besides i am sure everyone
will turn around and stare at me when they get to the crack about
the school principal because it is well known i am scared of her. i
got a check this morning from royalties for the bad children so
someone somewhere is putting it on. i can give it to the local high
school royalty free which is almost certainly why they are doing it. i
had another letter this morning, too; may i tell you a funny story
about it? yes?

  you must know, then (continued she) that during the summers i
spend one week in august at a garden spot called suffield connecticut where they run a reader-writer conference and several nice peo-

ple like louis untermeyer and william jay smith and shirley barker*
are permanent staff and so am i; we enjoy ourselves enormously. our
duties are light; all entering students are required to submit manuscripts and the first day we staff divide up the manuscripts, generously urging one another to take the heaviest ones; we then read the
manuscripts, you perceive, and we are expected to meet for an hour
individually with their several authors to discuss. (paddy colum† is
always there too but no one has ever managed to communicate with
him about reading manuscripts; we just sit and listen to him talk in
that wonderful voice.) at any rate i am regarded (complacently i say
it) as outrageous because i insist upon having a pitcher of water and
a bowl of ice delivered to my room one hour before lunch and one
hour before dinner and i set a bottle of bourbon on the table and
people tend to drop in for a drink before meals. so they put me in
what they call their guest house which has a little living room so i
can conduct my orgies away from the students. i think this is
charming but i do deplore their giving me a lady named marjorie
freer‡ for a roommate. marjorie is the sweetest person in the world
and i took a wholly unworthy sideswipe at her in that article on
children's books because she <u>does</u> write things like violet girl horti-
culturist and damn me she sells them too and teen age girls read
them except i told joanne she could read them in the library if she
wanted to but not to bring them home and marjorie sent joanne
one and it was about a girl (teen age) who opened a little bakery in
her home because her father was an invalid and her mother could

* Louis Untermeyer was an American poet, editor, and anthologist responsible for,
among many other things, a series of children's books published by Crowell-Collier in
the 1960s. He was a panelist on *What's My Line?*, was finally blacklisted by TV for taking controversial stands on social issues, and was named in hearings by the House Committee on Un-American Activities. William Jay Smith was a poet appointed Poet
Laureate Consultant in Poetry to the Library of Congress from 1969 to 1970. Shirley
Barker was a poet, author, and librarian. All became good friends of Shirley's after meeting at the Suffield conferences.
† Padraic "Paddy" Colum was an Irish poet, novelist, playwright, children's author, collector of folklore, and leader in the Irish Literary Revival. He was a beloved member of
the Suffield faculty and a dear friend of Shirley's.
‡ Marjorie Mueller Freer was the author of seven "teenage career novels." Over time, she
and Shirley became good friends.

not support the family (small brothers and sisters; our marjorie does not miss a trick) so dorothy girl baker soon owned her own factory. <u>you</u> know. but that is exactly what marjorie is like. she kept coming into my room at night and sitting on my bed while she put up her hair and we had what she called—i swear to this—girl-talk. my notion of girl-talk is somewhat conditioned by the hard-bitten faculty wives at bennington college but i honestly found myself solemnly discussing things like My First Dance and Should I Cut My Hair? (really i don't think so marjorie dear; it looks so nice the way it is). marjorie thought the world of me and told everyone what a sweet child i was (she was really only about three years older but there is a type of female which finds me childlike perhaps because i sit with my mouth hanging open while they talk about slip covers). marjorie and i got along simply wizard together from the very start. when we divided up the manuscripts at the staff meeting marjorie was supposed to take juvenile stuff and i was supposed to take short stories. the boss reads off the titles and everyone says oh give it to marjorie or oh give it to bill or why not save that big stinker for louis. he reads off a title "how Johnny went to the party" and everyone said juvenile juvenile give it to marjorie. marjorie accepted it, remarked with her usual martyred sweetness that it was not just one story, but three, but never mind, <u>she</u> would read them. there. this is a long introduction to a short story.

marjorie and i took ourselves off to our shack, and marjorie sat down in her room—good old marjorie—to read her manuscripts because she had said she would. i, having managed to leave my stack of manuscripts in the dining room (i always lose them and don't think it isn't on purpose) was lying on my bed drinking bourbon and reading a mystery story when marjorie strode into the room, dead white, eyes flashing, lips trembling. "this," she said tensely, "<u>this</u> is NOT A JUVENILE." she was holding "how johnny went to the party" and other stories by one corner, at arm's length. "so?" i said. "how <u>dared</u> he?" she said and she does honestly talk like that. "how dared he? he knew there were ladies at this conference." "yeah?" i said, interested now, and reaching out for the stories, "let <u>me</u> read them." "no, no," said marjorie, backing up, "you mustn't read them; they're not fit for you to read. you have a good clean ladylike mind and—" "i have <u>not</u> got a good clean ladylike mind," i told her, and snatched them.

well, she wrung her hands and entreated me not to sully my pure mind with such trash but of course i was already reading them. the second story was called "luanne and the hired man" and the third one was called "jenny's profession" and while there was not actually anything in them i have not read before i do have to admit marjorie could have made a good case for the mind-sullying. they were also abominably written. because i am a nasty sadist I told marjorie i would keep them and maybe even read one in my class and i presume marjorie went in and cried herself to sleep. the author—a gentleman named (stanley says i made this up) wolf, was in my class, as it happened, and was exactly the kind of shy, nice-mannered fellow you would expect; what i had in the stories was his dream world and outwardly he was a mouse. Understand, the stories were not obscene, or pornography, but simply the racy fancies of a timid fellow. one who reads exclusively—he told me later—playboy and the various men's magazines. i did not have the gall to read one in class, but toward the end of the week he came up to me after class and asked if we could have a conference about his writing. i said certainly, although i wondered if i was quite qualified to pass judgement, and it developed that the only time he was free was at five that afternoon and i—not thinking, and determined not to give up my before-dinner cocktail because you had to have <u>something</u> before facing that crew at dinner—said come down to the guest house at five, then.

i forgot to tell Marjorie that he was coming.

at five he knocked on the door and i opened it and said "come in, my wolf, come in," and turned and went into the living room; when i realized that he had not followed me i looked around and he was standing in the doorway holding his hat looking terrified. he was looking at the coffee table where there was a bottle of bourbon, two glasses, a bowl of ice and a pitcher of water. i suddenly began to feel a little bit like theda bara* and i kind of wished there were silken hangings around instead of the pictures of the last ten graduating

* Theda Bara, known as "The Vamp," was a famous actress in early silent movies.

classes from suffield academy, but i made myself very brisk and said, "do come in and have a drink." "i have a wife and two children," he said with a sick little laugh. oh, for a tiger skin or at the very least a snake bracelet. "doesn't your wife let you drink?" i asked him. (i couldn't help it.)

"<u>you</u> go ahead and have one," he said, still with that little weak smile.

"well, sit down anyway," i said.

"i'd rather stand," he said.

"of course," i said. "Well, mr wolf, about your stories—"

"i just <u>write</u> that stuff," he assured me hopefully.

"of course," i said. "what I wanted to say—"

"I <u>only</u> write that kind of thing for—well—fun. i mean, i only write it because—well. i mean—"

then the door to the bathroom opened and marjorie, clad in an inadequate bathtowel, came tripping into the doorway. "hi, sweetie," she said, not perceiving mr wolf who, his worst nightmares come true, was looking from one of us to the other with the most outrageous terror i have ever seen on a man's face. then marjorie saw him. "yeek," she said distinctly, and took off; mr wolf, clearly thinking she was taking off <u>after</u> him, scrambled wildly for the front door and out. i don't know what he ever told his wife. he dropped out of my class, though, and enrolled in bill smith's poetry. marjorie was cross with me for about two days because, as she said several times, she didn't see anything <u>funny</u> about it and she had heard me laughing. she had, too. i was draped over the arm of the chair gasping and howling with tears in my eyes. and this morning, six months later, i have a cold note from mr wolf. "I note," the man writes, "that playboy magazine is publishing a story of <u>yours</u>. my congratulations." a good loser, mr wolf.

i have dined out since on marjorie and mr wolf. marjorie writes the darlingest letters but she is pretty busy now. she is deep in a new book about this girl who makes these ashtrays and things out of seashells. her mother's sick, see, and . . .

of course i would not go into a haunted castle with twenty schoolteachers. i would not go into a haunted castle with even <u>one</u> schoolteacher. and can you see stanley in greece trembling grapes with his beard? (no, <u>no</u>. no.) i cannot really remember what it is like to have a child under two, and glad i am for it. i realize abruptly every now and then that barry is taking on that "really, <u>mother</u>" tone they get at a certain age and then they suddenly get into a discussion at dinner about town planning and i look at them and think goodness they are four people. also now it is nice to do things as a family, where it used to be something of a chore; we can all go out for dinner together, or have a family poker game (did i tell you about that? they play rough poker, particularly barry) or communicate through family jokes. i got kicked out of the city planning discussion because i said i liked our town better since the movie house burned down. stanley, red-faced, shouts in arguments, "everything in this world is either true or not true or one of your mother's delusions," and the children nod, all together.

my birthday is december fourteenth, sagitarius. (i do not know which of those letters should be doubled.) lilydale? lilydale?* i have heard of <u>down with skool</u>,† but not <u>the skin</u> or <u>the eighteenth ostrich</u>.‡ you do not live in a city? in a suburb? (let me tell you a thing or two about city planning.) we are all house-happy and i ordered a fourteen-foot couch to lie on and listen to music to except laurie explains patiently that if it goes into the room at all we will have to stand it on one end.

"and all that season it snew." from a contemporary account of Richard 3's military campaign.

my book is so completely bogged down that i am almost frightened. quite seriously, writing these long letters to you (and, oddly, i do not write <u>so</u> to anyone else, perhaps because <u>your</u> letters are so <u>delightful</u>) <u>does</u> more good for me (selfish) than anything i can think of; it somehow relaxes and directs. i hope you will not find this too horribly conceited, and consequently will excuse long rambling incoherence. anyway i cannot get the book moving although the experience is hardly new; i have started so before. i have only a year and a

---

* Lily Dale, New York, is a tiny upstate town founded by spiritualists that hosts annual conferences and demonstrations on mediums and mediumship.
† *Down with Skool!* by Geoffrey Willans, a series of children's books first published in 1954.
‡ *The Case of the Eighteenth Ostrich* (1944) is a children's novel by Colin Curzon.

half left to write it in, and so must get going. I do a page here and a page there and it is like modeling clay.

if you are interested in stuff i am doing for magazines now let me know and i will lend you the carbons. i only read the magazines for the recipes. They send me copies but only a month or so after publication.

i have decided since i am still shurly (surly shirley) that i must be catching barry's cold. good. i <u>want</u> to catch cold. what? the rotary club? oh. well, he is president of the senior class and got asked. they had veal cutlets.

valentines, valentines

s.

• • •

[To Jeanne Beatty]

[early 1960]

dear jeanne,

i have been invited by the new publisher of the oz books to do a long article on same; they will send me various unpublished materials and such; imagine the chance of spending a few weeks <u>again</u> in oz?

no no—i hasten to the typewriter—i cannot agree with you about peanuts; the indefatigable sally wrote that man—schultz?*—and got back a letter about how We Cartoonists (and he may even have said Artists) have an Obligation to You Young Folk and i swear he called himself We throughout. the very early stuff, perhaps, before he got to be We. sat in a bar one night (tim costello's, third avenue, new york) and listened to walt kelly curse the people who were trying to put out pogo sweat shirts and pencil boxes. he says while he lives they will not. he made me a picture of albert alligator chasing a lady alli-

---

* Charles Schulz, prolific cartoonist and creator of the "Peanuts" comic strip and marketing empire.

gator (how can you tell it's a lady alligator? well, it scandalized my mother) and it says "i love shirley jackson" and i had it framed and hung it over my desk and a great consolation in times of dreariness. he made sally a valentine of pogo proffering a motheaten bouquet.

i had to take down the picture of frank gifford* on the refrigerator and burn it; i have now a picture of richard III and unless i am enticed into putting a bet on the roller derby it will stay. this is because stanley (stanley edgar hyman, my husband, professor of literature at bennington college, vindictive winner of bets, poker player, writer of profiles for the new yorker, stern bearded disciplinarian, who will not read hill house because he is mortally afraid of ghosts) has a knack for picking the losers and making me bet on them, he is also afraid of the electric blanket i gave him for christmas.

barry—our spaceman-elect—says that 2+2=4 is not a universal absolute, since the mathematics of other planets may be non-euclidian (he learns this kind of thing from his father, who probably hasn't got it quite accurately) but i do agree with you that children are the thing to send into space; at the very worst, it should keep them busy for decades in their little space ships, and the very concepts of space travel and non-gravity and light years belong more properly to the world of children than of sensible grownups; i personally have enough trouble running the automatic timer on my new stove. (they kept trying to attach an egg-timer and i kept trying to tell them that after cooking for twenty years i just knew by myself, somehow, when the eggs were done; you put on the eggs and plug in the coffeepot and set the table and put in two slices of bread to toast and those are four-minute eggs.)

we moved out of westport because they always used caterers who made sweet martinis; everybody liked them. huysmans, yes, although he gives me nightmares. (so does proust. and most modern english writers.) i dwell these days happily in tudor england (all imposters if you really fancy richard III) and wander sideways into eighteenth century crime; i think my new book (which goes poorly, thank you) will be about a nice girl who murders simply everybody.

* Halfback and wide receiver for the New York Giants (football) 1952–60, 1962–64.

i do not like peter pan. i don't very much like button-bright,* either. do you?

you are clearly not yet forty years old; one begins to perceive by then that both ends of the circuit are closed.

oh dear. i went to bid jannie goodnight and she was trying to stand up in her new highheeled shoes (glee club concert, high heels required). laurie just got word that the band he plays with has a job on a liner next summer; they sail from new york the first of july, land in rotterdam, wander europe for six weeks, and sail home. i always thought somehow to see london before my children did; we do not go until summer after next. i go into a state of anxiety when i have to visit new york; how will i do in the capitals of europe? i want to see the tower of london, though.

it is a wonderful pleasure to write to you. i go from month to month and year to year never writing letters because i cannot write little letters which are polite and unnecessary mostly because i can't stop, as you see. you provoked me, you did; if you write to a professional writer a lovely long letter you are apt to get a rambling long letter back. it's like sitting down to talk for an hour, and far more agreeable than most conversations. all best wishes to all of you.

Shirley

• • •

[To Jeanne Beatty]

thursday [February 25, 1960]

dear jeanne

frabjous day, sadly needed. your letter in the mail, which i read before the herald tribune then agent carol called and good house has taken both the things i sent them and something called family circle (as

* Button Bright was a character in the Oz books.

opposed to me, family square) has bought an old old story for some
fantastic amount of money and stanley will be home one week from
today. so, cheered, laurie decided to finish building the record cabinet, and except for the jolly sound of the power saw things are at
peace. i have been deep in gloom and guilt; since there is no school
this week and stanley is not here to enforce discipline i have been not
waking up in the morning and then not able to sleep at night so i
watch television which always makes me feel degraded and a trifle
blind. just to get even with the world i told carol (now do i get even
with the world or the word? they are both foul) that i was throwing
out the new book* and—lip trembling—that i just didn't see how i
could ever ever _ever_ write it so there, and got back the old tantrum-
soothing routine, about put it aside for a week or so and get a new
perspective and you know darling you always get discouraged at first
and just don't let me down on this because we both know it's going
to be great. bah. this before i had finished my coffee.

whine whine

damned book is nagging me so i wince. it is a perfectly splendid
book, nicely planned, and if done carefully should work out true and
complete; it has only one disadvantage—

everything in it has been done before, by me or someone else. it is
as unoriginal as an old sponge. you ask whether hangsaman started
like this. yes it did. all of them do. but each one is worse because i
nag myself by remembering the others. if i can get it off the ground
at all it will go lofting until about page seventy and then come down
with a crash. then this will all happen over again and carol will en-
treat me not to let her down and stanley will say put it aside for a
week or so and then i will kick it to life again and about page one
hundred and fifty the end will be in sight and i will be so encouraged
that i will go back and start over. the hell with it, actually. it's no
more degrading than watching television. and now i think of it why
should i steam at _you_? you never said anything about getting a new
perspective, or did you?

i will endeavor to recollect myself. surely this loving dwelling on

* _We Have Always Lived in the Castle._

The Problem of the Artist in Modern Society is not fitting on a morning when i have had your letter. did i say anything that might indicate that i would write to you into a vacuum without getting your letters? no fair. i wait for your letters (what are you laughing at at breakfast) and won't be deprived of them. anyone who can spoil three batches of fudge in a row might better be writing letters anyway. my habits irritate stanley because he sits down at the typewriter and says today i will write ten pages with half an hour for a cigar after lunch and today he writes ten pages and on tuesday he writes letters every tuesday and answers all the letters he has gotten since last tuesday and on sunday he files everything. and in the evening he says i will read these three books and take notes. and on wednesday he trims his beard. and if you think that on tuesday in detroit stanley is <u>not</u> writing letters you are drearily mistaken. so when he sees me spending a Working Day making a doll house out of an old carton he gets very nervous. or sometimes i look at pictures of houses or sing to myself or sit on the back steps telling myself stories and stanley frets. people were put into this world to keep busy at constructive things. he has always been driven by the nightmare of time; there are so many things he will never have time to learn, so many books he will never have time to read. i find this a Good Thing.

how shall i say this? the playboy story. dylan.* did you know that they were not unconnected? stanley says sure as anything that whole pack around dylan is going to sue me for libel but i am outwardly innocent; i could not be supposed in actuality to have known anything about dylan's death. (and don't you tell.) john brinnin† (who will someday meet, i hope, the fate he deserves) took a crack at us in his book on dylan; among other things he remarked that our children were noisy. i feel i still owe him a little something. they were not any noisier than usual the day he brought dylan over.

now later

---

* Shirley's story "Weep for Adonais" appeared in *Playboy* magazine and is believed to be about Welsh poet Dylan Thomas's death.
† John Brinnin, a poet and critic, brought Dylan Thomas to the United States for a book tour in 1950, during which he visited Westport and was invited to the Hymans' for dinner. Brinnin was the author of *Dylan Thomas in America*.

joanne called; this conversation:

me: dear, any plans for next summer? any chances?

j. yes; listen, is it all right if i work in a bar in chicago?

me: DOING WHAT? DOING WHAT?

j. i'll ask. i'll let you know. but is it all right?

and stanley called and it is storming like anything in detroit and he is supposed to be flying tomorrow to akron (are these places real? you live out that way, you should know) for another lecture and i believe that one or another of these planes will fall down and i wish he would take a bus or something.

previous ill-temper some modified. nice to know that faraway family is still remembering. Do you—oh, pussycat, do you—know flanders and swann,* the drop-of-a-hat cats? stanley said to me go out at once and get that record and i did and they are lovely lovely. or do you know dylan's records? they sound like him. he taught me to say "not bluidy loikely," and i can do it fine. you say it when someone tells you it's time to go out and vote on city planning. no' bluidy loikely, you say, no' bluidy loikely. no' me, myte. this is all welsh, except for city planning. someday i will know clearly how i felt about dylan. how far away?

when <u>we</u> hitchhiked it poured rain all the time.

you didn't tell me about your course in architecture. did you major in it? (laurie is going to, i think; my family is one whole maggoty heap of architects) and at what college? laurie designed a house which to my eye looks wrong but i only like eighteenth century houses and baroque but at least i know when a kitchen has no wondows. (wondows are spaces for wondering in and any kitchen needs them.) my kitchen wondows are dirty and i will not clean them and neither will joanne because the house is so old that panes of glass fall out into your shoes when you rub hard. oh, about the picture of bix. how kind of you not to point out the scuff marks on the door beyond. what you so cavalierly call traffic marks are actually the boards of our fine old mansion floors, uncleaned, and they do not go out into the hall because vermont farmers were nothing if not sensible,

* Flanders and Swann were a British comedy act who composed, sang, and recorded more than one hundred songs, including their musical revue *At the Drop of a Hat.*

and did not see any sense in using good wood to floor a hall where everyone was going to track snow anyway and besides we could not afford the sander for just <u>every</u> room, for heaven's sake. that is an artificial doorknob which laurie is fond of sticking up just anywhere and hopelessly confusing stanley on the coat closet which he uses every day. (wait, wait, it is not the coat closet down <u>there</u>, no, really; the coat closet is . . . no. the <u>coat</u> closet which stanley uses every day—to hang up my coat which i leave on the floor—is somewhere else. <u>that</u> little low closet is. . . . now wait. i knew just a minute ago. we use it all the time. it is a little low closet.) there is a definite cold spot in the hall because one of our several back doors opens upon it. melting snow lies deep just beyond the picture's border.

oh, jay.* or rather abrashkin; he does the research, is sick (in some fashion i never knew) and is largely unable to function; has to have everything read to him, cannot feed himself, etc. incurable. jay is an old and close friend of his, and so does the writing, so the style to which you object must be largely jay's. jay was not originally a writer, but an entertainer, and still relies for his effects on sharp fast punches, which of course makes his style jumpy. privately, we both think it a shame that he took to writing at all, although his work with kids is incredible (they adore him) and some of that gets into his books, but he is such a great entertainer that he is really now a talent lost. his real love is medieval history. i suspect i am partial to the books because i am fond of the man; i can quite see your objections. he has blind spots, and in his adult books these are clearer; he loves to tell all about the witch cult in england in the times of james I, and so loses all perspective in character and ends up with what you rightly call "formula," although it is formula in character rather than plot. what does come through, i think, in both adult and children's books, is his genuine love of learning and enthusiasm for all kinds of off-beat ideas. the first time i met him was in college, and he—at that time apprentice to an african witch-doctor in new york—conjured up a silver tiger with emerald eyes in the living room of the house where i was living; many of us saw it, chanting mama

---

* Jay Williams.

loi, mama loi. he introduced himself as my father. We drank sour wine and danced on the top of a hill, and many years later he gave me the jade ring he wore that night because it was magic. i am to give it to sally someday. he introduced himself as my father so i could get out of the house because i was condemned to get in every night at eight unless my parents came. he sang all the time, jay. he knows a little something about everything, and a song about that. he is desperately anxious to be a success as a writer, and i do think the children's books are far above most stuff being done today simply because of jay's love for kids. i wish somehow you could meet him; you would know better what i mean.

i am going to take off right here and now and get into the tub with lots of bath salts.

fri

oh, listen. in the mail this morning is a letter from some woman who lives on a paw paw lane in indiana and she is going to review hill house for her Fortnightly Book Club and she wants to know will i please answer the following questions like is the early haunting telepathy a quatre and what ever happened to the dog they chased out of the house? (you know, i went and forgot that dog? i don't have the faintest idea how it got there or what it was but i do think telepathy a quatre is a lovely name for a dog.) she also wants to know why i said luke was a liar and a thief when he seemed like such a nice young man; she should know that luke is my dearest secret idol like essex in sundial and he is bad because i choose that he should be bad. he is named luke because stanley, who teaches the bible in one of his lit classes, was re-reading luke one evening and we got to talking about lucan devices* and the idea charmed me. but how can i tell this to a lady living on paw paw lane in indiana? i don't have anything to say about the movie stuff, and don't want to, but now—i may have told you—someone wants to do sundial as a movie, and a friend here in bennington is working on a project for making three stories

* Reference either to the epic Roman poem by Lucan titled *Pharsalia*, detailing the civil war between Julius Caesar and forces of Pompey the Great in 48 B.C.E., or to Luke 15 and the parable of the Prodigal Son/lost son.

(demon lover, pillar of salt, tooth, which were originally written as a trilogy) into a kind of art movie. do you know the stories? what do you think of this: they have been talking of running them together, not in sequence, so that the story lines interweave and the stories are separated by the use of different symbols and colors for each, with the same actor playing all three men, the james harris character (who is luke of course) and three different women.

one of my difficulties with the new book is that luke has gotten into it. i am perhaps obsessed. i tried naming him charles but he comes through even so. i could name him king charles' head couldn't i.

do you read jane austen or not since high school? i am sending you the carbon of the short good house piece because i like it; i have to have it back fairly quickly so that will make you write sooner. also it will make this letter look pretty odd, coming in a story envelope. sally and barry have just made a welcome home sign for joanne's door. those fiendish cats.

meow

s.

•   •   •

## [To Geraldine and Leslie Jackson]

monday [March 1960]

dearest mother and pop,

this is going to sound crazy. prepare yourselves. our lawyer is forcing us to make wills, on the grounds that our estate (get that!) is now of such proportions as to need handling, and if we did not make wills the kids would be involved in enormous tax and red tape problems if anything happened to us. also, we have to provide for the disposition of the books and the coins which are both collections of considerable value and—this is the kicker—my literary estate.

stanley's literary works are fairly static; they bring in a small regular sum, but my royalties are growing every year and from them money is to be put aside for the kids' education and such. it all sounds very pretentious, particularly when the lawyer gets it done up in that fancy language. anyway, my private papers are the point at issue now. stanley and sally have already arranged to publish my letters as joint editors. anyway the important thing is my letters to you over these years, which i pray you have kept, and will arrange for them to get back to me. stanley is most urgent about this, since he puts a higher value on them than i do, and i promised him and the lawyer that i would write you at once and make sure that they would be returned to me eventually. since i hope i have a couple of years still to go the problem is not very pressing, but the vital thing is that you not throw them out. since I only write long letters to you they must be a long detailed record of many years. i am almost embarrassed when i think of the mountains of pages they must make.

we were both charmed by the will-making. of course it was nice to know that we were worth so much, and infuriating to realize how much the government will take away. the children were delighted and spent a long pleasant morning dividing us up. if sally gets the literary properties then laurie wants the coins and joanne wants the books, leaving poor old barry with the house and land, and he finally decided he would make the house into a laboratory. joanne said well then, she would take the house and make it into a ski lodge. i felt absolutely like a character in a mystery story making a crazy will to get everyone fighting. will you let me know about the letters as soon as you can?

we have had near-spring the last couple of days; the snow has not gone, of course, but it has been warmer. it means our season of mud is coming. and summer plans are in the air; joanne has been accepted as a counselor in training at the camp where barry and sally will be. laurie of course will be in europe, and stanley and i plan to take a couple of short trips; i still want to get to salem, and we both want to go back to newport for a few days.

still no word on the movie of hill house. i suppose the hollywood strike has held everything up. i've told you, i know, about the art movie the drama people up here want to make of three of my stories; they have backing and a script writer and we are all to work together and they keep saying it will be great fun and referring to this fellow bergman who is apparently the greatest right now and has pictures playing all over new york and they discuss things like his mastery of symbols and such; we are to do a movie just like bergman. unfortunately, the college brought bergman's <u>seventh seal</u> up here for a special showing and stanley and i went, all eagerness, to see the great art movie and about half way through i walked out because it made me actually sick. there is no question about his being great, but he is too rough for me. it was about the plague in denmark in the fourteenth century and altogether too graphic.

i had a rough weekend of it because i can't walk. last week i slipped on the ice on our steps—like a fool, really; after a winter of walking on ice i should know better than to run up the steps in high-heeled shoes but i was in a hurry—and banged my knee; after a couple of days my whole leg turned purple and stanley called the doctor who spent two minutes looking at my leg, announced that i had bruised it and it would go away and there was no sense trying to do anything about it, and then sat for two hours telling us about his trip to the virgin islands. then on saturday i got my foot caught in our heavy metal storm door and got a bad gash in the heel on my <u>other</u> foot and for a few minutes i was hopping around the kitchen first on one foot and then on the other wondering how people could limp on <u>both</u> feet and so now i kind of shuffle around, unable to wear boots or even stockings. thank heavens they are nicely brought up; joanne did most of the work around the house this weekend, funny sally voluntarily scrubbed all the bathroom floors, and barry dusted. they were like a pack of little goblins, all busily telling each other what to do. and of course once i did the cooking, most of which i did sitting down, the girls were able to deal with serving and dishwashing.

laurie has made us the most beautiful cabinets for the stereo set; they are going to make the room look so nice. we have ordered a new sectional couch for what used to be the front room but is now the music room (where we have the television set) and new drapes, and laurie is going to make a huge coffee table and it will be beautiful, we are also having the house painted again as soon as the weather allows, and the living room chairs recovered. now that we are finally able to put some money into the house i am cutting down the cat population—over the strenuous objections of the children i got rid of all cats but seven who were close personal friends of one or another child, and had them all fixed so there will be no more kittens. also i am advertising again for someone to clean the house. stanley says to offer unusually good pay, since everyone is so discouraged when they see the size of this place. (this is all the money from the reader's digest, by the way; when the movie money starts i don't know <u>what</u> we'll do.) it is nice to be able to fix things up. we may find that we have to get a new furnace, since this one is getting very old, but the idea doesn't worry us half as much as it would have a year ago.

well, i must start my trip downstairs. it takes me quite a while. but i suppose they will want lunch as usual. write soon, and we are still hoping to see you in may.

lots and lots of love from all,

s.

•  •  •

[To Jeanne Beatty]

monday [March 1960]

dear jeanne,

i have been wanting to write for days but somehow things move too fast. college opened last week and this morning stanley had to drag himself out of bed and go teach and the campus, which has been so clear and empty all winter is now full of screeching girls always eating and wearing skin tight pants. it means the end of our peaceful winter; bennington, as you probably know, has a three-month off-campus winter period, when the girls are supposed to be pursuing their educations at various jobs and research projects, and the faculty hibernates. now it has begun again and already i feel tired. last night was the faculty cocktail party, officially opening the social season, and people who have lived within a mile of one another all winter emerged and blinked and greeted one another after three months. we have such an odd community; we are so isolated with no trains and only an occasional nasty bus and roads not fit to travel on most of the time, so we are forced to find all our social life in one small college community. it means we see the same thirty-odd couples all the time. now that the term has begun we have to be social again. that means a dinner party every saturday night, and all the invitations in return. it also means—which is worst of all—being entertained by students, either way it's a headache. i stay rigorously away from the college, rarely mix with students, don't know any of their little names, and so before any such function stanley has to spend half an hour or so briefing me on who i am going to see and what to talk to her about. i can manage the faculty pretty well, and even have some close friends among the faculty wives, but rarely see them; an affair like last night's usually leaves me shaken up for two or three days because the impact of a big room full of people all talking hits me harder than the cocktails. i have luckily managed to establish a reputation for mild eccentricity, and now no one minds if i go and sit by myself in a corner for half an hour, and no one insists on coming up to make bright conversation because i am sitting alone. they are all nice people and i like them very much but they certainly do all talk all the time. also i invariably fall down, not from drinking but from nervousness and unaccustomed high heeled shoes, and last night was no exception although i did manage to hold out until i was coming up our own steps and slipped on the ice. it is so beautifully quiet here in my study this morning, and no one <u>talking</u>. stanley is trying to make me learn to talk to people, particularly since i am giving more lectures and readings now than i used to and you can hardly give a lecture and not talk to people. i do all right, not even nervous, with the lecture itself, but then afterwards they ask questions or come and talk to me and i am numb and dumb. but i did lecture at williams college last week and stanley said that afterwards i answered at least

two questions quite intelligently. mostly, at the party afterward, stanley answered all the questions for me; i just smiled charmingly and
nodded. i never remember any words when people ask me something.

now i will have to leave this and go make lunch. why <u>do</u> they have
to keep eating? that damn school keeps sending them home every
day at twelve. hot dogs.

thursday

have been trying to work but barry has a friend, loud david, here, and
polished prose goes out the window. david brought a tin whistle. depend on david.

so many things i keep trying to remember to write you but mostly
when i am not writing i sit and dream about my castle. my big problem now is <u>how</u> to kill him; after reading ten million mystery stories
i still don't know a good way. i want something highly suspicious but
possibly natural, like mushrooms but i don't really know one end of a
mushroom from another. some highly poisonous garden plant (not
oleanders i just happened to find that by chance in the children's en-
cyclopedia) but i read somewhere larkspur.

oo let us make a orchestra cries david you bang on the wastebasket. her name is jenny. she lives with her sister constance in a big old
brown house saturated with family memories and her husband lives
there too; they have been married for seven years and her sister constance still calls him mr harrap. they are going to kill him because he
is a boor i think.

oh. lottery is out of print. unbuyable. i cannot even get copies for
myself or else i would send you one. they keep saying they are going
to reprint it but that is the publisher i had such a fight with because
they wouldn't give me a lot more money and so they are most incivil
and never reprint my nice books. and we don't know who is going to
make the art movie because all that has happened is this fellow and
bill alton* from bennington and me all sitting around drinking all af-

* William Alton was a member of the Bennington College drama faculty, and a family
friend.

ternoon and saying what if we did this? this fellow whose name is i think sparks and he had a black eye and he talked all the time he said why didn't i put more sex in my books and i said my mother reads them and he said how old is your mother darling and i said if he was going to make any movies with me he was going to keep sex out because art movie sex is bad enough without sparks obvious trype sex and he said but it was (no not trype, type) very important to put sex in a movie and i said the sexiest scene i ever wrote was toward the end of hill house where luke is describing what he may or may not do to the house all the time sneering at eleanor and sparks got a light in his eye and said hey he better read that and i am very anxious to hear from him what he thought. high up in the list of people i do not understand as i may have said before come drama and acting people. sparks told bill afterward that he thought i was going to be very very wonderful to work with because i did not insist upon intruding my own ideas into the script talk but of course sparks has not really had a chance to find out because that man is going to lay one finger on the plot of tooth—my favorite—and i am going to black his other cyc. anyway it ought to be about six years before we even get a script much less start making any movie and they have several backers interested but are not committing themselves yet because every time they get together they talk big and convince each other that this thing is really too great to give to anybody for certain right now.

did you know i once saw groucho* plain? he was the father of a bennington student for a while. (she was only here for a while, see, and anyway she would have traded him for any other father going.) she was a good friend of mine—perhaps the last student friend i ever had—and said that he was the most dreadful vulgar sadistic man she had ever known. she adores the other brothers.

yes. know dylan thomas records. do not listen.

i have been reading pride and prejudice because stanley has been playing harpsichord records every evening.

* Groucho Marx, of the Marx Brothers comedy act, was the father of Bennington student Miriam Marx. Miriam was often Laurie's babysitter when he was five, and took him to see *A Night at the Opera*.

i have suddenly thought that if i hurry and send this then it will be <u>my</u> turn. kind of cheating but who doesn't cheat?

david if you cannot treat barry's toys gently you will have to go home. "we have always kept male cats, mr. happap," constance said politely, "but of course they have always been fixed."

cooking now is putting something into a casserole and sitting on my red stool making notes. ("constance sends christmas cards. jenny gardens.") about one third of this will get into the book* and the rest is just saturating myself with the two of them and trying to get ivy compton-burnett† out of my system. i always start like ivy and have to write it off. i am not yet talking like jenny but i will be soon. on the old filing folder for hill house there is a note saying "theo has six toes."

your friend's letter (for which thanks) said you wrote stories. where are they?


tuesday

i hope you do not mind if i do this kind of a page at a time. i am feeling so odd tonight (oh look single space; that is because i wrote a letter to poor marjorie freer whose husband died very suddenly and about whom i cannot make any more jokes because i am so sad for her; she idolized him like not many women do their husbands; poor poor marjorie) because we have spent the day making wills. it is very odd. i mean i never made a will before. our lawyer is a charming lady named elizabeth and she said we had to make wills. so we went. and she said now how would you like to be buried, and what kind of service? i said a wake with lots of people drinking and stanley said certainly a wake but no services, and i said no services but lots of people drinking and elizabeth said never mind i personally will see to the lots of people drinking as a matter of fact i will throw the party myself but in the meantime you must be serious and decide what you

---

* *We Have Always Lived in the Castle.*
† Ivy Compton-Burnett was an English novelist who specialized in dissecting the social mores of the upper classes in late Victorian and Edwardian times with melodramatic stories told largely in formal dialogue.

want them to sing at your funerals and i said i do not want a funeral because it will be rough enough for the kids fighting over what we leave without having a funeral to go to too and stanley said we are going to be cremated together and elizabeth said but suppose you don't die together and that thought was so appalling that we looked at each other and said then what the hell we won't die at all. and elizabeth said look you've got to make this will, friends, and so we are to be cremated. no services. good god what a thing to do on a sunny day.

shirley

•   •   •

[To Sally, Barry, and Joanne]

thursday [summer 1960]

dear sally/barry/joanne or whatever your names are,

we got nice letters this morning from sally and barry but there seems to be someone missing; weren't there three of you when we left? is the third too busy with the fancy hairdryer to sit down and write a letter?

(harlequin, sitting on the dining room table to watch me type: i can't find sally. where is sally? why doesn't sally ever go to bed any more?

me: sally is at camp.

harlequin: oh.)

barry's letter, while not very informative, is consoling; at least, it doesn't say that he has lost his knife, his good pants, his compass, or his sleeping bag yet. sally's letter is fine, except who is rupert of hentzau?

(harlequin: i just went up and looked in sally's room. where did you say she was?

me: at camp.

harlequin: oh.)

the attic is going on beautifully. it has been considerably cooler so laurie hasn't suffered so much, and most of the insulation and dirty work is done. the carpenter is here now, putting in a skylight, and they have ordered the fan. there is no point in my trying to clean the upstairs hall (even if i could find the broom and dustpan) or any bedrooms, because so much sawdust and scrap wood keeps falling down the trapdoor. if they ever finish i will go to work up there. if i can find the broom and dustpan. meanwhile i am getting some work done on my book and dad is working hard between feeding the fish and clearing the bar and carrying laundry.

we had a lovely time after we left you at camp. we drove on down to connecticut where we were expected at the gills'* 25th anniversary party, and what a party it was, to be sure. they have a big garden (this is in their <u>small</u> house; the <u>big</u> house is down the road and has an even bigger garden, but it is <u>too</u> big to open for just the summer) and they had set up a tent on the grass and there were about a hundred people and about a hundred cases of champagne. dad says he drank one case. we saw some old friends and stayed on after the party— never did get any dinner except cocktail sandwiches—and had a nice evening with the gills and the next morning visited their lake cottage for a few minutes (they do not own quite all the lake; four other families have little pieces of it) and then came home. the road there is so narrow that when last year they had a fire at the cottage and the fire engine came charging down the road and got thoroughly stuck between two trees and could not get out, so the neighbors put out the fire and a wrecking crew came and got the fire engine. i was very much impressed with the outfits the gill girls were wearing; there are five of them although only four were there, and they were dressed alike in white pleated cotton skirts and colored blouses; the skirts were so handsome that i asked one of them where to get them and

* Brendan Gill was a good friend and *New Yorker* writer for more than sixty years, known best as the magazine's longtime drama and architecture critic, and author of *Here at The New Yorker.*

she said everyone wore them and you could buy them everywhere in new york, so if i get a chance i will try to find a couple. I will guess at the sizes.

(harlequin: where did you say she was?

me: at camp.

harlequin: oh.)

applegate is furious at dad. the other day applegate caught a splendid bird, slightly larger than he was; we think it was a blackbird, and he brought it live into the bathroom where it promptly flew up onto the coatrack and sat there yelling and cursing and applegate sat on the floor and wondered what to do with this thing. i finally persuaded dad to help and he worked out a plan; the idea, he said, was to get the bird outside, which seemed very reasonable, so he cornered the bird and kept it at bay with the buggy whip, while i snatched applegate and put him in the front room and shut the door. then dad shut the door into the kitchen and opened the back (study) screen door and with the buggy whip herded the bird into the summersalt room and finally gave him a little flick with the whip and the bird shot out the door smack into faun malkin who was just coming in. faun malkin, who is not used to being hit in the mush with a blackbird, fielded it like barry on a low grounder and went tearing off with a mouthful of blackbird and no idea what to do with it and when i let applegate out of the front room he could not understand why dad had taken away his bird and given it to faun malkin. he was so angry that he went out and got two mice one after another and left their heads in the kitchen and when dad reminded him that mice were an unclean sacrifice he got another mouse and drowned it in bix's water dish, so it would maybe get clean that way. he now believes that nothing will please dad and i think he has given up.

i have almost gotten my voice back which is good because i have to lecture at the college in ten days. we are going to new york next week leaving laurie to feed the fish and i am going shopping and to see some movies and we will celebrate lulu and gramp's anniversary with them. laurie is doing all his own cooking; he doesn't want to go to restaurants with us, so he cooks himself cube steaks and hamburgers. last night he made steaks for Corinne* and she said they were good. dad and I have been wandering all over for dinners.

love,

mom

• • •

"Dear, you know the doctor said you weren't
to carry anything heavy—"

## [To Geraldine and Leslie Jackson]

wednesday [August 1960]

dear mother and pop,

first of all i want to tell mother happy birthday—little early, I know, the new yorker subscription is renewed with our love, and a record

---

* Corinne M. Biggs, from the town of Bennington and now a Bennington College student and occasional babysitter at the Hymans', is now dating Laurie; they will be married in 1962.

will be arriving which i do not recommend your listening to.* anyway, happy birthday from all of us.

everything is fine here, and the kids are all well. it has been a wonderful summer for all of us. stanley and i have kept busy here at home, writing, although not so much as we should have, and i have not cooked a meal except breakfast since the kids left. we have been going out for lunch at some small local place, and then go exploring for dinner. there are only one or two good restaurants near here, but during the summer of course new england comes to life. we have been as far as fifty miles away to try a special place. we got a list from friends and from books, and are really having a lovely time at it. we are trying to get to a place which life magazine's cookbook calls one of the fifty top restaurants in the united states, but although it is only about seventy miles from here, there does not seem to be any way to get there. we would have to go to brattleboro and then turn around and come back down another road; very confusing. we are getting to know the country around us, which we never did before. we always left town in one of two directions— either into new york state, going to the city, or into massachusetts, going to the kids' camp or to boston, so we never explored further into vermont. half the fun of going, of course, is the little open car. we spent a week in new york city early in the summer, seeing agents and publishers and such, which is always a tiring experience (everyone drinks before lunch, which is very hard on us rustic types). we also spent a week in suffield, connecticut, where i go every year for my writers' conference, and this year stanley came along as kind of semi-staff, which meant that while i was out teaching every morning he stayed in our room and worked on his book, and then sat in on a couple of panel discussions and gave one evening lecture. that was a lot of fun, since i love suffield and have a lot of good friends there and this year stanley was able to meet them and see the place.† i also gave an evening lecture, which i am

---

* Shirley's Folkways record of her reading "The Lottery" and "The Daemon Lover."
† 1960 was clearly the first—and only—time Stanley accompanied Shirley to Suffield. It evidently did not go very well, as is reflected in a long letter to Stanley that Shirley will soon write.

getting to enjoy doing. i am much less nervous about public speaking than i used to be, and may end up doing lecture tours yet.

our plans are to go to salem next week; i have always felt that i ought to see salem since i wrote a book about it, and am very anxious to see the old houses there. we are trying to decide whether to go to new york to meet laurie's boat;* he has apparently been having the time of his life. he has written twice, long excited letters. he and one of the boys spent about ten days in greece, staying with the boy's relatives, and laurie had a chance to see how a greek family lives. he was shocked at how poor they were, and how much we take for granted here at home that they regard as luxuries. they got into trouble with the police in yugoslavia, since they tried to go through the country without proper visas, and got hauled off the train and scolded, neither of them understanding a word, and the police took away all their cash—about twenty-eight dollars, laurie said—and they can't seem to get it back without going back to yugoslavia and fighting all that red tape. the american counsel in athens told them to forget it; the last we heard they had left greece and were hiring a car to go through italy and briefly to paris and then on to holland where they sail from rotterdam on the fifteenth. the boat trip was also great; the boat was a kind of college cruise ship, full of american college kids, and laurie and the other boys in the band were just part of the crowd, rather than being made to feel like the hired help. it has been, altogether, a great experience for him and i only hope he comes home prepared to settle down to college.

we saw the other kids in camp last sunday, and hardly recognized them. barry is so tan that it is a shock, and his hair has been bleached by the sun so he looks very different; he is also two inches taller; the girls are both tan and have been concentrating on taking off weight, which is an improvement in both, although i never thought i would see the day when sally worried about weight. sally is what they call a senior girl, which is the oldest girl's group in the camp. she is the youngest of the senior girls, but fits in with them beautifully, and has surprised everyone this year by being more interested in the camp

* Laurie and his jazz band were returning from their European trip on a Holland America ship.

dances than in climbing the roof of the recreation hall. joanne is doing astonishingly well as a junior counselor, and the kids are very fond of her. the camp director says they can use her any year she wants to come. i think she is a little bored by it, however, and would prefer something else next summer, something more like a real job. she still wants to try summer theatre, but there doesn't seem to be much chance.

it hardly seems possible that summer is nearly over; i wish the two worst winter months went this fast. we are getting lonesome for the kids and it seems too quiet now, although we liked it for a while. oh, we have a new floor in the kitchen, back hall, and bathroom. we bought a new fourteen-foot couch for the front room where we have the television and stereo, and it looks beautiful; sectional and curved, with finally plenty of room for people to sit down. stanley and i sit every evening and listen to records; we are particularly interested in harpsichord right now, and it's wonderful on the stereo records. no more jazz, not until laurie gets home. we have been buying lots of records on what we save on the phone bill with all of them gone.

remember, i do not advise your listening to the record we sent you, but a very happy birthday, anyway. lots and lots of love,

s.

· · ·

[To Geraldine and Leslie Jackson]

wednesday [fall 1960]

dearest mother and pop,

i thought that just for amusement you might want to know the current standing of HILL HOUSE; perhaps it is because i never had a book so successful, but I just love to count it over.

anyway, (i just <u>love</u> this sum) the movies paid $67,500. my share of the reader's digest is going to be about twenty thousand, with a possibility of more if it sells beyond their average figure. they have also taken an option on foreign sales for another four thousand. the paperback rights have been sold for a sum which the agent said i didn't need to know because it would only make it harder for me to add. the english rights have sold, and the agent said sadly that she had felt it wiser to close the hollywood deal without going further into the broadway rights. on top of everything else, sales on the book itself are great; it has paid off its advance and is making a profit. sold four thousand copies last week. it might even make the best seller lists.

the publisher is now talking about a new book, which he expects will do as well on the strength of this one. he is so pleased because you know they took me on and gave me a prodigious advance on faith, and this has paid them off well.

we do look forward to paying all our debts. once we are in the clear with the world we can save the rest for things like college for the kids. it will be wonderful to know that everything is paid. mostly it's the mortgage on the house and a bank loan, and things like dentist bills. also, one item is eighteen hundred owed to you, accumulated over the past twenty years, and you can expect that to be coming along.

i don't know anything at all about the movie itself. the contracts have not even been signed, but i expect i will know something early next year. all i do know is that it will not be a low-budget movie, like the last one, because they could hardly pay me so much without expecting to get it back.

i have arthritis again, in the ends of my fingers, and cannot type for longer than a few minutes without trouble. i have had it off and on for the past several years, and the doctor says that eventually i will have to use an electric typewriter but i am afraid of them. anyway it's lucky that i don't have anything to write. my agent has been after me for a long time to come into one of the big new york hospitals with a specialist to see if something can be done but that is silly, since i would probably end up not able to type at all. it's your fault, anyway; it's inherited. the doctor says it's also an occupational disease, that pianists have it, and the only practical relief is aspirin, and applications of oil of wintergreen, which is an awful cure. i smell like a bubble gum factory, and the wintergreen gets into the sheets and the pillows and the chocolate pudding. anyway except for smelling awful i don't really mind it. it is a great excuse to sit around and read.

i want to get all this money changed into gold pieces and sit on the floor and play with them, but stanley says the government would find out.

lots and lots of love to you both.

s.

. . .

[To Geraldine and Leslie Jackson]

monday [September 5, 1960]

dear mother and pop,

this being labor day i am in the last stages of the confusion of school clothes and laundry. the weather has turned quite cold and now they say that we may be in the path of that new hurricane.

mother's letter came this morning, and so i will answer all the questions in it; i have the feeling i have written you all this before but will try again; laurie is building a bookcase just behind me and the sawing makes it difficult to concentrate.

here goes:

the paper edition of the lottery was done without any reference to me. all reprint rights belong to my former publisher who does not like me and so is trying to squeeze every possible nickel out of what rights he has. he has authorized reprints of several books, all awful as far as cover pictures and copy are concerned, but i can't do anything about it, and probably won't get any money to speak of.

the record sounds funny because i was concentrating on going slow; the tendency with something like that, particularly the elaborate setup with mikes and recorders, is to hurry up and get it over with as fast as possible. i will never make another record, if i have any say. i think this one is horrible, and cannot listen to it. also the legal complexities are awful; most of the recordings or readings are by poets, whose material is not usually copyrighted in more than one form, but these two stories i read are copyrighted as plays and as stories and nbc owns right now the television rights to lottery and raised a howl when they heard that it was being recorded. the record company blandly assumed that my agent would okay their contract which has always been all right for the poets, but the contract automatically gave folkway records all dramatic rights to both stories, and it took two months of lawyers fighting to get a contract which would save the stories for me. now the record cannot be played publicly at all, not even on a radio program. you can buy it in record stores, but it costs six bucks.

the book about the cats and children is what i was calling the baby-book. i did it for money. i was asked to do thirty thousand words and the idea was that my name would only appear in some small note somewhere; the book was not in any sense to show that it was by me or edited by me or anything, but they went ahead and put my name all over it and there's nothing i can do. i have not even seen a copy, but have asked that i be given the author's regular complimentary copies and will send you one when i get them. it is called special delivery and i am not very proud of it.

my new book is coming along slowly; i had lunch with the publishers in new york this summer and they asked if i could finish next spring. i don't think i can, but they are wonderful and always give me as much time as i want. i have a couple of good housekeeping articles scheduled; i am now doing one for them every other month, and am in october and december, i think. that is just about the only magazine work i am doing.

the kids are all well, and busy as usual. laurie, who leaves for college tomorrow, is trying to finish up all his odd jobs, hence the bookcase. he is going to goddard college, in upstate vermont; it is a very small coeducational college, very new, modeled after bennington. he has bought himself a model a ford, which is his dearest love. it will not go faster than thirty-five, and he has had it patched up—brakes, for instance—and is going to have it painted and will then take it to college. next weekend he comes home again—it is about a three hour drive in a real car—because he is playing an important job with his band, the last one for a while.

wednesday

i had to give up on this letter because the hammering got so loud. now laurie has gone, and everyone else is back at school. laurie drove up yesterday and called last night to say that everything was fine, except for a slight flat tire on the way. he likes the college, says nearly everyone plays the guitar, and the place is full of folk singers, but he has found a trombone player and a piano player.

most of our summer plans fell through because stanley had a slight accident; he tripped over a light cord and fell, smashing his jaw against a radiator, although thoughtfully missing the fireplace and the iron woodbox. he did not, for some strange reason, break his glasses, but he did break one tooth and a dental bridge, which snapped and cut his mouth. he was an awful mess altogether, and—since of course it happened on sunday morning, when not a dentist is to be found in bennington—had a perfectly terrible time with the broken tooth. the doctor finally gave him some dope that got him through sunday and on monday morning our local dentist took one look at the broken tooth and said it required a surgeon dentist, and since the only surgeon dentist stanley trusts is in new york, we took off for new york that afternoon. at the very best it is a four hour trip, and this was about the very worst; we drove, of course, and about halfway hit a cloudburst, one of the kind that is so heavy you can't drive, no visibility, and have to pull over to the side of the road. we were on the taconic parkway, so of course there was no place to go inside and have coffee or anything, so we just sat, stanley getting more and more unhappy as the dope began to wear off, and me just cursing. the unspeakable cloudburst followed us all the way down; it would stop raining for ten minutes or so and we would go tearing off down the road—covered with flashing signs, every mile, reading SLIPPERY WHEN WET CAUTION DANGER—and then the rain would start again and we would have to stop. it finally took us about six and a half hours, and by the time we checked into the hotel stanley was very miserable, so we filled him up with dope and then sat and had three drinks each and then he began to feel better. the next day he went to his surgeon dentist and they found that they had to take out five teeth and make a new bridge. they took out the five teeth and we drove home, stanley considerably happier, and the following week he had to go down again to have the bridge put in, and i said i just couldn't make that drive again, but would drive him to albany where he could get a train and be in the city in three hours. my plan was to drop him at the train station and come home, driving back to albany—about an hour's trip—the next day to meet him; consequently i was wearing an old skirt and sweater and old shoes; luckily i had my enormous pocketbook which has just about everything i need in it, because about half an hour from albany we hit a cloudburst, worse than the week before. i made a few choice remarks about never never driving him to a dentist again and we came down the hill which leads to the albany road into a flood. i have never seen anything like it. the cars were bumper to bumper for about five miles, with water flowing by like a river. we were three blocks from the railroad station with about ten minutes to catch the train, when the car stalled, just stopped dead. i said i would get out and get help and opened the door and the water outside was level with the car floor, so i closed the door again and we sat there, with a line of cars in back of us blowing their horns. traffic was going the other way in the other lane just as slowly and then a taxi driver stuck his head out going the other way and said lady you better move that car; the fire engines are coming. i said it was just too bad about the fire engines; they would have to run over me, and then the first fire engine came whipping down the road with the sirens screaming, but the taxi driver and a truck behind him skittered over to the far side of the road and the engine zipped around me and got itself somehow down the middle of the road between the two lines of traffic, and so did two more engines behind it.

i was so thoroughly demoralized by then that i just sat there staring and stanley remarked that well, he guessed he had missed his train. finally a policeman came by and arranged to have us pushed off the road onto the side. i knew the car would start sooner or later when it dried out so after a while i tried it again and it started and off we went except it turned out the brakes were wet too and wouldn't hold. i crawled that car all the way to the railroad station, and finally turned a corner and let it roll to a stop in a parking lot. when i got out of the car my knees were shaking and i was soaking wet. i told the attendant at the parking lot that i was giving him the car for good and stanley finally told him to keep the car until i came for it, and i took my pocketbook and we went into the station. stanley had missed his train by half an hour, but had another in about forty-five minutes, so he suggested that either i come to new york with him or go to a hotel in albany until he came back the next day. i was hardly dressed for a hotel anywhere, much less new york city, but i was too upset to drive back home alone, so i elected the hotel in albany. i certainly felt like a fool walking into the fanciest hotel in albany and asking for a room. i told the desk clerk i wanted a room with air conditioning, television, a bottle of bourbon and a bowl of ice, and he asked if my pocketbook were a suitcase and i said no, so he made me pay in advance. i certainly didn't look like anyone who belonged there, and the bellhop made a great production of carrying my key upstairs while i carried the pocketbook. i had them send my dinner up and i had a lovely evening all by myself watching television and drinking bourbon. and the next afternoon i met stanley at the station and the car was fine and the streets were dry and we drove home peacefully, him with a new bridge.

    this is the kind of adventure that kept us from doing a lot of the things we wanted to this summer. we did spend a couple of days driving through massachusetts and maine because i had never seen the seacoast, and i fell in love with those little fishing towns in maine. we stayed away from tourist places and just wandered looking for houses we would like to buy someday.

    i am going to burlington to lecture in october and the kids will take their lunch to school for two days, lovely. two days off. and stanley and i are taking an evening off on saturday and going to a wonderful new french restaurant* about twenty miles away; we

---

* L'Auberge, run by the Berends, who became good friends.

found it this summer and the owners have read all my books and insist on sending us bottles of wine. consequently we keep on going back.

lunch. must stop writing. write me soon, and lots of love from all.

s.

•  •  •

[To Jeanne Beatty]

monday [September 1960]

have been wishing you would write but suppose sadly that you are too busy. somehow end of summer comes. our trees are turning; are yours? i love fall. i love red leaves and apples and pumpkins and generally getting tucked in against the winter, and it has been a good, a great, summer.

sally and barry both came home with colds, and joanne came home with four stitches in her right hand. laurie came home with tales of far countries and vague, laughing reminiscences of the girls in florence. "in greece we used to . . ." and then sudden, stricken silence. "cracked up the motor bike outside barcelona but the doc patched me up okay. no, mom, no. no, mom, i tell you i'm all <u>right</u>. mom, I'm all <u>right</u>, <u>honest</u> i am." but the girls in florence, and the goat's milk in greece, and paris . . .

and we went to salem, stanley and i, to see witches but there weren't any witches not anywhere there. but there was the Witch City Auto Body Wrecking Company and the Witch City Dry Cleaners and the Witch Grill. and seagulls outside the hotel window and i sat at the window looking out over old lovely houses now the home of the See-Rite Framing and Window-Working Company, and packs of young hoods on street corners where the salem city fathers would have forbidden them to loiter if the city had not fallen upon ill days. they would have been in church. after much searching i

got to see a manuscript written in court of the trial of rebecca nurse*
and she really did say all those heartbreaking things; "can you really
read that old writing?" said the neat girl at the desk, adjusting her
harlequin glasses; "yes," said i, "i know much of it by heart." "really?"
said she, "is it interesting?" i don't know much of it by heart, actually.
i was showing off. i wouldn't sign any guest books because i was
ashamed to say that i had been there. i would have sent you a post
card but you hadn't written for so long.

new york. i bought lots of clothes because i had none. i went into a
store and bought six skirts and two coats and five blouses in twenty
minutes and raced back to the hotel and put some of them on and
went out to lunch with editors who said of course the book will be
ready by next dogwood day? dogwood day is a day made up by my
publishers because i am afraid of real days so this is the day when the
dogwood blooms in central park and it is not real because of course
the dogwood never does bloom in central park, and i was eating eggs
benedict and drinking martinis and pretending that i was a lady
being taken out to lunch. the book will not be ready a year from dogwood day. the heroine is named merricat; do you like it? mary catherine really, but we who know her best say merricat. i am trying not to
let her be sub-normal mentally. tell me a good man to use; i am desperate because i need a man and cannot think of a kind of one i want
to use; "let your material guide you," i said to the school-teachers-
who-want-to-write at suffield, "do not impose your own prejudices
upon your story; let your story tell itself." i told them and told them.
marjorie freer said to me do you remember that funny little man who
came here for cocktails one day? yes, i said, his name was wolf. of
course, marjorie said, i wonder whatever happened to nice little mr
wolf. i broke all records for their evening lectures, a big big audience
and very nice. i had a nice speech, too. stanley and marjorie kept giggling off on the side and i frowned sternly.

if you write me a letter i will tell you about hazel at suffield. and
the new scandal in north bennington. and my mother's new car.

well, yes. she does drive, in a manner of speaking. but a jaguar? my

* Rebecca Nurse was one of the Salem women accused of witchcraft and hanged in
1692.

mother? nice little old lady, whipping down the california highways at a hundred and fifteen miles an hour? she said she just saw it and liked it and of course they are keeping the Cadillac for city driving. dammit i am going to get a ferrari and we can have drag races mother and i.

it is such a dreary nasty rotten stinking beast of a day and your letter brightened it considerably. it has rained for two solid days and nights (a solid day and night is one where it doesn't really make much difference which it is because it stays dark and everyone sniffles) and down around the store they are saying ominously that this here hurrycane might well be worse than thirty-eight. (thirty-eight it blew away the stone catamount (for mounting cats) from in front of the catamount tavern; forty-three the airport blew away, it really did.)

thursday

it missed us. by golly. in pittsfield forty miles away they had tornadoes and like everything else except tourists from new jersey the storm daintily avoided setting foot over the vermont border and took the scenic route through massachusetts. and down at the store this morning they were opining darkly that it don't often happen twice and here is this new hurrycane building up and it is probably worse.

not that the sun is shining or anything like that. me, i left this letter monday after being so happy to get your letter and have been walking around in blackest gloom, sighing, scowling, snapping. it is somebody's fault, of that i am sure. mine.

good housekeeping turned down my last article (and rightly; it missed by a mile, but that doesn't help my self-esteem) and even though it's the only one they've refused in the two years i've been writing for them and the editor practically cried over the phone and my agent was soulfully indignant on my behalf i still don't like it because it was a lousy article and i knew it. and i had one of those searching self-inquiries all alone here with applegate the cat to listen and of course that always makes you feel worse and i decided at last to give up on castle and i put it all in a filing folder and hid it away in my desk and called my agent back and told her so she immediately changed and became heartily falsely cheerful and slapped me on the back over the phone and said don't force yourself to do anything you don't want to do darling and i'll tell the publisher for you that there won't be any manuscript for him next spring and you take a nice long rest. so then i felt even worse, of course and applegate staring at me coldly. so stanley came home and i told him, woebegone, lip trembling, blinking fast, and he said you take a nice long rest over my dead body you rested all summer you don't have to write this novel if you don't want to but you get the hell up to that typewriter and write <u>something</u> or your fingers will fall off. so i began to feel better right away and he has invited me, my nice husband, to dine with him tonight at our fanciest restaurant and so maybe i will write another book.

i am really seared by all this, although the clouds are lifting slightly. i have spent eight months trying to make a novel out of that thing and almost convincing myself i could, and it is an absolute relief to be able to look at it and say there isn't any novel there. i have only done this once before and then it was a novel i liked but no one else did* so i put it away. this one i plain didn't like, from the beginning i didn't like it. now i am like a kid let out of school. there. enough moaning.

applegate the cat is in high esteem right now because his brother gentle shax committed an unpardonable offense: he slept in stanley's filing cabinet and mixed things up ("these cats have GOT TO GO") and it took a lot of pleading and promises never to do it again to appease stanley and finally he allowed as how he would overlook it if he got a jar of macadamia nuts from the cats so he did but applegate the cat, dissenting, felt that one jar of macadamia nuts was hardly adequate for the magnitude of the crime so he brought four mice one after another and gave them to stanley to play with and the dead ones i got into the garbage can but (although i am afraid of mice i was wearing a long housecoat) after stanley had formally accepted the live mice and thanked applegate the cat the mice went under the bookcase and i spent the evening sitting up on the back of the chair.

* *Abigail.*

stanley was pleased and applegate felt that he had done the Right Thing, but the mice were gone in the morning and gentle shax had a stomach ache. so does justice triumph.

monday

   i know your letter went on for months and months but you were not as sorry for yourself as i am. i am now in the i-don't-have-any-real-friends-and-my-children-are-becoming-country-hicks stage. that means it ought to wear off about next friday.

   i now want to send joanne away to school, and am quite earnest about it, although she and her father think no. she went to a high school dance on friday and no one asked her to dance and she came home brave but hurt and i was sick; we have a distinct town-and-gown problem here and we are among very few college faculty who live in the village and the kids suffer for it. even barry, excited over joining cub scouts, confessed that he was timid because a couple of the other boys didn't want him. stanley and i can put up with being regarded as a couple of local freaks but it is awful for the children. my great consolation is laurie, who has been completely staggered by the sudden encounter with higher education. he is at goddard college, which is even more progressive than bennington. he writes raptly that there are so many wonderful subjects to study he can hardly choose; he wants to take them all. he found a drummer and a piano player and a trombone player and they entertain the entire community (only 150 students and 30 faculty) and he really thinks he will try to learn to read music. stanley and i have not even seen the place; it is very strange to think that he is really gone for good, too. the college plan includes sending them out for three months each winter to work, like bennington, so he will be home only for a day or so at a time, at christmas and such. and i find it shocking that next month he must register for the draft (why do i say draft as though it were still 1914? i think because when he was very small i used to look at him and think someday they will make you be in the army, never supposing then that he would grow up exactly the kind of boy who would enjoy army life) and he is so tall.

   because you were so kind about my stew recipe and seem to enjoy it so much i am sending you two more. one of them is from my mother-in-law, the other is from a repulsive lady. she was the mother of an entering bennington student and because she was vaguely related to friends of ours we were charged with being Nice to her and her husband so we took them out to dinner and she confided during the onion soup (confided to me and to the owner-chef of the restaurant, a brilliant cook and a good friend of ours and i was so embarrassed because damn it i do know something about cooking and never had the nerve to ask him any such questions) that she was an expert cook and she thought his food was very nice indeed and would he please give her the recipe for his salad dressing and he, eyebrows-ish, said naturally madame and wrote down with care the recipe for an ordinary french dressing and said but of course madame will be sure to get wine vinegar and she said ardently that she never used anything else and he shrugged and gave me a glance which can only be described as enigmatic and poured another glass of wine for stanley and said then madame's salad dressing will be as exquisite as mine. which of course his salad dressing is nothing much and he prides himself upon his chocolate mousse which is genuinely exquisite and which she never noticed being still all tearful about the salad dressing. anyway she got to pulling rank on me about cooking ("darling even if you're not much of a cook i always say why worry? now take me, i couldn't write a story if i tried." and she kept patting my hand until i was ready to bite off her fingers and serve them up with a mornay sauce. "darling," she said finally, "let me give you a couple of good recipes; they look like a lot and they only take twenty minutes to prepare and really no one will know what they're made of.") she patted my hand again and said but "remember i couldn't write a story if i tried."

i am a standard size but it is nobody's damn business what; stanley and i are a pair of stout-, good-eating burghers, and the diet is permanent when I remember or feel conscience-stricken. i am in a condition of permanent envy, too, at the people who can gobble. our doctor (who never gains a pound) shakes his finger warningly under our noses and we glance gleefully at one another and call to make a reservation at l'auberge. so it's hard to buy clothes; who needs clothes? my mother is still a size eighteen but she never had any fun.

monday again

   i mean, it was no use going on. it simply was no use going on. because i took the winter clothes out of the moth bags and my two best (best? only) winter suits had been devoured. why—beating my head vainly against the laundryman's strong shoulder, why, i cry, why? barry's raggedy old winter jacket which should have been thrown out was untouched.

   perhaps i will go and live on an island somewhere.

   anyway after that which i will bravely go on believing was the last and cruellest blow came what has never yet failed me which was louis untermeyer. it will be all right when louis comes, i kept telling myself, and so it was. except the untermeyers have never been here before and there were sand fleas in the guest room and we went to the poetry section of our books to make sure that one or two of louis' anthologies were prominently displayed and we had none. none. stanley went wildly through the college faculty begging to borrow untermeyers to display for a couple of days and finally we turned up one collection which the wife of the physics teacher had used in her freshman lit course at swarthmore. prominently displayed. he is the funniest man i know. oddly he was completely enchanted by barry, a grave little boy who sat compactly on the fireplace step and explained with barry soberness to louis that he wanted to be a nuclear physicist when he grew up and a human biologist in his spare time but recently he had begun to wonder if he would have enough spare time and he might have to make other plans. what kind of other plans louis wanted to know. well, barry said, considering, i will probably have to give up football.

   he is not humorless, that barry, he is thoughtful. he was explaining to sally about genes and sally thought he meant djinns. also when his counselor at camp tried to order him around barry announced that he was going to re-wire the counselor's electric blanket and electrocute him and after that barry ran the cabin. they go to the same camp, by the way, all three. joanne was a junior coun- selor this year. nice small disorganized camp with a lovely lake and dirty old clothes.

larkspur was used, by the way, in a lovely old english mystery whose name i cannot remember. i never had much faith in mush- rooms. i just made brownies (and onne his shinne a normale hadde he)* and came from louis scher a big package of books for the kids.

i wish you had come to suffield. next time you think of coming let me know and i will try to get you a scholarship. we still expect to be abroad next summer but i am going to try to squeeze in suffield for a day or so if i can. (oh, a fine and private place.† well, the publishers sent it to me and i looked at it and thought my god whimsy and with a raven yet and i didn't read it and then it turned out that the unter- meyers are doting friends of this beagle's and he is their protegee and i promised them i would read it and now you like it too so i guess i will. but i will go cautiously because i am actually reading h. rider haggard‡ right now because graham greene said that he was a better historian than walter scott which is not really saying much is it. but i always use any excuse to reread haggard and have you by any chance picked up the pocket book of the incompleat enchanter?) hazel is young and cannot write at all and is possessed of a wholly unwar- ranted arrogance and belief in herself. before she came to suffield she sent in three-quarters of a novel, twenty-six poems, a novelette and eleven short stories. all terrible. shirley barker got the novel and i got the novelette and the stories and if i were ever going to write another book i would use hazel.

hazel is armenian, born and living in boston in one of those tightly-bound communities within communities; until she grew up she really did not perceive that there was a boston beyond the arme- nian settlement. her whole life was spent in a culture completely de- rived from the old country—food, manners, furniture, language,

---

* From Chaucer's *Canterbury Tales,* though "normale" should be "mormal"—a scabby ulcer. The original quote describes an unpleasant cook.
† A 1960 novel, by Peter S. Beagle.
‡ Nineteenth-century English writer of adventure fiction set in exotic places.

tradition, everything. her father was lower-middle-class armenian which meant that there were strata above him right up to the extremely wealthy big-luxurious-house-with-servants level. (i bet the servants were irish, though.) hazel was okay—played with her cousins, sassed her mother—until she was twelve. then (yep) she developed second sight. in that community it was really something. she began predicting the future, accurately, terrifying her cousins and thoroughly awing her parents and her uncles and her aunts and her grandparents and eventually friends of the family and finally the whole community. people used to come to consult her, bringing gifts for her father in payment. she was a kind of priestess, and finally one of the very wealthy families wanted to consult her, so of course she had to be taken to them since they would not come to her, and every week for nearly a year her father took her to their beautiful home where she had a special chair and table and spent an hour or so writing in a big book (i gather it was automatic writing and self-hypnosis) and then she was given a sweet and sent home, her father having been paid. this lasted, i gather, for about a year and then she began having nightmares and hysterical fits and her father most sensibly put a stop to the whole thing and she lost whatever gift she had and has never tried it since.

i learned all this because of an accidental reference in one of her stories; i spent a couple of hours wheedling the story of her childhood out of her. she has forgotten almost all of it, and is thoroughly ashamed of what she remembers, because she has repudiated her armenian background and is now an american housewife, married. no, it never occurred to her to try automatic writing these days, she was too busy. no, she had no idea whatever happened to the big book of her writings. no, she didn't think it was very interesting anyway. no, she didn't think a writer ought to use her own experiences because who would be interested in stories about armenians? miss barker had her <u>real</u> work, the unfinished novel; <u>that</u> was the kind of thing that would sell.

poor miss barker went and read that novel. it was the story of a beautiful glamorous manicured brittle wife of a madison avenue advertising man whose life is so empty that she decides (and decide is

the word) to have an affair with one of her husband's junior execu-
tives who has cool amused eyes and a crooked grin and the novel
takes them through the preliminaries (cookout in westchester, you
know how they live, those people) and ended, abruptly, in a hotel
room where the errant wife and the crooked grin had just checked in
and had a drink (wicked) sent up from room service. now came the
part that was hard to write. hazel's television watching and movie
magazines had taken her this far, but beyond the first drink together
most of her sources had left her to her imagination with nothing but
a line of dots to go on. . . . please, hazel wanted to know, how do i go
on from here?

shirley barker is a tough old biddy with gold-painted toenails and
when you look at her pictures of hotel rooms and assignations and
whispers in the dark simply leap to the mind but actually she dresses
that way because she thinks it is funny and keeps beagles all alone in
a white cottage in new hampshire. you're married, she kept saying to
me evilly, clutching me with her gold nails, you're married, you tell
hazel what comes next. the hell i will, i would say, edging away, if my
husband found out i knew anything about strange men in hotel
rooms he would be cross with me, and anyway hazel is married, so
just being married doesn't seem to be much use and anyway you're
supposed to be helping with the novel, not me. but i have never married, shirley kept saying, casting her painted eyes virtuously heaven-
ward; i have never married and i keep beagles and i cannot think of
half a dozen times when i have been in a hotel room with an amo-
rous young man and anyway it is without doubt the worst novel i
have ever read and what she should do is burn it.

the distant soft murmur is barry practicing his cub scout oath; he
is the type who will keep it, too; "i will obey the law of the pack"—
what a vision it raises; the translyvanian wolves coming blackly down
the snowy hills raising their voices in an agonized howl for human
blood at the gates of the castle dracula; after the Bobcat badge the
loup garou. laurie became a cub scout in westport where the parents
signed away lavishly without reference to the boy's achievement and
so silver arrows were handed out like television contracts.

i sat up till four this morning (and why? i have to get up at six-thirty; what perversity lures me into sitting talking late at night?) gossiping with our college psychologist; we have a tradition around here of puring (oh, dear and him a freudian) pouring out one's heart, not unlike group therapy, really; there are some of us who love to sit up late and drink and say the kind of thing we would not say earlier, and the custom is corrupting; one drops in late at another's house and says i-want-t-talk. i frankly love it. group therapy in that we all repeat shamelessly what we heard last night. anyway i convulsed the psychologist—as stanley had been earlier enchanted—with your story about the condoms and the liquid nitrogen. apart from stanley, who has to, and you, if you have read this letter at all, he is the only person who bears with my whining about writing. i told him i had only been saved from some frightful temperamental demonstration by a golden letter from you and he asked if he could read it and i said no. (he wasn't being nosy, just wanted to know how a letter could be so brightening.)

there is no punch line to the hazel story anyway. shirley finally ducked the whole problem by a kind of evasive chat on the writer's imagination (as if hazel had any) and hazel all but snapped her fingers under my nose when she reported that miss barker "liked" her novel and thought she ought to finish it. i said civilly that miss barker was an excellent judge of novels and wished her well and hazel has presumably gone off to do field work in hotel rooms. i do not think we will see her again at suffield, and shirley and i both protested to the boss there about having to endure this woman.

you are not going to vote for mr nixon are you? i liked him on television because he looked unshaven and just like a villain from gunsmoke which should lose him lots of votes. are you?

i did—and thank you—get the cookbooks which i read with joy and had already found your lovely recipe but have not tried it. what are crawfish? (is?)

i don't think my chaucer spelling is correct. write, write. best,

s.

•   •   •

"Flotsam and Jetsam"

[To Stanley Hyman]

september 9 [1960?]*

dear stanley,

i am writing this down for three reasons, one (you name it) ignoble. first, i may always be able to use the material for something else. second, i still hope and believe that if i write things down they will somehow go away. third, there are going to be, eventually, reasons why our marriage ends, and you ought to know that it will not be a vague sudden emotion, or quarrel, which drives—has driven—me away. i am of two minds about writing it down, embarrassed at reading it and very much afraid that i will not be able to wait, but will show it to you on some sudden impulse, although i have no reason to believe you would then read it, do i?

the material, the complaints, the worries are familiar to you; they

---

* It has been challenging to discover when this letter was written, but it seems clear by the Suffield references that this comes shortly after they attended the Conference together for the first, and only, time in August 1960.

certainly should be, by now, and you can recite them back to me cru-
elly and nastily, surely, however, a state of mind which has endured so
resolutely (and you have no idea of the lengths i have gone to to suppress it, and would probably not believe me if i tried to tell you)
ought by now to be dignified by a recognition of its permanence.
when we talk about it, i cannot keep from sliding into self-pity and
recrimination, and you are always so ready to belittle and call names;
perhaps if i write it down and then read it over some months or years
from now i will be able to put a name to it—something like para-
noia, or jealousy, or self-destruction. (i know: reading, you would stop
here, and say unpleasantly that we call them all schizophrenia now.) i
am writing about myself, however, and can call my own names.

the truest name for it is loneliness. i am so lonely now that i am
shocked when i remember being a child and an adolescent; i thought
i was lonely <u>then</u>. it was frightening to me when you pointed out
that our sudden rush of company at the end of the summer was due
to your presence at home, because it was true. i was so used to being
lonely that i spent the whole summer alone without realizing that i
was talking only to myself and to people in the store; occasionally i
would come to the surface and realize that it was necessary for me to
see someone—anyone, really—and i would call one of those professionally lonely creatures, helen feeley or pat sherman, and spend a
dutiful evening with them at the drive-in. the rest of the time it was
hard to remember that i was more alone than usual. i tend to think
of myself (as i suppose most people do) as intelligent, witty, a good
companion and an agreeable person to talk to, imaginative, sensitive,
and so on—all the valuable successful attributes, in fact. to a large extent i expect this is true. i would, however, rather drink as much and
as fast as i can than face the fact that it might have been true once,
but no more. i am afraid to talk to people because i have that nagging fear that i am actually what you have told me so often i am, a
tedious bore. i think i see it in people's faces sometimes—the eye that
wanders, the impatient gesture, the alert false politeness.

indifference breeds indifference, stanley. i hear you say that every
action has a reaction, and you use the firing of a rifle as an illustration, and yet you never see the concrete illustration in your own bed.

how can i be a dim silent meaningless creature, hovering in the background (and hovering, of course, is the wrong word; one of the things i try most to do is hide myself out of sight; i am no more real by the magic of having a room of my own, but i can go there, at least, and be useless in private)—how can i be nothing at all for hours and days at a time, and then suddenly create myself into a real person for ten minutes at bedtime? i wonder, even then, what or who you are really thinking about. you have said positively that our sexual difficulties are entirely my doing; i believe you are right. i used to think, this summer, with considerable bitter amusement about the elaborate painstaking buildup you would have to endure before getting one of your new york dates into bed; you would of course have less trouble with them than with me because they had personalities to start with. they had been sought out, even telephoned, invited, spoken to and listened to, treated as real people, and they had the unutterable blessing of being able to go home afterward.

of course there was also the unspeakable effort of reading their stories and taking chocolate apples to their children and finding them jobs, but, as you have pointed out to me, you <u>liked</u> these people, they were your <u>friends.</u> you called them not because you were stuck with them but because you wanted to see them. (and here another point troubles me; do these women make themselves look nice, put on pretty clothes, because they know someone is going to be looking at them? i can't think of a better reason for concerning yourself with your appearance, any more than you ought to concern yourself with your conversation when you know that no one will be listening.) i am still bitter when i hear you speak of those women as "unhappy" or "lonely" or "sick;" i would have changed places with any of them for the evening you <u>invited</u> her out to dinner, making the gesture of phoning and issuing an invitation, taking the trouble to arrange something, making a decision, enjoying yourself, listening to her, interested in what she was doing and thinking. well, we can't have everything, can we? they were supposed to be unfortunate because they had been deserted by their husbands. do you have a good adjective for me?

one of my devices for suppressing these—no doubt—unworthy

pangs has been telling myself about other wives, the ones you read about in magazines, your mother and mine, whose husbands stayed away all day at the office and came home to settle down to read the evening paper or watch television; i argue with myself that this is the lot of wives and i have no cause to complain, but i can't win this argument either, because neither your father nor mine spent his working day in the company of three hundred-odd wives/mistresses/mothers/children, to whom he was devoted to the exclusion of his family. there it is, i guess. your "work" leaves no room for other emotional involvement, not even a legitimate one at home. i have quarrelled with your teaching theories hopelessly, because i see you change from your usual glum preoccupied personality at home, change during the short space of the ride up to college, into someone eager and happy and excited, almost unable to wait until you can get into the world you love. then at night you come home, preoccupied again, irritable and tired and bored, with no time for anything but the mail and work. you complain that our children never say goodnight to you; why should they? how can they compete with your children, your three hundred beloved babies? you have heard me say this a hundred times, but it is still true. if anyone comes to see us, you are too bored to talk unless that talk is about the college students. time grudged to your wife or your children or your friends is lavishly spent on a student who drops in to borrow a book. perhaps you are right in saying that this is what makes you a good teacher, and you can only do your work well if you love your students, but you must then admit that your children are justified in thinking you are indifferent to whether or not they say goodnight, and your wife is justified in thinking you are indifferent to whether or not she intrudes on your bed.

do you know, i think the worst single part of it is your unguarded delight at getting to the college in the morning? i am not flattering myself that you are so pleased at leaving me, since you hardly realize that i am there, but i think i even prefer the unguarded boredom with which you greet your home.

i also do not believe you realize the brutality of your constant small reminders, to me and to the children, of our insignificance; you invite guests into <u>your</u> study, absent-mindedly shutting the door in my face when i follow, you assume that a question about "your girls" refers to college students, your interest vanishes abruptly, in any conversation, when anyone asks about my book, and you constantly interrupt my answer with some new topic of your own; it is <u>your</u> study and <u>your</u> hi-fi and <u>your</u> college; you are incredulous if you discover i am planning to attend some college function to which you have not specifically invited me and of course when it was a question of my reading to an audience there i was genuinely afraid to have you come because it really takes very little to destroy my public-speaking voice, and i could not have stood the kind of belittling you employ when you suspect that i have wandered even slightly into your own preserve. incidentally, i do not want you to come to suffield with me next summer, because it is now one of the only places where i feel i have a personality and a pride of my own, and i cannot see that go, too, under your mockery.

i am not going to talk about my writing because i am afraid to; in any case, you already know how badly i have been hurt there.

i am laughing at what has just occurred to me; if i tried to tell you all this, even once more, even quietly and with restraint, even hoping desperately that somehow something can be saved, your answer would be, as always, that i am hurting your work. i am keeping you up too late, i am undermining your confidence, i am poisoning the atmosphere. at the very least, i am wasting your time which is so carefully budgeted. i am getting you, and myself, all upset over nothing.

well, it is enough. i don't think i have written you a letter in many years; as i say, my only fear about this one is that some time i am going to lose my head and show it to you. it has served its purpose, i think. i will betake me back to my own indifference, bred from indifference, living in the state so familiar and pleasant to you, of complete privacy (you would not know it for that, i think; when i am complimenting myself most ardently upon my rejection of this painful wanting to be loved and cherished you are most apt to turn to me and say approvingly, "you seem so much more calm these days; are you happy?" and cannot understand why i am caught at a loss for an answer). if it is a mature attitude, i don't want it. did you know that we were commonly regarded as a happily married couple?

you once wrote me a letter (i know you hate my remembering these things) telling me that i would never be lonely again. i think that was the first, the most dreadful, lie you ever told me.

[unsigned]

•    •    •

[To Carol Brandt]

October 5, 1960

Dear Carol,

I have been wondering about Roger Straus; is there any way to short-circuit his seemingly limitless control over most of my stuff— specifically, "Lottery"? It has just been reprinted in a collection of short stories with his permission in a section illustrating dishonesty in story-writing, which I do not find pleasant.

Although my morale has improved considerably I still find it impossible to do any writing at all. The road to hell is very likely paved with my notes for stories and books and articles. I am clinging doggedly to the conviction that it will pass eventually.

I am very happy about the Sundial progress, and as you know would simply love to see it done as a movie. It has always been my favorite.

Best,

Shirley

•    •    •

[To Jeanne Beatty]

wednesday [November 2, 1960]

how enchanting to have your letter on hallowe'en while i was making octopus costumes; i resolutely put it aside unopened because of course duty to the little ones comes first and all the time i was stapling tentacles i was thinking ha a letter to read as a reward for all my sacrifices and working my fingers to the bone making octopuses and what thanks do i get. stanley says the plural is octopodes and i suppose it might very well be. it was very fine. i read my letter and giggled and wriggled (she swallowed the spider to catch the fly.) and sally went to a hallowe'en party and barry went trick-or-treating (you be home by eight i don't care how late david can stay out and don't cross any streets without looking first and if the big boys from shaftsbury are hanging around the center of town you go the other way, you hear? and don't step on your tentacles). he did, though. step on his tentacles, i mean. pretty soon barry was trailing tentacles far far behind and he said bitterly they got caught in every single door and he left tentacles behind all over town. How do octopodes manage I wonder.

such an eerie morning we have got today. it began when stanley found a tooth in his breakfast rolls (friehofer brown and serve salt sticks) and got worse when he discovered that the tooth was not his own. i have only seen him so shaken once before and that was because gentle shax took to sleeping in wastebaskets and stanley got up in the night to go to the bathroom and glanced down at the wastebasket and found it was filled with a pool of black fur. "i mean," i said in the grocery, "the friehofer people have always seemed so sanitary." "i'll speak to the delivery man today," said larry. "do you want a fresh box of rolls?"

well it didn't really begin then. it really began during the night with my dream. which is the third (and don't get all college-psych on me and say i imagined dreaming the other two because i wrote them down yah only i can't find them and stanley says it's because he was reading milton aloud last night over my protests and i hate milton except satan but stanley says it is only the great rolling lines which

stayed in my head but it wasn't because i have heard people read milton before and it never gave me nightmares and anyway i think a
husband who reads milton aloud in the evening when his wife wants
to take off her shoes and settle down with an old <u>unknown</u> ought to
be shut in the cellar) and it scared me. i id (what the <u>hell</u>. that's three
times i've tried to write <u>did</u> in that spot) did did did fancy briefly
that i might be only a character in an old novel from unknown but
actually that might be worse.

what? oh, it's a kind of pact-with-the-devil series of dreams. the
first, nearly fifteen years ago, was so frightening that when i wrote it
down a friend of mine went home and dreamed it herself scaring
both of us even more. i woke up from that first one screaming "i
didn't sign i didn't sign" and the second—a recreation of what i
thought was a scene from my childhood leading inexorably into the
same dream—was about six years ago and i got so worried that i
wrote to my mother (you don't write my mother things like this)
asking her if i had ever been criminally attacked as a small child because i had been dreaming about it and she wrote back not to me but
to stanley asking if he knew i had been Imagining Things and Was
There Anything Wrong Between Us? now the third last night and i
was standing there at a sabbat shouting prophecies. how silly it
sounds. i almost asked stanley to cancel his class this morning because i was afraid to be alone. frightening because of the sneering little voice that keeps saying you go right on thinking it's a dream if
you want to, dearie.

what a shame that dreams are not the stuff that stories are made on.

i think i will spend a very sensible day, just in case. i will read the
new yorker. i will finally sew on that button. i <u>will</u> take the chair in
today to be fixed, i promise i will. i will make chocolate pudding. i
will bring faun malkin and applegate the cat upstairs after lunch. i
will get out the soft blue puff and i will turn on all the lights because
it is a kind of dark day and i will take a nap. i will tell barry that yes,
david may play here today. i will get a boy to rake the leaves. i will
persuade sally to do her homework this afternoon in her room. (did i
tell you that sally-magic is in bad repute? because some friends who
were building a house asked her for lawn-magic when they were put-

ting in the lawn and they wanted it to grow fast and she gave them magic to sprinkle on the bare ground and now the lawn grows so fast it is ankle deep most of the time and there is a real fairy ring in the center? and recently we were expecting week-end guests and they didn't come and they didn't come so i asked sally for a little guest-bringing magic and she gave me some to sprinkle on the threshold and our guests came almost at once but that evening eight more people dropped in?) because with the tooth and the dream anyone knows that one more will happen. stanley will not be home until six. i have asked him most politely not to read milton aloud again tonight and he has promised and even offered to get off a little swinburne if i thought it would help but i rather think i will watch television. something sane like the untouchables perhaps.

i do not think you will believe this: laurie writes that he has been reading the oz books at college because some girl lent him several. he says they have been having oz-and-jazz readings and especially dig the munchkins. i do not believe it either, but i have written urgently to know more about what kind of girl brings oz books to college and passes them around.

we are having such a joy of a time with stanley's tooth (the tooth of my husband's salt stick). larry in a state of high righteous indignation turned over the tooth to the pepperidge farms salesman that afternoon and the salesman, pale and trembling, telephoned his main office on the spot to report tooth found in salt stick; larry gave them our name and address and the salesman tottered off on his appointed round after assuring larry that i might have a brand new box of salt sticks on the house. larry said he rather thought not, thank you, at least not for a day or so. then i got a splendid letter from mr pepperidge himself, referring guardedly to my "horrible experience" and pointing out that the most extreme care was taken in their bakeries to avoid such things: employees were not allowed to drink out of glasses, but must use paper cups, no one was allowed to wear watches or rings or hearing aids, hair was always covered, and so on. nothing was said about checking teeth at the door. he was very careful to indicate that this was probably something that had been put into the rolls by a bad magician long after they left the factory. and he finished by saying that he was "taking the liberty" of sending me some of their products which he hoped we would eat with confidence. confidence he said. and lo! came the next day a box from pepperidge farm with a loaf of hovis bread therein. special delivery. cost of bread thirty-seven cents. cost of mailing eighty-three cents. the children are boiling; they had expected those lovely cookies. i am boiling because i badly wanted to write back "dear mr pepperidge farm, thank you very very much for the lovely loaf of bread . . ." and stanley won't let me. the poor people are probably terrified that we are going to sue but i think i will content myself with just telling everybody about it. stanley has taken to wondering idly what happened to the <u>rest</u> of him; after all, we only found one tooth and there ought to be cuff links and perhaps a watch charm in the coffee cake or the dinner rolls.

dear mr pepperidge farm: oh, boy! a free loaf of bread! how did you <u>ever</u> . . .

("look, peppy, there's this dame up in new hampshire or somewhere and she found that tooth mannie lost the night of the office party and it got into that batch of salt sticks the way we were worried it might of, and we better do something, the way i figure, we send her like bread, maybe—those people are always so crazy to get something for nothing, like free samples, you know? so maybe she hasn't gotten to a lawyer yet and you get that young fellow in copywriting to send her the same letter we sent that guy with the caterpillar last year and i'll go through the salt sticks to see if i can pick out mannie's glasses.")

it is true about the oz books. all true. laurie came home last week for a day with a friend and they knew all the countries but not the rulers in order and they tried to steal a copy of the little engine that could ("man, figure that i-think-i-can chorus against a cool bass") but barry wouldn't let them have it.

sally got a tankful of tropical fish for her birthday and we gave joanne a canary for her birthday; barry says that on his birthday, which is next, he confidently expects a cluster of microbe bacteria. he cornered us; he brought home a report card all a's, and barry—who is not modest—requested a present, our standing offer for an all a's report card. (stanley never got so low as a b in his life until the year we took shakespeare together in college and he says that was my fault.)

we had put away a microscope set for his birthday but stanley, carried away, gave it to him for his report card. he is the only child i have ever seen who attacks a microscope set by reading the enclosed booklet before he touches anything. he got a feather from joanne's bird and some algae from sally's fish and last night he seems to have been staining cells in the bathroom. the purple dye will of course not come off the soap dish.

sally has asked me to send you a recipe. i made it up several years ago during the broadcast of a brooklyn dodgers baseball game and the winning pitcher for brooklyn (now long since retired) was named lasorda* so when everyone liked their dinner they named the dish lasorda. it is a particular favorite of sally's and she asked that year that it be served at her birthday dinner for her friends and they all liked it so well that it has become a standard for sally's birthday and everyone wants the recipe but it is difficult since i never know how much of anything i put in.

do you know about the paula welden case? an account of it turned up recently in a cheap collection of sensational articles on missing persons, and i was reminded of how i always wanted to write it, but can't, of course. she was a bennington college girl who disappeared about ten years ago;† i'm sure i have told you about it. it is such a lovely story and every now and then around the store people will get to talking about it again and going over and over all they remember; they were talking about it today. she walked out of her dormitory room on a sunday afternoon, telling her roommate she was going up local mount glastenbury on what is called the long trail and the last anyone saw her she was going out the college gates heading for the hills. odd thing was that by the time—the next day—she was reported missing and boy scouts and hunters and firemen and such were out combing the long trail for her, everyone already knew positively that she had never

---

* Tommy Lasorda was a professional baseball pitcher and later manager of the Los Angeles Dodgers for twenty years. He was inducted into the Baseball Hall of Fame as manager in 1997.

† Paula Welden disappeared on December 1, 1946, about a year after the Hymans first moved to Vermont. It was quite sensational, and there was much press coverage. She was never found.

reached the long trail; larry-at-the-store and a couple of other scout-mastering types had been up and down the trail all afternoon clearing out a scout camping spot and at the time when she was last seen heading for the trail they were coming down, walking, so that she actually vanished somewhere between the college gates and the start of the trail. (someone saw her getting in a car, someone saw her on mount anthony, someone saw her in a shoe store in albany, someone saw her hiding in a college cellar.) i love the story, we all have our theories, of course. we were also talking about our other classic case, which is the story of middie rivers, a local man of seventy-seven, who still lived in the house where he had been born and had never been farther away from home than the nearest town. he had hunted and fished the woods around his house since he was old enough to walk and yet one day he wandered into a woods on his own land and vanished like paula. they are still searching for his body in an area of perhaps ten acres; he went seven years ago and there has been no sign of him. i keep wondering where they are, paula and middie. i could maneuver paula's story around so it wouldn't be about bennington but i am puzzled about police procedure; the police in paula's case did most of their investigating sitting around the sheriff's office drinking hard cider and even the f.b.i. put in a half hour of pointless questions, but it wouldn't be nice to write it like that.

i am awed by your control of your washer; i am afraid of mine. when it goes pocketa-pocketa i get barry to go in and turn it off. my electric coffeepot blew me across the kitchen for the second time and i got mad and went out and bought a good oldfashioned five-and-ten percolator and stanley said at last a cup of coffee strong enough to taste. effete, that's what we all are, effete.

did you know i had four thousand old post cards? i don't exactly know why. stanley gave them to me for a present.

writewritewrite.

best,

s.

•    •    •

[To Geraldine and Leslie Jackson]

friday [May 1961]

dearest mother and pop,

haven't written because i expected to be talking to you on mother's day but although we put the call through several times you were always out, so happy mother's day anyway and lots of love from all of us. i was brought breakfast in bed in honor of the occasion and was presented with a most magnificent bouquet of yellow flowers, yellow being my favorite color, so i had a lovely morning reading the sunday paper in bed admiring my flowers.

we are still in the midst of spring which means that the mud season is over but it rains every other day; overnight the grass turned green and the leaves came out on the trees, and we had one spell of very hot weather.

i have had a most unpleasant time since february with something called colitis; i apparently picked up the bug while i was still getting over the flu; it is a kind of intestinal flu that hangs on and on and although i am nowhere near as uncomfortable as i was a few weeks ago i am still troubled and taking pills. for a while i was very poorly, enough so that oliver was considering packing me off to the hospital but the mere threat of the hospital was enough to make me better. i had to take paregoric* six times a day and as though that was not bad enough i had sulfa pills the size of the eggs to take and about four other things and just to top it off there was nothing i could eat except cottage cheese. it is not at all serious, merely very uncomfortable, and annoying because it keeps on so long. oliver told me cheerfully that some people have it for months and months. i had a harrowing three days last month when stanley and i went to farleigh dickenson university in new jersey to do a dual lecture stint; we drove down on the throughway for five hours but i made the trip all right

* Paregoric, a tincture of opium, is a patent medicine used at the time for the treatment of diarrhea.

and then the next day we had to perform and imagine me on this schedule: at lunch time we left the inn where we stayed and drove five miles to the college where we had lunch and i smiled politely and had a cheese sandwich and tea while everyone else had wonderful curried chicken. then there was stanley's performance, a panel discussion which lasted for nearly three hours and i had to sit in the audience and of course could not leave without being very conspicuous. then a coffee hour with the students (no coffee for me, thanks) and then a cocktail party (that they didn't take away from me, thank heaven) and then i finally got back to the inn for half an hour to change. after that dinner at a very fancy restaurant and the combination of my ailment and knowing that i had to lecture in the evening completely destroyed my appetite so that i sat there looking at an eight-dollar steak and absolutely unable to touch it and of course the people who were taking us to dinner were english teachers with salaries not always equal to eight-dollar steaks and i felt perfectly awful with no possible way to apologize. i had been dreading my lecture although i usually enjoy lecturing, but this time i had to make arrangements with stanley so that he would carry on if i suddenly got up and ran out. the funny thing was that in all this time i had no trouble at all; oliver had given me a great bagful of pills to take and there was no problem. the lecture went beautifully; there were about five hundred people and i sat on a platform with a mike and stanley, alert, in the front row; afterward they asked stanley to come up onto the platform too and we both answered questions from the audience, although i make stanley do most of the talking when i can. the next day we drove home and as soon as i got home my difficulties returned.

i seem to have spent a long time discussing my own health, sorry; it's because it has kind of influenced everything i have been doing. we are going off again next week, this time to bard college, but only stanley performs this time. i will sign autographs and smile politely. i am a great autographer because my handwriting is so poor that no one knows whether it is my name or not. we both autographed dozens of books in new jersey and stanley is always so neat and careful and i just scribble. next year i think i will be doing a good deal more lecturing. up till now it has always been hard to leave the kids but we have found a nice bennington girl who loves to come and take over while we are gone and the kids like her and most of what corinne has to do is cook with joanne's help and keep an eye on things at night. and i certainly like going away for a day or so and staying in hotels. these days the kids take their lunches to school so my life is considerably easier. three days a week stanley is at the college and i am all alone all day and manage to get a lot done. i have finally started my book* and i think it is going quite well. i get in a couple of hours of work every morning and then at twelve i get in the car and drive to a little restaurant and have lunch; it is such a nuisance making lunch just for myself and going out makes a welcome break after working. then i come home and go to sleep until the kids come home from school, although these days all three of them have so many outside activities that there are days when no one comes home and then i am apt to sleep and sleep and sleep. as you can see, it is a nice easy life, and the book is getting written. it is only a year late. the publishers keep sending me money, though.

the director and the writer who are doing the movie of hill house flew here from hollywood to see me and talk about the book and the poor fellows naturally assumed that vermont in april would be fair and balmy and they wore their california clothes and there was still snow on the ground. they took me out to lunch and i had two cocktails and probably said a lot about hill house that wasn't true. it is going to be what they call a big-budget picture, although it is still in the writing stage right now. i was dying to know who would be in it, but no one has been signed yet. i did learn a lot about how to make movies, and they expect to do their location shots in new england, since they think there are no california houses worth haunting, so perhaps we can see a little of it being made. joanne and sally made a great point of being introduced to a hollywood director (he is the director of "west side story" although i forget his name)† and we had a very agreeable day. the movie will be in color with a special musical

* _We Have Always Lived in the Castle._
† Robert Wise.

background and we are all to go to new york for the premiere. in
about three years.

    we hear from laurie frequently; he is a great letter writer and calls
us weekly usually to ask for more money. he is doing fine, loves the
college, and is doing a lot more with his music this semester. he
turned down the spring trip to bermuda with his band because it
would interfere with his school work and although the band is
signed up to go to europe again this summer he thinks he will not
go; he has been offered a regular playing job at a local roadhouse and
prefers that. the only one who has visited the college is joanne; stanley and i have never been there because laurie wanted to make his
start by himself. we have met a good many of his friends, since he always brings three or four home with him when he comes and all
they do is eat. oddly enough, (well, why oddly, come to think of it?)
several of them have taken a fancy to joanne, and a couple of them
write to her and come down with laurie just to see her. it was so
funny; most of the other girls in her class went to the high school junior prom and joanne was not invited to go, but the same week one
of laurie's friends invited her to come to goddard for a two-day visit.
she went to goddard, of course, and had a lovely time. she has become quite grownup. her conversation is more suited to laurie's
friends than her own, since she is interested in books and the theatre
and music—she still plays the guitar and sings nicely. sally has grown
up almost overnight. she wears the same size clothes as joanne and is
an inch taller. she is still very babyish in her manner and habits, however, and we are hoping that this summer at camp will calm her
down a little. she also is reading at a furious rate, she is writing a lot
and is on the school paper this year; joanne has been on it for three
years and the two of them do a lot of feature articles; sally also does a
regular cartoon for them. besides that she is writing her own stories
and poems and putting together quite a collection. barry continues to
grow and become more of an elder statesman every day. he is still
very serious and thoughtful and does algebra problems for fun. he
pestered stanley until stanley taught him the rudiments of algebra
and found him an old textbook and barry loved it. he is still at the
top of his class. all three of them go to camp on july first. joanne will

be a counselor and waterfront assistant. when they go stanley and i
are going back onto our last summer's schedule of no-cooking, having dinner in restaurants every night. it was so much fun last year,
and we managed to see a lot of our neighboring country. i am going
to my regular writers' conference at suffield, connecticut. stanley will
spend that week in new york, since writers' conferences give him the
creeps.

we have spent this spring making improvements in the house; had
it painted again, and put new drapes in the living room and dining
room and—thank heaven—had the bathroom upstairs redone. we
got a new washer and dryer and a new typewriter for stanley and are
thinking vaguely of getting a television set; ours has been broken
down for months but now the baseball season has started and we like
to watch the games on weekends so we may get one. best of all, we
have our new player piano, spinet size but a full keyboard. we heard
about a firm in new york that was now making player pianos, so we
bought ourselves a player piano and never had so much fun. we
bought fifty rolls and they sound lovely. the darn thing is so loud that
you can hear it all over the neighborhood. also it is very stiff to pedal
and the only one who can really work it for hours at a time is barry.
stanley and i wear out after one roll. it has a very nice tone for regular
playing, too, and we are happy to find that sally is interested in making up little tunes to play, and perhaps as she grows more pleased
with herself she will take to music as laurie did. we are saturating
them with music anyway; stanley and i play records every evening
and sometimes the kids lie awake and listen. we are getting the records from the vivaldi society, vivaldi concertos, mostly for lute and
harpsichord. (that should be concerti, shouldn't it.) we are both very
fond of harpsichord music and have been gathering up what we
could; the kids go around whistling or humming fragments from the
music we play in the evenings. when laurie comes home he plays the
trumpet along with the piano, and one of his friends plays the flute
and the guitar, so we sing and have trios.

we completely gave up the idea of going to europe this summer.
we decided that we would rather wait and go another year with all
the children. also stanley got very much annoyed at the kids because

none of them knew anything about the bible, so we are reading the bible aloud every evening after dinner. first i read a chapter and then stanley reads a chapter, and we started at the beginning and are now nearly at the end of exodus. it is slow tough going because everyone argues about what is going on.

as usual i have to cut this short to go make lunch. write soon, keep well, and lots and lots of love from all,

s.

•  •  •

[To Libbie Burke]

Sept. 5 [1961]

Dear Lib,

As you know, family troubles* have put a lot of confusion and sadness into our routine recently; I don't mean that as an excuse for not sending your books back sooner, but I <u>did</u> have them out ready to send.

Many many thanks for all the help they—and you—have given me. The book progresses very slowly but at least two chapters are done and now that things are calming down I can get back to it. I only hope you have not been picking mushrooms without your handy guide.†

Best to you and to himself; see you soon? Please.

Love,

S.

•  •  •

---

* Stanley's father, Moe Hyman, died in August 1961, at the age of seventy.
† Shirley has been researching poisonous mushrooms for her new book, in which they will appear.

[To Geraldine and Leslie Jackson]

sept 5 [1961]

dearest mother and pop,

i realize it has been a long time since i wrote but it has been such a hectic and confusing summer that i have not even made much progress on my book and i am beginning to get sharp little notes from my publisher saying he doesn't want to push me or anything but the book is announced for publication in 1962 so let's see the manuscript. anyway the movie money is running out so i had better get moving.

it is half-past ten and joanne is just lying in bed luxuriously; the other kids got up at seven and went off to school; today is their first day. joanne doesn't have to go until the fourteenth and she wanted to get up this morning and sit on the front porch and wave to her friends going by but i gather she changed her mind. we are all very excited about her school; it is a very good one, highly recommended. she will find it very tough going after the north bennington high school but they will see to it that she works hard. the school itself is lovely, in the hills outside weston massachusetts with a little lake for swimming and ice skating, and good modern buildings. it is small, about one hundred fifty kids, coeducational, expensive (ouch) and only moderately progressive. it is about ten miles from boston. the big disadvantage of the school is distance; boston is a hundred and eighty miles away, and it will mean a lot of driving. people from bennington college go back and forth fairly regularly to boston, though, and there is a bus of sorts. we are dreading getting her stuff there next week because she plans to take everything she owns. i cannot imagine what it will be like with only sally and barry home.

laurie is now in new orleans with his college roommate. a friend of ours has offered them the use of her air-conditioned house. laurie has taken a job with a local band for this fall to earn himself some spending money; it means he will have to come home weekends and although we don't like it he feels that he can manage the job and college too. he has promised to quit the job if it interferes with his school work as i am sure it will. he is eager to get back to college after a summer of hard work. we finally opened up our third floor; it has always been a dingy attic reached through a trap door in the hall ceiling and only laurie and the television man had ever been up there, but we badly needed the space for books, of which we now have about twenty thousand. we had a carpenter come and put a stairway up and put in a skylight and install a huge fan which not only cools the attic but the whole upstairs. the fan did not come until a week ago so poor laurie worked up there all summer in the heat, and it was certainly hot. he insulated it and put up wallboard and sanded the floor and painted it and built four hundred feet of book-case and earned enough money to take him to new orleans and still leave him a bank account. and now the attic is beautiful; there is a lot of floor space so we turned it over to sally and barry and barry has his electric trains there and sally has a painting studio. this past week stanley and the children have moved every book in the house, rear-ranging. the shelves look lovely and at last there is room for expansion.

the other kids had a good summer at camp, and joanne has been asked to come back next year as a full counselor which means she gets paid. sally was of course constantly at odds with her cabin mates because as she said they talked about nothing but boys. but sally found one friend who hated this as much as she did, and the two of them were very happy together. barry is getting to be a leader type, and was easily the head of his cabin; he is a quiet, popular, respected boy, and seems able to adjust comfortably to anything. he has none of sally's rebelliousness and he is one of the camp favorites. he is the same at home and in school, goes along getting all a's in his studies. he is also a miser. he kept track of every minute he worked moving books, because stanley was paying them by the hour, and once he collects, his money goes right into the bank and stays there.

stanley is finally finishing his big book;* it goes off to the publishers this week. he has gone over it so many times that i think he can

---

* *The Tangled Bank: Darwin, Marx, Frazer and Freud as Imaginative Writers.*

recite large sections. he really hates to see it go; he has been working on it for so many years. the job of reading galleys on it will be enormous, and we both will do it.

barry just came home with the information that he could only take his lunch to school if he lived more than half a mile away or had a working mother so i had to call the principal and explain that i was a working mother and she agreed that writing a book qualified me as a working mother so now barry can take his lunch.

stanley is feeling considerably better about his father, although it was a terrible shock. he had been in bad health for so long, but everyone believed that he was much better, and he was getting out much more and seeing friends again. it happened early in the morning, very quickly, and stanley's brother was able to get over there right away and take care of everything. we took laurie and joanne down with us, because they both wanted to go; they were both very fond of him, and laurie was particularly upset. i did not go to any of the ceremonies because i have a real terror of such things and will <u>not</u> go; everyone in the family understood perfectly because crazy old aunt bella used to be the same way, so they just left me home. of course the place was packed with relatives, and arthur's wife and i, as the two daughters in law, were expected to handle the food and drink department, which was considerable. we handed out coffee and cake and scotch and iced coffee and beer until we felt like a lunch counter. considering that it was 96 that day in new york, and the apartment is quite small, with a tiny kitchen, we had a man-sized job. the family—about thirty of them—has to be served a traditional lunch after the funeral, so bunny and i did that too; it was the first time stanley's mother has ever sat still in the living room while someone else used her kitchen, and she suffered, poor woman. we used the wrong dishes (put cheese and stuff in the dishes which are supposed to be reserved entirely for meat) and put everything back where it didn't belong. after everyone left that night and lu was alone with just two of her sisters there she went out into the kitchen and washed everything over again and straightened up; it probably did her more good than anything else.

i was fascinated by the ritual of the thing; even though stanley's parents have given up most religious observances for a long time the funeral still had to be done right. the strangest thing was the cohen tradition, which stanley had to explain to me; cohens are hereditary priests and cannot come anywhere near a dead body, so that even the present day members of the family named cohen—who are very far from being priests, considering that one of them is a small-time gangster—could not come to call on stanley's mother and could not come to the funeral. what they did was dress in their best dark clothes and stand outside the temple while the service was going on, and when the family came out of the temple there were the cohens including the gangster standing just far enough away to be safe but they had come to the funeral as well as they could.

stanley's mother absolutely refuses to live with either of her sons, wants a small apartment of her own, and as long as arthur takes care of all her business and financial matters, will be quite all right. since she has thousands of sisters and many good friends, she will never be completely alone. also the family business will continue to support her.

as usual everyone is clamoring for lunch. write soon. i am knocking wood because i haven't had any hay fever this year; hope you are as lucky. everyone sends love.

s.

•   •   •

[To Carol Brandt]

October 21 [1961]

Dear Carol,

The answer to your letter is definitely NO.

Although it is most flattering to think that Mr. Arnaz is interested in having me work on a screenplay* both my inclinations and my ex-

---

* Desi Arnaz invited Shirley to develop a new movie story for his wife, TV star Lucille (Lucy) Ball.

perience are definitely against it; as you know, I do not want to write teleplays or screenplays, but only books. And Hollywood holds no charm for me.

Book is growing and growing and growing.

Best,

Shirley

. . .

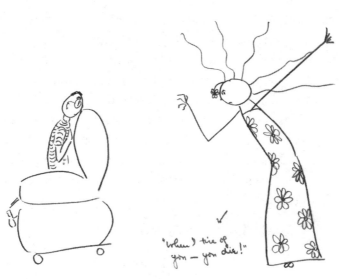

"When I tire of you—you die!"

[To Geraldine and Leslie Jackson]

monday [November 13, 1961]

dearest mother and pop,

we keep thinking what a nice time we had while you were here. it was such fun seeing you and the children are still drawing pictures.

we are all concerned over joanne's knee, which happened just after you left; she was jumping over a fence (why? why?) and threw it out of joint; now she has a real football player's trick knee, which keeps going out of joint. they thought she would need an operation and luckily the headmaster at the school stepped in or loony joanne would have gone right ahead and entered herself in a boston hospital and gone through the operation without ever bothering to let us know. so we are now planning for her to have it checked at christmas time and if she needs the operation have it done here with our own doctor supervising.

i have not been well again; i had a return of my friend colitis, and oliver put me right back on my former medicine, but even though it helps i have a side-effect which i don't really care for: he figures it this way: the colitis includes a sudden attack of nausea, which is all right; that is what it's supposed to do. but the sudden nausea causes an abrupt drop in blood pressure of perhaps twenty degrees, which is exactly like getting kicked in the stomach, and i all but pass out; i get dizzy and sick and staggery and shaking, and of course very scared; all i have to do is sit still for a few minutes and it goes away, but he says if i didn't fight it so i would simply faint and that would be it. but i have never fainted and am not going to start now. silliest thing is that although my blood pressure is normal (and he checks it every time) i always supposed that it was <u>high</u> blood pressure i would have to worry about, not pressure going <u>down</u>. so i am being careful about smoking, particularly in the mornings, which is when it seems to happen. it would go away much faster if it were not, like most fainting spells, entirely a matter of suggestion: once i start thinking it might happen, then of course it all starts. i stay home as much as possible in the mornings, and so am making fine progress on my book; there's nothing like being scared to go outside to keep you writing.

we are waiting and waiting to hear from the movie people who want to buy <u>sundial</u>; their option ran out last week and they wrote that they were "optimistic" although i suppose in hollywood talk that just means they are broke. no news on the other movie yet.

the weather has been quite cold, and there is already snow on the hills. our foliage was quite as lovely as ever, the week after you left. now the kids have been out raking leaves, which is a considerable job on our lawn. we are having stanley's mother here for thanksgiving. we will also have stanley's brother, without wife, who is driving his mother up here, and very possibly stanley's ancient aunt anna and uncle harry, the banes of the family; they are both in their eighties, completely crazy, and just as lively as they can be. they have no children, and spend all their time and energy keeping themselves healthy. anna and harry are quite strict, and the kids have been looking up the dietary laws in the bible, which ought to stagger harry some. it makes for an odd thanksgiving dinner. and i wish the bible would tell me how to make mashed potatoes without butter or milk.

dear old mrs king has just left, after brushing around ineffectually in the living room for two hours. i can't possibly fire her because she needs the money so desperately, but she really accomplished very little. sally and i do the dusting and are just thankful that the rugs are vacuumed. the game of where-did-mrs-king-put-it goes on all the time; i finally found the bathroom wastebasket but stanley's desk ashtray has eluded us for two weeks. if i ask her she doesn't remember.

i am to be one of four speakers holding forth at the bennington library this wednesday night; we are supposed to talk about writing and i haven't the slightest idea what to say. twenty minutes i have to talk. i enjoy lecturing now; i used to be terribly nervous but now i have done enough so i like it. both laurie's college and joanne's school have asked me to lecture; the trouble is they expect you will do it for nothing as a favor to the kids. the library will be fun; i will know everyone there and it will be quite informal. i said i would go if they would cancel my overdue fines on my library books.

the children keep asking when you are coming again. meanwhile, lots of love from all.

s.

# SEVEN

. . .

## Magic Wishes: 1962–1965

one world is writing and one is not, and from the one which
is not, it is not possible to understand the one which is.

—Letter to self, 1963

*After a period of writer's block Shirley has begun work again on* We Have
Always Lived in the Castle, *and is pleased with its progress. Her agorapho-
bia keeps her confined to the house except for trips to visit her psychoanalyst in
Bennington. Laurie is spending his Goddard College non-resident work
term loading trucks at L. Hyman and Sons Paper Company in New York,
and living in a furnished studio apartment on West Eighty-fifth Street.
Corinne Biggs, also on her N.R.T. from Bennington College, is now secretly living for two months with Laurie. Joanne and Sally are at boarding
school, and Barry attends the North Bennington grade school.*

[To Jeanne Beatty]

jan 3 [1962]

dear jeanne,

i know i know i have owed you a letter for a very long time and i
pray your indulgence because merricat is ending chapter four and
sailing along and the publisher says it must be finished by dogwood
day in april and four people have read the first two chapters:

stanley        sally        louis untermeyer        the publisher
and all independently announce that it is the best work i have ever
done so if i could only stop with the first two chapters and publish
those it would be fine but no they want another two hundred pages.
it is hard. very hard. i finally got it into a kind of sustained taut style
full of images and all kinds of double meanings and i can manage
about three pages a day before my eyes cross and my teeth start to
chatter, and i shall be late i shall be late.

so i am really writing to thank you for the cookies which are incredible and of course all eaten with furious excitement. my

mother-in-law was here for christmas and personally accounted for about a third of the cookies, stanley digging about in the box and snatching at "those wonderful little round fellows" and the kids deciding that the gingerbread creature was a grinch. thank you. thank you.

and happy new year.

best,

s.

• • •

[To Geraldine and Leslie Jackson]

tuesday [February 13, 1962]

dearest mother and pop,

have just been decorating valentine cookies for the kids, and a happy valentine's day to you, too. it was twelve below this morning and our furnace works so well that right now my room is nearly eighty but the study downstairs where stanley is working is barely seventy. he is wearing a sweater and warm slippers and i am thinking of putting on a summer dress.

i am writing mainly to thank you for the insurance check, which was very welcome indeed; and to thank you, too, for the new dishwasher, which is what your christmas check bought. the dishwasher was not planned, but my old battered one broke down, and after four weeks of washing dishes by hand, even with rubber gloves and special hand creams, the ends of my fingers were so cracked and sore that i could hardly type. stanley said he figured it was costing us a couple of thousand dollars a day to have me wash dishes, so saturday morning he told me to call and have them bring over a new dishwasher. my hands are already better, and yesterday i mailed off chap-

ters five and six to my publisher. he will get them today, read them
tonight, and call me tomorrow morning to say it is wonderful, great,
marvelous, keep going. Stanley likes them too but sally, who has been
reading chapter by chapter, is very angry over one of the characters
whom she thinks i am doing wrong and wants me to change. i finally
did make some of the changes she suggested and Stanley was furious; he says he is a professional critic and i take the advice of a
thirteen-year-old girl over his. i think sally was right, though. last
night when i came upstairs i found on my bed a document from sally
suggesting a new interpretation of the character and proposing that i
go back and make him entirely different. i have put her document
with my notes; i always make pages and pages of notes typed in all
different directions so that i have to read through all of them to find
the one i want, and i tape the pages of notes in a line along the book-
shelf right by my typewriter. one of sally's notes points out that as
long as charles thinks everyone is "conspirating" against him the
reader is going to sympathize with him. i am so pleased that she is so
deeply involved in the book because it encourages her to write herself.

stanley's mother sent me a clipping from a new york paper about
the movie of hill house. it is to be called "the haunting" and will be
directed by robert wise who did "west side story." the clipping also
said that they were trying to get someone named dick breymer for
what they call the "romantic lead," which i suppose is luke although i
never thought he was very romantic, and—this delights me—peter
ustinov is doctor montague. stanley says he wonders who doctor
montague could have been modeled after if peter ustinov was a natural for the part.

talked to laurie last night; he is well and thriving. he goes over to
see stanley's mother once a week and she sees that he gets a decent
meal. he and the friend he lives with believe that they are doing their
own cooking, and stanley's mother lent them a frying pan and a coffee pot but i think he is very pleased to go see her and have a steak.
stanley's brother and his wife are separating in march; they have
planned things so carefully that arthur decided exactly which day in

march he would leave their home in new jersey and move into a new york apartment. they cannot separate sooner because of an important business convention to which arthur must take his wife to avoid comment. one result of all this marital confusion is that arthur spends most of his time in new york and only goes to new jersey weekends, so he keeps inviting laurie to have dinner with him and go to a show. i think arthur wants laurie to introduce him to a couple of girls.

the u.s. government has asked for permission to print part of stanley's chapter on karl marx from his new book; the part they want is the description of communism as described in das kapital, which will go into a government handbook on communism and what it is. this is secret, by the way; please don't tell anyone. stanley is very pleased to be a government authority on karl marx. his book comes out in april. the index alone was a hundred and twenty pages.

sally turned out to have inherited a fine talent from her grandmother; in home-ec in school she had to make a blouse and she did a beautiful job and loved it, and now asks for a sewing machine of her own. if she is still interested we might get her one for her birthday next fall. any advice? since i never owned one i would not even know what would be practical for her.

joanne is quite well now, and very happy at school. she seems to have settled down there nicely, and is all excited over an invitation from laurie's college roommate to come up for a weekend when college starts again in march.

barry is going to get me up at six-thirty tomorrow morning to see the astronaut again. it will probably be twenty below at that hour.

lots of love from everyone here and write soon.

love,

s.

• • •

[To Carol Brandt]

February 21 [1962]

Dear Carol,

I assume you knew that the Book of the Month Club has chosen THE WITCHCRAFT OF SALEM VILLAGE as their April selection for its Young Readers of America Club. What a mishmash. They wrote me asking me to do a letter addressed to DEAR YOUNG READER presumably telling them to read the book, so I did. Are we all going to make a lot of money from this?

My book goes along so well it scares me. I am now in the sad position of seeing the end a hundred pages away, and I am most reluctant to give up my characters. Stanley suggests an infinite number of sequels.

Best,

Shirley

•   •   •

[Generic "Note to a Young Reader" Shirley was asked to write upon republication of *The Witchcraft of Salem Village*]

[February 20, 1962]

Dear Young Reader:

No one is really very much afraid of witchcraft any more. If the bewitched children of Salem Village came screaming and writhing into a modern courtroom it would probably be assumed—and with some reason, too—that they were the willing victims of a new teenage dance craze. Fashions in fear change, but do people?

We are not more tolerant or more valiant than the people of Salem, and we are just as willing to do battle with an imaginary enemy. Santayana says that "if we do not learn from history we are sentenced to repeat it," and if we cannot see clearly how the good people of Salem were deceived by their fears we cannot act honestly today. The people of Salem hanged and tortured their neighbors from a deep conviction that they were right to do so. Some of our own deepest convictions may be as false.

We might say that we have far more to be afraid of today than the people of Salem ever dreamed of, but that would not really be true. We have exactly the same thing to be afraid of—the demon in men's minds which prompts hatred and anger and fear, an irrational demon which shows a different face to every generation, but never gives up in his fight to win over the world.

Sincerely,

Shirley Jackson

•  •  •

"Mr. Ross is outside, sir, and wants to know if
you can spare him five minutes."
"Stanley carries on at The New Yorker—the way I <u>hear</u> it."


[To Carol Brandt]

March 6 [1962]

Dear Carol,

As you probably do not know, I am intensely superstitious about
things turning up when they are needed. I am at the moment puzzled in the middle of the climatic scene in my book and badly in
need of some way of handling it better than I have so far. Now you
write that you are sending me four old manuscripts of mine. I have
no doubt at all that my solution will be in them somewhere. I am on
page 124, expect to have about another hundred pages, and to finish
by the end of April. I thought it would be some small sign of my
gratitude to Pat for his patience all this time if I asked if I could dedicate the book to him, and he seemed pleased. He has six chapters

now and says he still can't guess the ending. I think I am going to surprise him.

Best,

Shirley

•  •  •

[To Carol Brandt]

April 20 [1962]

Dear Carol,

It's done, it's done. I sent the manuscript to Pat this morning. He wanted two copies so I have only one copy left which I will send you in a day or so; I want to look over it once more.

Now he owes me a lot of money.

Hope you have a pleasant trip. Also hope to see you in June.

Best,

Shirley

•  •  •

[To Carol Brandt]

April 23 [1962]

Dear Carol,

In a veritable frenzy of terror, I hasten to place this in your hand with all possible speed. And I am sorry about having deprived you by even a day of the bliss of reading it.

Best,

Shirley

•   •   •

[To Geraldine and Leslie Jackson]

monday [April 1962]

dearest mother and pop,

it's really too much to have a monday morning after school spring vacation <u>with</u> daylight saving <u>with</u> pouring rain <u>with</u> a leak in my car roof so that i sat down in a puddle. the children went drearily off to school in raincoats and rubbers and stanley went drearily off to school in raincoat and rubbers and the bird—who is moulting and won't sing—is doggedly taking a bath in his water cup and ignoring his nice bathtub. we do need the rain badly but i wish they could have put it off till tuesday.

this is actually my first unoccupied morning and i have spent an hour just wandering around. i finished my book on friday april 20, but with the kids home all last week i had no time to relax and sit back and take it easy. after three years devoted to that book i can hardly believe it's finished; it's exactly like having one of the kids leave home. the desk is so empty without my folders of notes and the wall is bare; i usually make pages and pages of odd notes and taking them down makes the room look funny.

everything is moving fast with the book; once they got past me as the bottleneck they really went into action. it is at the printer now, and i'll see galley proofs in a few weeks. they are publishing it in september. pop: the heroine of this one is <u>really</u> batty. my editor, pat covici, to whom the book is dedicated, called me last week full of enthusiasm: not a word needed changing (except could they please change the spelling of "grey" to "gray" and marshall best, head of viking press, cried when he read the book; pat swears marshall was crying. stanley says if the book can bring tears to those mean old publishing eyes it ought to make a million dollars; it's foolproof. my agent is talking big, as agents always do. agents are supposed to say about each book that it is a natural for the book of the month club, and the national book award, and probably the pulitzer prize, so my agent says all these things very politely and then gets back to reality and goes out and tries to sell it for money. the silly part of it is that i don't want the national book award or the pulitzer prize and i most particularly do not want the money. stanley says a movie sale on this book would finish us. the money on the last book finally ran out this past january and we were just settling down comfortably with enough to live on and all we really want right now is enough for a new car. stanley is having a terrible time with the college because [president] bill fels is trying to raise his salary and stanley is trying to stop him. it really is crazy, although it is such an unusual and wonderful situation to be in that we are enjoying it thoroughly.

actually—although the foregoing is just a slight exaggeration—i do not think this book will go far. it's short, for one thing, and stanley and the publisher and the agent all agree that it is the best writing i have ever done, which is of course the kiss of death on <u>any</u> book, and then there is that batty heroine. my little group of regular readers will buy it and the local library will feature it on the table they reserve for books by local authors and my friends will write me nice letters and it will be published in england and get panned.

as you can see, it's practically all i can think about. this is the worst time, when the baby has been sent out into the world, and you don't know how it's going to get along. poor stanley just got jolted by a vicious review—written by an old friend, of course—in the new york herald tribune, but then he had two nice reviews, in the times and newsweek. most of his reviews, naturally, come in the little magazines and the scholarly journals, so the times and newsweek reviews were a pleasant surprise. he is keeping a list of people he hears of who actually spend ten bucks for the book, and there are fifteen already. he was very pleased that you read about the sex life of the worm, which he says is really the most exciting part. by the way, hill house is coming out in a paperback this june, and i hear they are actually going to start the movie. my agent tells me that ghost stories and the supernatural are definitely in this season.

well. it's wonderful to have the book done, anyway. around this house, when i say <u>the</u> book i mean mine, but when stanley says <u>the</u> book he means his. sally and barry followed my book chapter by chapter, reading each one as it was finished, so they are deeply involved in what happens to it.

by the way, the day i sent off my book i stopped taking my pills. the colitis is just about gone, and all my other symptoms disappeared. so now until i start a new book i am fine.

must stop writing. it's so nice not to have any pressure to get back to the book. keep well. write soon. keep soon. write well.

lots and lots of love from all.

s.

.  .  .

[To Geraldine and Leslie Jackson]

thursday [June 14, 1962]

dearest mother and pop,

i have started three letters to you and torn them all up, so now i will try again. stanley thinks i should write you this, and so do laurie and corinne; as you must have guessed, they are expecting a baby in the fall, which is the reason for the early marriage. they had the good sense to come directly to us, instead of trying some silly solution of their own, and we are every bit pleased and happy as i told you. they have been talking of marriage for a long time, and consequently this is not just some unlucky accident which ties up two people who would not otherwise consider marrying; now they will go back to college as married students, or at least laurie will go back; corinne will be pretty busy for a while.

i know it sounds awful and it was something of a bad shock to us at first, but actually we have been so accustomed to the idea of laurie and corinne getting married sooner or later that after the first gasp we decided that we were really delighted. joanne, who is very close to corinne, knows the truth, but of course sally and barry do not, and i am afraid that corinne's mother is not taking it well, although both mother and father are extremely fond of laurie.

we have been in a wild mess all week because corinne's family are all devout catholics; stanley has been referring to the whole situation as a soap opera called "laurie faces life, the hard way." at first they thought that the only way they could be married was in church, because of course corinne's mother and father couldn't see it any other way, but then laurie discovered that to be married in a church he must sign away his kids and even take a course of instruction in the catholic religion himself, and guess who turned out to have all kinds of scruples i never knew i had, and i raised such a howl ("i will not go to any popish wedding or put on a hat or see my grandchildren raised in ignorance and fear and i will never vote for john f. kennedy again . . . and so on") that even stanley was impressed, since he remembered our marriage and thought that any alternative was preferable to alienating parents from their children because of a mixed marriage. we were actually saved by the lord high priest of the area, who refused his consent to the marriage under these circumstances. laurie said he talked to every priest in vermont and he doesn't think much of them. corinne is not at all strong in her faith (after two years at bennington college, she hardly could be) and surprised and stunned her parents by siding with me. but corinne took a beating. so she is being married in sin, by a justice of the peace, and her parents are sinning by coming at all. the result of all this is that it is to be a very short small ceremony, with only immediate family present, and with a small reception afterward, provided corinne's mother can stop praying long enough to arrange for it.

about corinne: we have known her for so long that she is quite one of the family. the other kids are extremely fond of her, and joanne thinks of her as a close friend. she has been one of stanley's students, and he and i both think highly of her. she is one of the few local girls to attend the college, and has done fairly well. she is quite intelligent, very lovely, and—until she met her mother head-on in the church battle—we thought of her as quiet and docile. she is very well-bred, with good manners and dresses well. since she is an only child her parents have devoted everything to her, and insist upon her education because they have none themselves. the college has turned her from a bennington town girl to a bennington college girl, and the result is fine. she surprised me a little by her enthusiasm over the baby; she apparently wants nothing better than a home and a family, and when i read her the section of your letter about silverware she was overjoyed, and dumfounded laurie by saying that their own silver was somehow the first step in settling down. laurie still thinks of their lives as wandering europe in the summers and going to school in the winters, but he is going to be surprised by finding that he is being turned into a husband and a father. i think it's wonderful, and stanley—who is still giggling over the idea of being a grandfather— thinks it's terribly funny, and has been giving laurie dire accounts of how i did the same thing to him.

once the religious question was solved—which it only was yesterday—everything seemed much smoother. they are not sending out invitations, since the family has already been notified by phone but corinne is planning announcements; her mother points out that she hardly wants to tell her friends that her daughter is being married in sin, but corinne says her father has already come round to accepting the idea, and she thinks her mother will be all right in a day or so; corinne refused to tell them about the baby until the quarrel over religion made it necessary, so her mother got all the shocks at once. anyway they are really very nice people, and devoted to both the kids, and her father finally admitted that he certainly wasn't going to let anyone else give his daughter away no matter where she was married.

naturally there is talk whenever any two kids announce a sudden marriage, and we have gotten a little bit of it already, but our friends, who will certainly know the truth soon enough, have already mostly guessed it, and the general tone seems to be one of polite indifference. i think that our public and immediate support of laurie, and the fact that this is no fly-by-night affair, has already done a good deal to take the sting out of the gossip. laurie and corinne will be in europe all summer, so they will be pretty much all right, as far as gossip goes, and stanley and i simply couldn't care less. among all the difficulties that is the brightest note—we are adding to our family exactly the person we want.

and of course the rest of the world continues to move along. sally goes tomorrow on the bus to new york to visit her dear friend betsy for the weekend, and the rest of us drive down on sunday, laurie following us on monday. we are coming home on thursday, marrying them on saturday, and seeing everyone off to europe and camp the following week. i am seeing my publisher and agent in new york and will get the latest word on my book. publication day has been set back to october because of a heavy printing schedule; i may very well have a book and a grandchild at the same time.

laurie very much wants to enter bennington as a special student in literature and drama, and bill fels, our president, has said that he would be very much in favor of it, since laurie made such an impression here the year he took one literature course. if laurie should be admitted (and it is a much better college than goddard) then corinne would also be re-admitted whenever she wanted to come.

i have interrupted this letter a dozen times to answer the phone and run errands; the whole thing has been great for me personally; i am so busy i don't have time to worry about my anxiety problems.

i hope you will be as pleased and happy about all of it as we are. i am sure the baby comes as no surprise to you, but i hope it comes as a great pleasure. you will like your new granddaughter, i know. and much much love from all of us.

s.

p.s. corinne is smallish, very dark, with enormous dark eyes and a nice voice.

•   •   •

[To Geraldine and Leslie Jackson]

wednesday [July 4, 1962]

dearest mother and pop,

your letter arrived this morning; surprisingly, since it was postmarked july 2 in hawaii. i am sorry that you are cutting your vacation short; i hope it was because of the weather and not mother's wheezing. i do hope that mother is well and comfortable.

things seems so quiet and uneventful around here after the past few weeks. stanley is typing away downstairs and the canaries are singing and cat applegate is asleep on the chair and mrs king is cleaning the bathroom and it's all just like an ordinary day with the kids at school, and hard to remember that they are all gone. somehow each year they go to camp it seems less going away than just switching homes; they know what and how to pack by now and when they arrive everything is just the way they left it last year and they move right in. joanne will enjoy being a counselor; she had to go three days earlier than the others to help get things ready and was getting along quite nicely with the boy counselors, which is of course why she took the job.

the thought of describing the last three weeks appalls me; i cannot even remember clearly what happened when. first, sally went to new york to spend a weekend with betsy, and we saw her off on the bus with considerable apprehension, since it was her first trip anywhere alone. joanne and barry and stanley and i drove down on sunday, going to a hotel in brooklyn across the street from stanley's mother's apartment, so that she could take over the kids and stanley and i could spend at least one evening in the city visiting friends. it was ninety-five degrees in the city when we arrived about four o'clock. the hotel had messed up our reservations. we finally got settled with us on the ninth floor, barry on the tenth floor, and joanne on the fifth floor, and they had a lot of fun telephoning each other and driving the telephone operator crazy. we got all the air-conditioners turned on, too. on monday stanley doggedly started off with barry and joanne, to see the planetarium and the museum of natural history; i headed off into new york where i had lunch with my agent and pub-lisher and heard lots of nice things about my book except the reader's digest didn't take it and no book club wants it, which made us all very sad but didn't really surprise anyone, and we ate cold salmon with capers and drank whisky sours and had a lovely time. after leav-ing them i thought this was a good time to do some shopping, and in order to get as much done as possible i hurried and hurried and suddenly about half past four i found myself loaded down with pack-ages standing on a street corner in that searing heat and feeling very awful indeed, and a man passing took my arm and said was i all right and i said no i was not and he said stand back here in the shade and i will get you a taxi and the poor man stood on the corner for fifteen minutes trying to get a taxi while i kind of sagged against the wall with people going past staring at me. (i have asked oliver about this of course since i came back and he said it was probably mostly the heat and the hurrying with a spot of anxiety thrown in and wasn't i silly to rush in and out of air-conditioned stores?) anyway i finally

got a taxi and the poor man was mighty glad to see the last of me
and i thanked him earnestly and wanted to give him money but he
wouldn't take it. when i finally got out of the taxi in front of our
hotel and saw barry standing in the doorway i nearly cried. barry
took my packages and took me upstairs and i sat down under the air
conditioner while stanley made me a drink with lots of ice cubes.

the next day they went off to the metropolitan museum and i simply stayed in the hotel room. it was lovely; i had my lunch sent up
and i read and washed some clothes and did all my business with editors and such on the phone. i never had such a nice day in new york.
about seven in the evening, when it was cool again, we all went out
for dinner with stanley's mother and his brother, and came back to
stanley's mother's apartment to find laurie sitting on the couch
drinking beer and watching television. he moved into the hotel
room on ten with barry and it was fun to have everyone together
for breakfast, particularly since laurie had come down for only two
reasons—to buy a wedding ring, and to go to the baseball game with
stanley and barry. they had tickets for a double-header that afternoon, and we then went into one more of our complicated ballet se-
quences; laurie drove stanley and barry to the polo grounds and i
waited in the hotel with the girls until sally's good friend jay williams
arrived; he had invited sally to come out to their home in connecticut
overnight. he was going to take her out to lunch and then back to
connecticut and give her a fencing lesson, and he wanted sally to
meet his little girl vicky who is ten. she loved jay's wife and the little
girl, and she and jay wrote a poem and fenced and he taught her how
to use a crossbow. in the meantime joanne and i took stanley's
mother into new york to lunch and we very daringly let joanne order
a tom collins which made her feel very old and sophisticated and we
had a very gay time, and then came back to brooklyn. i was expected
to meet stanley in new york so joanne and stanley's mother had tea
and peanut butter sandwiches in the apartment, on the terrace,
which is nice and cool.

this is where i picked up my scottish sea captain; i was trying to
get a taxi in front of the hotel in brooklyn and so were a lot of other
people, including one man who was clearly in a hurry, and so was i,

so when the doorman got a taxi we both headed for it and the man said why don't we share it and i said fine. we were both going into manhattan but he was already forty minutes late so i said by all means drop him first and he said he was late because his ship had only docked an hour before, and explained that he was scottish, which we already knew perfectly well from his talk, and during the hour trip into new york the driver and the sea captain and i had a perfectly lovely time; it was as though the three of us were old friends who had gotten together for a talk. the sea captain ran a freighter up and down the amazon, and his main cargo was missionaries. he said that he always took out more missionaries than he brought back, but they always kept coming. last trip he had taken out six, but when he came to pick them up there were only three left. i said kind of timidly what had happened to the other three? and he said "och, they werrrrre eaten." the driver thought that was a good thing, because missionaries had no right to go around trying to convert cannibals anyway. we surprised the doorman at the commodore hotel because we were all three laughing so the sea captain could not get out of the taxi and had to wait to control himself and then the taxi and i drove off still laughing. so i met stanley and we got taken out to a Real chinese dinner. when we got back laurie and joanne decided to take the car and go into new york—in the middle of the night—to hear some jazz, so they went to a village night club and i gather that joanne had another tom collins.

the next morning stanley and barry and i left, and joanne went off to help laurie buy a wedding ring. i gave him my chargeaplate* which is good in most of the big stores. he was actually a little more imaginative. he and joanne went first to rogers peet where he bought himself a suit to be married in (laurie simply goes to the man who has sold clothes to stanley and stanley's father and stanley's brother and all his uncles) and then on to tiffany's where he had decided he really wanted to buy a wedding ring. no one knows how he did it, but he opened a charge account in his own name at tiffany's, bought his two wedding rings, and charged them. so laurie has now become the only

---

* An early form of credit card. Shirley preferred to charge things in stores whenever possible.

person we know of who has a charge account at tiffany's. then he and joanne got into his car and headed for new jersey where they picked up laurie's ex-roommate, bob, who was going to be best man at the wedding, and started home. we meanwhile had met jay and sally in a selected rondevouz outside danbury, gathered in sally and her bags and her souvenirs and got home in time to feed the cats. laurie and joanne and bob got home about ten, having picked up corinne in bennington on their way, and we all sat around talking about weddings and admiring the rings and easing bob's stage fright; bob was the chief actor at the college, and starred in all their productions, and had just finished off his senior year with five performances of <u>macbeth</u>, but this was his first wedding.

joanne and i suddenly discovered that what with coming back from new york on thursday and the wedding being on saturday we had only one day to get ready. late friday night laurie's godparents, our old friends june and frank, drove up from new york, and on saturday morning stanley's mother and brother arthur arrived and by ten o'clock saturday i was serving breakfast right and left to thousands of people; everyone except laurie and bob, who had gone out for a final private party, just the two of them, the night before, and were both feeling tired and frightened. laurie had also invited the negro band leader with whom he has been playing for a long time, and who has taken very good care of him for three years, keeping an eye on him in roadhouses and bars and such, and we all like dave and feel very grateful to him; dave brought his wife [Frances] and my, how they were dressed. absolutely the most beautiful clothes i have ever seen, and at the end of the day there still was not a wrinkle in dave's suit. laurie kept assuring everyone that he was not the least bit nervous, and bob went back three times to make sure he had the rings, and the rest of us kept drinking coffee and wondering if it was going to rain, which it was. they had finally decided to have the wedding in one of the college gardens, a traditional spot for student weddings, where there is a little fountain and pool, and flowering bushes all around to make a little private spot; very lovely, but not the place to be if it rains. people were dressing all over the house, and barry had on his good jacket and tie, and was helping dress laurie, who kept telling people he was not nervous and of course it was not going to rain and did bob have the rings, was he sure? there were corsages of roses and orchids for stanley's mother and me, and carnations for laurie and bob and stanley and about quarter to twelve we got ourselves sorted out into cars and drove to jennings, the music building at the college with the lovely gardens, and we were supposed to meet corinne and her crowd there and of course it was raining. laurie kept saying he thought people were supposed to be nervous when they were getting married and here he was not nervous at all, and he went up and said hello so glad you could come to mr macguire, who is the college handyman and was there to see that there were enough chairs and then laurie said how do you do so glad you could come to another man and the man said i had to come i'm the judge who is marrying you; we rehearsed it all yesterday; don't you remember? and laurie said well anyway, one good thing is i'm not nervous. stanley, who was also not nervous, went up to corinne's mother and said i'm sure laurie and joanne will be very happy when they are married, and then he brought his mother over and said i'd like you to meet my grandmother and his poor mother was furious. there were about twenty of corinne's people there and they all looked exactly alike, all the women wearing flowered hats. laurie kept saying it would not rain but then the judge said let's go on outside then and we went out and it was sprinkling but they decided to go on with it in the garden anyway and we went out and just as corinne came with her attendant into the garden the rain stopped and the ceremony began; the poor judge who i guess was not nervous either, got both their names wrong, calling laurie laurence jackson ryan. and got corinne all tangled up, and bob gave them both the wrong rings, and thank heaven corinne seemed to be fairly self-possessed because she exchanged the rings without any difficulty and of course everyone cried and thank heaven the ceremony only took ten minutes because as it ended the rain came down again. the photographer took a lot of pictures but they are terrible, mostly because of the bad light. laurie was by then in a complete daze and bob was not much better because of mixing up the rings, but we got ourselves back into cars and drove over to the four chimneys, the inn you liked so much, in old bennington.

they had arranged for a private dining room, and it was beautifully set up; because the entire group was only about thirty-five the biggs family had decided to have everyone sit down and to serve a regular luncheon, and they lined the bride and groom and parents and grandparents and best man and bridesmaid up at the head table and then had smaller tables for everyone else. before we sat down poor bob—he was sitting between laurie and me—had to propose a toast to the bride and groom, and just as everything was ready, with the photographer waiting and all, bob said i think i'm going to cry, and laurie said five performances of macbeth and you're going to blow this line? and bob burst into tears and managed to say it with tears going down his cheeks and everyone drank the toast and laurie and i revived bob but there is a fine picture of bob's tearful toast. after that everyone was eating and drinking champagne except barry who was allowed to have milk and me, because i loathe champagne and the head waiter, who knows us of old, brought me a nice glass of bourbon. the funniest thing happened sometime during lunch, when the door opened and a vaguely familiar character came in, smiling and nodding to everyone, walked up to laurie, held out his hand and said "i'm the governor of vermont;* i came to congratulate you." turns out he—he's the oiliest crookedest republican scoundrel in politics—had been having lunch and heard there was a wedding party and couldn't stand the idea that there were more than ten people in a room without hurrying in to do a little political campaigning, so he went up and down the head table, shaking everyone's hand and beaming, and when he came to us he said so you're the parents of the groom; nicelooking boy; i do like to see young people getting married and being so happy, and stanley said this pair is going to raise a fine family of democrats, and the governor looked surprised and then went off and shook hands with someone else. by the time laurie and corinne cut the cake everyone was feeling very happy and gay. we then invited the entire party to come back to our house, and by three o'clock everyone was here and we had quite a party going. one of corinne's old aunts had always wanted to learn to play the trumpet so laurie was

* The Republican governor of Vermont then was F. Ray Keyser, Jr. He lost the election that November 6 to Democrat Philip H. Hoff.

giving her trumpet lessons in one room and in the front room joanne and dave's wife were teaching corinne's mother how to do the twist, and stanley's mother and another old aunt were hitting it off fine in a corner and corinne's grandmother, who is eighty-seven and speaks and reads only french, (french-canadian) was happily in a chair in the corner reading "life among the savages" in french.

the biggs family and friends had given laurie and corinne a good deal of money, which they had put into the bank with what we gave them, and at one point stanley's brother, who had already given them some beautiful luggage, handed corinne a hundred-dollar bill to buy herself something in paris. i have never seen laurie so happy; he is not a demonstrative boy, as you know, and yet he was so excited and just plain delighted with the world that he couldn't stop laughing; he was so proud and joyful it was good to see. by this time both families had decided that they loved each other, and even dave and his wife, who are so nice and so sweet that everyone likes them, and then mr biggs, corinne's father, announced that he had lost his only daughter but by great good luck she had married into a family with plenty of daughters to go around and he was formally adopting joanne. they are very nice people, friendly and very good-hearted, and once they had given up the idea of the church wedding they decided to be as nice about it as they could, and they simply settled down to enjoy themselves and i suppose do penance afterward. about eight o'clock most of them were gone, and then laurie and corinne and bob and dave and his wife decided to go; they were going to drive as far as al-bany, where dave was taking them out to dinner, and then on to new york, where they would stay in bob's family's empty apartment until wednesday when their boat sailed. then bob, who is acting in sum-mer stock in burlington, would bring the car back and keep it to use this summer.

after everyone left stanley's brother invited us all back to the four chimneys for dinner, we went and sat on the terrace and relaxed and we all agreed that it had been a perfectly charming wedding, and quite the nicest we had ever seen.

laurie and corinne called on tuesday night before they sailed and they were still dazed and wildly excited. bob stopped by on thursday on his way to burlington and said that he had seen them off okay, and that since this is a college cruise ship they have no accomodations for married kids, and laurie is in a cabin with the band and corinne in a cabin with six other girls, just like being back in bennington college. he had brought back all the announcements, which they had taken with them to "do on the way" and he and i finished them off and sent them out.

friday

we had a week after the wedding to get the kids ready for camp, and then after i had taken them up on saturday we went out and had a quiet dinner all by ourselves and then both of us slept for twelve hours. we are back on our schedule of dining out every night, and it is very pleasant. we have friends staying with us for the summer, barbara and murry karmiller; they were both working in new york, no children, and suddenly decided that they had had enough; barbara came into a small legacy and so they packed up and went to europe to wander and live for as long as they liked. they stayed nearly two years and then got homesick, so when they wrote this spring they were coming home we asked if they wanted to spend this first summer home living in our back apartment and doing their own cooking and taking care of our livestock when we were away, and they wanted to very much, so they came. they are thinking of renting a house near here, or even buying if they can, and staying around north bennington. barbara is a former bennington college student, and loves the country, and murry, who used to be a television writer, wants to try his hand at magazine writing and likes this quiet life, so we have been spending afternoons wandering around our pretty countryside looking at houses. they come out for dinner with us occasionally, but mostly they make their dinners here, and barbara and i make breakfasts and lunches together. with three of us typing away in separate rooms barbara gets most of the table-setting to do.

next saturday stanley and i take off for michigan, where stanley will lecture in ypsilanti and i will lecture in east lansing. and then must hurry back here saturday and wash out some clothes and then leave again on sunday, me to suffield and my writers' conference, where i give another lecture and stanley to new york and a week at the new yorker. then home again for two weeks, and at last in mid-august off to quebec and the st. lawrence river. that will be our real vacation, just lazy driving from one little town to the next, stopping where we want to, and if possible taking a boat up part of the river.

i will stop now, and write a lecture, and once i get the lecture done i can be completely lazy.

keep well, write soon, and much much love from all.

love,

s.

•   •   •

[To Carol Brandt]

July 11 [1962]

Dear Carol,

I am very curious about the little book, NINE MAGIC WISHES.* For such a very small thing it is kicking up quite a fuss. Do you know anything about who is illustrating, when they publish, or any such thing?

You still did not send me a plot. I am tired of cleaning closets and want to start a new book. Writing is easier than housework.

Best,

Shirley

•   •   •

* Shirley's first children's book, published in 1963 by Crowell-Collier, with illustrations by Lorraine Fox. It was republished in 2001 by Farrar, Straus & Giroux, with illustrations by Shirley's artist grandson, Miles Hyman.

[To Libbie Burke]

sept. 5 [1962]

dear lib,

you have not read my new book because i have not sent you a copy
because although the publishers assure me that copies were mailed
out in mid-august i have still not received any. as soon as i have them
a copy will go to you, you of course deserving the first because of
providing me with a good half of the book.

they are making a fuss over the book including dragging stanley and
me down to new york for publication day—september 21—and giving
a cocktail party at the st. regis (i put your names down to be invited
but i bet they didn't judging from their apparent way of doing things
but i bet you feel the same as we do about literary parties anyway; i
plan to get plastered real fast) and two days of interviews and such. i
am quite excited about this publication, i think because the book matters so much to me, and i am very curious to see how it is received.

also very excited because (who's counting) we are going to be
grandparents this fall. stanley can never shave his beard now because
he looks so grandfatherly, and i am already preparing to be insuffer-
able with advice and theories of child-raising. laurie and corinne are
still in europe, where they have been all summer, laurie traveling with
a band (did you see the article in the recent Sat Eve Post on the
band, with several fine pictures of laurie?) and for the past month
have been in frankfurt where the band has a steady job. they come
home next week just in time to enter bennington college, although
corinne will of course be on a part time basis. laurie has been admitted as a special student, and we have rented them a tiny house out on
overlea road. corinne's mother and i are competing in studied indifference about the house; both of us are dying to get over there and
put in furniture and hang drapes and both of us are resolutely assuring each other that after all it's the kids' first home and they ought to
furnish it themselves.

barry went reluctantly back to school today, stanley starts next week, and the girls go away on the fifteenth. the summer has gone, and i did not do any of the things i planned, like clean the pantry and rearrange the linen closet and now i want to start a new book so i suppose the pantry will never be done.

see you soon? best from all.


love,


s.


•   •   •


*Returning home with Stanley from the New York publication party put on by Viking on September 20, 1962, at the St. Regis Hotel, Shirley finds an unpleasant letter from her mother criticizing her over her appearance in a photograph by Alfred Statler in* Time *magazine that ran with a very favorable review of the new book. She dashes out the following letter, never mailed.*


[To Geraldine Jackson]

[September 25, 1962]


dear mother

i received your unpleasant letter last night when i got back from new york, and it upset me considerably, as you no doubt intended.

i wish you would stop telling me that my husband and children are ashamed of me. if they are, they have concealed it very skillfully; perhaps they do not believe that personal appearance is the most important thing in the world. as far as the picture in time is concerned, i think it is strange to blame me. time sent a photographer from new york, who spent a morning taking sixty or seventy pictures of me, most of which were presentable and pleasant. time chose this one, which was by far the worst, from some perverted sense of humor. i do not think it was kind of them, but i had no authority whatsoever in the matter—beyond refusing to let them do this again—and as far as i am concerned it is a very minor thing. i am far more concerned with my book and the very good review which accompanied the picture.

i am also tired of being told that i am ungrateful and thoughtless. naturally you would have heard from me and from the children if the silver had arrived.

you were sent a copy of my book as soon as i had a copy to send. that was about ten days ago.

will you try to realize that i am a grown up and fully capable of managing my own affairs? i have a happy and productive life, i have many good friends, i have considerable stature in my profession, and if i decided to make any changes in my manner of living, it will not be because you have nagged me into it. you can say this is "wilful" if you like, but surely at my age i have a right to live as i please, and i have just had enough of the unending comments on my appearance and my faults.

love to you and pop.

s.

. . .

[to Joanne and Sally]

wednesday [September 26–28, 1962]

my dear captive princesses:

the doc has taken away my big boss pills because they were no longer boss and has given me the prettiest, most explosive great black and blue things of which i have just taken one so let's see if my typing improves.

have been meaning to write for several days but taking these pills uses up so much time that i hardly do anything else except play duets with barbara. and new duets arrived this morning so we will play twice as long tonight. also arrived this morning without warning a check for french rights to savages and hill house in the reader's digest. very very nice.

i am still feeling a little bit like a visiting movie star after our trip to new york but i suspect that will wear off quite soon. not that i ever intend to go back to new york ever. i found that even with double boss pills i could not go out of the hotel without wild panic attacks so the publishers got me a nurse kind of to watch me. she was actually the publicity girl from the publishers and a very nice person named julie and it was her job to see that i got where i was supposed to be going and stayed there once i got there. she kept grabbing my arm when i got up and started madly for the door. we worked out a system—dad actually figured it—for transporting me; she would go out onto the street and look for a taxi while i cowered in a doorway and when she found a taxi she would bring it directly to the exact spot where i waited and i would make a mad dash while she held the door open and then she would persuade the taxi to stop directly in front of wherever we were going and i would race for the doorway and hide. i really made a very interesting impression on new york; people kept thinking there was something wrong with me, of all the silly ideas. i dwell on this to such an extent because it was the governing system of our whole visit. we had a magnificent suite in the hotel, a big living room with an alcove containing a refrigerator, and a small bar set up for us (we had to give drinks to visiting newspaper men) and a big bedroom with a three foot stone lion which it turned out we were unable to get into the elevator to bring home. when we arrived there was a big bowl of roses waiting compliments of the publisher and copies of the early reviews of the book, most of them very favorable indeed and a picture in time magazine which my mother is cancelling her subscription because you would not believe it if you saw it because that photographer got sent up from new york and he took sixty-eight pictures of me and this must easily be the worst it is ghastly. anyway the first reviews were great although most of them think merricat is crazy. then there were a couple of reviews not so great but all in all the general feeling is that the book will sell very nicely. the understanding was that i was to be interviewed in my suite drinking with the interviewers and it worked out very well, except each day i had to go out for lunch with someone. the first day it was arlene francis* and this luncheon at sardi's thing and julie and i were secretly very amused although terrified. luncheon at sardi's with arlene francis is actually without arlene francis. julie and i after identifying ourselves were taken to a second floor dining room which was largely empty and we sat in a little alcove (very fancy restaurant, all red plush and caricatures of people in show business all over the place) and across from us was a table full of tape recorders and microphones. so julie and i sat there in lonely state and had a cocktail and lunch by ourselves, since it is arlene francis' policy to arrive after lunch for luncheon at sardi's. we were just debating whether to order dessert when arlene francis' assistant arrived, a very very oh very charming young woman who gushed at us and said how much arlene had <u>loved</u> my book just <u>adored</u> it darling. she was wearing a handsome pinkish wool suit cut very severely and lots and lots and lots of dangling bracelets and a big garish pin and a large elaborate costume ring. after about ten minutes arlene francis arrived. she was wearing a handsome white wool suit cut very severely and lots and lots and lots of dangling bracelets and a big garish pin and a large elaborate costume ring except arlene francis' bracelets and pin and ring were all real diamonds. her assistant apparently copies everything she wears and says and even the tone of her voice and the big hearty laugh which is just as phony as it can be although actually the woman is very pleasant. anyway arlene francis sat down at the table with the microphones and said "darling, where's the book, what did you say the name of it was?" and the assistant brought her a copy of my book and arlene francis turned the pages very quickly assuming that we could neither see nor hear her and she kept saying yes but what's it about i never did read more than the first page. and the assistant whispered to her and they both made notes.

so then they called us over and sat me down by another microphone and arlene francis said for god's sake don't listen to the com-

* Arlene Francis was a popular radio and TV talk show host.

mercials darling they will literally turn your stomach. she was right, and she read them in an exaggerated eager voice which made them worse and i could not imagine how any audience could possibly believe she was serious about somebody or other's pork sausages. so she asked me a lot of damfool questions and i gave her a lot of damfool answers and they taped it all and julie and i got away. laurie heard the program (it was broadcast last monday) and said that arlene francis sounded worse than i did, but not much.

thursday

laurie called at eight this morning and said he had taken corinne to the hospital during the night; they are not yet sure whether this is really the baby or a false alarm but laurie said he would call as soon as he heard and of course i will call the school and get word to you as soon as i hear.

sc for the rest of the new york trip in a capsule: we had a wonderful cocktail party because they do these things very well at the st. regis hotel and there were about sixty people including frank and june and ralph and fanny and various other friends whom we had invited, and a number of publishing and newspaper and magazine people. i liked it because i came in with the two heads of viking press and the waiter came up and asked me what i wanted to drink and he came back with my drink on a silver tray. then i stood in a corner propped up against a doorway and smiled and said thank you very much to all the people who said they liked the book. and they had wonderful food: little sausages (not from arlene francis) and hot cheese tarts and smoked salmon and tiny hamburgers and all such but i was too frightened to eat. everyone had a fine time even me after a while and then the publishers took us to dinner at a fancy restaurant. and about ten-thirty i suddenly realized that i had had it and i said to dad please take me home to my stone lion and we went back to the hotel where dad fell asleep and i sat up most of the night massaging my feet. and wondering what was going to happen to poor old merricat who had somehow gotten lost in all the fuss.

except that two of the big new york bookshops had full window displays on publication day and another jumped the gun on sales and had sold out their first order the night before publication.

we saw lulu and arthur the first night in new york and poor lulu will never go out with me again because she simply would not believe that i was afraid to go outside and kept trying to argue with me and she had kind of an idea we would go to the tower suite or some equally fancy restaurant for dinner but dad explained that i had to go into an empty restaurant because i was afraid of crowds and consequently we were having dinner at sheik* and lulu could have a nice order of stuffed grape leaves which lulu nearly fainted but she was a very good sport about it.

we came home on saturday and found that barry who has been staying at barbara and murry's was all set to go right on living there because the food was great and murry played monopoly with him every night. sunday night we had to go to the malamuds† for dinner and barry spent the early evening with laurie and corinne. he is enjoying being the only child but it is hard to pass things at the dinner table; we tried all sitting at one end but it was too crowded.

i wish that phone would ring. probably nothing at all will happen until late this afternoon and i will have spent the whole day staying by the phone.

SALLY: as you know i am to write another book for beginning readers, and dad thought it would be a wonderful idea to use your jay-hex about ten cities knowing your name,‡ okay? it is permitted? little girl named sally trying to get her name known in ten cities, writing it big on a kite and flying it over the rooftops, persuading bees to fly up and down the streets saying zally zally zally, making stars get in formation, and such. well?

although my new pills seem quite powerful i am still not equal to any large scale shopping and mostly just call the store and larry pow-

---

* The Sheik, a tiny Lebanese restaurant on Twenty-ninth Street in New York, was greatly favored by Stanley; he and Shirley became good friends with the owner-chef.
† Bernard and Ann Malamud were close friends and the families visited often.
‡ *Famous Sally,* published posthumously by Harlan Quist (1966).

ers has everything ready to carry out to the car when i stop by. so i cannot yet send you packages of food although i hope you got the apples.

call just came. laurie too excited to talk; it is a boy, eight pounds, everything fine. you will know of course before you get this letter; i will call the school and leave messages for you. must call dad at college. lulu. arthur. yippee.* i will finish this later. i can go to the hospital and see corinne right away and maybe they will let me get a look at the baby so i can tell you all about it later.

friday

i must finish this letter today or the baby will be ready for school before you get it. barbara and i went to the hospital yesterday, taking along a few necessities of life for corinne—a box of candy, donated by larry powers, a bottle of nice cologne, a very fancy lace-trimmed nightgown and bedjacket ("what does she need a nightgown for?" laurie wanted to know, "aren't the hospital nightgowns good enough?") and, from barbara and murry, a bottle of dry cinzano, of which corinne is particularly fond, and which had to be hidden under the blankets. the baby looks just like a baby; he is quite big, weighed eight and a half pounds, quite long, little reddish fuzz on his head; we could not see his eyes because they were squeezed tight shut and he was yelling and yelling and laurie kept saying will he yell like that at home? they have definitely decided to name him miles, after gramp. he is fine and healthy and barry thinks he looks quite intelligent. we got barry in to see him last night by cornering oliver and begging him to put a little pressure on the head nurse; oliver got him in long enough to see the baby for a couple of minutes and to say hello to corinne. barry was enchanted with his nephew and is easily as excited as laurie; he went off to school this morning yelling at passing friends that he was an uncle.

corinne is fine. she apparently started having bad pains about five in the morning, and about eight laurie called the doctor, who said

* Miles Biggs Hyman is born September 27, 1962.

bring her over to the hospital; they still thought it was a false alarm—she is about a week early, after all—until around nine o'clock, when it became clear that she was going to go through with it. she simply took it all in stride, had almost no anaesthetic, and polished off the whole business in half an hour, practically a hospital record. by last night she was beginning to feel a little tired, but she was wearing her nightgown and drinking cinzano and eating candy. they will let her sit up today, walk tomorrow, and come home probably on monday.

lulu is practically beside herself, and so is arthur. i made laurie call them from here yesterday morning; he could hardly talk but neither could lulu. they are coming up the weekend of october sixth.

when laurie called me yesterday morning i called the college and left a message with dad's secretary and she took it to him in class and he read it aloud to the class and they all cheered and dad went around the rest of the day giving away his good cigars. he thinks the baby looks like his uncle louis feinberg.

the college movie this saturday night is called torero, about bull-fighting; one of the best and most authentic documentaries and star-ring a real toreador and i am most anxious to see it but of course cannot go into the theatre. dad talked to ben bellitt,* who is in charge of movies at the college, and ben has arranged a private show-ing on sunday afternoon for me and my little theatre party, which will now include barry and the karmillers, dad, and laurie. corinne and miles will have to miss it.

the combinations of my new explosive pills and the heady effect of being a grandmother has seemingly strengthened me considerably; i got to the hospital twice yesterday and even into bennington to do some shopping. barbara came with me, of course, but i did fine and even walked down the block and across the street and this morning i sailed down and got the mail without a qualm.

we are all delighted with your accounts of school. corinne was most anxious to know that you were sent word about the baby and

---

* Ben Belitt, well-known poet and translator, taught literature at Bennington and de-lighted in bringing rare and unusual films for College Movie Night every Saturday.

sends you her love, as do laurie and probably nephew miles and the new grandma and grandpa and man do we feel like fools.

lots and lots and lots and lots and lots and lots of love.

m.

.   .   .

*This is the first letter Shirley actually sends to her parents after the St. Regis party trip.*

[To Geraldine and Leslie Jackson]

tuesday [October 2, 1962]

dearest mother and pop,

laurie and corinne will of course be writing you, but in their present circumstances it may take a while, so i thought i would write right away and tell you that the silver arrived yesterday and is perfectly beautiful. the kids are enormously grateful and pleased, and tonight will be their first ceremonial use of their handsome silver, since corinne and the baby come home from the hospital today. i said i would take them over a little casscrole and a bottle of wine and laurie will have the table all set, so they will have a fancy private party to celebrate.

we were supposed to go for dinner last saturday night, actually. it was to have been their first company meal, but corinne managed to get out of it. poor child; all things considered, she didn't need to have the baby two weeks early.

stanley and laurie pass one another at the college and sometimes have coffee together. laurie is doing very well indeed, and is fascinated by the music program he is taking; he is composing and playing in an ensemble and actually learning the piano. after six years as a professional musician he is finally learning to read music. corinne is taking only an art course, and had a paper to write for that, due thursday which is the day the baby was born, so her teacher, who is paul feeley, generously gave her an extension until the following monday, by which time, he said, she should be through having babies and ready to get back to work.

we were in new york for three days, guests of my publishers, who had a fancy suite for us and all day i was interviewed in our suite, serving drinks to newspaper men and giving silly answers to silly questions, and i was on arlene francis' radio program called luncheon at sardi's. the head publicity girl from the publishers was with me all the time to make sure that i kept mentioning the name of my book. the book has been getting simply fantastic reviews—a new batch came in yesterday, making about twenty-five altogether and only two unfavorable—and is selling well.

this summer quite by accident barbara and i were looking over some of our old music; barbara is a first-rate pianist and she had been without a piano for so long she was homesick, so i got out the music and there right on top was one of the old piano duets dorothy* and i used to play and barbara dared me to try it and of course i am hopelessly outclassed but we had so much fun that we went to the music library at the college and took out great volumes of bach and haydn and now spend evenings sightreading this stuff; i am playing

* Shirley's childhood friend Dorothy Ayling.

far beyond anything i ever thought i could, but of course barbara is good enough to help me out.

the girls are very happy at school; sally's letters are so joyful and enthusiastic that it is a pleasure to read them; she has made several friends and has for the first time met kids who are not ashamed to say that they like to read and to write, and she met a boy who actually boasts that he writes poetry, which in north bennington would get him laughed at. sally was asked to make a special poster for a dorm party and it was put up in the dining hall, to her great pleasure, and their only complaint is that now that sally is three inches taller than joanne everyone thinks sally is the older sister.

the oddest thing about being a grandmother, i find, is that you are so wholly unnecessary. i am dying to run over to laurie's house and help dress the baby and play with the baby clothes and fold diapers but i do not seem to be needed. they both seem so competent and so confident, and corinne has no worries or nervousness about handling everything, that it is a real pleasure to see them. corinne's mother was all set to move in with them for the first week, and take care of everything and was told most politely to stay home. they were surprised when i said i would bring them over some dinner tonight because they both assumed that corinne would come home and get right back to work cooking and taking care of the house.

must stop. lots and lots of love from all.

s.

•   •   •

[To Carol Brandt]

October 23 [1962]

Dear Carol,

This does not seem much like a morning when grandchildren or contracts or books or practically anything else can possibly matter.

After the President's broadcast last night* my poor young Barry, who used to dream of being an astronaut, fled back to the Oz books for comfort. I feel the same way.

As far as the Holiday magazine piece is concerned, I am most definitely interested, since my present unfortunate position is that of enormous inclination and time to write just anything at all, and not one solitary idea.

I am continually amazed at the reviews of CASTLE; I am also a little puzzled at the weekly Viking ad in the Sunday New York Times which makes no mention of any such book; aren't they going to advertise it any more?

My grandchild grows; I have reached the stage where I babysit for an evening and thankfully return him to his mother. He is a very sweet boy and I am delighted that he belongs to somebody else. His mother just arrived to dump another load of diapers into the washer.

As I say, I cannot, this morning, find any of these things very real. I will go and bake a cake; at least I know where I stand there.

Best,

Shirley

. . .

[To Joanne and Sally]

tuesday [October 23, 1962]

dear whatever-you-are-calling-yourselves-this-week:

i hear from hattie fels† that you are both well happy and beautiful which was nice to know. i also hear that joanne took care of her and saw that she got dinner and was most efficient and charming; very

* President John F. Kennedy had announced the Cuban Missile Crisis.
† Wife of the college president, William Fels; Shirley was close friends with her and the couples socialized.

good, joanne. i further hear that my food packages arrived, which surprises me a good deal, since i had only mailed them two days before.

as far as bringing friends home goes, of course your friends are always welcome and we would be delighted to have them, but are you sure that you want them here for your birthday celebration? the weekend will be very rushed, what with visiting laurie and corinne and big mo,* and seeing barbara and murry, who are most anxious to see you, and i don't know how much entertainment we could offer guests.

sally you never gave me any word on whether it was okay to use your ten cities for a little book.

our social life is wild these days, what with our three houses entertaining each other. laurie and corinne carry big moey around in a basket and when they both have to go somewhere they simply drop him either here or with barbara so we see a lot of the baby. ralph ellison came by on sunday so naturally we all went over to laurie and corinne's and ralph got to hold the baby and then in the evening laurie and corinne and barbara and murry came here and laurie and ralph played trumpet duets with barbara at the piano while big moey slept sweetly on the couch with a trumpet blasting on each side of him.

barbara and i play duets nearly every evening and quite often laurie and corinne and child drop down so laurie can use dad's books and somehow it seems that things are going on all the time. last night we had a big (forty people) party for kenneth burke, who has just finished a series of lectures here. it was very lively and we could not invite laurie and corinne because they are students but we apparently had all laurie's teachers and heard a lot about how well he is doing. dad has taken over the big cook's apron one of you girls stole from camp and he wears it to tend bar and looks very professional.

merricat is sailing along. third printing, which makes twenty-five thousand in print now, although no one knows how many sold. they are running a contest among bookshops for the best hallowe'en win-

* Shirley started calling three-week-old Miles "Big Mo" or "Big Moey" after Moe Hyman.

dow featuring the book which although i think it is kind of silly will certainly get the book into bookshop windows. poor old jonas will be a hallowe'en cat.

wednesday

as far as your summer plans are concerned, joanne, both dad and i agree that the apartment in boston idea is out of the question. even if you could find an apartment and a job. you simply cannot spend a summer on your own. we would like to have the family together next summer, anyway, and are still talking of getting a summer place on a lake. that of course depends on money money money. merricat is working hard to get us a lake.*

i have been turning on the news every hour to hear about the cuban situation; i hope people up your way have not gotten as upset as some people around here. at our party monday night almost everyone came fresh from hearing the president's speech and they were terribly depressed, but somehow the longer it goes on the less real it seems. by the time you get this i suppose we will know what is going to happen. we have a radio because dad wanted a little transistor to take to school to hear the world series so i got him one. barry's is working again but he will not listen to it as long as the news is so scary.

every day i drive along main street at noon time i am thankful that you two are at cambridge. i see the old north bennington girls, looking just as dull and bored and silly as usual. and the boys throwing junk at each other and everyone standing around with nothing to do.

must go make lunch. lots and lots of love to both of you from all of us. see you soon.

love.

m.

•   •   •

* Shirley and Stanley are thinking of buying a small lake, with others, and are considering Lake Shaftsbury.

[To Carol Brandt]

November 6 [1962]

Dear Carol,

Mr. Ehrlich* suggests writing about superstition or witchcraft, or anything else except children, and I have two ideas. One is our little country store, which in my time here has changed from a really country store to an emporium featuring delicacies and French wine. The other is the story of the two English schoolteachers who visited Versailles and stumbled into the eighteenth century; it is a case in which I have always been interested and would love to write about. If neither of these sounds right, I will try to think of something else.

I was charmed by the story in Vogue; I had completely forgotten it and you are amazing to have found it after all these years and sold it besides. It was a favorite of mine, I now remember.

Isn't it nice how Merricat is best-selling? Pat Covici called me to tell me, and I did not like to tell him that Bernard Malamud, now at Bennington, and a man who takes his Writing Career very seriously indeed, subscribes to the Advance Times Book Section, and calls me every Monday to let me know how I stand.

Now. The little baby book for Collier Books. I have a lovely idea and most of it is written but about one-tenth of the words are not on their arrogant little list. I simply cannot manage to bring it down to their level, but I hate to give it up. Is it worth my finishing it and sending it along to you (and I should of course send a copy to Louis Untermeyer with a note of explanation) on the chance that they might want it for slightly older readers? My illegal words are not difficult—"share" for instance, or "wonder," both words I am

* Arnold Ehrlich was an editor at *Holiday* magazine.

shocked that small children should not know. Please do let me know what to do.

Shall I send you some Vermont cheese?

Best,

Shirley

•  •  •

[To Geraldine and Leslie Jackson]

tuesday [November 1962]

dearest mother and pop,

it's high time you met the young gentleman enclosed. laurie took a lot of pictures of him but this is the best. he looks unbelievably like laurie as a baby. he is beginning to be more alert and alive now, turns his head to watch people and knows when he's being spoken to, smiles, and eats like a horse. he's trying to turn over, and for one wild morning corinne and i were sure he was getting a tooth, although it turned out that even this baby couldn't produce a tooth at five weeks. he still wanders around everywhere with his parents, and no one really knows where he is going to turn up next. yesterday he was over here visiting. i made dinner carrying him around under one arm while his mother was outside pushing laurie's model a ford to see if they could get it started.

they have certainly changed a lot of things about babies even since barry's time. do you know that there is instant formula now? like instant coffee. i suppose disposal clothes are next.

we are not finding it too difficult to be grandparents. he is a nice baby and we like having him around for an hour or so but we are always very glad to give him back to his mother and father. i find it very difficult to change him because corinne is left-handed and i have to turn him over to get the pins out of the diaper and then corinne can't get out the right-handed pins i put in.

things continue much as usual in our three houses. we visit back and forth constantly, and it seems as though we never see anyone except family, barbara and murry now being included as family members. last weekend june and frank came up for a couple of days and laurie and corinne invited everyone over for sunday breakfast, using their lovely silverware and we had a fine time. miles sat in the middle of the floor in his baby seat and we all sat around eating scrambled eggs and drinking orange juice with vodka. on saturday everyone went over to barbara and murry's for cocktails and then came here for dinner. we have the only dining room that can seat nine people. miles came to dinner—he went to the cocktail party too, as did barry—and slept happily while we ate and played the piano and sang.

the girls came home the weekend of november third, which was halfway between their two birthdays; both girls are well and happy, and we were particularly pleased with sally, who is enjoying the school and looks so much better and acts so much happier than she did in this terrible town. sally had received your nice gift, and i hope has written you, although she is not much on writing these days with her concentration on her school work. she intends to spend the money on books; she has found a little old second-hand book shop and apparently spends a good deal of time and money browsing around there. much of her wildness is going. she is still a little batty, of course, but a much nicer sally.

joanne is of course running the school and doing it very well. she hates the idea of leaving next june, but has applied to several colleges in case she doesn't get into bennington. she is very happy at the school, not doing her best in the work because she is so busy manag-ing things for everyone else and arranging the seating at assembly and being president of the dorm and chairman of the recreation committee and keeping up her busy correspondence with half a dozen boys.

neither of the girls has more than the slightest interest in the baby, which surprised everyone. both of them admired him, held him for a minute, remarked on his little hands and feet, and then forgot him completely.

laurie is doing unbelievably well at bennington. laurie himself is full of enthusiasm, working hard, and just generally taking on anything that comes to hand. he set up a painting studio for corinne in their basement. now he is interested in photography; he bought a good camera in europe, and for his birthday we gave him photography stuff (i don't know what it is; he named it and we bought it) and he has set up a darkroom and is developing his own pictures. now he says he needs an enlarger, so there is his christmas present. i have never seen him happier or busier. he has a job playing regularly every sunday afternoon at a student-type restaurant near williamstown, where they play modern jazz from four to eight, not at all like the roadhouse kind of job he used to have. he tried working saturday nights at his old job but found he couldn't manage it. he gets lots of offers of odd jobs playing with various bands, and has the satisfaction of earning some of his own money and being less dependent on us; he is taking just as little from stanley as he possibly can.

wednesday

mother, do you still have the genealogy you once had put together for the d.a.r.? i was talking to a miss bugbee who works for the bennington library and she was most curious to know what branch of the family we were, and joanne met a girl at school who claims they are related through the field family. i would love to find out more about it; bugbee is a very common name around here.

i discover that i never sent you the picture of corinne i had for you. the picture loses her usual lively expression, but at least you will recognize her when you see her. we are just as fond of her as ever, although i still jump when she calls me mom.

merricat is really swinging along, still getting the most fantastic reviews, and three weeks now on the new york times best seller list; started at fifteenth and now up to thirteenth. this does not really offer much of a challenge to "ship of fools"* or "fail-safe,"† but it is right good for merricat, who is also twelfth on publishers weekly's best seller list. this means it is selling about fifteen hundred copies a week. our local bookshop has re-ordered four times, which is about on a par with our electing a democrat governor of vermont. the new york times called me yesterday for a picture (which i do not have) to use in their christmas issue; merricat is one of their recommended books of the year. the side effects are odd, too: a paperback company has picked up "sundial", which never made a nickel, and is reprinting it, and my agent dug up a ten-year-old story out of the files and sold it to vogue, who turned it down ten years ago. holiday has asked me to do a piece, and my agent is begging me to go into the desk drawers and find old stuff she can sell, or at least to write something new.

thursday
    must finish this today. cannot do anything else. yesterday, after repeatedly warning everyone that the back steps were icy, i skipped blithely across the porch, hit the ice, and went down magnificently, terrifying barry, who was helping me unload the car. it knocked the breath out of me and of course barry immediately concluded that i was seriously injured and, true to cub scout training, tried very hard to persuade me not to move until he had called the doctor and improvised a stretcher, but i finally convinced him that the only injury i could locate was a twisted ankle and he let me get up and hobble into the house. i had completely forgotten that my daughter in law had been a nurse's aid in the hospital for a year, and when she called a few minutes later i casually remarked that i had fallen and twisted my ankle and in ten minutes she was over with bandages and epsom salts and you should see me. i told her i was going to soak it in bourbon instead of epsom salts and had a great deal of difficulty persuading her to let me make dinner. this morning i am far less bruised and

* *Ship of Fools* by Katherine Anne Porter (Little, Brown, 1962) was the Book of the Month Club selection, and its film rights were immediately sold for $500,000 ($4,226,073 adjusted for inflation).
† *Fail-Safe* by Eugene Burdick and Harvey Wheeler (McGraw-Hill, 1962) was a bestseller and adapted many times for film and TV, starting in 1964.

battered than i expected to be, but now mrs king is after me to let her make the beds and run down for the mail and what not. in all of this while they argue i walk around doing exactly as usual; my only real difficulty is in driving because it is my foot for the clutch and of course my little car has to be shifted constantly. also the only thing i can wear on my foot is a furry red bedroom slipper and i simply will not walk into the post office wearing it, so i just won't get the mail, and the store will send up my groceries and i will spend a happy day with my foot on the hassock reading a mystery story which i had just picked up at the library before we came home and i fell.

did you know i got a new car? another morris minor convertible, exactly like the black one, only it is a 1963 model and is white. i kept the black one, of course—joanne will be driving by spring.

friday

i was too optimistic yesterday about not feeling any bruises; i should have remembered that these things take a day or so. this morning i really feel it.

we have most unexpected house guests. a friend of laurie's, who played with him in europe, a scotsman* (he says i must say scotsman) who spent a good deal of time this summer questioning laurie and corinne about this country; he and his wife had very serious thoughts of immigrating here. yesterday they called corinne absolutely without warning; they had just landed in new york and were on their way to vermont. corinne was a little taken aback, but they were good friends and lovely people, so she said come ahead, and then called me frantically; could they sleep in our guest room, since laurie and corinne have not the luxury of even one extra bed? and of course i said sure, so corinne and laurie brought them over in the evening and stanley and i were both charmed by them. he is ken and she is gwen; she is german, an experienced secretary who speaks english and french fluently and does not anticipate much trouble finding work in the united states. he is so very scottish that she frequently has to trans-

---

* Ken Ramage and his wife, Gwen; he was a jazz trombonist picked up for a month by Laurie's band at the Storyville Club in Frankfurt, Germany, but stayed on with the band and accompanied them back for a scheduled recording session in New York.

late what he is saying. music is only a hobby with him—he plays trombone—and his actual work was "in whisky" which we have somehow come to believe means he had a still in the back yard although he insists it was imporrrrrting. he is a country boy, from near edinburgh, and fell in love with vermont. we may very well find a new couple settling in our community. he sounds exactly like something from an english mystery story. ken swears he has a kilt in his luggage which is stored in new york. i served them pancakes for breakfast, a good old yankee custom which puzzled both of them. she was a little more equal to pancakes, since they are served in germany, but ken pointed out that pancakes were more usually served for tea, were they not?

now i must stop. i have to fill out a form for the international who's who, listing my clubs.

much much love from all, and write soon. keep well. i will soon send more data on our growing international family.

love,

s.

•  •  •

[To Stanley Hyman]

november 20 [1962?]

stanley, here is a prediction for you. as soon after christmas as possible, with the utmost discretion and thoroughness, you will provoke a quarrel with me, on whatever subject, in spite of all pacific attempts of mine (and i will be extremely cautious, having this prediction in mind). you will therefore arrange to go off to new york in december in a state of domestic warfare, justifying you in whatever big city plans you can make.

•  •  •

## [To Sally]

wednesday [December 5, 1962]

dear sally,

the first part of this letter is going to be very critical indeed, and i want you to read it twice and pay attention to it. i have waited this long to write because i did not want to write an angry letter, but you can hardly suppose that we are delighted with you.

we were simply heartbroken over your reports. you know what they said, and i imagine you agree, but what i am afraid of is that you will revert to your old habit of ignoring what seems to you unpleasant, and not profit from the very good suggestion that your teachers made. you cannot get passing grades in a good school without making a real effort to understand the work and learn.

understanding these things may make the difference between staying at the school or coming back to north bennington. and remember that you are not giving in, or humiliating yourself, or yielding in any way; you stay the same sally, only nicer, if you try to get along better.

there. now no more. perhaps all of this has been unnecessary and you have already begun a reform. i think perhaps this may be so, because you certainly seemed at thanksgiving to be sweeter and prettier than when you went away in the fall. i do not like to say that we have higher hopes of you than of our other children, because that implies a comparison i think is ridiculous, but there is no doubt but what you are enormously talented and intelligent, and i have always hoped, as you know, that you will be a writer. there are lots of good books just waiting to be written, and i can hardly write them all myself, you know.

here is a funny story: a week or so ago, on a saturday night, three carloads of f.b.i. men drove up to arlington and arrested one of the ten most wanted criminals in the country,* who had been staying

---

* David Stanley Jacubanis, arrested November 21, 1962.

quietly at the green mountain inn there. he had been there since last april, arriving in a stolen jaguar which he parked in a barn and never used, and with lots and lots of money which turned out to be the proceeds of a bank robbery in boston. he told the inn people that he was a business man recovering from an operation, so he went for long walks, and went fishing, and hung around the village of arlington until everyone got to know him quite well, and altogether he got to be a very familiar character, and everyone liked him very much. he made friends with one of the waitresses at the inn, and took her out several times, bringing her down to bennington college on saturday nights to the foreign movies, and afterwards to the rain barrel for a cup of espresso. he was finally caught because the f.b.i. had traced him approximately to this section of the country, and had put up special posters in all the local post offices with his picture and offering a reward. the rumor is that many of his friends in arlington recognized his picture at once, but being good vermonters they minded their own business and would have thought it contemptible to turn in a neighbor for a reward. at any rate, some rat finally did turn him in, so the f.b.i. arrived with machine guns and searchlights and surrounded the house of the waitress where he was waiting for her to get on her coat and hat to come down to the college to attend the modern dance recital. naturally he was not carrying a gun to a dance recital, so when the f.b.i. turned the searchlights on the house and shouted for him to come out quietly he came out quietly and surrendered without any trouble, although i gather the waitress made quite a scene and no wonder, since she was all dressed up to go out. they have taken him off to boston to jail, and he will no doubt be given a stiff prison term, and his arlington friends are already gathering together a collection of greeting cards and cartons of cigarettes and baskets of fruit to send him.

the punch line to the story is that the f.b.i. of course took apart his room in the inn to see if they could find the rest of the loot from the boston robbery; they cut up the mattress and took out the linings of all his clothes and tested the floor for loose boards, and so on. what they found was a copy of merricat on his bedside table, with a bookmark showing that he was about halfway through. it belonged to the owners of the inn, who refused to let the f.b.i. take it away with his other stuff, so the poor book was tested for fingerprints and given back. many people in arlington think it would be a nice gesture if i sent him another copy, autographed, and i think i will, as soon as i find out which prison he is in, and which alias to autograph it to.

I wrote about this to my publisher and they were very much amused, and the story will probably turn up as a publicity release. all the new york newspapers are on strike, however, and we have not had any papers for several days. poor merricat. she was tenth on the new york times list last sunday, sixth week on the list, but there will not be any list next sunday and maybe by the time the list is out again we will have dropped off the bottom. it is still selling very well indeed, and as a matter of fact is seventh in publishers weekly, which is the other important listing. there are still rave reviews coming in, and the publishers have just ordered a sixth printing, which is very good indeed. it has sold nearly forty thousand copies.

barbara has just arrived with the mail. she gets it every morning. i no longer go out of the house.

love,

m.

•  •  •

[To Geraldine and Leslie Jackson]

january 2 [1963]

dearest mother and pop,

just a short letter to say thank you very very much for the check and for the most handsome plates; they are beautiful.

we had a wild and exciting christmas, and even young miles seemed to enjoy himself.

my book has been nominated for the national book award, which is very exciting. the award will almost certainly go to katherine anne porter* but even being nominated is a great compliment. there is some great plan afoot to make my book into a broadway play, although no one quite seems to understand it, play producers being the kind of people they are. imagine how it would feel if it turned out to be one of those things that ran for two nights and closed?†

the temperature has stayed below zero for about four days now, down to twenty below one night, and of course the only car around that started was my brave new morris.

must stop writing and make lunch. happy new year, thank you again, and much love from all.

s.

• • •

[To Jeanne Beatty]

January 13 [1963]

Dear Jeanne,

Since I am not an absolute fool, it is beginning to get through to me that there is something very wrong, although I never before knew anyone too ungracious to acknowledge a book.

Pride would of course prevent my ever writing again, but I confess that I am far too curious to know what has happened, and why. Do you think you could possibly bring yourself to offer some explana-

---

* Other finalists for the award included John Updike, Dawn Powell, and Vladimir Nabokov. The winner was *Morte D'Urban*, a debut novel by J. F. Powers (Doubleday, 1962).
† How prescient Shirley was—David Merrick's big musical would open and close soon afterward. There were only nine performances, and it was a critical flop. None of the family got to see it.

tion? Break off all communication if you like but find some way, if you can, to end my absolute bewilderment.

Best wishes, in any case.

S.

*This letter is never answered and their correspondence ends. Ruth Franklin, who uncovered the Beatty letters, reports that Beatty never opened one of the last letters, but it was saved, along with all of the other letters Shirley had sent.*

•  •  •

[To Carol Brandt]

January 27 [1963]

Dear Carol,

Your nice letter did more for our Sally's morale than anything you can imagine; she does not really think that the story will sell (although, like all of us, she hopes), but the knowledge that she is one of your clients, and is taken seriously enough to have An Agent, is world-shaking. She is, of course, working on another story.

Which is more than you can say for her mother. I am on the fringe of an idea for a new book. Just kind of circling around it. I am anxious to get to work, and in that irritable state where I am furious with myself because nothing happens. I could have used that idea of Sally's but I suppose swiping plots from your own daughter is not cricket.

I have known Barbara Lawrence* for twenty-five years. We had not seen each other for many years until sometime ago when I had lunch with her and Betty Pope, and we had a lovely time remember-

* Barbara Lawrence was a features editor at *McCall's* in the 1950s and 1960s.

ing old days. I'd very much like to see her again, although the very thought of coming to New York sends me into a quite serious parox-ysm of terror.

Best, and thanks again for Sally's boost.

Shirley

. . .

[To Geraldine and Leslie Jackson]

friday [March 1963]

dearest mother and pop,

i have not written in a long time, i know, and i am sorry, but things have been so tumultuous around here that there just seems to be no time at all.

i want to start right off by explaining my present situation to you, this being one of the main reasons i haven't written. i have started psychoanalysis, after fighting and arguing and protesting; i never believed in it or trusted it (i always felt it was a little bit like christian science) and yet now here i am, and all sorts of queer things are happening to me. stanley, and barbara and murry, plus our doctor, prevailed on me to try, and there is a very good man in bennington, although for the life of me i couldn't tell you what he looks like or what his office looks like, so off i go twice a week at twenty-five bucks an hour. now i am appalled at how far gone i was before i would agree to see him. last thanksgiving was the last time i had been out of the house until i went to see him in february. it was literally impossible for me to go through the door; if i tried, i would start to shake and my legs would give way and everything would go around and around and i would begin to pass out, unless i got back inside fast. it was very strange and most unpleasant, and it kept getting worse, with all kinds of wild attacks of panic and

nightmares and finally i could not even answer the phone. oliver
had me taking tranquillizers all day long but all they did was keep
me kind of stupid but still frightened all the time. it's a classic case
of acute anxiety, i know now. i once read somewhere that acute
anxiety is one of the most terrible ailments possible and i would be
willing to go along with that. my first appointment was on a friday
afternoon at five-thirty, and i was fortified with my usual tranquillizers, a sedative injection from oliver, two stiff drinks, and stanley
and barbara, barbara to drive and stanley to get me from the car
into the office. i think getting out of my car in front of the doctor's
house was the most terrifying minute of my life. his office is part of
his house, and luckily the doctor was waiting for us because i was
ready to turn around and head for home. the doctor was most reassuring and comfortable and i think the most wonderful minute of
my life was when he said quite casually that of course this condition could be helped; why had i waited so long? stanley and barbara
came back for me at the end of the hour and when i got home i
looked around the house and got a sudden very clear happy picture
of what it might be like to be free again, and i told stanley i was
going to have the fastest analysis on record because i was in such a
hurry to be well. as it happened—i understand it is frequently this
way—the first weeks i moved with astonishing speed. at the end of
two weeks i took my first step, which was driving myself with stanley along to get me from the car to the office, and my next trip i
went alone. my big fear was that the car would get stuck in the
snow while i was alone, but it didn't, and since then i have been
driving over and back by myself. my next steps were really funny.
stanley and i got the car one morning, and drove to the post office,
and then, with stanley practically leading me, we went in and i remembered the combination of the mailbox and opened it—thank
heaven it opened the first time around—and then ran like crazy for
the car while stanley got the mail. the next day the same thing, only
that time i waited until he got the mail and we went out together.
the next day he sat and waited in the car and i went in and got the
mail alone. each time i took a new step i would have a terrible

after-effect of terror and trembling and gasping for breath but each time i did something a second time the after-effect was less. finally there was a day when i drove down alone, went into the post office alone, and got the mail. that one was a bad day afterwards but i was so triumphant that i didn't really care.

we tried the same process with my going into the grocery, and that was nice because i got a rousing reception there, and i even bought a loaf of bread the first day. after that we went through the same process with my going into bennington and into a couple of stores there, so that now, although still at considerable cost in fear, i can function almost normally. i was amazed and fascinated by the whole process, because it was so completely learning to do things <u>alone</u>, like a baby learning to walk. i am writing it in detail because i think it might interest you, too. also i am determined not to write a book about it. anyway i could watch myself getting frightened and each new step was a great triumph. along with all of this has gone a kind of unbelievable confusion, walking the floor all night crying and feeling perfectly dreadful over something i can't even remember the next day, and the most horrible, perfectly obvious delusions. i see the doctor on fridays and mondays, because he spends the middle of the week in new york, and around about tuesday night things start to get bad, and i start inventing delusions and of course when stanley tells me they aren't true i get furious and altogether give him a very bad time. i have the doctor's new york phone number in case i get very bad but so far i have not been desperate enough to call him and as i seem to get better (it changes back and forth; one day i am fine, and the next depressed and desolate, with no cause at all) i am hoping never to have to use it. when college started and stanley was away all day i had some very bad times because i was so afraid of being alone, but that is going too,

> [unfinished and unsigned, and
> probably not sent]

·  ·  ·

[To Sally]

saturday [spring 1963]

sarricat.

i hope by now you have dad's letter and the rejection slip and know that we are really still here. i have not written because my hands have been bad, because i have been all wound up with the doc, because i have been trying to write a review, because i am lazy.

since last monday i have:

DRIVEN TO THE POST OFFICE WITH DAD AND WAITED WHILE HE GOT THE MAIL.

DRIVEN BARRY TO SCHOOL.

DRIVEN TO THE STORE WHILE BARRY WENT INSIDE.

DRIVEN MYSELF TO THE DOC WITH DAD.

DRIVEN TO THE POST OFFICE WITH DAD, GONE INSIDE, OPENED MAILBOX BEFORE RUNNING AWAY.

DRIVEN TO THE POST OFFICE WITH DAD, GONE INSIDE, OPENED MAILBOX, GOTTEN MAIL AND PACKAGES.

DRIVEN MYSELF TO THE DOC WITH DAD.

GONE ALL ALONE TO THE DOC BY TAXI, ROADS BEING BAD.

DRIVEN TO THE STORE WITH DAD, LEAVING DAD AT DOOR OF STORE, GONE INSIDE, COLLECTED PACKAGE OF GROCERIES.

it gets easier and easier. when i ordered my groceries this morning i told them i believed it was the last time; next week i want to do the shopping myself. also get the mail myself.

wait till you see the new kitchen. and the new dining room. and the new living room. and the new hall.

all send love. work hard keep well try to get some sleep and enjoy yourself.

new stories?

love love

m.

. . .

## [Letter to self, 1963?]

it is now clear to me—after a year spent hoping and endeavoring to make sense from an impossible situation—that stanley intends at all costs to obstruct my serious writing in any way he can. he is perfectly happy with my money-writing, happy to think that after so much work i have at last achieved a point where I can make a great deal of money, which he cannot, by simply writing. that i should do anything more, anything he cannot participate in, is horrible to him. consequently he will not allow me to write anything in which I feel that i am doing more than only writing for money.

please, that i should remember. remember, first, that what i write or want to write is to be kept to myself. remember, second, that judgment warped by dreams of money, and visions of envy, is not judgment, but handicap. remember, third, that one world is writing and one is not, and from the one which is not, it is not possible to understand the one which is.

the beauty of words coming is mine. let me not talk about it. this is prayer. please make it come all right. please make it say the things it should. please make it be good. please let me not tell him or show it to him or answer him when he asks what i am doing. please let it be mine, and not soiled, and not ruined, and not hurt, by jealousy. please just let me write what i want to, and not be stopped.

i will not be afraid. i will not run away again.

it should be clean now, clean enough to start again and keep going without fault. without feeling it right i should not start, and so often i have been confused, but i will not be confused any more. i am proud and alone and i will not be hurt by stupidity which only knows what is going on afterwards. i will be not afraid. i will not be afraid. i will do what I am set to do and nothing else. i will not be afraid. i can not be afraid. i will do what i am set to do and nothing else. i will not be afraid. i will not be afraid. i will do what i am set to do and nothing else. i will not be afraid. ever again. i will not be afraid. i will not be afraid. i will not.

[unsigned]

.   .   .

[To Sally]

[March 1963]

dr sarricat

short letter because you will be coming home so soon.

i've been going to the doc by myself these last few times and today i daringly went into bennington and actually into two stores. i can go to powers and get the mail without much trouble.

very difficult for me to write because when they fixed my typewriter they made it too tight and the paper won't move smoothly but catches and pulls, and all the keys are stiff. i can't write unless the typewriter is rattling and shaking and pieces are falling off.

lots and lots and lots of love.

m.

.   .   .

[To Abby Fink, one of Stanley's literature students at
Bennington College, and later a close friend of Shirley's]

friday [April 1963]

dear abby,

i am at present enchanted by a lady named edith thompson who
with a young sailor named bywaters did to death mr thompson. edith
and byw. were both hanged in england in 1922, and ever since earnest people have been trying to say that edith was innocent and that
she was convicted because byw. foolishly kept the daily letters she
sent him when he was at sea and because they are passionate love
letters she was actually convicted of immorality and not murder. her
letters are full of passages about how she is going to have to wait for
her lover boy to come home because she gave her husband the stuff
in his tea that morning and he noticed the bitter taste and she is
afraid that she will not be able to give him anything with a bitter
taste any more and she tried the ground glass in his oatmeal three
times but the third time the glass was not fine enough and he got a
piece caught in his tooth but she is saving a brand new lightbulb
which she just bought to use after he stops being suspicious and she
wishes to hell bywaters would come home so he could help her because she is having a tough time trying to swing it alone. this among
long passages about how she loves her sailor boy and how she hates
her husband and how happy they would be without him. the earnest
people who say she had nothing to do with the murder of her husband read all the bitter taste and ground glass passages as kind of poetry and at the trial bywaters said yes, he got the letters and yes, he
read the parts about the ground glass etc. but he thought mrs
thompson was just kidding. she did not save any of his letters and i
am trying to make up for this by sketching out his probable answers.
thus:

dear mrs thompson,
got your last and thanks for writing. it is nice of you to call me

darling and lover boy just like my mother does, it makes me very homesick. no, i will not be back in england for another six weeks, but will surely phone you when i get in and maybe we can take in a show or something if mr. thompson would like to. please do not write me any more, though, about light bulbs and ground glass and tea with a bitter taste, because my stomach is already quite upset what with being at sea the way i am, and always delicate anyway. well, must close now the captain is calling me.

Best regards to you and mr. thompson,

very sincerely,

p. bywaters.

they stabbed poor old thompson on the street corner near his house, when he was coming home with his wife from the theatre, and mrs thompson told the cops right off that bywaters did it and they read all the letters in court and bywaters spent the whole time with his face hidden but mrs thompson was pleased and kept nodding at the good parts. poor bywaters tried to say he was not guilty at first, but mrs thompson kept saying he did it and she was very much surprised when it turned out that everyone thought she was in on it because she said she just stood there wringing her hands. I am very glad they hanged her. She must have been extremely clumsy, but I wonder about bywaters; he was hanged on mrs thompson's evidence, and he finally pled guilty and tried to get her off.

[unsigned, and probably not sent]

•   •   •

[To Sally]

thursday [April 1963]

salliblu

i was delighted to hear that you are working on that story. i am still finishing my notes for you, but somehow there has not been much time to get to the typewriter. we have had a very busy social life which shows no signs of ending.

nine magic wishes is to be published on april 29; i should have copies of the book any day now.

carol called the other day to say that the movie of hill house was finished and the company said it was breathtaking, superb, absolutely faithful to the book, a great movie. they want it to open at radio city. they have a print of the movie at their offices in new york and we were invited to come down for a private showing any time. i lost my nerve at the idea of driving to new york but carol says that since the movie will not be released before summer we can come down any time for the private showing, so i can wait and gather courage. the doc gave me a new pill. it's bigger than the others at least.

so write soon. much much love from all; work hard, work hard, work hard.

love,

m.

. . .

[To Geraldine and Leslie Jackson]

wednesday [April 1963]

dearest mother and pop,

it was good to get your nice letters and to talk to you the other day. i am glad you are reassured about me, since there really is nothing to worry about now. i am making very quick progress, my doctor says, and my big trouble now is that i am not yet strong enough to hang on to the gains i make, so that i backslide very often. also one result of all this is a complete mental tumult, so that i cannot trust my own reactions or opinions; everything changes from day to day and there is no sense of proportion, so that i felt perfectly awful a day or so ago because i broke a dish and went around feeling miserable all day and looked like a tragic heroine when stanley came home and thought he was unkind because he could not see how serious it was to break a dish. he learned quite a while ago not to laugh out loud when i did this. and some days i am so happy it is unbelievable and it becomes terribly important to do something like making a cheesecake for laurie and corinne. these are perfectly "normal" reactions to my present stage, and i only wish i could write them down as they happen but it is impossible; i can only write the barest details because of course i know really that these things are not sensible.

what "ails" me, pop, is what they used to call a nervous breakdown. and the really surprising thing about it is that it started perhaps eight years ago, as nearly as i can discover, and has been getting worse ever since. oliver points out that his records show that it was eight years ago when he first started giving me tranquilizers because i was so jumpy all the time, although we agreed that if he had suggested my going into therapy then i would have thought he was batty. anyway the analyst, perhaps the only irish psychoanalyst in the business, says things are going fine.

tomorrow night we leave for michigan, which is a big step ahead for me. i have been in the car as far as north adams, about thirty miles away, but otherwise not away from home for more than a trip to bennington. we have a bedroom on the train (i am still not equal to flying) and we get on at nine-thirty with a bottle of bourbon and a bottle of scotch and wake up at six a.m. in detroit. then on to east lansing where stanley gives a lecture and attends a conference and where i am a kind of visiting writer, and then home saturday night. i am very much excited at going and not at all frightened. laurie will drive us to albany to the train.

our friends barbara and murry karmiller have been unbelievably kind and helpful during all this bad time, and having both been in analysis and come through it all right they are quite a steadying influence on me. they keep telling me don't worry; it will all go away in time.

laurie has gotten a job for the summer. he will be a cashier at our new race track, and make fourteen bucks a day. the race track is the first in vermont, and we are all very excited about it; it is about ten miles from here; now we can do our betting nearer home. and laurie will pay us off if we win. although he still loves music, his new great love is photography. he has his own darkroom, and his senior thesis at the college is going to be a picture book; he will write a text and then illustrate it with photographs. he has barry camera-happy too, and they go off together on photographing trips, taking pictures of old barns and snowfalls and rusty farm equipment.

corinne and the baby are fine, corinne still managing to keep up with her painting and doing very well at it. we see a good deal of them, naturally, and grow more and more fond of corinne. young miles is becoming a terror. he has two teeth with which he bites people and is just starting to walk and pull down everything in sight. he is big and strong and very handsome, and very happy almost all the time.

joanne has been admitted to bennington this coming fall. she is wildly happy because it was the only place she wanted to go, and we are all very pleased. she will of course live on campus, and come home perhaps once a week for dinner. she will not take stanley's courses. she is planning to spend the summer at home just relaxing. she is learning to drive, and wants to help out at home (i think it is high time she learned to cook, and i plan to leave her in charge when stanley and i go away).

sally is not doing at all well at school, but she called the other night and was most encouraging; her grades are better and she is working hard. we are very happy to find that she is making friends and is quite popular at school. we are praying that her grades will be good enough to let her go back to school next year. it would be ruinous to send her back to north bennington.

barry is doing fine and is quite happy with lots of friends and he is a boy scout and delighted with the little league, and busy all the time. he is off on his bike every saturday morning and is gone all day unless he gets hungry. i took him shopping with me yesterday partly because i do better with someone with me, but mostly because he needed shoes. he can go into the stores by himself and buy things, in case i feel like staying in the car.

as you can see the news is almost entirely good, and everything goes well.

everyone sends love, and write soon.

lots of love,

s.

•   •   •

[To Sally]

tuesday [May 1963]

dr salliblu

enclosed: allowance checks, for you and joanne. also enclosed: the sallirules.* let me know what you think of them.

came this morning a press release from the movie company about hillhouse. the movie is made—was photographed in england, partly at hatfield house, where elizabeth I was kept prisoner for several years, and partly at another great old house which was <u>already</u> haunted although only on fridays. they used the grounds at hatfield house which elizabeth always thought of with great tenderness. theodora is played by claire bloom who was the female star in olivier's richard III. julie harris is eleanor and someone named russ tamblyn is luke. i don't know who plays the doctor except in the press release he is no longer doctor montague.

<u>my</u> doctor is very well thank you. there seems to be progress. at any rate i keep going.

* The first draft of "Notes for a Young Writer," written for Sally and published posthumously by Stanley in *Come Along with Me.*

dad wants to tell you that he has been very busy and so could not write. he is sorry not to have had more time but when things let up a little you will hear from him.

lots and lots and lots of lv.

m

. . .

[To Carol Brandt]

July 2 [1963]

Dear Carol,

I know I should not complain of the Vermont heat but there is no doubt that it is hard to type when your fingers melt into the keys. Many thanks for checks, information on THE HAUNTING (and have you seen the little ads asking people who have seen ghosts to write in to MGM?), and information on English CAS-TLES.

We come to New York, I think, on July 30. I will have to let you know a more complete schedule as soon as I know myself, since I am apparently giving a lecture at Columbia one evening. Stanley now thinks that he will pass up the viewing of THE HAUNTING; the photograph on the cover of the paperback was too vivid; he loathes ghosts and scary things. I am very anxious to see it, and prepared to be terrified. And of course delighted to know that others are coming too.

My two big difficulties, which should be improved by the time I come down, are a reluctance to be packed in tightly anywhere (as in cocktail parties or traffic jams!) and a reluctance to go alone across open spaces (like walking down a street). Both are far easier if I am not alone, and perhaps if necessary Pat may let me borrow Julie again.

As far as THE FAMOUS SALLY BOOK is concerned, Stanley still likes it and thinks it is worth publishing. perhaps we should wait and talk about it when I am there.

I'll have a chance to see you and Pat, won't I, apart from the movie?

Best,

Shirley

•   •   •

[To Geraldine and Leslie Jackson]

wednesday [September 6, 1963]

dearest mother and pop,

happy birthday to mother; i hope it was one of the best.

everyone is well; young miles has eight teeth and is starting to walk. he is so big it is hard to believe he is not quite a year old, and very strong.

i am doing fairly well; i have not been doing any writing at all, not even letters—as you already know—and am beginning to have to accept the fact that i have a long siege ahead of me. i have done very well about traveling this summer, but still cannot do much alone. i am going to try to drive sally back to her school next week; joanne will come with me.

we saw the movie of "the haunting" in new york at a special preview. it is actually a very poor movie, the plot of the book changed radically, and far too much talk, but there are a couple of terribly frightening scenes in it and a lot of exciting camera work. stanley and i were both really scared, and the house is wonderful. it opened for some reason in albany, also when we were out of town, which was good, because we avoided the premiere; all the actors were there, and the director, and they made a big fuss which we were very glad to miss. it opens in new york on september 18.

big news now is the broadway play,* which is definite. at least they paid me a retainer of ten thousand dollars, which makes it definite enough for me. this is an advance against box office receipts; they expect to open the play either december or january, and everyone is very optimistic about it. i don't know how they could possibly make a play out of "castle" but they seem to think they can. i signed a thirty-four page contract in which i am called The Novelist and the guy who is doing the adaptation is called The Writer. The Writer gets flown economy fare to any city where the play opens but The Novelist has to get there on her own.

glad to get pop's letter this morning and know that you are well and looking forward to your trip. you'll have a wonderful time, and no asthma. our little trips have been fun, although mostly business; i did do a lecture in new york at columbia university, and it went very well. i was quite nervous ahead of time about getting frightened in the middle and having to stop, and stanley was ready to take over but actually once i started i forgot all about the panics and enjoyed myself. i have never been nervous about lecturing and have never minded doing it, so it's nice to know that i still can. i saw my doctor at his new york office the day after the lecture and he was very proud of me.

we took the children to atlantic city on an odd trip. they loved it because we traveled up the coast and stayed at seashore resorts which all seemed to have ferris wheels and wild rides, and the evenings were spent careening from one ride to another while stanley and i sat and watched the waves come in. and we all—even me—went swimming in the ocean.

stanley and i went to pennsylvania to see amish farmers and eat shoo fly pie and look for hex marks on barns. the country is perfectly lovely, but the shoo fly pie is awful and all the hex marks were on gift shops. the amish farmers were there, though, riding in buggies and blocking traffic. we stopped at tamiment, which is a big fancy sum-

---

* David Merrick's *We Have Always Lived in the Castle*.

mer resort where stanley has been asked to lecture next summer, and they asked me to lecture too; it means we would stay at the resort for a week, since the lectures are held on monday nights. we are not sure whether we could take a whole week of resort life, but the food is marvellous. we were invited to stay for lunch and it was the only good meal we had in pennsylvania. i am always surprised at the way these resorts are like little cities set out in the mountains, with new york papers delivered every day.

i will try to write again soon. i am trying to get back to work, have agreed to do a review for the herald tribune and have promised to start work on a new book this fall. since money still comes in every month from the last book it is hard to find an incentive to write a new one!

lots and lots of love to you both from all of us, and have a wonderful trip.

love,

s.

•   •   •

[To Libbie Burke]

October 24, 1963

Dear Libbie,

Thanks for your words about "The Haunting," although since I got paid in advance I don't really worry whether or not the movie is successful. I saw it last July at a private showing at the MGM place in New York, and found it quite scary, although very talk-y, and then took young Barry to see it here in Bennington, and nearly went to sleep; scariest part of the whole thing the second time was the parking ticket I got while I was in the movie. And Barry had not a bit of trouble sleeping afterwards.

I do love the house, though. It's a real house, decorations and all, an inn near London. Someday I will stay there.

Are we ever going to see you? It's been so long. Love from all,

Shirley

Part of my current writing block is a complete inability to write letters; I can barely manage.

. . .

[To Geraldine and Leslie Jackson]

nov. 4 [1963]

dearest mother and pop,

i imagine by the time this reaches you, you will be home and tanned and relaxed from your trip.

pictures of your great grandson enclosed. he celebrated his first birthday the end of september, and the following week his father celebrated his twenty-first, so we had some fine partying.

everyone here is well and as usual working hard. i have been doing some book reviewing for the new york herald tribune, and am now hopelessly involved in a review of the new critical parody about winnie the pooh, which has had me reading winnie the pooh for the last few days; before that i did dr. seuss, so i seem to be reading nothing but children's books. stanley's book of essays was published this week, to very good reviews, and he is quite pleased. you will have a copy soon.

laurie and corinne are doing well. corinne has left college because she simply couldn't manage with the baby, and is now learning to cook. she is doing fine, too. she has borrowed some of my cookbooks and she keeps turning out all kinds of delicacies.

joanne loves bennington college, although right now she seems to us to be rather more boy-crazy than education-crazy. she has a charming roommate and several very nice friends; they come here to dinner once a week.

sally, unfortunately, could not make a go of it at school. she came home last week and will not go back. we are very sorry, but at the same time we are convinced that she is better off at home. she is now going to the same doctor that i do, and is already considerably more calm. she is back in the north bennington high school, does not like it, but is working hard. the important thing, of course, is getting her to college in three years, and i think that the combination of hard work and the doctor will do it for her.

barry is growing up very fast. his two great interests now are boy scouts and his weekly dancing class, which he loves. he is getting so big and so busy that we hardly ever see him; he is home long enough to do his homework.

i just got a letter from a young actress wanting to know if i could help her get the lead part in the play of CASTLE. i had to write her telling her she had as much influence as i did. they are planning to start rehearsals early in january, which means the play should open in february. i am very curious about it, and am hoping to see the script. sorry this is such a short letter; i must get back back to winnie the pooh. but i did want to say welcome home, and to send you the pictures.

much love from all,

s.

•  •  •

[To Carol Brandt]

November 7 [1963]

Dear Carol,

I am in the disagreeable position of being most eager to get to work, with nothing at all to work on. If I do not find an idea soon I will have to steal one.

Best,

Shirley

. . .

[To Carol Brandt]

December 2 [1963]

Dear Carol,

I promised Pat that I would try his system of writing just anything at all for an hour or so every morning, so I will. He swears something will come of it, and I am ready to try anything.

I am heartbroken at the probability that I will not after all be able to come to New York this winter; I was looking forward to coming, but it does not seem possible to make arrangements.

Best,

Shirley

. . .

[To Carol Brandt]

February 21 [1964]

Dear Carol,

Stanley and I got home this morning from Indiana, and I got your telegram and letters. I am thrilled and happy over the story, and feel back in business again. Wonderful, wonderful; now I will write more.

Thanks for arranging things with Barbara Lawrence; I am happy to be seeing her again. We used to know each other quite well many years ago. And lunch at the Four Seasons awes me; I have never been there and would love to see it.

Stanley lectured at the University of Indiana, and because we are Professional People they gave us a tour of the Kinsey sex archives; I have never encountered such a mass of pornography in my life. (In all my varied experience!) Some of the material would make an interesting book; you couldn't show it to your mother but my, wouldn't it sell.

Best,

Shirley

. . .

[To Geraldine and Leslie Jackson]

tuesday [spring 1964]

dearest mother and pop,

everyone here is well, and looking forward to your coming in may. the weather should be lovely then and it will be just fine to see you. i will reserve rooms in the motel for you; i know our guest room bothers mother, with animals around.

there has been a man here taking my picture for the saturday evening post. i know it will turn out to be just as awful as my pictures always do, but they insisted. i have done an article which they are running probably in june, on the unpleasantness of european travel. of course i have never gone to europe so that made me the proper person to write it; i talked to everyone i could find who had gone, and made up a lot of interesting things and the post loved the article except they said it was too authentic; it sounded as though i had really been and was pretending not, so i had to go through and put in all kinds of disclaimers. if what i said sounds true i never want to go. i have also sold a story to the ladies home journal; these are the only things i've written this spring so i am selling one hundred percent. i am getting back to work very slowly; the doctor keeps urging me and so does stanley, but it is very hard to start again. things keep moving in spite of me, though; my agent found an old old story* and sold it to vogue and it has now been picked up for the best short stories of 1964; considering that it was written somewhere in the fifties it does sound silly. and my last book is being translated into french and things are coming out in paperback all the time.

sally and I go to the doctor twice a week, and one of us sits and reads in the waiting room while the other one goes in. he has done simply wonders for sally (for both of us, of course) and it is sometimes hard to remember what she was like six months ago. she is so much more relaxed and happy and cooperative, and quite pleasant. she has been trying to get into more activities around the school, although she hates the place, and her grades have improved. she helped to direct the senior play. she and i have planned an adventure; i am lecturing at new york university next week and am taking sally with me. i still do not dare go many places, particularly new york, alone, and of course sally is delighted to make the trip. we will be there for three days, and will go shopping and see movies and go to strange restaurants.

thanks again to the doctor's insistence i have accepted lecture dates right through the summer and winter and into next spring, and

---

* "Birthday Party."

at the end of the summer i go to the bread loaf writers' conference as short story lecturer, and i go alone; that is going to be the big test; i will be there for two weeks and stanley will come up to visit but not to stay. we are both visiting lecturers at columbia this summer; we only accepted if they promised to find us an air-conditioned room. and in may i lecture in chicago, to which i will have to travel by plane. stanley has a sabbatical so he will come too and we may spend a few days around chicago; in the meantime stanley has also lectures to do, and whenever possible i will go with him, so we are going to keep busy; each of us has three prepared lectures and they have to be carefully calculated not to overlap. we went to indiana where stanley worked, and we went by train, which was fun; stanley got the upper berth. we also spent two days at indiana being shown around the kinsey sex insititute, which has an enormous library of all kinds of pornography, and was fascinating. all of this i do with great trepidation, and batteries of pills, but i've been doing it. i can do almost anything i want at home, and i go to college functions, and out to lunch, and shopping in bennington, by myself; the only place i can't go is the grand union supermarket because it is so big. each adventure takes a little less pushing from the doctor. i am on a fairly strict diet—it can't be too strict, on top of everything else—and am losing weight slowly but regularly, so much so that none of my last summer's clothes will fit me now.

stanley is working very hard, and teaching goes well. his class is still the biggest at the college. we have had his tutees for brunch the last two sundays, four at a time, and they eat everything in sight, and curtsey politely when they leave.

joanne—now known as jai—is very happy at the college, and we seem to hear of her everywhere. she has two roommates, and they share a suite of two rooms which they have decorated with photographs of the beatles. they invited us for cocktails the other day and we had a lovely time, although it is an awful lot of beatles to take at one time. she and sally have become quite close, and sally goes up to visit her often; they still sing together beautifully.

old barry is the busiest of all of them, i think. he rides his bike into bennington to visit a redhead, and goes to all the school dances. his dearest friend right now is a young english boy, the son of a visiting sculptor at the college,* and barry has developed an english accent. the most wonderful part of it is that he has been invited to visit timmie in london next august, and it looks like he will go, and he will stay for a month. he has more than enough money saved up to finance the trip.

i am sending you two books. one is for each of you, but you must decide yourselves who gets which.

everyone sends much love, and it will be so good to see you.

love,

s.

•   •   •

[To Carol Brandt]

May 5 [1964]

Dear Carol,

Sally and I were disappointed at not seeing you in New York last week, but I hope your trip was as pleasant as ours was; we did an enormous amount of shopping and Sally met Pat and was vastly impressed. She almost promised to send him a manuscript. I almost promised too.

Right now it looks as though we will be spending a good deal of time in New York this summer, so I do hope we can get together.

I have a new typewriter, one downstairs now and one upstairs. I can type with both hands.

Best,

Shirley

•   •   •

* Sir Anthony Caro, a modernist British sculptor who preferred to use "found" industrial objects, taught for a year at Bennington College.

[To Carol Brandt]

May 8 [1964]

Dear Carol,

I have a problem. After my lecture at NYU the other day, a lady named Carol Drexler of Doubleday stayed for a few minutes to ask me if I was interested in doing juvenile for them. I was not until she suggested a fantasy, perhaps in the manner of the Oz books (which I confess without shame I love dearly) and this did tempt me. I told her that under no circumstances could I possibly agree to do any book until I had written a novel for Pat, but that I was definitely interested in, say, a year or so. She has now written me confirming her interest and asking if I will continue to think about it for after the novel.

Can I agree to do the book for her? I do really find the idea fascinating (not a book like the Oz books, but an individual juvenile fantasy) and would love to do it, but am wondering if you will okay it and if any such book ought to be submitted to Pat first; might he even like it instead of a new novel?

Best,

Shirley

•  •  •

[To Carol Brandt]

June 2 [1964]

Dear Carol,

I am writing that I am happy to grant the extension on the play of CASTLE.

Now I do not know whether this will please you or not. I became so enchanted with the idea of the fantasy book for children that I started making notes and then writing a little and have now started it and like it very much.* I would like to go on with it (on assumption that it will not take more than a couple of months to finish) and hope that Pat will want it. Since I do not seem to be writing any other kind of book I thought this might be a good running start. What do you think?

I expect to be in New York the second week in July; hope I can see you then.

Best,

Shirley

•  •  •

*After Shirley writes the satiric essay "No, I Don't Want to Go to Europe" for* The Saturday Evening Post, *she receives a torrent of angry, insulting mail reminiscent of what she received after "The Lottery" was published, sixteen years earlier.*

June 25 [1964]

Dear Carol,

We are coming to New York on Sunday July 5, leaving Thursday July 9; I would love to see you any of the days between, whichever suits you; I will hold things open until I see you or hear from you.

Something bothers me. As you must know, I have never paid much attention to letters or reactions on any of my stuff, and generally can ignore nasty letters. The Post piece, however, has given me a very bad three weeks, and I am a little sick. In the first place, they printed my married name and address on the piece, so that every

---

* *The Fair Land of Far* (unfinished).

crackpot in the world could write me freely, and I have had letters which it shames me to read, and which are full of the most unpleasant personal abuse. Now the Post appears this week with a column and a half of further letters, not as abusive, but still disagreeable. I do not, heaven knows, think much of the Post's readership, but I am now feeling that I would never like to be so exposed again. I feel as though my other work is jeopardized by this ugly response. I am really quite upset.

So. I will retreat to my lovely imaginary country.

Best,

Shirley

•  •  •

[To Geraldine Jackson]

sunday [August 1964]

dearest mother,

we got home from new york last night, to find pop's letter, and i am so concerned and sad to hear that you are still not well. it is such a miserable thing to have, and so uncomfortable, and stanley and the kids all want me to send you their love and sympathy.

we put barry on the plane for england last thursday, and he looked very small indeed in his new raincoat getting on that enormous jet, but we got a cable saying that he had arrived and loved it, so i guess he is having a wonderful time. stanley and i spent the week at columbia university being visiting lecturers at their writers' conference, and except for stanley's not feeling well we had a fine time, meeting people and talking about books and i was made an honorary member of the men's faculty club and allowed to sign checks there.

no new grandchild yet, although corinne would be just as glad to get it over with. laurie is still up in the air about jobs and moving. he is now working at the race track and enjoying it; stanley and i went to the track one night (i broke even!) and watched laurie paying out vast sums of money and looking efficient.

we keep busy. if stanley is well i am going to the bread loaf writers' conference on wednesday, where i will lecture and give forth with profound words about Writing, and spend two weeks being cool on top of bread loaf mountain, although perhaps a little stir crazy. it is only about a hundred miles from here, so i can get home without too much trouble.

we spent last weekend at a big fancy home in long island, where i rang the bell beside my bed and the maid brought my breakfast on a tray, and where they had an electrified tree; when they wanted coffee they brought out the coffeepot and plugged it into the tree. we want a tree like that.

please do feel well very soon; i will try to write as soon as i can, and in the meantime everyone sends much much love. all our very very best,

s.

• • •

[To Carol Brandt]

September 8 [1964]

Dear Carol,

We were in New York, at Columbia, and left in considerable haste and worry; Stanley was suddenly so sick that it was necessary to get him right home and—we thought—into the hospital. Just to steal some of his thunder, I fell downstairs going all the way sitting down and it is only the last day or so that I have been able to do anything that required sitting, like typing; I take my meals standing and manage to drive with extreme caution. I am now getting back to work, though, and since I did some work on my little book earlier in the summer I am quite optimistic.

We have a new granddaughter,* two days old.

Best,

Shirley

•   •   •

[To Geraldine and Leslie Jackson]

monday [September 1964]

dearest mother and pop,

i have been doing stories for the past couple of weeks and have not had time for much else. it is also a very busy time of year, with school getting under way and the college social season starting. although we are staying far away from most social events right now. we are in a most conservative, bed-by-eleven state.

i don't know if i told you quite how sick stanley was. the doctor in new york really frightened me about getting him home and into the hospital at once, and then when we got home oliver, our doctor, managed to scare stanley about a coronary, so that even though the hospital was not necessary stanley went to bed docilely and stayed there and now is firmly in oliver's clutches. oliver comes once a week to give him a shot, and poor stanley has lost forty pounds and is taking all kinds of pills and going to bed early and not working so hard and generally reforming in all directions. we are all, except barry, staying on the diet with stanley. sally has lost about fifteen pounds and so have i. stanley lost so much in the first week or so; by giving up salt and taking dope. i finally left him in care of sally and joanne

* Gretchen Anne Cardinal Hyman was born September 6, 1964.

and went off to work at bread loaf; by the time i left he was up and around but very grouchy and the girls apparently had quite a time with him; i was gone two weeks and it was during that time he lost all that weight, so i got quite a shock when i came home. i am now getting to be quite a low-calorie cook. i have ransacked our local supermarkets and brought home all the diet foods i could find. since this diet is more or less permanent i have just settled down to live with it.

i actually had my last good meal at bread loaf, when a group of us went to the blueberry hill inn and had a wonderful dinner. since then i have been hungry. bread loaf was most enjoyable; i did my work well enough to be invited back next year, and i spent a lot of the two weeks sleeping. this entire summer was somehow devoted to stanley's illness, since it began with the asthma early in the summer and got worse and worse. as a result i realized as soon as i got away that i was worn out, so bread loaf turned into a vacation. i lived with the rest of the staff in a lovely old house on campus, and since it is one of the traditions there that the staff never mixes with the paying customers, we got to be a little private group, eating together and gathering every day at twelve and at five in our private little bar, where we had a bartender and an inexhaustible supply of bloody marys. i gave four lectures, conducted three reading sessions, and had conferences with six students, which meant that i had something to do every day. i also got some writing done.

i'm working very hard right now, and enjoying it more than i have in a long time. i divide my time between stories and the children's book. i give two lectures in new york state this month, and then in the spring stanley has a sabbatical and we are going to chicago and michigan and eventually to georgia; stanley has been asked to do a memorial introduction to the books of flannery o'connor, a very good writer who died quite young a month or so ago, and she lived in georgia so we must go there to meet her family. neither of us has ever been in the south, and it will be an interesting experience. we will drive down, and take our time about it, and see some old southern mansions.

sally has changed so that you would not recognize her; one result of her going to the doctor has been that she has gone out and made friends, and is now involved in a great social whirl.

laurie and corinne are quite discouraged about the job situation. laurie spent last week in new york seeing people and had not much luck, and the people who own their little house are raising the rent considerably so laurie and corinne are most anxious to move. right now laurie is still working at the track, but he must find something this month. the new baby—gretchen—is charming and as a result of being so late she is not red and wrinkled, but perfectly beautiful. she looks very much like corinne. miles is lively and cheerful and talking a lot.

as i say, we are being very quiet. we are cutting down on holidays, too, so that we have already decided on a much quieter christmas this year. stanley's brother and his wife, who were separated for several years, are now together again, so stanley's mother will spend christmas with them this year. they will all be up thanksgiving, though.

must stop now. please write, keep well, and go out and have a piece of chocolate cream pie and think of us.

much much love,

s.

•  •  •

[To Carl Brandt, Carol's son and an

agent at Brandt & Brandt]

September 28 [1964]

Dear Carl,

I am frankly a little stunned at the idea that of all the stories I have ever written Martha Foley* should choose PEANUTS† as one of the

---

* Martha Foley founded *Story* magazine in 1931 with her husband, Whit Burnett.
† "One Ordinary Day, with Peanuts."

fifty best stories. Also nothing is said about payment. I am signing the contracts, however, and returning them to you.

I would be grateful if you could explain to Houghton Mifflin that I do not think that my religious affiliation is any of their business.

I am sorry to sound so grumpy, but this whole business seems faintly odd to me.

Best,

Shirley Jackson

•   •   •

[To Carol Brandt]

October 3 [1964]

Dear Carol,

Welcome back, and here is a story for you. I do hope you had a wonderful time and ate and ate and ate.

Eating is at present the center of our lives. Stanley is much recovered, and on a very strict diet; he has lost a great deal of weight and must keep on, so we live in a low-calorie atmosphere.

The little book goes well, although I set it aside to do some stories.

I am sitting down again, and working hard and joyfully. We have a new granddaughter, by the way, and our maples have all turned gold.

Best,

Shirley

• • •

"The Neurotic Personality of our Time"

[To Carol Brandt]

October 14 [1964]

Dear Carol,

I really do not think the story is what he has in mind, but I'll get it off to you in a few days and you can decide. It's really quite a nasty little story.*

I wrote Pat, and Sally, who adores him, made him an enchanting little card. Have you any word on how he is?

* "The Possibility of Evil" will be published (posthumously) in *The Saturday Evening Post* in December 1965. It will win the Edgar Allan Poe Award for Best Short Story.

I find that every now and then I lift my head from calorie-counting and dream of that dessert at the Four Seasons.

Best,

Shirley

Just heard about Pat.

*Editor Pat Covici (1885–1964) has just died. Shirley had become very fond of Pat, had dedicated* We Have Always Lived in the Castle *to him, and is deeply affected and saddened by his death.*

. . .

[To Carol Brandt]

October 30 [1964]

Dear Carol,

Here is my new story—not the one I thought to do for the Post, but a <u>newer</u> one—and I do hope you like it.

I am very sad that you are confused over Sally's story, because Stanley and I both thought it was a beautiful job, difficult and disturbing; I suppose you could say that it was about the myths of the changing of the seasons. I did not show her your letter, of course, nor mention that you had written about it. The poor child made the mistake of handing in the story as an assignment in English and is still smarting over the treatment she got from the teacher, who read half of it to the class and then stopped and asked "Does anyone really want me to go on with this?"

Anyway, I hope you'll want to send it to one or two places just to see what happens. I have one more story to do, and then I think another book. I have put the children's book aside for a while; it got me started writing again but I would rather do a more grownup type of thing, I think.

Best,

Shirley

• • •

[To Corinne, Laurie, Miles, and Gretchen,

now living in New York City]

tuesday [November 1964]

dear c/l/m/g,

i am writing although there is no news at all. joanne is coming for dinner tonight, which makes for a pretty exciting day.

i hope the records* come before saturday. thank you very much for getting them, and will you let us know how much they cost so we can reimburse you. i hope they are not too ghastly. barry let me watch the beatles on television the other night and i think they are fine but then he made me listen to people called the animals and the rolling stones and my goodness. they are all twelve years old, i think.

we solved the storm window problem by ordering two metal windows for the study. we figure at the rate of two windows a year we may have all metal windows before the house sinks to the ground. i do feel that all the beams are loose as a result of barry's records.

the handle fell off the refrigerator again.

dad hit 180 pounds and now he won't weigh himself anymore.

barry is borrowing a car motor from bennington college (why does

* Probably bullfight music, which Shirley loved and could not find in the Bennington record store.

bennington college have a car motor?) and is going to put it in the cellar and teach me how to take it apart. i will then be able to make all repairs on morris.

i spoke to corinne's mother the other day and invited them for thanksgiving but they have family coming. we are going to miss you. you are coming for christmas aren't you? it's very lonely without you.

everyone sends love; write soon; keep well. all our love to m and g.

m.

• • •

[To Carol Brandt]

November 6 [1964]

Dear Carol,

I am very curious indeed to know who my new editor will be. Since my son Laurie and family are now living in New York City, I have been looking for an excuse to make a flying trip there, and may manage it to meet a new editor.

Working, working.

Best,

Shirley

• • •

[To Carol Brandt]

November 17 [1964]

Dear Carol,

I am quite excited about having a new editor, and from what you say I should think that Corlies Smith would be the wise choice, since I do of course want someone who is interested in fiction and knows my work. I would very much like to meet Mr. Smith but don't know when or how I can come down, since from now until Christmas things keep quite busy around here. We are planning to come down in January; is that too late? I would like to get down to see Laurie sometime, but am afraid that that will have to be put off. And, too, I would like to have some kind of book started to show a new editor.

I gather that my two stories are not doing well. I am discouraged but not entirely. And blessings on you for sending out Sally's story; she was wild with excitement when the letter came from The New Yorker.

I may honestly end up writing a low-calorie cookbook.

Best,

Shirley

•  •  •

[To Laurie and family]

thurs. [November 1964]

this letter came back because i—of course—had the wrong address. so i can now put in the green stamps.

snowing.

they fixed the refrigerator but dad's desk chair fell apart again. it was once too often; i am ordering him a new one today. you remember how it happens: first the chair cracks and joggles and then slowly comes apart and dad leaps up and the chair goes out from under him and he leans over and his lighter falls out of his pocket and he leans over to pick up the lighter and his cigarettes fall out of his pocket and he leans over to pick up his cigarettes and cracks the side of his head against the desk . . .

love to all.

m.

•    •    •

[To Carol Brandt]

November 24 [1964]

Dear Carol,

I have decided to put those two stories completely out of mind and I am making little tentative pokes at a book. I want to have something for you before I come down in January.

Best,

Shirley

•    •    •

## [To Geraldine and Leslie Jackson]

january 11 [1965]

dearest mother and pop,

am sorry to be late writing you but we just got back from new york; i am using my new typewriter and nothing is where it ought to be, so my typing is odd, to say the least.

we loved all your wonderful presents, and many many thanks. The check is going to go into our summer fund; stanley has a sabbatical this year, and we are thinking of england, or taking a cruise, or some such wild crazy thing, and putting aside money for it now.

we had to go to new york on business; my editor at viking press died this summer (pat covici, whom i have known for a million years, and whose death upset me terribly) and it was necessary for me to meet and decide on a new editor, and a terrible thing it was. my agent interviewed several nice ambitious young men at viking, and finally decided on one and he took me to a fancy lunch and it turned out he has a thirteen year old son just like barry so it will be all right; we can work together. all he really has to do is send me free books and take me to lunch and write me timidly that they are correcting my grammar. anyway the new typewriter is to start the book,* and i have a year and a half to write it in. the saturday evening post just bought my new story;† i am back in business.

we are still dieting, although it is difficult in new york. we are all well, had a wonderful christmas with grandchildren, and only wish you could have been here.

many many thanks and love from all of us. write soon.

s.

•　•　•

* *Come Along with Me,* unfinished, published by Viking Press in 1968.
† "The Possibility of Evil."

[To Carol Brandt]

January 20 [1965]

Dear Carol,

The advance from Viking is wonderful, and I am full of awe for you. I should finish the book easily in eighteen months, and certainly with peace of mind under these terms. Many thanks for planning it so thoughtfully.

Seeing you in New York was lovely, and I have had a nice note from Cork Smith saying how much he enjoyed lunch that day; so did I, and I look forward to working with him.

I hope that you notice that I am seriously at work at last; I have a new typewriter ribbon.

Many thanks again.

Best,

Shirley

•   •   •

*In February, Shirley develops pneumonia and is briefly hospitalized.*

[To Carol Brandt]

March 5 [1965]

Dear Carol,

Much to report. We are home from the south, after a splendid but tiring trip; I am supposed to be convalescent, cannot go up stairs, cannot lift anything or overdo in any fashion, take eight different kinds of pills and so on. It is a pleasure, anyway, to be half back at work; the hardest part of all of it is taking it easy.

I am getting to work on the Journal story, and it should not take long, although I must go slowly. I am supposed to keep telling myself "Slow slow" whatever I am doing; a person could go crazy.

I have not looked at the book for a while and am most anxious to get back to it.

I am sorry to sound so sloppy and self-absorbed. My whole life has been turned upside down in some lunatic fashion, and I can't seem to come to terms with things quite yet.

Best, and many thanks,

Shirley

I do sound sorry for myself—it's not really this bad!

• • •

[To Carol Brandt]

March 18 [1965]

Dear Carol,

Here is the Journal story. I realize that I must apologize for the abominable typing; I am working on a strange typewriter and we do not seem to get along.

All best,

Shirley

• • •

[To Carol Brandt]

April 8 [1965]

Dear Carol,

Delighted to hear that the story is okay for the Journal. I am feeling better and livelier every day, and so long as I don't get tired I can do anything I want, so I have been working. We have just come back from Wisconsin, where I read the first ten pages of the children's book and the first ten pages of the grownup book to a student audience, and they were very enthusiastic. As a result, of course, I am even more excited about both books.

The Viking check has still not come; are they just dragging their feet? Do you think we could get it regularly on the first of each month? I hate to bother you with this, but we depend on it.

Have a wonderful trip. I tried plane travel for the first time in years on this trip to Wisconsin and I must say the food is awful. Your route makes me believe that all those places really exist, and can be really visited.

Best,

Shirley

•   •   •

"Dear, you look so strange tonight."

*This is the last letter Shirley will write to her parents.*

[To Geraldine and Leslie Jackson]

may 12 [1965]

dearest mother and pop,

as you can imagine, we are both exhausted and have had enough traveling and lecturing to last us for quite a while. we have just come back from a trip that took us first to syracuse, where we both lectured, then to rochester, where stanley lectured at nazareth college then to akron, south bend, and finally chicago,* where i was resident lady lecturer for four days, meeting students and Talking about Writing, and giving a lecture and doing a radio program and having dinner with the president and going to teas and sherry parties (i loathe sherry) and brunches, then stanley went to macmurray college in illi-

* University of Chicago.

nois and lectured and then he lectured again in urbana and then we took four days driving home. from the day we left syracuse the weather was constantly over ninety. in chicago it was almost impossible to go outside in the heat. i lectured in an auditorium so hot i dripped all over my manuscript and the audience was visibly suffering; all the doors were open but the temperature in there must have been over a hundred. part of my job in chicago was living in a student dorm where stanley felt very ill at ease; we had to have <u>all</u> our meals in the student cafeteria, as part of the bargain, so that students could come over and talk to me. food was terrible. we got out once to dinner at the president's home, where the food was worse. we drove up westminster road in rochester, and i almost didn't recognize the old house; rochester has changed so that i was completely lost; our hotel reservations (made by nazareth nuns) got confused so we went to the sheraton where we had been told to go, and ran into a convention of embalmers or some such who had of course filled the place, and then got sent to the manger hotel which i dimly remembered as highly unsavory and in a bad part of town but it seemed all right now. i was interviewed by the democrat and the chronicle, enclosed, and the times-union, which i haven't seen; don't think i said all the things they say i did. the interviews took place in the nuns' reception room and sister margaret mary was plying us with the bottle of cutty sark they keep for the priest.

i hated chicago; i loved the city but the university is a mess. they were very nice to me but the schedule was so wearing that i thought i wouldn't make it; they want an awful lot for their money.

because the little morris was beginning to be kind of shaky i went down to the car store a few days before we left and bought a brand new mg sedan, bright red, and we took it on the trip; that was the nicest thing of all, because although the car is officially a sedan it is really a sports car, and drives like one. on those long flat midwestern roads i had a wonderful time. also all our expenses were paid and we made enough in lecture fees to pay for the car. everyone at syracuse was very full of hints and suggestions, because although it is an official secret everyone knows that they are giving

me an arents medal in june; i got the official announcement just
before we left. they give three medals and it is the occasion of our
class' twenty-fifth reunion. what they don't know is that i would
have to be out of my mind to go and get it; i wouldn't go back to
that reunion for anything. also such an acknowledgement from syracuse after all these years is not really as much of a compliment as
they seem to think it is. they want me to show up in formal clothes
at a banquet and all kinds of reunion events and i am writing to say
no thanks.

we left two college girls with sally and barry while we were gone
and everything went fine except that barry badly needs a haircut; the
college girls couldn't persuade him.

corinne is here for a week with the kids, laurie coming this weekend, they are all fine but glad to get out of the city for a while. laurie
is not at all happy in his job and is trying hard to get something else,
but without much luck. both children are getting so big and so handsome, and miles is going to nursery school in the fall. gretchen is very
pretty and looks very much like corinne.

can you imagine: dinner at the home of the president of chicago
university, twelve people, lovely table setting, and the hostess announces that oh, she is very sorry, but there isn't enough roast beef;
anyone who really wants a second helping can take scraps from the
platter.

i have to write them a thank-you letter.

we went to places like columbus ohio, which is a crazy city, full of
wild architecture, and for some reason a mining town in west virginia
which was ghastly, and we were at elmira new york, about three hundred miles from home, when the heat finally got to both of us and
we gave up and checked into a motel and turned the air conditioner
on full and just sat there. and we got caught one day driving along
the banks of the allegheny which we mistakenly supposed would be
a resort area but was instead deserted and uninhabited and finally
came to a horrid little joint called peg's tavern and motel, six pink
stucco motel units and a roadside tavern, and had to stay there and it
was incredibly clean and the air conditioning was new and very

strong so the room was like a refrigerator but otherwise very primitive and we spent the evening sitting at the bar in the tavern with peg and her husband al, talking about pennsylvania and vermont and raising kids and cats and peg took some hamburger out of the freezer and made us dinner. it was a better dinner than the president's, and i am going to write peg a thank-you letter.

i am supposed, again as part of my resident lecturer bit, to write a confidential report on what i thought of chicago and the students and their life. i am afraid that if i did write such a report they would not be pleased; i never saw such dull drab creatures as those students; we are spoiled by the bennington girls who are full of ideas and enthusiasm; these kids in chicago only wanted to get their papers written and their homework done so they could get out of the place. they rarely see their teachers, have enormous classes with no individual attention, and during their first two years at least they are not encouraged to do any individual work; one of the girls said she wanted to write and i said then why didn't she and she said if she wrote a story there was nothing to do with it; no one to read it, no one to criticize, she would have to leave it in a desk drawer. and i asked another if there was any student rebellion, as there has been in every other college we have visited, kids up in arms about civil rights and such, and these kids just stared at the idea, completely apathetic. it was really bad to see them without any excitement or enthusiasm at all. and no interest in anything.

well, as you can see i disliked chicago. no child of mine will ever go there. neither will I ever go there again.

but i must write them thank-you letters. right now. the laundry has piled up while we have been gone and i can't find anything in the kitchen and i am supposed to be writing a book. back to work.

love from all,

s.

•　•　•

"There's an old proverb says I cannot dismount."

[To Libbie Burke]

June 14, 1965

Dear Lib,

The eye doctor said I needed bi-focals. So instead I got two pair of glasses, one near- and one far-seeing, and now I have to change glasses to look up a number in the telephone book.

We were sorry we missed your dinner party and even sorrier to miss you before you left, but surely we will get together soon? Everyone said your dinner was lively and gay, which is certainly more than one could say about our entertainment at Bard, although the students were most earnest and sincere and had lots of real good questions to ask. We stayed in a boys' dorm and after we were put in for the night I was not allowed outside the door, although the Clay-Liston fight was being broadcast in the room across the hall. By the time Stanley managed to sneak me in the fight was over.

Our big news right now is that our young Sally has sold her first story, for $250 to something called The Gentleman's Quarterly. She wrote the story when she was fourteen—sixteen now—and it is a good start. I sold my first story for $25; there is a moral in there somewhere.

We are still pursuing Lake Shaftsbury;* it is so beautiful and so perfect and so possible that we are very excited; you are interested, are you not? Stanley will keep you posted on our progress.

Commencement week, with parties, parents, and papers, is upon us. Our Jai stage-managed "The Balcony," which was well stage-managed, but my, what a lousy play. Towards the end of the first act it occurred to me suddenly and vividly that if i heard the word "illusion" or the word "function" once more I was very likely going to be publicly sick, and then I realized that if I was publicly sick I would no doubt be regarded as part of the play's action, so I got up and fled to the open air and never went back. The rest of our crew stayed till the very end and said it got worse and worse. But it was very well stage-managed.

I must start making lunch now, which means I must change my glasses.

Love from all to all.

Best,

S.

•  •  •

---

* Shirley and Stanley are negotiating to purchase nearby Lake Shaftsbury with the Burkes.

[To Carol Brandt]

June 8 [1965]

Dear Carol,

If nothing goes amiss, we expect to be in New York the week of June 20th. Any chance of seeing you? Ought I to write Cork Smith?
     Working hard.

Best,

Shirley

•  •  •

[To Carol Brandt]

August 2 [1965]

Dear Carol,

Sorry that neither Sally nor I has been in touch with you; Sally has been sick and all her plans for coming to New York are kind of in abeyance. I am still hoping to bring her down for a day or two during August, but if this is not possible—and I am afraid it may not be—we will have to try sometime during the late fall.
     In any case, we both hope to see you sometime; everything this summer seems to have been conspiring to keep me from working, but I do make progress.

Best,

Shirley

•  •  •

*Six days later, on August 8, 1965, Shirley Jackson went upstairs to take her customary afternoon nap. When Stanley came to wake her, she was unresponsive. He called Sally and Barry, who also tried to wake her. Shirley was dead, at the age of forty-eight.*

*Her biographers have reported that there was one last letter written by Shirley to Carol saying that she was soon leaving alone on a wonderful journey and would meet many new people. That letter was received by Carol a day or two after Shirley died, and was shown to at least one member of the family, but it has since disappeared.*

*Taped to Shirley's wall above her typing desk was a handwritten note:*

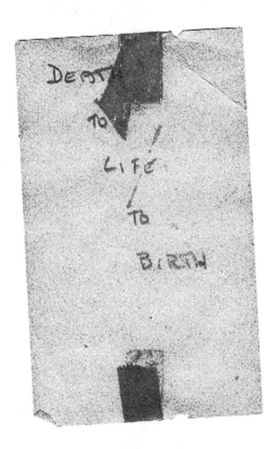

# ACKNOWLEDGMENTS

. . .

I would like to thank the following people for their help making this book possible:

Cynthia Kane Hyman, for support and encouragement throughout.

Bernice M. Murphy for her insightful scholarship and spirited collaboration.

Murray Weiss of Catalyst Literary Management for years of belief in this project, and for finding a welcoming home for this book.

Caitlin McKenna and Emma Caruso at Random House for helping me shape it.

Benjamin Dreyer for his vital early formatting advice.

Ruth Franklin for her discovery of letters written by Shirley to Jeanne Beatty, Virginia Olsen, Louis Harap, and others.

Sarah Hyman DeWitt for yet one more trip to the Library of Congress and early reading of the letters.

Barry Hyman for locating and photographing more than eight hundred Shirley Jackson drawings at the Library of Congress.

Jai (Hyman) Schnurer Holly for occasional name- and fact-checking.

Nichelle Wyatt-Whyte and Rebekah Thomas for their careful typing of often near-indecipherable pages.

Loretta Deaver, Reference Librarian, Library of Congress, for making scans of the drawings.

Michael Shulman at Magnum Photos, Inc. for help with Erich Hartmann photographs.

Steven Wolff and Ryerson Image Centre Toronto for the photograph by Werner Wolff.

Tanya Kalischer for Clemens Kalischer's photograph.

# PHOTOGRAPH CREDITS

. . .

# INDEX

. . .

SHIRLEY HARDIE JACKSON was born in San Francisco in 1916, and grew up in Burlingame, an affluent suburb of the city. In 1933 the family moved to Rochester, New York, and Shirley finished school there. She enrolled at Syracuse University and met Stanley Edgar Hyman, and they graduated in 1940, moving to an apartment in New York. Their first child was born in 1942. Shirley published numerous short stories in national magazines but finally received wide critical acclaim for "The Lottery," which was published in *The New Yorker* in 1948. Between 1945 and 1951 their family grew from three to six, with four children spaced with almost mathematical precision within three years of one another. Shirley is the author of six novels, including *The Haunting of Hill House, We Have Always Lived in the Castle,* and *The Sundial;* two best-selling family chronicles, *Life Among the Savages* and *Raising Demons;* hundreds of short stories, many published in five collections; several children's books; and two plays. Her work has been adapted for film, television, stage, musicals, and ballets. She died in 1965, at the age of forty-eight, while working on a comic novel, *Come Along with Me,* published (unfinished) posthumously.

## ABOUT THE EDITOR

Laurence Jackson Hyman, the eldest child of Shirley Jackson and Stanley Edgar Hyman, has spent most of his professional life in publishing—as a writer, photographer, editor, art director, and publisher. More than sixty of his black-and-white photographs are collected by the Bennington Museum in Vermont. He is the author, editor, or co-editor of dozens of books and monographs, including *Going to Chicago* (Woodford, 1989), *Really the Blues* (Woodford, 1996—winner of a prestigious W. C. Handy Award), and *The Great Jazz Day* (Woodford in 1993 and Da Capo Press in 2000), and Shirley Jackson's *Just an Ordinary Day* (Bantam, 1997) and *Let Me Tell You* (Random House, 2015). He founded Woodford Publishing and Woodford Press in San Francisco and managed them for nearly three decades, and in 2018 he was an executive producer for the film adaptation of *We Have Always Lived in the Castle*. He has also worked as a professional jazz trumpet player for more than sixty-five years.

BERNICE M. MURPHY is an associate professor/lecturer in popular literature at the School of English, Trinity College Dublin, Ireland. She edited the collection *Shirley Jackson: Essays on the Literary Legacy* and has written several articles and book chapters on Jackson's writing. She is also an expert on American horror and gothic narratives. Her current work in progress is a monograph entitled *The California Gothic in Fiction and Film.*

ABOUT THE TYPE

This book was set in Caslon, a typeface first designed in 1722 by William Caslon (1692–1766). Its widespread use by most English printers in the early eighteenth century soon supplanted the Dutch typefaces that had formerly prevailed. The roman is considered a "workhorse" typeface due to its pleasant, open appearance, while the italic is exceedingly decorative.